Refiguring
ENGLISH
STUDIES

Refiguring English Studies provides a forum for scholarship on English Studies as a discipline, a profession, and a vocation. To that end, the series publishes historical work that considers the ways in which English Studies has constructed itself and its objects of study; investigations of the relationships among its constituent parts as conceived in both disciplinary and institutional terms; and examinations of the role the discipline has played or should play in the larger society and public policy. In addition, the series seeks to feature studies which, by their form or focus, challenge our notions about how the written "work" of English can or should be done; and to feature writings which represent the professional lives of the discipline's members in both traditional and nontraditional settings. The series also includes scholarship that considers the discipline's possible futures or that draws upon work in other disciplines to shed light on developments in English Studies.

Changing Classroom Practices

Resources for Literary and Cultural Studies

Edited by

David B. Downing
Indiana University of Pennsylvania

Refiguring English Studies
Stephen M. North, Series Editor
SUNY at Albany

National Council of Teachers of English
1111 W. Kenyon Road, Urbana, Illinois 61801-1096

Manuscript Editor: Robert A. Heister/Humanities & Sciences Associates

Production Editors: Michael G. Ryan, Michelle Sanden Johlas

Interior Design: Tom Kovacs for TGK Design

Cover Design: Pat Mayer

NCTE Stock Number: 05289–3050

It is the policy of NCTE in its journals and other publications to provide a forum for the open discussion of ideas concerning the content and the teaching of English and the language arts. Publicity accorded to any particular point of view does not imply endorsement by the Executive Committee, the Board of Directors, or the membership at large, except in announcements of policy, where such endorsement is clearly specified.

Every effort has been made to trace the copyright holders and to obtain all permissions. In the case of those copyright holders who could not be located or those, if any, who did not respond, the publishers will be pleased to make the necessary arrangements upon receiving notice.

Library of Congress Cataloging-in-Publication Data

Changing classroom practices : resources for literary and cultural
    studies / edited by David B. Downing.
        p.   cm. — (NCTE Refiguring English studies series, ISSN 1073-9637)
    Includes bibliographical references (p.   ) and index.
    ISBN 0-8141-0528-9
        1. English philology—Study and teaching—United States.
    2. English literature—Study and teaching. 3. Language and culture—
    United States. 4. Culture—Study and teaching.   I. Downing, David
    B., 1947–   . II. Series.
    PE68.U5C4   1994
    420′.71′073—dc20   93-50205
                                                                       CIP

Contents

Foreword   *vii*
    James A. Berlin

Preface   *xiii*

I. Configurations of Teaching Lore   1

1. Configurations of Lore: The Changing Relations of Theory,
   Research, and Pedagogy   3
       David B. Downing, Patricia Harkin, James J. Sosnoski

II. Social Class in Classroom Discourse   35

2. Human Labor and Literature: A Pedagogy from a
   Working-Class Perspective   37
       Janet Zandy

3. The Cultural Work of Teaching Noncanonical Poetry   53
       Cary Nelson

III. Feminist Transformations   73

4. A Room of Whose Own? Lessons from Feminist
   Classroom Narratives   75
       Paula A. Treichler

5. Two Women on the Verge of a Contextual Breakthrough:
   Using *A Feminist Dictionary* in the Literature Classroom   104
       Barbara DiBernard and Sheila Reiter

6. Local Struggles/Partial Explanations: Producing
   Feminist Theory in the Classroom   122
       Ellen E. Berry and Vivian Patraka

7. Feminist Sophistics: Teaching with an Attitude   149
    Dale M. Bauer and Susan C. Jarratt

    **IV. Negotiating Authority and Difference: Radical,
    Oppositional, and Collectivist Pedagogies**   167

8. Pedagogy of the Distressed   169
    Jane Tompkins

9. A Pedagogy of Counterauthority,
    or the Bully/Wimp Syndrome   179
    Gerald Graff

10. The Teacher's Authority: Negotiating Difference
    in the Classroom   194
    Patricia Bizzell

11. Collective Pain: Literature, War, and Small Change   202
    C. Mark Hurlbert and Ann Marie Bodnar

    V. Toward Cultural and Rhetorical Studies   233

12. The Role of Rhetorical Theory, Cultural Theory, and
    Creative Writing in Developing a First-Year Curriculum
    in English   235
    Alan Kennedy, Christine M. Neuwirth,
    Kris Straub, and David Kaufer

13. Transforming the Academy: A Black Feminist Perspective   263
    Beverly Guy-Sheftall

14. Cultural Studies, Literary Studies, and Pedagogy:
    The Undergraduate Literature Course   275
    Anne Balsamo and Michael Greer

    Index   309

    Editor   321

    Contributors   323

Foreword

James A. Berlin
Purdue University

Some indication of the diversity and scope of this remarkable collection is revealed in the evolution of its present title, *Changing Classroom Practices: Resources for Literary and Cultural Studies*. Most of these essays were first presented at a conference entitled "The Role of Theory in the Undergraduate Literature Classroom: Curriculum, Pedagogy, Politics," held at Indiana University of Pennsylvania in 1990. Those of us who attended that gathering quickly realized that this designation was not quite right. First off, there were numerous presentations that had little to do with literature. Some dealt with rhetorical texts, others with media such as television, film, and popular music. Even those who talked about literature often referred to texts not usually included in college English courses—for example, the noncanonical works of women and workers and people of color, including the English-language literatures of postcolonial nations. And if the notion of the undergraduate literature classroom that was being described at the conference was unexpected, so were the theories that were offered, the pedagogy, and, yes, even the politics. In short, the truth-in-advertising standards that we have come to take for granted in attending academic conferences had been violated. Yet, there were few complaints. There was, instead, a general feeling that this new agenda was indeed just what was wanted. And it was this experience that made necessary a new title for these efforts, a description more adequate to the changes in our conceptions of the relations of literature, culture, and the classroom that are now unmistakably in the air.

David Downing has assembled some of the best essays from this conference and included one or two others that form a part of their dialogue. Taken as a whole, they engage the most pressing issues facing us in English studies today. And while they cannot be said to be in total theoretical accord, they do agree about the problems most in need of our attention. They also insist on situating the solutions to these problems within the context of the classroom.

Theory remains central to the classroom strategies described here. Despite the diversity and complexity of the theories called upon, however, the most obvious feature of the volume is that, in every case, they are made accessible to nontheorists; in other words, this is not theory for its own sake. In keeping with the commitment to a classroom that always starts with the experience of students and teachers, these essays offer formulations that have proven themselves useful in enabling students and teachers to become better readers and authors of their everyday activities. Thus, while the essayists call upon structuralist, poststructuralist, deconstructionist, Marxist, feminist, African American, gay and lesbian, neopragmatist, and other schemes, they do not assume an audience conversant in any of these schools. Indeed, just the opposite is true: the essays are designed for serious teachers willing to learn about the new possibilities that the intersection of theory and the classroom offers. They are never meant to tax the patience of the teacher, insisting instead that the teacher's classroom experience is the starting point for any discussion of theory.

Thus, theory is not here considered a white knight (the color and gender choices are intentional) come to save us from the enemy (who is us). Instead, it becomes a set of reflections, a way of thinking about our entire range of experience, to be tested in our daily lives. As teachers, this means centering this interaction between reflection and action in our encounters with students in the classroom. Most important, as pointed out by Downing, Patricia Harkin, and James Sosnoski, as well as by Ellen Berry and Vivian Patraka, this means that theory is something that teachers and students do, not something done *to* them. Whether we are invoking Jacques Derrida or Michel Foucault or bell hooks or Donna Haraway, theory is valuable only insofar as it makes sense in our experience and transforms it in the service of more humane personal and communal arrangements. Theory is never, then, considered for itself. It is likewise never regarded as final and irrevocable. Instead, a central argument about the theories forwarded here is that they are disposable, to be used only so long as they are useful in understanding and improving the character of daily behavior. And so the range of theories invoked is extensive, with no final agreement on the best versions to be forwarded. The proof of their value is finally in their usefulness in the classroom.

The emphasis is thus on theory subordinated to the needs of learning as an instrument of personal and social change. This brings us to the political dimension of the projects offered here. Most would agree that the English classroom must address the failure of our democratic society to realize its promises to all of its citizens. As teachers and students examine the interactions and mutual corrections of theory and practice, they situate their study within larger social contexts. And so all of these essays are preeminently contextualist: they locate the experiences and theoretical frames they consider in the classroom within larger economic and political categories. They may not all point specifically to the historical role education has played in the democracies that extend from ancient Greece to the twentieth century, as do Dale Bauer and Susan Jarratt. They do, nonetheless, explicitly agree that to be educated in a democracy is to be an active critic of one's experience and the institutions that influence it. Preparation for citizenship, for engaging in economic and political change, is a crucial part of every project offered here.

This engagement insists on examining the performance of democracy in the entire body politic. Thus, Janet Zandy and Cary Nelson share with their students the literary texts that speak to the experience of the working class, the group that comes into view only when one looks beyond the twenty percent of the work force consisting of the professional middle class—that is, the class position most prominently represented in the schools. Paula Treichler in her essay and Barbara DiBernard and Sheila Reiter in theirs show how their classrooms address the experience of women in the economic and political arrangements of our moment. Here students and teachers explore the ways language and institutions constrain women's lives so as to limit their economic, political, and personal possibilities. Beverly Guy-Sheftall challenges the "erroneous notion that the normative human experience is Western, European American, white, male, Christian, middle class, and heterosexual." Her students transgress the limits of the university, enriching their understanding of political activity by taking part in community projects. And Patricia Bizzell argues that all activities in the composition classroom should be organized around teachers and students negotiating political values.

These classrooms are thus student centered without focusing exclusively on the narrow experience of the individual learner. As indicated earlier, all of us live within contexts that influence and limit us. Awareness of the possibilities of our experience is available only through understanding the ways these contexts operate upon us. Thus, whatever independence and uniqueness are available to the individual can be understood only by coming to terms with the conditions of experience that work against becoming independent and unique. Students achieve a measure of freedom and possibility only by facing the limits that continually circumscribe and constrict their autonomy and singularity. And as we have already seen, these limits are greater for some groups than they are for others.

These essays thus chronicle a shift away from the exclusive and myopic preoccupation with the individual, a common failure of certain innovative pedagogical practices of the sixties (as a number of contributors note). The corresponding move to a larger concern for the individual in context is demonstrated in the collaborative nature of the classrooms described here. Students and teachers are constantly working together in setting classroom procedures, agendas, and methods of investigation. Authority is dispersed. This does not mean, however, that the teacher abnegates all responsibility, a move, after all, that the institution simply will not allow. This does, nonetheless, involve a different attitude toward authority within and outside the classroom.

No set of institutional practices is declared immune from interrogation. All are to be investigated for their contradictions, concealments, and exclusions. And this inquiry extends to the classroom itself. Collaboration then—and this is crucial—does not necessarily lead to consensus. Indeed, the most striking feature of the courses described here is that they are frequently scenes of discord and struggle. The traditional narrative for an experiment in pedagogy demands a happy ending, a moment of completion in which all conflicts are resolved in a celebration of difficulties successfully overcome. As a number of teachers here demonstrate, however, this harmonious unity is usually achieved at the expense of silencing members of the classroom community, of refusing to allow certain experiences to enter into the discussion. This often involves ignoring failures that our society refuses to acknowledge, injustices in employment, wages, housing, health—in general, inadequate opportunities for a secure and safe life. Such openness, of course, means that inequalities of race, class, gender, sexual orientation, age, and ethnicity must be addressed. All students, however, do not agree that such disparities exist. And so the central conflicts in the classroom that must first be taken up are often not between class members and an unjust society—they are instead the conflicts among class members themselves.

It is here that the standard of collaboration without consensus is demonstrated, the commitment to creating a climate that allows for dissent. While students and teachers work together, they do not always agree with each other. Furthermore, they cannot be expected to agree with each other. These essays strikingly illustrate one of the contradictions of the recent attacks on those who would bring economic, political, and social conflicts into the classroom. The purpose of entertaining these conflicts is to acknowledge them in all of their complexity as a necessary step toward addressing their cruel consequences. No English studies course can by itself finally hope to end the injustices of our society. Our discipline can only serve as a democratic forum for developing the literacy practices—the activities of reading and writing—needed to address our disagreements about them. Ironically, it is those who ignore these conflicts who themselves, then, engage in repression, denying our obvious discords in the name of a general civic harmony that simply does not exist.

Facing up to our differences means that students may often be uncomfortable. This is an inevitability that teachers must address. As these contributors recognize, students are not evenly equipped to deal with classroom discord, so the teacher must develop strategies for enabling equal participation. All of the essays accordingly deal with this issue, offering a broad range of devices for encouraging dissent without a destructive contentiousness.

One complementary feature of many of these essays is that they demonstrate a commitment to collaboration in the very act of their composition. And these collaborative efforts, once again, are meant to cross boundaries, to bridge disparities. In the opening essay, Downing, Harkin, and Sosnoski join their separate roles of literary critic, rhetorician, and literary theorist, finding common ground in the realm of classroom lore where theory, research, and pedagogy are brought together. Dale Bauer and Susan Jarratt are at different institutions, Barbara DiBernard and Sheila Reiter write from the perspectives of professor and graduate student, and Mark Hurlbert and Ann Marie Bodnar cross the lines between teacher and undergraduate student. In all three, different perspectives are brought together to create a dialogue, an interchange that in the latter two essays is marked by offering separately authored sections. Finally, the essays on cultural studies by Alan Kennedy, Chris Neuwirth, Kris Straub, and Dave Kaufer and by Anne Balsamo and Michael Greer are collaborative efforts to break the boundaries between poetic and rhetoric, aesthetics and politics, the passive reader and the active writer, disinterested and interested texts, and, finally, low culture and high culture. And with the mention of "culture," we are entering one of the ruling concerns of this collection.

The meaning of the term has occasioned one of the most lively debates in considerations of English studies today. The traditional designation of culture as a set of canonical texts and reading practices is found in the work of E. D. Hirsch and Allan Bloom. Here authentic culture is always "high" as distinguished from "low" or popular culture. In a practical sense, experiences judged not universal in their appeal are excluded from the privileged category and are banished to the local and temporary. Such experiences are then to be ignored or even openly condemned as pernicious. It is not difficult to see what happens to most of the texts—written and electronic—that form a part of our students' daily experience. They are simply not to be allowed into the classroom. Officially, despite their great influence in our students' lives, they simply do not exist.

The contributors to this volume accept an alternative definition of culture. For them, culture has to do with the ordinary ways of life of our students, with their everyday lived experience. Because of its historical commitment to teaching reading and writing practices in the service of the good and just life, English studies cannot ignore this ordinary experience. After all, our previous devotion to high culture—to canonical texts and reading practices—arose out of our concerns for teaching students methods for discerning value. Today, many of us realize that this exclusive commitment prevented a consideration of the actual cultural conditions of our students' lives, of their positions in cultures not represented in the canon. Thus, in teaching students to read and write so that they can discern the values operative in their daily experience, we must turn to a consideration of new texts and new ways of interpreting them. This does not banish literature from our purview, but, quite the contrary, expands the horizon of the literary to include previously marginalized written texts. (Indeed, the literary is given a privileged place in the title of this collection, even though all of its contributors might not agree with this move.) Of equal importance, this revised conception of culture dramatically enlarges the kinds of texts to be considered—the discourse of film, television, music, advertising—and, of course, the methods of considering them. To echo the opening essay of this collection, English studies then becomes reading and writing as equipment for living in making decisions about conflicting cultural values.

This collection suggests promising new possibilities for English studies, and it does so in the most concrete of terms. Teachers doubtful about the value of the culture wars that we have been witnessing in school and society can see one fruitful product in this effort. As is argued throughout these essays, conflicts freely examined often result in the discovery of rich possibilities—this text itself is palpable proof of this assertion. *Changing Classroom Practices: Resources for Literary and Cultural Studies* is coming at exactly the right moment in our cultural conversation. It deserves a close hearing.

Preface

This book had its beginnings in a conference I directed in the fall of 1990, "The Role of Theory in the Undergraduate Literature Classroom: Curriculum, Pedagogy, Politics." Most of the contributors to this book participated in the conference, and many of the essays included in this volume are revised versions of their earlier presentations. One of the key issues that emerged from the conference was a wide-spread belief that the traditional models of scholarship and publication no longer served very well to promote the serious exchange of ideas related to changing classroom practices. Indeed, the almost sudden interest in pedagogy (especially for teachers of literature) after more than two decades of intense theoretical debate signals an important moment in the changing shape of humanities classrooms and curricula as we near the end of the century. In our introduction, Patricia Harkin, James Sosnoski, and I offer an explanation for this important turn toward pedagogy in our profession. If the shift toward postmodern and post-structuralist theory has been broadly named the "linguistic turn," it seems appropriate to call this most recent refocusing of debate the "pedagogical turn." In short, the old models for teaching as the trans-mission of cultural value (as in the "banking" model of education) have given way to broader questions relating education, knowledge, pedagogy, and literacy to the very creation and construction of social as well as personal relations. "Pedagogy" can then no longer be con-fined to the classroom, the curriculum, the university, the school. Sec-ondly, the very division between "research" and "teaching" that fairly dominates work in higher education now comes under intense pres-sure. As we argue in the introduction, by reconceiving teaching "lore" as serious inquiry into reconfiguring social relations, we need to find new ways to promote, circulate, and revalue a whole arena of our professional labor as professors which has traditionally been given little reward. This is an especially pressing need given the now more widely held belief that "pedagogy is politics" in the broadest sense of that term.

This book begins with the acknowledgment that pedagogy is a form of social and political transaction. The central question I have posed is

"What do we do now?" once we accept the theoretical arguments for the sociopolitical significance of teaching. Indeed, many books now testify to those arguments, but it has become increasingly clear that the professional models of scholarship lend themselves to the theoretical debates much more than to the lore of the teacher-practitioners who are actually working out the consequences of their actions as teachers in the classroom and of the curricula. In short, we have been much more able to invest in the theoretical critique and critical negation of the work of others than we have to work out the "thickly" configured dimensions of our actual teaching practices.

The sense of this book as a resource for literary and cultural studies emerges from the commitments of the contributors to an exploration of their own changing classroom practices, the narratives by which they have configured their own teaching lore in a time of considerable cultural uncertainty. The tentativeness (as well as the boldness) of some of these essays suggests the widespread lack of many concrete, well-developed models for reconfiguring our teaching of literary and cultural studies once we have opened the canon and questioned the relations between knowledge, power, and authority. As we argue in the introduction, it is time to acknowledge the force of teaching lore as a kind of postdisciplinary inquiry into the possibilities of changing social relations in a multicultural world.

For this reason, I envision as the primary audience for this book teachers seeking the kind of lore that will help them to realize their own desired changes in classroom practices. If the "pedagogical turn" in our profession signals the wide-spread reconsideration of the very processes of acculturation, then every teacher's theorized practices become the occasion for inquiry, research, and understanding. And such reconsiderations will no doubt reveal that our uncertainties, our hesitancies, our vulnerabilities are a much larger part of the learning situation than our traditional notions of authority and knowledge have ever led us to believe. In a multicultural world, displacement and change seem to be the one constant that we can count on to call us back to theorizing in self-critical ways about those practices that may help us work for a more democratic nation. Finally, despite our apparent sense of autonomy in our individual classrooms, our teaching practices have never really been isolated from the curriculum, the institution, and the profession. Accordingly, some of the essays included in this volume focus on these issues as an essential phase of pedagogical reform.

One of the ways that the contributors to this volume worked through their revisions and reconsiderations of their work was to exchange their drafts with each other. This proved beneficial in many ways as it led to a more truly collaborative book in which many of the contributors address the relations between their own work and that of the other contributors, and such exchanges helped to prevent the kind of speaking at cross-purposes that often happens in collections of diverse essays. I wish to thank all of the contributors for their willingness, often eagerness, to consider such additional labor in the preparation of their own essays. I also wish to thank Michael Spooner for his immediate positive response to this project and his ongoing support of it. As editor of the series "Refiguring English Studies," Stephen North offered just the right kind of insight and foresight that I found valuable to complete the editing of this book. Finally, Robert A. Heister has, once again, served as a perceptive, meticulous, and efficient manuscript and project editor.

I Configurations of Teaching Lore

1 Configurations of Lore: The Changing Relations of Theory, Research, and Pedagogy

David B. Downing
Indiana University of Pennsylvania

Patricia Harkin
University of Toledo

James J. Sosnoski
Miami University

"The Pedagogical Imperative: Teaching as a Literary Genre," a special issue of *Yale French Studies* which included Paul de Man's essay "The Resistance to Theory," was published in 1982. As Barbara Johnson points out in her preface, the "collection is designed to probe the theory and practice of teaching in an unusual way. While discussions of pedagogy generally deal with classroom procedures for the teaching of texts, this volume studies the ways in which texts themselves dramatize the problematics of teaching" (iii). By contrast, *Changing Classroom Practices* is concerned, not with a *literary* genre that represents teaching, but rather, with genres of teaching practices. Whereas in the *YFS* collection texts are the sources of theories of teaching, in this collection teachers are the sources of theorized practices. The *YFS* issue presents us with a view of relations between literary theory and teaching practices in which the latter is an application of the former. *Changing Classroom Practices* subverts this familiar hierarchy.

Since 1982, many collections of essays have focused on relations between theory and teaching practices: *Practicing Theory in Introductory College Literature Courses, Contending with Words, Theory/Pedagogy/Politics: Texts for Change,* and *Pedagogy Is Politics* (1991); *Reorientations: Critical Theories and Pedagogies* and *Conversations: Contemporary Critical Theory and the Teaching of Literature* (1990); *Reclaiming Pedagogy* (1989); *Professing Literature* and *Tracing Literary Theory* (1987); *Theory in the Classroom* (1986). This flourishing theoretical attention to teaching has

3

blossomed in the last decade in a relatively contentious climate. Renewed interest in pedagogy is supported by voices from both the left and the right. The left calls for more critical attention to teaching as a process of enculturation. They object to classroom practices that reproduce the production/consumption modes of capitalist patriarchy. From this perspective, hierarchy, privilege, exclusion, and the effacing of cultural differences sustain what institutions call the "dissemination of knowledge and/or truth." On the other hand, conservative voices have countered in the media with charges of "political correctness" and have painted dissident intellectuals as resorting promiscuously and tyrannically to intimidation.[1] From the conservative perspective, more attention to teaching, including, for example, rewarding "master teachers," is intended to lead to a widespread literacy that will better serve the national economy in a competitive global market.

Why has teaching become a subject of national controversy in recent years? What purpose does a renewed interest in pedagogy serve at this moment in history? The circulation and dissemination of information has become a far more economically significant process in our society than it was just a few years ago. One explanation is that it addresses a knowledge crisis perceived to be far more consequential than the concerns Sputnik evoked thirty years ago. Signaled by the electronic revolution, the postmodern period has precipitated drastic reconceptions of knowledge. In technological fields, information has become a more important resource than manufactured goods or even industrial raw materials. Nonetheless, it is an unexpectedly scarce one. Japan threatens to corner information markets, an unforeseen consequence of what many perceive to be its more effective educational systems. In the humanities, on the other hand, renewed attention to teaching is a likely result of and a probable response to a different aspect of postmodern reconceptions of knowledge which Fish, Rorty, and others have labeled "antifoundationalism." In traditional foundationalist epistemologies, objective knowledge could be sought and secured only at the very moment when it severed all connections with social and political history. Indeed, such objectivity carried with it stipulations of a "disinterested" pursuit of knowledge "for its own sake." Traditional scholars fear that postmodern students and their antifoundationalist teachers are losing the races for crucial knowledges whose traditions must be maintained to preserve the social and economic status of the United States. For many other teacher-researchers, however, the traditional view of knowledge has little credibility, especially in cultural studies. Much of the influence of "theory" in the last thirty years is the consequence of antifoundationalist discourses. More specifically, the work of

Foucault, Lyotard, Bourdieu, and others has resulted in the scrutiny of institutions that claim to produce objective knowledge. Teacher-critics no longer ignore the connections among knowledge, power, and politics that give shape and meaning to the very "subjects" and disciplines they are supposed to teach.[2] They have become skeptical of arguments allegedly "based on," "grounded in," "supported by," "validated through" some unshakable "foundation." At the same time, such skepticism is disquieting.

Once the foundations of knowledge production have crumbled, are we merely to occupy ourselves with questions of how to transmit the news of their demise? If literature departments can no longer provide students with disciplinary principles as the foundation of knowledge production, what can they do? Lately, several reformists have suggested that we turn our attention to the values that form our "culture," those fractious subjective judgments previously outlawed by our methods.

Unfortunately, it is often asserted (or assumed) that when such changes become curricular reforms they liberate students from the claims for objectivity that we associate with logic and science and, instead, empower them to use rhetoric to form not only values (and therefore selves) but also knowledge. But of course, to realize that knowledge is discursively produced and then to make that realization the "foundational" principle of a reformed curriculum is to re-establish, on a more abstract level, the problem the reforms were meant to solve. In short, antifoundationalist critiques of authority can institutionalize themselves in traditional structures of authority. New umbrella terms like "rhetoric" have a way of becoming foundational terms. We used to have the logical principles of valid arguments to govern our entire discipline; now we use rhetorical principles to regulate our studies. The question becomes how to prevent the new curriculum or even the new course content from becoming yet another totalizing foundation.

One way that seems to work is to refuse to separate our theories from our pedagogies. Though we recognize that no system can master another, we know, too, that in the institutional settings in which we work and live, attempts at mastery are constantly being made. When research materials become the content of courses, they become credos. Hypotheses become dogmas. One way of avoiding such fossilization is to reconceive teaching, to reject the old transmission model of knowledge in favor of a more pragmatic approach to learning in which the problems students have with cultural values are the subject matters of their teachers' research. Thus, pedagogy becomes particularly important as a response—not a solution—to the problem of foundationalism, because, by focusing on the concrete problematics of the classroom, the reformist can avoid, or at least bracket, "master discourses." This response collides with the responses of teachers who believe that traditional approaches must be upheld and who thus advocate a more disciplined transmission of knowledge. Understood conservatively, teaching is the transfer of information. Understood antifoundationally, teaching is the formation of culture. Both sides, however, see the need for pedagogical research.

The integration of research and pedagogy is hastened by the fact that state and national legislators call for more teaching and less research from the professoriate. Hence, while responding to the call for more attention to teaching, educators on both sides of the political spectrum can in good conscience turn their attention to the ways in which *culture is the discourse that educates,* one remarkably important instance of which occurs in their own classrooms. From this vantage point, the relations between writers or speakers and readers or listeners is an appropriate subject for scholarly investigations.

Other forces also abet such changes. The national economy has moved from industry to arbitrage, now producing more "services" than things. Instead it commodifies information, and information about information, and analyses and evaluations of information about information. Similarly, the profession has moved from raising questions about authors, to raising questions about texts, to raising questions about readers, to raising questions about the conditions of possibility for any reading, to raising questions about how we teach students to read. Indeed, we have now moved to raising questions about the social and political consequences of reading and teaching in a troubled culture. Since many extramural changes have dramatically but subtly affected our intramural habits, it is necessary to provide a historical perspective on the changing relations of classroom practices to that "other" form of scholarly conduct called research.

Changing Classroom Practices and Their Effect on the Paradigm of Literary Research

At mid-century, the model by which literary studies was most frequently understood could be found in M. H. Abrams's (1953) "coordinates of art criticism" in *The Mirror and the Lamp* (figure 1). From the time of its publication, this simple chart of the relations thought to be constant in every aesthetic situation guided discussions of schools of criticism. It functioned, however loosely, as a kind of paradigm of research endeavors. With Aristotelian rigor, Abrams described the four causes of the work of art: material, formal, efficient, and final. Attention to these causal relations generated four distinct perspectives: mimetic—focused on relations between the work and the universe; pragmatic—governed by relations between the work and its effects on its audience; expressive—attending to the work as an expression of the artist; and objective—deliberately narrowed in its concerns to the relations within the work itself, "in its parts and their mutual relations" (26).[3] This simple scheme was presupposed by innumerable research endeavors in literary criticism. New Critical research was construed as a formal concern with intratextual relations. By contrast, psychoanalytic critics were understood to study relations between the artist's unconscious and the work of art as a species of dream work. Historical criticism investigated relations between the work and its contexts. Reader-oriented criticism was declared to be an account of relations between the work and its audience. These four examples, however, did not exhaust the possible research endeavors. Though concerned with the extra-textual contexts of literary works, sociological critics nonetheless could be distinguished from literary historians, and so on. For many, Abrams's diagram outlined the legitimate areas of literary research. Like other objects, the work of art could be explained as the result of the underlying causal principles that generated it.

Abrams's scheme was immensely influential. From our point of view, it is noteworthy that critics like Wayne Booth demonstrated how the plurality of views Abrams delineated relies on incompatible foundations, yet, nonetheless, provided reliable "facts" upon which interpretations could be based. Abrams's schematization of Aristotelian causality was widely respected as a justly pluralistic view of literary study in which four substantive relations were thought to give rise to discrete schools of research, each with its own set of foundational principles or methods. If a historical third dimension is added to it (as Abrams intended but was not able to diagram), then it also reflected the *fields* of typical literary research—the romantic period (Abrams's main concern in *The Mirror and the Lamp*), the eighteenth century, and so on. The scheme was liberal, yet rigorous. But defenses of such pluralism have been superseded by "antifoundationalist" complaints and postmodern critiques of totalizing systems.

Given Abrams's "coordinates," it is hard to imagine how pedagogy might be charted. The diagram plots the intersections of research methods or interpretive strategies. But introducing relations between teachers and their students into the diagram (figure 2) dramatically alters Abrams's graphic. In this new graphic representation, the entire "object of research" becomes the content of the dialogue between the teacher and the student. Notice, though, that even in this "plotting," teaching figures as a mere transmission of information. The configuration conscripts teachers for the role of walk-on's—disseminators of research to which they make no significant contribution. Thirty years ago, pedagogy did not belong in the organization of literary research.

Indeed, as Cahalan and Downing argue in their introduction to *Practicing Theory in Introductory Literature Courses* (1991), "The hierarchy of advanced research versus introductory teaching is deeply embedded in the higher education system of this country, which in turn is deeply embedded in the ideological differences of race, class, gender, and ethnicity of U.S. social life. . . . In short, the traditional scholarly models still operate as powerful constraints on . . . the very pedagogical alternatives being recommended . . ." (3–4). Teaching was simply regarded as something you already knew how to do; it had no place in the serious study of literature, mere teacher's tips, "lore," not knowledge.

In the thirty years that have passed since Abrams first delineated his coordinates, the artists' relation to their work, the formalities of New Criticism, the historical contexts of the work, the audience's response have all undergone immense rethinking. We saw Lacan take the place of Freud as the interpreter of dreams, Derrida take the place of Cleanth Brooks as the master reader, Fredric Jameson or Stephen Greenblatt take the place of F. O. Matthiesson or M. H. Abrams as historians of letters, and Stanley Fish or Janice Radway take the place of I. A. Richards or Louise Rosenblatt as arbiters of interpretive communities. Throughout the period, however, the relations implied by Abrams's diagram still identified the legitimate areas of literary research and still excluded teaching. Over the years, research came to mean almost the opposite of teaching. Those who could, did research; those who couldn't, taught.

Only recently have we witnessed a groundswell of research interest in pedagogy.[4] Today, many scholars regard pedagogical research as the study of the most crucial of textual and social relations. For lack of better terms, we might describe this groundswell as an influx of *cultural pragmatism,* if only in the sense that it is *a response to a public problem*—cultural literacy. Public outcries against illiteracy happened to surface at a moment when the foundational paradigm of literary research was crumbling. Thus, an academic movement responding to the needs of the public could safely abandon the literary object of research and focus instead on the transmission and formation of cultural understanding. But the notion that teachers simply transmit "knowledge" as the results of literary research to their students (the sector of the public put under their keeping) was regarded by postmodern scholars as naïvely simplistic. It became infamous as the "banking" model of pedagogy (figure 3). This configuration mirrors Abrams's implied conception of pedagogical relations, thus revealing how easily traditional models of literary study adapt to the banking method. According to this model, teachers deposited symbolic capital as investments into student receiverships. But this notion did not always correspond to what went on in actual classrooms. Thus, in an antifoundationalist climate, the banking model quickly gave way to the realization that the transaction between the teacher and the student was a dynamic instance, not of preserving, but rather of actually forming cultures discursively. If teachers were supposed to be transmitting our cultural foundations, they were either failing miserably or something else was happening. Over this issue two views collided. Some teachers accepted the idea that their task was to transmit the foundational texts of the culture and that they were failing in that task.[5] Others rejected the nineteenth-century pedagogical goal of cultural transmission as a naïve view of how enculturation and acculturation take place. By implication, the unspoken premise that a modern system designed to transmit supposed cultural foundations was inadequate to these postmodern times insinuated itself into the plans of many scholars. In some quarters of the academy, research interest shifted dramatically away from texts (as our cultural foundation) to the ways in which pedagogical transactions (vs. transmissions) actually shaped or formed the culture.

More and more scholars have become concerned with cultural transformations. Many of them assert that when readers read or watch or listen to such cultural artifacts as image-making telecampaigns, they are predisposed to live out the myths they learn to inhabit. Rather than construe literary study as an impersonal, highly abstract theoretical venture, accompanied by esoteric readings intelligible only to a coterie of initiates, cultural pragmatists work directly with the ways in which the lives of persons in the culture are shaped. Their attention is given, not to the text alone, nor the theory alone, but to *persons* and the problems they experience in their cultural habitats.[6] The "object" of research is no longer an isolated text but a cultural transaction—often on stage, "live" in the classroom. The main research question becomes what's wrong with this transaction? Why do people feel disassociated from the culture they inhabit? Why is this painful? Attention shifts from lifeless texts to the discursively induced pains culturation inflicts upon its subjects.[7]

This shift involves nothing less than an entire reconstruction of the humanities in a move away from the text-centered, method-oriented,

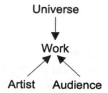

Fig 1. The coordinates of art criticism.

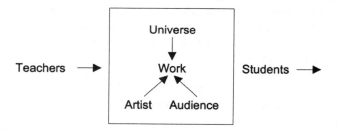

Fig 2. The teacher-student transaction .

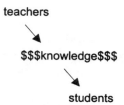

Fig 3. The"banking" model of pedagogy .

scientistic principles of disciplinary study toward a person-centered, postdisciplinary exploration of the processes of culturation. By "culturation" we refer to the ways individuals (subjects) form their identities within the often contradictory and differing conditions of literacy. In short, illiteracy is more deeply understood as inarticulateness. Literacy is more deeply understood as normalization. What had once been the study of writing or reading is now the study of readers reading writers writing readings. What once were books now are texts, that is, anything that can be interpreted. Though the world has become everyone's library, it still is available only to those who could read it. For cultural pragmatists literary study is ineluctably pedagogical and schools have no walls.

This new "pragmatic" attitude about culturation is a response to public needs, variously interpreted. The term "cultural illiteracy" is one account of, or interpretation of, such a need. Publicity about cultural illiteracy has changed the traditional "model" of the organization of literary research for many scholars. Both in composition and rhetoric and in literary studies, many teachers have shifted their emphases to cultural studies where engagements with texts are no longer thought to take place in a theoretical vacuum unrelated to social contexts. Rather than depersonalize writing and reading as a field of objects for study, teachers personalize their practices. Following suit, scholars began to look at the traditional research paradigm as a reduction of their subjects. Instead of asking, "How should this text be interpreted?" they asked, "How does this text help or hurt persons?" Teachers think about their students as persons whose lives do *not* change much as a consequence of being in their classrooms. The pedagogical isolation of the individual classroom thus opens to the social and political conditions of living, teaching, and learning in late-twentieth-century America.

Moreover, what used to happen behind the closed doors of the academy is now a public matter. Our high-tech culture has made the study of literature a national issue. The recent furor over the PC phenomenon, for example, may be seen as a reaction to a reaction. Academics have slowly but steadily turned their attention to public spheres ever since the "literacy crisis" made national headlines. Asked to heed the needs of a public finding itself culturally illiterate, academics have responded overwhelmingly. But this response cannot be extricated from the changes that had taken place within the academy, for instance, from the development of antifoundationalist theories. As the government turned from neglecting education to demanding that the citizens who pay for schools be made more literate, teachers responded to that challenge; but, of course, they were more thoughtful about what illiteracy involves than the government anticipated. For many the solution to illiteracy was to bring into the fold those persons who were not literate in the ways of middle-class white America. Instead, the more academics looked at the problems of illiteracy, the more they saw problems with the cultural literacy that was being promulgated (see Stuckey 1991). This volume shows how teachers have responded to public needs by changing their classroom practices. Literacy is, after all, nothing more than a synonym for culturation. Yet, the problem of illiteracy cannot be reduced to the issue of how to enforce cultural norms.

Norms are not unproblematic. They deserve research. We need to know how cultural norms normalize through institutions like schools. Literacy thus becomes as problematic as illiteracy. Once normalization is identified as a condition of literacy and as an effect of schooling, then researchers have to consider how pedagogical practices must be changed to counter the force of institutional normalization. Our task in this volume is to consider the impact of counternormalizing or counterdisciplinary practices. We give the name "lore" to the practices we examine. This volume configures the denormalizing teaching practices that address cultural illiteracy not by enforcing obsolete cultural standards, but by examining and then dismantling them.

Before we can take up the pedagogical alternatives the essays in this volume offer, we need to demystify the traditional view of relations between theoretical research and pedagogical practices. This next section cautions our readers *not* to understand the changing classroom practices presented in this volume as applications of the most recent and fashionable postmodern theories.

The Trickle-Down Theory of Theories and Its Channels of Refutation

It is widely assumed that cultural research follows the same pattern of development as most disciplinary studies, for instance, as the pattern of research that spawned the computer revolution. Computers are thought to have their origins in purely mathematical work resulting in highly abstract theories (e.g., Turing). These extraordinarily abstract theories, often unexpectedly applied in demanding historical situations (usually wars, as in this case, WWII), later influence engineers doing applied theoretical research (e.g., von Neumann).

Finally, practical engineers are brought in to work out the details. In short, first the abstract theory exists as a theory inspired only by other theories. Next, some application is discovered. Then, it gets disseminated by popularizers of the newly contextualized theory. Finally, it bears practical fruit in the everyday practices of ordinary people who make no contribution whatsoever to its development but only extend the range of the theory's applicability.

In our own domain, the pattern would look something like this. First, Jacques Derrida (or Lacan or Foucault) develops an abstract theory. Next, someone applies that theory to a particular context (de Man using Derrida to re-read existing readings of literature). Then, it is disseminated to a wide audience by scholars like Culler, Scholes, or Atkins, who seek to make the theory accessible. Lastly, it is put into practice by ordinary teachers.

We wish to challenge this trickle-down theory of theories. Let us begin with the nefarious and infamous "watering down," "bastardizing," and general "misreading" of the theories that invariably take place once the theory is transported into a practical context like a classroom. Deconstruction no longer looks anything like the reading strategy Derrida used to interpret Lévi-Strauss or Rousseau. What's worse, it totally distorts his strategy. Even more horrible, apparently anything under the sun becomes "deconstruction." Not only is Harold Bloom a deconstructor, and Stanley Fish and Jane Tompkins, but so is Arnold Schwarzenegger in *Terminator II*. In fact, the "original" theory is so battered as to be unrecognizable.

The professional advocates of the theory industry often work to defend against such bastardization and dilution of theoretical discourse when it gets "applied" in classrooms. To understand how and why they do so, it will be useful to remember that the institutionalized mechanism by which theory is supposed to trickle down operates according to a pattern we describe as "cutting edge negation." It works like this: since, in an antifoundationalist context, you can't prove directly what you know, you negate what others have authorized.[8] If your negation succeeds, you then occupy the position of the authority you dethroned. The "cutting edge" of your arguments proves the superiority of your beliefs. This strategy works in many ways. If Derrida successfully negates Saussure and Husserl, he occupies the field in which they once were the authorities and thereby authorizes a new discursive terrain. Once in place, the newly authorized discourse can be used by sycophants to refute the impure or bastardized forms of the theory that trickle down from the prestigious places where they originated. This is often a concerted effort. The adherents of one school customarily work to refute the beliefs of rival schools.

Let's pause for a moment and reflect upon the terms we are using: In the preceding paragraph we have used the terms "negate" and "refute" as synonyms. Of course, they are not. By overlapping them we wish to emphasize that, in certain social practices, the *format* of refutation is used to gain power by lowering a competitor's professional status as a means of raising one's own. Normally, arguments are intended to be persuasive, to influence audiences. Rebuttals of likely objections are an aspect of such suasion. Discourses are not, however, merely logical artifacts; they have social effects. In situations wherein rebuttals are not logically permissible (owing to the lack of any grounds for refutation), they may still be stated and nonetheless have interpersonal consequences. Socially, rebuttals (with or without grounds) are most often experienced emotionally as rebukes. When rebuttals lack logical force, "refuting" is indistinguishable from admonishing, reproaching, reprimanding, chiding, or rebuking. In literary theory, where there are few grounds for refutation, rebuttals are frequently conscious or unconscious attempts to gain academic status at the expense of others. This is the most deleterious aspect of the cutting edge negations which propel the trickling down of theories—to the discussion of which we now return.

As an original theory trickles to less privileged places, "informed" critics always seem to surface just in time to refute alleged "misuses" of the original theories by the "uninformed." These encounters follow typical scenarios: for instance, a lecturer from a prestigious university speaks to an audience of "uninformed" mainstream teachers. The discussion period divides the audience into two groups: those already initiated in the theory (the "informed") and those who are not. At such events, it is easy for those on "the cutting edge" to rebuke the uninformed for their misunderstanding of the novel theory. Teachers not already in privileged institutional positions rarely practice such refutations (rebukes) because teaching allows very little time to sharpen "cutting edges." It *appears* that very little of what counts as "theory" can take place in other than the most privileged and elite institutions. Consequently, the trickle-down theory of theories that legitimizes "cutting edge negations" ironically legitimizes hierarchies of exclusion even when the ostensible "cutting edge" of the theory offers itself as a critique of those very structures of oppression. In other words, it functions less as radical critique than as the usual business of aggrandizement by exclusion.

Who is being tricked here? Whereas theorists respond to the concepts of other theorists, teachers respond to the problems of the persons they teach. And the problems students have in writing and reading are rarely resolved by the cutting edge negations of their beliefs. Fortunately, few theories survive classrooms in their pure formulations.

Almost all are watered/trickled down. The pure form of a theory is rarely germane to the exigencies of the situation in which it is allegedly applied. In different contexts, not only are different theories required, but different versions of the same theory are called for. What helps, helps. Hence, there is no need to worry whether the theory is in its correct, pure, or "original" form, thereby maintaining its "cutting edge" force.

In fact, the original theory (deconstruction, reception theory, etc.) is not what gets circulated anyway. Abstract ideas do not circulate well. By contrast, the new and somewhat threatening configurations of social relations that a "cutting edge" theory seeks to legitimize may be protected by the umbrella of theory. The social relations that kept traditional authorities in power, in other words, get deconstructed along with the privileged texts that legitimize those relations. Deconstructive readings make an interesting example because they are less revolutionary than they sound but more revolutionary than they seem. As a reading strategy, deconstruction has many parallels with New Criticism in its formal investigation of textuality, shifting the critic's focus merely from intratextuality to intertextuality. At the same time, deconstruction configures cultural differences affirmatively and thus becomes a critique of hegemonic social relations. And yet, just as easily, deconstruction can be a cutting edge negation and perpetuate exactly that which it claims to dismantle—hierachization. Contexts dramatize theories. As R. Radhakrishnan (1991) suggests: "To alienate and denaturalize the pedagogy of the privileged is one thing; alienating and denaturalizing the pedagogy of the oppressed, quite another" (129).

There is no "pure" or foundational form of the theory that will inherently prevent its use for oppressive purposes. A postmodern theorist who insists that we must circulate down to "ordinary" people the concepts of "suture," "supplementarity," "the little 'a,'" "differend," or even, "ISA's," may be engaging in nothing more than the practice of a cutting edge negation, a practice that may very well be painfully experienced as arrogance and elitism for those not so well versed in the purities of theoretical discourse. We ought to question the belief that such "radical" practices bring about desired social changes.

Though abstract concepts circulate in tidy conceptual frameworks, the reformations of social relations they entail is a messy affair requiring ad hoc, illogical, and intuitive adjustments to the original ideas. To take one example, new conceptions of teacher-student relations become widespread teaching practices, not because they trickle down as ideas, but because they become the subject of lore. Faced with oppressive and demanding situations, teachers invent tactics to alleviate some of the oppression and pain their students experience, and, when these are successful, they enter the lore of teaching practices. Such pedagogical innovations are born out of self-reflection and self-criticism; teaching lore is not foolish or thoughtless. In other words, some teachers and students work *as theorists* even though they are not recognized as professional or institutional "Theorists." Their theories, however, are rarely abstract generalities. More often than not, they configure their experiences in generally helpful ways, and these configurations enter the lore of changing teaching practices.

By using the term "configure" in speaking of lore, we promote what the word suggests. Figures are perceived together (in relation to each other). Most theories invariably have a "configural" dimension. The clearest example is Foucault's theory of discipline as it is configured in the Panopticon. Althusser perceives ideology as an "apparatus." Lacan understands subjects in terms of "the mirror stage." Derrida deconstructs meanings and decenters texts. These images all configure human relations. Schools, to a reader of Foucault, look like prisons. Readers of Althusser feel bound to institutions as binding apparatuses in which relations of power constrict their lives. And so on.

From this point of view, the force of humanistic theories derives from their power to reduce painful human problems in local situations. But local action presupposes a global perspective. When a local plant is petitioned to clean up its act because it is contributing to the destruction of the ozone layer, that local action has global consequences. Similarly, in a cultural pragmatics, theories are heuristic devices whose metaphorical configuration of potential relations suggests, not an application, but a tactic, an act, an image that fosters creative solutions to the problems addressed. This brings us to our main point: *At the level of practice, the ad hoc contingent activities brought to bear on pedagogical situations are contributions, not to some "cutting edge" theory, but to the reformation of social relations in the polis.*

What we earlier described as the "watering down," the "bastardizing," the "misreading" may actually be powerful insights institutionally misdescribed in "cutting-edge refutations" as errors. "Theory," usually quite conceptually rigid, often works because it is bent and twisted into a usable tactic. Regardless of their force, tacticians know how to trick institutions into believing that their work is legitimate because it is authorized by a high-profile theory. In cultural studies, theory is "empty" *unless it can be turned into lore,* that is, into tactics that resolve, however temporarily, difficulties in the relations among personal, institutional, and global concerns—hence, the term "cultural pragmatism." In its most potent form, lore exists as a set of anecdotes implying tactics or strategies. These anecdotes exist in their richest form as stories about human interactions. By configuring them, lore achieves theoretical force.

Lore as a Reconception of Research

The term "lore" designates teaching practices. In *Rhetorical Traditions and the Teaching of Writing,* Cy Knoblauch and Lil Brannon (1984) use the term to mean the untutored, ahistorical, nontheoretical, even uninformed classroom practice that prevents composition studies from being taken seriously. But in *The Making of Knowledge in Composition: Portrait of an Emerging Field,* Stephen M. North (1987) attempts to recuperate lore by defining it as "the accumulated body of traditions, practices and beliefs in terms of which Practitioners understand how writing is done, learned, and taught" (22). Lore is a group of stories about teaching practices that "work" at solving local and contingent teaching problems. Using Mina Shaughnessy's work at CUNY as a paradigmatic example, North calls for the profession to take lore more seriously. He calls attention to lore as the profession's procedure for circulating knowledge. Virtually every reviewer of North's book called attention to his account of and interest in "lore," and most (e.g., James Raymond, Richard Lloyd-Jones) hailed it as a welcome shift in emphasis for composition studies. Even Richard Larson, whose review was largely negative, comments with interest on North's argument for the "re-establishment of Practice as inquiry" (North 1987, 371). David Bartholomae, however, objects that North is like an anthropologist among the natives, taking a scientific higher ground as he describes the work of teachers, urging them to adopt the procedures of science so that they can be taken seriously. In "Taking Practitioner Inquiry Seriously: An Argument with Stephen North," Elizabeth Rankin (1990) suggests even more strongly that North's "analysis of practitioner inquiry rests on assumptions that have been seriously called into question by such theorists as Foucault, Derrida, Rorty, and Geertz" (261), that is, that knowledge can be "made" in positivistic processes of falsification. Rankin asserts that lore is validated when it is able to demonstrate that it "works" at achieving the teacher's objective. Of course, as both North and Patricia Harkin (see below) note, lore or practice may not be inherently liberating. Lore's political effect depends on its configural uses within specific social relations. If the teacher's objective is to transform students into New Critics or business executives, nothing prevents a teacher from drawing on such lore.

Whereas North values lore in spite of its difference from scientistic means of knowledge production, and Rankin asserts that these differences are only apparent, we value lore because of these differences. In "The Postdisciplinary Politics of Lore," Patricia Harkin (1991) asserts that lore is "non-disciplinary: it is actually defined by its inattention to disciplinary procedures" (125). In her analysis of Shaughnessey as the paradigmatic instance, Harkin construes lore as teachers' ability to use, but not be constrained by, existing institutional and disciplinary practices as they try to solve local and contingent (cultural) problems. Thus lore can be seen as an alternative to foundationalism and even as an antidote to foundationalist tendencies to reduce complex cultural situations to simplistic problems amenable to disciplinary solutions. She proposes that we construct "concrete accounts of proposed changes in institutional procedures that tell us what kind of knowledge teachers make, how they make it, and why it should count" (125). Louise Wetherbee Phelps offers such a model in "Practical Wisdom and the Geography of Knowledge in Composition" (1991), where she sees lore as "phronesis . . . the exercise of practical intelligence to take right action in particular cases" (864). Phelps undertakes to map a geography of knowledge in composition studies, using as her model a "teaching community collectively developing and testing a curriculum" (866) which she construes as a hypothesis about the "nature" (867) of knowledge, teaching, and learning. To this descriptive task, Phelps finds North's conception of lore "inadequate" in that "it seems to conflate an empirical analysis—what teachers typically do, more or less skillfully, in particular political and historical circumstances . . . with a phenomenological analysis of the essential defining qualities of practical wisdom" (868). Specifically, according to Phelps, North does not fully account for the ways in which teachers' accounts of their own (private, or at least individual) classroom experiences make "a public claim on others for attention" (869). Phelps invokes a tradition of philosophical distinctions embedded in disciplinary procedures to refine North's concept by discriminating procedural knowledge (knowing how) from propositional knowledge (knowing that). Through a complex system of diagrams and charts, Phelps shows how one can understand the informal and ad hoc attributes of lore through the formal and systemic contexts of traditional academic inquiry. This reliance on disciplinary constraints to describe lore, however sophisticated and thoughtful, limits, for us, the extent to which lore can be thought of as counterdisciplinary. We prefer, instead, to understand lore as the circulation of pedagogical research.

However, as we suggested earlier, changing classroom practices have redefined the research that takes place in literature departments housed in universities. The pedagogical situation, the transaction between students and teachers, is no longer a simple matter of the transmission of knowledge. Rather, since culture is the discourse that educates, research into pedagogy is synonymous with research into the struggle to re-form culture. Writing reading and reading writing are culture-making activities. When texts are no longer perceived as books, and libraries are no longer buildings, lore circulates our understanding of cultural reformations.

Given these formulations of the significance of lore, the cutting edge negations that stifle its circulation can be seen to be counterproductive. In dismissing lore, theorists and researchers alike usually understand it to be nothing more than the anecdotes teachers tell each other between classes. This is most notable in differences between publications on literature and their counterparts on composition. Whereas lore as such rarely sees print when literary texts are the topic, it is not uncommon to find lore-ic essays about teaching practices when writing is the topic. A variety of institutional constraints may explain these differences. Indeed, the very underprivileged status of composition within departments of English has ironically provided it a relative degree of freedom from the disciplinary constraints.[9] But even when teaching anecdotes appear in journals dedicated to composition or rhetoric, they are often dismissed as mere gossip of no theoretical value. In our view, however, the anecdotal character of lore is what gives it its theoretical value. Narrative presentations of teaching practices are not only circulated as anecdotes in the corridors of schools but are increasingly published in journals. To take lore seriously, then, is to alter the agonistic practice of disciplinary argumentation as refutation, and the consequences of such institutional changes involve nothing less than reconfigurations of English studies which challenge the deeply historical division between composition and literature.

As we have already suggested, lore is usually formulated in a narrative logic: I did this in my classroom, then, as a result, my students did that. Its anecdotal character is ordinarily thought to be of insufficient generality to be of much use beyond the local scene. Yet, narratives can have considerable generality. Since we cannot argue this point in detail here, we will simply invoke Kenneth Burke's (1969) notion of "representative anecdotes." As a point of departure for his theories, he sought, not a conceptual framework, but an "anecdote." He writes, in a way that is quite relevant to our considerations, that "if our theme were 'communication,' we should seek to form our terms about some typical instance of communication, rather than selecting some purely physical model, as a highway system or telegraphic network" (326). But, Burke continues, that instance should be "sufficiently demarcated in character to make analysis possible, yet sufficiently complex in character to prevent the use of too few terms in one's description" (324). It must have scope but remain simple. At the same time, it must have sufficient complexity to prevent reductive simplifications of the problem under investigation. So, anecdotes can express considerable generality. In fact, they can be as general as any pedagogical theory needs to be.

Moreover, anecdotes generalizing pedagogical situations have an outstanding advantage over concepts. They are, to use Clifford Geertz's (1973) term, "thick descriptions" that make it easy to recognize the experiences described. Hence such anecdotes have remarkable interpretive force. They configure experiences in ways that are more accessible than the thin generalities of abstract theories. The theoretical felicity of configurations as thick generalities not only make pedagogical theory accessible, but also retain the complexity of the human relationships under investigation.

Because lore is configural, its generalities are best considered as genres. To speak of generic conventions is already to acknowledge that lore is institutionalized and that even proposals to reform or revolutionize teaching practice and curricula will inevitably take an institutional form. Nonetheless, to describe these generic conventions, to mark their difference from and affinity with the more typical conventions of knowledge production, will, we think, be useful.

Ralph Cohen helps us to understand how lore might be described as a genre. In "Literary Theory as a Genre" (1975), he explains that literary theory, as writing, is subject to and describable in the same generic terms as any other writing. Theory, therefore, says Cohen, should not be subjected to logical tests of falsification. Rather, he says, theory should be studied as a "mixed genre" of writing; like any genre, it changes in time. These changes can be discussed in terms of themes, narrative structure, motifs, etc. Cohen's use of the term "mixed genre" evokes Clifford Geertz's (1983) use of the term "blurred genres" to point to works that cannot fit into any easy taxonomy. For Geertz, these blurred genres are characteristic of, and necessary to, postmodern life. Teaching is thick; teaching is postdisciplinary. In lore's mixing of genres, the problems are delineated in such a way as to make it clear that no one disciplinary solution to them is possible. Lore does not need to be a unified field theory.

Some Lore about Changing Classroom Practices

This volume contains essays that describe, interpret, and "theorize" teaching practice in ways that permit us to begin to trust the available lore. At the same time, these essays are formulated in the rhetoric of arguments expected in such collections, so the lore they present is not always discernible as such. We therefore call your attention to the anecdotes, narratives, and other literary devices used to configure classroom practices. Some essays configure pedagogy as a quest romance. Others are more ironic. Most are generically mixed. Since teaching does what works, some write how-to narratives. Others write manifestos.

Part II begins with two narratives that confront the problems of class differences that tangibly affect classroom interaction even when they remain concealed. Traditional models of literacy have tended to efface social class as a significant bearer of "literary" meaning or of differences in student-teacher behavior. Janet Zandy and Cary Nelson address these broad issues in local contexts. Zandy (chapter 2) configures the difference between her own working-class background and her students' upwardly mobile desires to succeed as a "struggle in the camp of the enemy," with heroic implications: "How does one put one's head in the mouth of the lion, and cause the lion some irritation?" However, instead of condescending to her students' apparent lack of moral sensitivity, she portrays them responding to specific historical fears about employment and opportunity in a time of scarcity. Students come to recognize their beliefs in individual freedoms and their feelings of constraint intersect.

Cary Nelson (chapter 3) configures the cultural work of his own teaching as a "mission about overturning the modern poetry canon." Like Zandy, he senses a historically different teaching environment from that of twenty years ago, and he stresses that although such historical changes require "different pedagogical strategies," this in no way "renders the politics of an earlier moment meaningless." For Nelson, the pedagogical consequences of his laborious research in noncanonical literature follow upon his efforts to socially recirculate in the classroom those very suppressed materials, but at a historical conjuncture when some students just don't want to engage those social spaces. Thus, although students may need to be guided by their forebears, the teacher must now avoid reinscribing the traditional hierarchies of the authoritative teacher and the passive student. Nelson's solution is to configure his class as a "theater of contesting interpretations" rather than a battle to impose beliefs. The teacher remains in control of the course content, but is not to be confused with a proponent of "political correctness," since Nelson argues that "penalizing students for racism or sexism will [not] cure them of those qualities." Rather, students engage texts that provide the opportunity for the class to "feel a sense of injustice about the profession's selective memory" without imposing the teacher's beliefs on them.

Part III offers four different but interrelated narratives of dramatic changes in classroom dynamics, as well as course content, emerging from the feminist movement of the last thirty years. Paula Treichler (chapter 4) focuses on specific case studies and the institutional contexts that constrain efforts to change classroom practices, but those case studies take on the force of representative anecdotes. Treichler points to the accumulating lore by "women and other outsiders" that, although often "invisible and inaudible" as well as "anecdotal and experiential," helps to identify problems and "suggest possibilities for change." By drawing on much of her own extensive research in gender studies, Treichler identifies the narratives of idenity, power, and pedagogy that together "form a rich metanarrative about the purposes of a university and whose interests it exists to serve." Just as we argued against the "trickle-down theory of theories," Treichler questions the need for any single "feminist pedagogy as constituted by a set of practices": the ad hoc dimension of pedagogical work in different institutional contexts and social circumstances prevents the formation of a single body of pedagogical knowledge or practice. For Treichler, "language, speaking, teaching, and interaction are all difficult activities that need to draw upon whatever resources [lore] are most relevant."

Barbara DiBernard and Sheila Reiter (chapter 5) tell of their use of *A Feminist Dictionary* in the classroom. This dialogue, like Hurlbert and Bodnar's (chapter 11) co-authored contribution, does not pretend to be a scholarly essay in any traditional way. As a collaboration between a teacher and a student, it is a kind of lore useful for anyone interested in changing classroom practices rather than for furthering cutting edge arguments about disciplinary knowledge. For them, as for Bauer and Jarratt (chapter 7), the circulation of knowledge is not an epistemological but a political issue. In their narration of pedagogical experiments, "the distinction between teacher and student are blurred" as they move closer to "the eradication of classroom hierarchy and the shared experience of teaching and learning." This pedagogical journey becomes "an unconventional task, one that has no model of scholarship." Indeed, their essay produces a new kind of lore about a new kind of resource, one that has been excluded by the disciplinary models of scholarship.

Ellen Berry and Vivian Patraka (chapter 6) configure their classroom as a "laboratory of culture" which "enable[s] students to produce theory themselves and to interrogate the production of knowledge within particular frameworks." They discount the "trickle-down" model of the dissemination of theory by providing frameworks and taxonomies through which students describe their relations to theory. In cutting edge negations, their "frameworks" and "taxonomies" might be seen as reductive. But "bastardized" forms of theory do not worry Berry and Patraka—whatever abets theoretical reflection enters their classrooms. They stress collaborative and collective projects for "social transformation" without effacing conflicting agendas.

Dale Bauer and Susan Jarratt (chapter 7) offer a "feminist sophistics" to configure the troubled relations between pedagogy and politics without resorting to a repressive notion of "political correctness." In particular, familiar metaphors of "trace," "trajectories," and "growth," are reconfigured in feminist sophistics as "creations of counterauthority": students are "invite[d] . . . to trace their own trajectories of growth as they encounter feminist theory." Rather than force students to change their minds, students develop counterauthorities within their own discourses. But, as Bauer and Jarratt stress, "feminist sophistics does not demand that students adopt a politically correct position; in fact, it argues against any fixed agenda in favor of personally grounded and historically located exploration of social identities." Just as the original Greek Sophists were seen to battle the ahistorical idealism of Platonic dialogue, Bauer and Jarratt follow the Sophists in attempting to link civic virtue with personal experience and historical understanding. They cite Patricia Bizzell and Linda Brodkey, both speakers at their 1990 conference on feminist sophistics, who relate their respective versions of rhetorical authority and feminist activism to feminist sophistics, thus countering any fashionable postmodern skepticism with a sense of ethical commitment for the "exploration of difference." In other words, configuring the pedagogical situation as sophists speaking in the polis leads directly to the problems of enculturation we discussed earlier.

Part IV includes four essays that describe pedagogical experiments designed to transform the authoritarian structure of the traditional classroom and its correlative "banking" model of education. The possibilities for negotiating authority are always inscribed within the accommodations for difference available within any discursive framework and political context. Given the institutional settings in which power is distributed unevenly, pedagogically speaking, it is never a question of abandoning authority. In "Pedagogy of the Distressed," Jane Tompkins (chapter 8) tells how she came to abandon the customary performance model of education in favor of a student-centered classroom. Tompkins first explains why Freire's critique of the "banking" model of education does not apply to pedagogical situations in the United States. For her critique, she targets the "performative" model of teaching, wherein teachers act out the roles of superteachers to secure approval from their audiences. As Tompkins explains, the performance model exemplifies a deep-seated, institutionally sanctioned "fear of pedagogy itself" as exactly that which one didn't discuss in graduate school. This article may not strike many working in composition and rhetoric as so strikingly innovative as it will those devoted to traditional literary study. Nevertheless, this article generated considerable debate in the pages of *College English*[10] and thus bears historical interest for those interested in reconfiguring literary studies. Pedagogy is indeed a force of acculturation when, as Tompkins puts it, "The kind of classroom situation one creates is the acid test of what it is one really stands for." But Terry Ceasar (1992), in his *CE* comment, raises one of the key issues of this volume when he remarks that the ideological foundation for most discussions of pedagogy depends on the faulty assumption "that all classrooms in all institutions are basically the same, and therefore subject to the same 'distress,' the same pedagogy" (474). Rather, different stories, different configurations of power, and different kinds of lore emerge in different contexts: "Everybody knows that immense institutional differences exist, and powerful political inequalities. But no one is supposed to say so" (475). Likewise, we advocate the development of the kind of ad hoc, contextualized lore that will take us beyond the usual pieties about the interrelations of teaching and research.

Gerald Graff (chapter 9) takes Tompkins's description of the pedagogical problem of authority as his starting point. He narrates his own conflicted allegiance to the figures of the bully and the wimp: on one side is the bully who "over-asserts" his beliefs and intimidates his students who respond by assuming passive positions. On the other side is the wimp who "under-asserts" his beliefs through an "equivocating teaching persona" and a nonauthoritarian mode of discussion that leave him feeling that he defaults on his students' desire to learn from his experience and expertise. Teachers cannot resolve these problems so long as the classroom remains an isolated site of transformation. In short, "the autonomous course . . . inevitably keeps students dependent on teachers, regardless of how traditional or progressive the course may be in content or form." Graff therefore challenges us to reflect more critically and constructively on how our individual pedagogical practices are collectively structured in curriculum designs (the focus of part V of this collection). Rather than reproduce oppositional enclaves in isolated classrooms, Graff advocates a "more collective and integrated curriculum" that would foster a more open dialogue on university campuses.

Out of her own concern for dialogue and the negotiation of authority and difference, Patricia Bizzell (chapter 10) articulates a "third alternative" between the poles of those who advocate "value-neutral" teaching as a disinterested pursuit of knowledge and those who advocate "value-positive" teaching as a form of indoctrination and propagandizing. Just as we have argued that pedagogy is acculturation, Bizzell describes this alternative, whereby the "teacher-as-acculturator is provisional, shifting, and changing." As in Bauer and Jarratt's feminist sophistics, a teacher's negotiation of authority proceeds by way of persuasion, a notion of rhetorical authority, and the pursuit of civic virtue. As such, "the class becomes an ongoing exercise in collectively formulating and revising consensus on values," but these are not "simply those that the teacher prefers. Rather . . . these values should be those that are cherished in the society whose culture the educator is paid to reproduce." The classroom is then configured as a space for "modeling the practices of a participatory democracy, fostering civic virtue among the students, as much as direct teaching of civic virtue." In contrast to "cutting edge negations" or the agonistic practices of refutation, such civic virtue as Bizzell imagines depends on "the process of seeking agreement" in which differences are negotiated rather than denied. The diversity of our cultural heritages can be engaged in the ways that Mary Louise Pratt (1991) has configured the "arts of the contact zone": if a classroom becomes a contact zone, a social space "where cultures meet, clash, and grapple with each other, often in contexts of highly asymmetrical relations of power" (34), then the "arts of the contact zone" suggest the civic virtues necessary for pedagogy at the moments when, as Bizzell states, "language users are specifically trying to negotiate difference, to cross or blur socially constructed boundaries, to communicate across them." Such differences need not defeat the productive seeking of consensual values, but it does mean that pedagogy can be nothing less than "an attempt to refresh the inclusiveness of democratic values."

Equally concerned with teaching for a more democratic America, C. Mark Hurlbert and Ann Marie Bodnar (chapter 11) represent the most postdisciplinary writing in this volume. They narrate their experiences teaching and learning during the time preceding the Persian Gulf War, and for anyone who happens to have been a supporter of the war effort or of traditional teacher/student roles, this essay may prove especially challenging because of the obvious political differences. As a collaboration between a student and a teacher, Hurlbert and Bodnar describe in personally revealing ways the anxieties, fears, and pains that so many teachers felt but rarely found ways to engage in the classroom or in publication. Indeed, they confront the tension between the dialogical aims of their collaborative pedagogy and their moral feelings of outrage at their opposition to a war supported by most of their students. They configure their literature class as a kind of political as well as personal therapy: "Learning literature, then, is learning to come to terms with our collective needs and pains and how they foster local and world violence." Such an approach will no doubt seem abrasive to many readers, especially since Hurlbert and Bodnar do not simply narrate another success story, but reveal their own affective as well as intellectual journey. In their efforts to move Tompkins's basic directive toward student-centered classrooms toward "collectivist-like social relations through collaborative reading, writing, and evaluation activities," they demonstrate that the classroom is indeed a contact zone where genuine differences may have to be negotiated unless one returns to the traditional pedagogical models whereby such conflicts are suppressed in the name of a common "subject" and authority. As Kurt Spellmeyer (1993) has argued: "The teacher who gives students real-world problems—or better, real-world projects—the teacher who sets the stage for genuine collaboration runs the risk of what may look to some sensibilities very much like chaos" (248). Hurlbert and Bodnar have taken those risks of negotiating real-world problems in the classroom, and they have done so without claiming to sustain an idealized "collaborative community" such as one finds in the work of Kenneth Bruffee. The collaborative narrative which they offer here may serve as a kind of lore that might help others in the "collective investigation and intervention" of troubling social issues at both the local and global levels.

The three essays included in part V concern curricular changes, particularly in the directions of cultural and rhetorical studies. Alan Kennedy, Chris Neuwirth, Kris Straub, and Dave Kaufer of Carnegie Mellon (chapter 12) argue for curricular revisions of the innovations that brought so much recent national attention to their literary and cultural studies program. This essay can profitably be read as the sequel to Alan Kennedy's earlier "Committing the Curriculum and Other Misdemeanors" (1992) where he provides a general overview of the importance of curriculum revision in the present historical moment. As he argues there: "In a general way, departments of English are currently positioned to do some substantial thinking about their purposes and constructions in relation to a general set of educational responsibilities of the university in a postmodern world"(24). He concludes this previous essay with a section on "Positions, Argument, Interpretation," which leads directly to the proposals he and his colleagues elaborate on in their contribution to this volume. Rather than taking the posture of "cutting edge" revisionists and negating the previous work of their colleagues, they depict their work as an addition to an existing structure. They describe their department as a triad of literary and cultural studies, rhetoric, and creative writing so that they might intervene in the dualistic institutional hierarchy that has plagued all of the previous curricular innovations. Their narrative concludes by configuring all of these strands of development, argument, cultural change, and knowledge as discursive maps of a cultural terrain on which students and faculty need to learn to negotiate the intersections of self, other, power, and authority.

Beverly Guy-Sheftall (chapter 13) offers a moving account of working from a black feminist perspective at Spelman College to transform the academy. She presents her view of transformation as a process of undoing the "miseducation" that students have ingested through the normative educational models that legitimate "Western, European American, white, male, Christian, middle-class, and heterosexual" forms of knowledge. Unlike the other contributors to this volume, her students are primarily African American women, so the majority of her students have not had their identities valued in their previous education. Besides a shift in content of the texts assigned, Guy-Sheftall also makes central to her students' learning "the idea that knowledge is also experiential." She therefore asks students to choose sites where "gender/race/class issues are played out" and to visit them and incorporate their observations into their papers and oral reports. Clearly, such disruption of the isolated classroom reconfigures relations between textual interpretation and worldly activities. Concluding with a plea for a new kind of cultural literacy, Guy-Sheftall reiterates a belief shared by all the contributors to this volume that "in opposition to E. D. Hirsch's call for 'cultural literacy,' we must create educational environments which will produce multicultural literates." This is a challenge all of us will in one way or another have to meet as our culture changes demographically as well as politically in the upcoming decades.

Anne Balsamo and Michael Greer (chapter 14) imagine their efforts at revising curricula toward cultural studies as a kind of intellectual troublemaking within the precincts of traditional literature departments. As they explain, "Cultural studies is most usefully seen as a displacement of 'literature' and an interruption of the established practices of the teaching of literature." Cultural studies can never be smoothly integrated into existing literature programs without ceasing to become cultural studies. This is consistent with James Berlin and Michael

Vivion's (1992) sense that: "Cultural studies is integral to the current uncertainty in English departments, acting as both a catalyst and a response"(vii). Again, just as we spoke of pedagogy as culturation, so Balsamo and Greer ask students to "construct a working notion of 'acculturation' to name the process whereby people learn to reproduce dominant narratives of gender identity." Drawing on Graff's notion of teaching the conflicts, they argue that "institutional history and conflict ... rather than 'primary texts' and the canon, formed the essential backbone of the course." Though they do not use the term "lore," Balsamo and Greer conclude that "the cultural studies classroom is a place where the distinctions between theory and practice, politics and scholarship become hopelessly muddled." Lore often involves such postdisciplinary muddling, and Balsamo and Greer's lore about cultural studies undermines any "pedagogical 'model' for undergraduate teaching wherein the roles/positions of the teacher and those of the students are clearly defined or determinable in advance of the discussions that take place in the classroom." Given the contingencies of lore, "cultural studies," as Berlin and Vivion (1992) argue, "simply cannot be easily pinned down." But what we can count on is that the "disruption of the reading-writing (passive consumption-active production) binary opposition leads to a further set of related disruptions in the usual business of the English departments" (x). The task we must face is creating and constructing lore that will lead to reconfigurations of English studies productive of a better culture for all citizens, not just those who already occupy privileged positions.

Conclusion

Having described some varieties of lore about the changing classroom practices this volume collects, it might *seem* appropriate to conclude by suggesting how they all come together to form a new paradigm of research methods and present a new diagram to replace the worn out Abrams model. But if you have read this far, you'll know that such a gesture would contradict everything we've said. The configurations of lore presented in this volume *do not add up to some new paradigm*—quite the opposite: as convenient fictions, they remain ineluctably context specific.

It may, at first, seem shocking to call configurations fictions. After all, we have gone to great lengths to persuade you that configurations of lore are theoretical and heuristic outlines of our most crucial research endeavors. But they are also indispensable fictions.

Recall the debates about who or what "the reader" was in the early days of reader-response theories. There was Riffaterre's "superreader," Fish's "informed reader," Fetterley's "resisting reader," empirical studies of actual readers, and so on. Theories of pedagogy face the same dilemma. Who or what is *"the* teacher" and who or what are *"the* students" and what is *"their* relationship"? We need to recognize that any configuration of teachers and students is a fiction—but a purposeful one.

Whenever a configuration becomes a part of lore, even in instances in which it is a direct description of an actual classroom, it takes on a level of generality that turns the relationship configured into a generic one. It becomes what Kenneth Burke called a "representative anecdote." Configurations do not have a one-to-one correspondence to the "facts of the matter." It would be more accurate to say, instead, that they have a one-to-many relationship to possible situations. In short, lore's anecdotes are heuristic, not empirical. Though they are indispensable, they are disposable when their ad hoc usefulness withers. They are analogies. Like other analogies, they grow old but can outlive their usefulness and become clichés. They do not add up to a new paradigm. They come and go. They cannot be diagrammed.

We believe that it is as (1) impossible, (2) theoretically unsound, and (3) socially unfortunate to speak of "the student" or "the teacher" as it ever was to speak of "the author" or "the text" or "the reader." We hope only to mark a moment in a process that will be seen to have shifted the profession's attention from conceptions of to configurations of social relations that reflect the complexity of the actual people who occupy not only the subject positions, but also the chairs: Jason and Melissa, Stanley and Loretta, Tyrone and Star, Jesus, Ahmad.

Notes

1. In *Critical Teaching and the Idea of Literacy,* Knoblauch and Brannon (1993) offer a fine analysis of the ways in which the popular media representations of "PC" and the "culture wars" have debilitated public understanding of the issues: "And so our point: whether given a limited speaking role, or only allowed a walk-on appearance, or never being named at all except in such malevolent corporate references as 'thought police,' critical teachers don't tell their own stories; they are spoken of and spoken for, rendered evil or pious or silly, but otherwise silent" (30–31).

2. We place "subjects" within quotation marks to flag the ambiguity the term now holds. On the one hand, it remains a synonym for "the *object* of study." On the other hand, it is now more often used to mean "a discursive representation of the role *persons* play in social formations."

3. Our use of the term "pragmatic" bears little relation to Abrams's use. We derive our usage of the term "cultural pragmatics" from the progressive movement and the tradition of radical pragmatism of James, Dewey, and others. There are complex historical relations to these traditions and to the contemporary neopragmatist movement that deserve more space than this introduction affords. Nevertheless, our basic contention is that, historically speaking, the progressive movement was broadly defeated in the institution-alizing of New Criticism as the dominant paradigm for literary studies in America. Arthur Applebee provides a very clear historical analysis of how this happened. His book *Tradition and Reform in the Teaching of English: A History* (1974) documents the success and failure of the entire movement. Applebee concludes: "One of the failures of the progressive program in the late thirties was its inability to specify precisely its structuring principles, leaving the 'experience curriculum' subject to a continuing loss of focus and gradual erosion." The progressivist focus on experiential learning, narrative, and stu-dents' involvement in their education gave way to a text-centered, non-student-oriented, authoritarian model of a methodically studied body of "literary" knowledge. With respect to contemporary literature departments, Deweyan scholars like Louise Rosenblatt and Dorothy Walsh hardly had an impact on the New Critical hegemony and stood out as voices of resistance to the domi-nant text-based New Criticism that, in fact, still informs most all anthologies of literature and the pedagogies that parallel them (see Mailloux 1989). More-over, in our school system, the now deeply entrenched testing programs, tracking instruments, etc. testify again to the dominance of models now very at odds with progressivist education.

Dewey, for example, anticipated postdisciplinary, experiential learning and emotional engagement rather than disciplinary objectivity as modes of learn-ing. Our point of difference is that recent theoretical interventions draw on critiques of disciplinarity, power/knowledge configurations, and, as we will point out below, lore. It is not insignificant that none of this research was available to the earlier progressive movement. Moreover, our work is deeply influenced by the related work of Kenneth Burke, who joins contemporary interest in rhetoric with many of the implications of postmodern thought via a notion of dramatism.

We also use the term "cultural pragmatism" to distinguish our work from the neopragmatist movement that has been popularized recently by Stanley Fish, Richard Rorty, and others. While we agree with the basic "antifounda-tionalist" stance of these critics, the neopragmatists have generally articulated a fairly bland and politically conservative view of relativism that tends to reinforce the status quo more than challenge it in the ways that the radical strains of James and Dewey would lead. Again, this is also a complex histori-cal argument. See Downing's "Deconstruction's Scrupples" (1987) for a brief overview of these relations.

4. Our remarks here are directed primarily toward the role of pedagogy in literary study, which we have been focusing on throughout. Composition and rhetorical studies have long focused on teaching, and this is part of the insti-tutional division between NCTE and MLA that we wish to challenge. But even in the case of composition studies, until recent years most work in composi-tion was still dominated by "value-neutral inquiry," formalistic concerns with "discursive modes," writing styles, heuristics, and grammar. As Patricia Biz-

zell suggests in her essay in this volume, much of what counted—and still counts—for research on teaching writing sought "to analyze essays as models of so-called 'effective' introductions, 'vivid' descriptions, or 'well-organized' arguments." If we consider pedagogy as the wide-ranging cultural processes for the production and dissemination of knowledge and values by which we become "acculturated," then such a sociohistorical concern for pedagogy is, for the most part, of more recent origin in all of English studies.

5. Knoblauch and Brannon (1993) describe the social and ideological effects of these foundationalist arguments: "Arguments for cultural and functional literacy plainly dominate the American imagination at the moment, and for predictable reasons. In the main, they articulate the needs, hopes, anxieties, and frustrations of conservative ideology. They reveal in different ways the means of using an ideal of literacy in order to maintain the world as it is, a world in which the interests of the United States, and indeed particular groups within this country, dominate the interests of others, both within and without" (20–21).

6. We do not wish to reinscribe a familiar division between persons and texts, as if "persons" signaled a realm exterior to the conditions of textuality. Rather, we use the term "persons" as an orientation toward work in the humanities that highlights a shift from texts as discrete objects to persons in cultural transactions. In other words, despite the recent poststructuralist arguments for a study of textuality and "textual power," the disciplinary "power" to re-enforce a curriculum based on discrete textual objects prevails. Persons are deeply "written" by their cultures, but our rhetorical purpose for the term "persons" is intended as part of the need to reconstruct the humanities around persons rather than the scientistic orientation toward textual objects.

7. Kurt Spellmeyer (1993) offers a remarkably similar account of the shift of pedagogy: "We become aware of our potential to remake knowledge only after we remember that something is always missing, that learning starts with the sensation of being trapped" (187). Being trapped is indeed a socially and discursively induced pain, and we are only beginning to learn how it feels to start learning in such places.

8. We wish to emphasize the social dimensions of "refutation" as a cultural practice whereby one person refutes or negates another. Among the many meanings of "negate" we find "to render invalid," "to rule out," and "to deny." There are, indeed, social dimensions to such ruling and denying. Likewise, "refute" derives from the Latin *refutare*, which means to "rebut," or "drive back," thus revealing the aggressive and agonistic dimension of "refutation" as a social practice. In this sense, then, negation as refutation reinforces competitive American individualism. This sense of the word seems to contrast with the less rhetorical and more philosophical meaning of "refutation" as a logical process of falsification, disproving false assertions. Our point is that the two meanings cannot be easily separated. This is not the place to elaborate on the philosophical sense of "negation." We do, however, wish to distinguish the social consequences of "negation" as refutation from the more philosophical sense of "negation" as a force of criticism and critique. Thus, our essay is intended as a critique of the literary discipline. Nevertheless, as a form of social criticism, we believe that the development of alternatives is more productive than the development of critiques.

Interestingly, in a recent "Comment and Response" in *College English,* Mike Rose (1992) asks the reviewer of a collection he helped to edit, "[W]hy it is [that] we in the academy feel it's necessary to attack each other in this way" (81). He concludes his response by asking "the critical question": does the reviewer "think it necessary to reduce our work and attribute cynicism and irresponsibility to us in order to forward her own scholarship? Recent essays in *CE* by Olivia Frey and Jane Tompkins are asking us to consider the adversarial way we academics establish our authority" (83). This is exactly the question we are raising in this essay.

9. This is ironic for the obvious reason that "composition" has historically evolved as the less prestigious, "service-oriented" sector of English departments in comparison with the institutionally privileged domain of "literature." James Berlin (1991) offers an excellent historical overview of how the division between "poetic" (as new conceptions of this term emerged in the eighteenth and nineteenth centuries) and "rhetoric" shaped English departments into their "higher" and "lower" concerns. As Berlin explains, "[F]or English studies all that is important and central in the study of discourse falls within the domains of literary texts and all that is unimportant and marginal is found in the realm of rhetoric" (23–24). He goes on to argue that "English Studies is entering a new moment in its development, a moment in which the received poetic/rhetoric relationship is being deconstructed and reformulated along lines that attempt to restore the recognition of the relations between discourse and politics" (25).

10. Between April 1991 (*CE* 53.4) and April 1992 (*CE* 54.4) there were nine different letters from readers and one response from Tompkins in the "Comments and Response" section of five different issues. In fact, the editors of *College English* invited further debate around this article in *CE* 53.5. That such varied and intense response should be signaled by this article suggests how deeply literary study has been devoted to disciplinary models of canons, texts, and periods even though recent pedagogical innovations all call for revisions in this orientation.

Works Cited

Abrams, Meyer H. 1953. *The Mirror and the Lamp: Romantic Theory and The Critical Tradition.* New York: Oxford University Press.

Applebee, Arthur N. 1974. *Tradition and Reform in the Teaching of English: A History.* Urbana: National Council of Teachers of English.

Berlin, James A. 1991. "Rhetoric, Poetic, and Culture: Contested Boundaries in English Studies." In *The Politics of Writing Instruction: Postsecondary,* edited by Richard H. Bullock and John Trimbur, 23–38. Portsmouth, NH: Boynton/Cook.

———, and Michael J. Vivion, eds. 1992. *Cultural Studies in the English Classroom.* Portsmouth, NH: Boynton/Cook-Heinemann.

Burke, Kenneth. 1969 [1945]. *A Grammar of Motives.* Berkeley: University of California Press.

Cahalan, James M., and David B. Downing, eds. 1991. *Practicing Theory in Introductory College Literature Courses.* Urbana: National Council of Teachers of English.

Ceasar, Terry. 1992. "Comments on 'Pedagogy of the Distressed,'" *College English* 54(4): 474–77.

Cohen, Ralph. 1975. "Literary Theory as a Genre." *Centrum* 3.1 (Spring): 45–64.

de Man, Paul. 1982. "The Resistance to Theory." *Yale French Studies* no. 63: 3–20.

Donahue, Patricia, and Ellen Quandahl, eds. 1989. *Reclaiming Pedagogy: The Rhetoric of the Classroom.* Carbondale: Southern Illinois University Press.

Downing, David B. 1987. "Deconstruction's Scruples: The Politics of Enlightened Critique." *Diacritics* 17.3 (Fall): 66–81.

Fish, Stanley. 1987. "Anti-Foundationalism, Theory Hope, and the Teaching of Composition" and "Interview with Stanley Fish." In *The Current in Criticism: Essays on the Present and Future of Literary Theory,* edited by Clayton Koelb and Virgil Lokke, 65–98. West Lafayette, IN: Purdue University Press.

Freire, Paulo. 1970. *Pedagogy of the Oppressed.* Translated by Myra Bergman Ramos. New York: Continuum.

Geertz, Clifford. 1973. *The Interpretation of Cultures: Selected Essays.* New York: Basic Books.

———. 1983. "Blurred Genres: The Refiguration of Social Thought." In *Local Knowledge: Further Essays in Interpretive Anthropology,* 19–35. New York: Basic Books.

Goswami, Dixie, and Peter R. Stillman. 1987. *Reclaiming the Classroom: Teacher Research as an Agency for Change.* Portsmouth, NH: Boynton/Cook- Heinemann.

Graff, Gerald. 1987. *Professing Literature: An Institutional History.* Chicago: University of Chicago Press.

Harkin, Patricia. 1991. "The Postdisciplinary Politics of Lore." In Harkin and Schilb, 124–138.

———, and John Schilb, eds. 1991. *Contending with Words: Composition and Rhetoric in a Postmodern Age.* New York: Modern Language Association of America.

Henricksen, Bruce, and Thaïs E. Morgan, eds. 1990. *Reorientations: Critical Theories and Pedagogies.* Urbana: University of Illinois Press.

Johnson, Barbara, ed. 1982. "Teaching as a Literary Genre." *Yale French Studies* no. 63: iii–vii.

Kecht, Maria-Regina, ed. 1991. *Pedagogy Is Politics: Literary Theory and Critical Teaching.* Urbana: University of Illinois Press.

Kennedy, Alan. 1992. "Committing the Curriculum and Other Misdemeanors." In Berlin and Vivion, 24–25.

Knoblauch, C. H., and Lil Brannon. 1984. *Rhetorical Traditions and the Teaching of Writing.* Upper Montclair, NJ: Boynton/Cook.

———. 1993. *Critical Teaching and the Idea of Literacy.* Portsmouth, NH: Boynton/Cook-Heinemann.

Mailloux, Steven. 1989. *Rhetorical Power.* Ithaca: Cornell University Press.

Moran, Charles, and Elizabeth Penfield, eds. 1990. *Conversations: Contemporary Critical Theory and the Teaching of Literature*. Urbana: National Council of Teachers of English.

Morton, Donald, and Masúd Zavarzadeh, eds. 1991. *Theory, Pedagogy, Politics: Texts for Change*. Urbana: University of Illinois Press.

Natoli, Joseph, ed. 1987. *Tracing Literary Theory*. Urbana: University of Illinois Press.

Nelson, Cary, ed. 1986. *Theory in the Classroom*. Urbana: University of Illinois Press.

North, Stephen M. 1987. *The Making of Knowledge in Composition: Portrait of An Emerging Field*. Upper Montclair, NJ: Boynton/Cook.

Phelps, Louise Wetherbee. 1991. "Practical Wisdom and the Geography of Knowledge in Composition." *College English* 53(8): 863—85.

Pratt, Mary Louise. 1991. "Arts of the Contact Zone." *Profession 91*: 33–40. New York: Modern Language Association of America.

Radhakrishnan, R. 1991. "Canonicity and Theory: Toward a Poststructural Pedagogy. In Morton and Zavarzadeh, 112–35.

Rankin, Elizabeth. 1990. "Taking Practitioner Inquiry Seriously: An Argument with Stephen North," *Rhetoric Review* 8: 260–67.

Rose, Mike. 1992. "A Comment on 'On Literacy Anthologies and Adult Education: A Critical Perspective.'" *College English* 54.1 (January): 81–83.

Spellmeyer, Kurt. 1993. *Common Ground: Dialogue, Understanding, and the Teaching of Composition*. Englewood Cliffs, NJ: Prentice-Hall.

Stuckey, J. Elspeth. 1991. *The Violence of Literacy*. Portsmouth, NH: Boynton/Cook.

II Social Class
in Classroom Discourse

2 Human Labor and Literature: A Pedagogy from a Working-Class Perspective

Janet Zandy
Rochester Institute of Technology

What place does human labor have in the study of literature? What is the relationship between the flourishing of critical theory inside the academy and the decline of economic justice outside the academy? What pedagogical strategies offer some resistance to the expropriation of intellectual and cultural labor to proprietary interests? Or, how does one put one's head in the mouth of the lion, and cause the lion some irritation?[1]

For nearly a decade I have been experimenting in my writing and literature classes with the concept of work and workers' perspectives as subject and as strategy for study. My approach is not career training; actually, it is a form of career resistance. I am interested in fostering within the liberal arts a point of reference about what constitutes good work for human beings. I want to raise questions about the way work is defined, shaped, and controlled. I want to explore the relationship between work and leisure, to question the assumed dichotomy between the terms "work" and "leisure." I desire an investigation of worker artistry and worker spirituality, or to put it another way, the artistry and spirituality of good work. In short, I want to establish a beachhead of resistance to the usurpation and control of ordinary people's working lives by corporate America.[2] And, I propose to do this in literature and writing classes with students whose primary concerns and driving interests are in getting a good job.

Human labor as a subject in American educational practice is generally neglected, and as a perspective or theme in literary study is labeled either "proletarian" and/or dismissed. Literary anthologies claiming to present "the human experience" include innocence and experience, life and death, and other predictable universals, but they exclude work.[3] Workers are invisible—particularly in academic culture.

A small example: In a major American city, an academic conference is held. In the lobby of the hotel a professor of English makes small talk with me. He asks, "What is your field?" I answer, "American working-class literature." After a significant pause, he replies: "Oh, I didn't know there was a working class anymore." I suggest that there still is a working class as I glance around the hotel lobby to see people clearing tables, carrying food, cleaning ashtrays, washing windows, setting up chairs, etc. The lobby hummed with human activity, but individual workers blurred into the deep background of academic humanism.

Seeing is central to my purposes here. In *In Visible light: Photography and the American Writer: 1840–1940,* Carol Schloss (1987) describes our culture's "unequal distribution of visibility" as a "disturbing pattern of American experience, a pattern in which Rousseau's ideal of the state as a transparent community of mutually visible citizens and motives is rarely achieved," hence preventing "any truly reciprocal interaction in the world from becoming a reality" (266–67). This essay proposes a pedagogical practice that explores possibilities for reciprocal visibility. My intent is to use the commonality of work as a place from which I can practice a pedagogy that takes into account particularity and partiality without sacrificing consensus about what constitutes a just society.

Standpoint

As a first generation college student, a scholarship girl, I had to choose between "getting an education" and my working-class identity. I learned that the language of home was not the language of school, that family history and stories were far removed from what was officially labeled as historical or literary. I was taught to repress and devalue my working-class identity and believe in aesthetic perfectionism. This condition of doubleness, of equivocality, of bifurcation, of competing and multiple identities is an old story, hardly unique or particularly acute to me.[4] It is a much less submerged story now because we have theoretical tools to name that condition, and with them, the power of language to democratize educational practice.[5] But, I get ahead of myself.

Too often theoretical language either alienates those most inclined toward democratic pedagogy or languishes in a state of theoretical narcissism—the theoretician dazzled by the shiny brilliance of the tool.[6] I propose that we use theory as a map to trace those locations where different epistemologies intersect. These intersections, occurring outside and at the borders of the academy, are sites where outsiders can become visible to each other (and are not just points of linguistic pleasure). We can begin to reconstruct sites of reciprocal visibility by focusing on work and class identity.

I'm aware of how easy it is to betray working-class lived experiences. I do not wear my working-class identity as a trendy badge for academic conferences. Rather, I choose to keep that identity, particularly the realities of economic struggle, unsafe and dead-end jobs, and the memories of collective celebration and commitment. These memories serve to center me in opposition to academic elitism and enable me to see how the world of work is not separate from literary study.

In oral and written narratives, speeches, letters, essays, poems, and songs, we find evidence of how ordinary people pooled their resources in a common struggle against an economic system that prefers profits to people. Muted, fenced away from academic discourse, these stories are an inheritance of risk taking and mutuality. They offer a clarity about bosses and workers, a way of fusing worker consciousness with consciousness about race, gender, and ethnicity. But these central narratives are not public. They are hidden from working people themselves, obscured by narratives of minuscule possibility—stories of winning, stardom, and lucky breaks. Playing Lotto has replaced an earlier generation's belief in sainthood—a way to make it big. Class consciousness is thwarted by spurious narratives. What might happen if narratives of common struggle weren't blocked? What might happen if patterns of oppression were visible to working people, to students and teachers?

I am not interested in human labor as "theme" in literature; rather, I want to penetrate texts with a system of thought that concerns itself with work and the dignity of human labor. The historicity of work can be a tool to cut through those pedagogical practices that pen in rather than liberate consciousness. The theologian Dorothee Soelle (1984) offers this perspective on work and social relatedness:

> All workers act within a particular society and culture. All have inherited tools, technology, knowledge from past generations of workers. . . .
> To develop a historical sense of what work has been, to know what our grandparents did and the path they took to their achievements, is the aim of an educational process that puts self-understanding and human worth before capital. Yet this approach to work is almost unheard of in a nation like the United States, which evaluates labor primarily in terms of productivity. . . . Work is communal not only in the space of a given community but also in time, as the shared memory of what we have received from the past that accompanies us into the future. (94–95)

I make this distinction between work and class in my methodology: I use work in its broadest definition (including paid and unpaid labor, domestic and caretaking work) as an inclusive matrix. Work is common territory where differences of gender, race, and ethnicity can be visible and where questions of what constitutes good work can be raised. I use class, that is, human relations based on economic differences, to illuminate relationality, in particular, life at the border of difference, a site of disruptive fissures.[7] This dis/located position is a good place from which to question obedience, particularly accommodations to power that thwart self-knowledge. It is also an appropriate position from which to examine central and marginal stories.

In *Landscape for a Good Woman*, the British writer Carolyn Kay Steedman (1987) creates an autobiography about the tangled working-class lives of her mother and herself, and offers this insight:

> the processes of working-class autobiography, of people's history and of the working-class novel, cannot show a proper and valid culture existing in its own right, underneath the official forms, waiting for revelation. Accounts of working-class life are told by tension and ambiguity, out on the borderlands. The story—my mother's story, a hundred thousand others—cannot be absorbed into the central one: it is both its disruption and its essential counterpoint: this is the drama of *class*. (22)

This way of seeing, its relationality, is inherent to practicing a pedagogy of possibilities and liberation. What follows is a contextualization of this approach in relation to my students in an upstate New York technical institute and to the peculiar and particular historic moment of living in the United States in the 1990s.

Reagan's Kids

In December 1988, a bomb exploded on Pan Am Flight 103 over Lockerbie, Scotland. Two hundred and seventy people were killed, including a number of upstate New York students. In response to this event, one of my students wrote this in her journal: "[F]rom 31,000 feet they had no chance to save themselves. Thirty-eight students, thirty-eight fewer people competing for jobs."

How is knowledge so constituted for this American student that she might read the explosion of a packed airplane in terms of job competition? She does not speak for everyone, but she is not necessarily in the minority, either. Having read hundreds of journals, essays, and fragments of student thought, I am inclined to believe that this person voiced what others tend to think but not say aloud.

I call them "Reagan's Kids"; they are representatives of the generation who grew to adulthood under the reign of this ideological Mr.

Magoo, a cheerful gent who has no consciousness of his own destructive legacy. I don't assume that my generation is inherently any better; only, at the moment, the 1960s generation is getting better press, now that it has been rendered harmless.[8] But, Reagan's Kids have had to face a different set of historical circumstances and more rigid economic opportunities. Even governmental statistics indicate the shift of wealth, the decline in real wages, and the narrowing of economic choices. It is also an era in which accountability and mutuality, like savings and loan institutions, have been deregulated. Life is a game based on an ethos of scarcity, and the rules say that, if someone else loses, I may win.

So fearful of falling out of the middle class (Ehrenreich 1990),[9] these students don't have time for what John Willinsky (in a study [1990] of British nineteenth-century working-class literacy) calls "economically disengaged" knowledge, that is, knowledge without discernible market value.[10] Having had part- or full-time jobs since they were fifteen or sixteen, they are accustomed to earning and consuming, not contemplating. In harness, waiting to race down a narrow career track, functioning within a tight quarter system, dazzled by lucrative cooperative employment opportunities, these students don't have the leisure time or the inclination to question their goals, to ask about the ideological implications of the managerial positions they seek, or to wonder what is missing from degree programs shaped to corporate demands. Reality has been flattened for them in the homogenization of malls, news "shows," and popular culture. Small wonder that they are often emotionally flat; small wonder they resist knowledge, display symptoms of what James Moffett calls "agnosis," a fear of knowing.[11]

Mostly, these students want to find their place, to fit in. I want them to see that the world they are striving to fit into is much more complex, unstable, fragmented and endangered than their disembodied coursework might indicate. Or as Gwendolyn Brooks put it in a 1990 commencement address at Trinity College: "I shudder when I consider the possibility that squads of young people are struggling to fit in . . . Look at the craziness. Look at the fear. See the sickness. Into this you want to fit?"

I want to suggest that we recognize students' real fears about employment and use work as an epistemological position in the teaching of literature and writing. In *A Feminist Ethic of Risk*, Harvard theologian Sharon Welch (1990) describes responsible action as "the creation of a matrix in which further actions are possible, the creation of the conditions of possibility for desired changes" (20). I turn to human labor for such a matrix, a position where my aspiring engineers, hotel managers, and package designers can begin to see patterns of control and economic inequities. There is nothing new about looking at work from an owner's or corporate perspective; indeed, that is presented in most academic institutions as normative, not perspectival. I want students to recognize worker consciousness and identity, to develop new subjectivities, ways of discerning, through the juxtaposition of texts, their own replication of, or resistance to, oppression. I am not advocating economic determinism, that work is the central or only perspective, but rather that it is a site of intersection and mutual visibility of competing concerns and constituencies, where differences of race, gender, ethnicity, geography, and culture might be seen.

Pedagogy, Theory, and Curriculum

It is the rare student who has overt awareness of the "domestication" of his or her consciousness. When queried whether or not they are "free," most students react with ambiguity. They acknowledge the dogma of freedom, but, somehow, they don't *feel* it. It is in that fissure of doubt between the rhetoric of freedom and the experience of control that I wish to begin my conversation with students over literary texts. That fissure of doubt is also an appropriate intersection for theory, politics, and pedagogy—a place to ask if theory is aiding a liberatory practice.[12]

A pedagogy that insists on the visibility of human labor is also self-conscious about its theoretical girding. Jim Merod, in *The Political Responsibility of the Critic* (1987), draws the connection between "the world of everyday labor and that other world of intellectual exercise which seeks an essentially theoretical clarity" (1). In noticing the curious omission within critical practice of a "vocabulary for the world of human labor" (4), Merod draws attention to criticism as intellectual labor, as a kind of work, that can either reinforce or disrupt the status quo.[13]

There are no theoretical safe places. Theory, like technology, is situated within structures of power. The fragmentation of postmodern existence partially explains why workers in a hotel lobby may be invisible to humanities professors, and bombed planes might become job opportunities, but—as critical praxis—postmodernism offers little resistance to the further rendering of the fabric of human relationality. Linda Hutcheon argues, in *The Politics of Postmodernism* (1989), that it is not enough to "de-doxify" systems of meaning (153); there must also be a "move into political agency" (157).

It seems to me that any theory that holds relevance for the twenty-first century must move beyond an ethos of critique and an ethos of despair. We need theoretical hybrids that contain paradigms for reassembling as well as disassembling. We need to be less anxious about origins, philosophical parentage, and labels, and feel at home in the blurring of political, scientific, and literary theoretical boundaries. Interactive political models that go beyond monism (single-cause theories) and pluralism (celebration of diversity) offer the potential for coalition building (without erasing differences) by emphasizing intersecting rather than competing oppressions.[14] Human labor and literature, imagined as a site of interaction, allow for the recognition of difference without necessarily producing greater fragmentation.

An imaginative, startling, indeed, blasphemous paradigm for affinity rather than identity politics is Donna Haraway's (1985) reappropriation of the cyborg myth, "A Manifesto for Cyborgs." Haraway illuminates the conditions of human labor and the formation of culture by offering what she calls a "slightly perverse shift of perspective": "[a] cyborg myth . . . about transgressed boundaries, potent fusions, and dangerous possibilities. . . ." Instead of a cyborg as "a grid of control on the planet," Haraway imagines "a cyborg world [which] might be about social and bodily realities in which people are not afraid of their joint kinship with animals and machines, not afraid of permanently partial identities and contradictory standpoints" (585).

Such an imagined cyborg world might very well unsettle technological hegemony and offer a revolutionary and democratic interplay between the liberal arts and the sciences. But in the meantime, I must acknowledge my students genuine concerns about their economic futures, and, at the same time, warn them that trading education for job training will not deliver them into the promised land of secure employment—not to mention what restrictions it may impose on their development as human beings. It seems to me that my task in teaching literature at this historical juncture is to practice a pedagogy of visibility and resistance that would offer opportunities for students to deconstruct false promises of easy fits, and simultaneously to construct alternate realities of mutuality and accountability, to move from self-serving individualism to relationality and toward community. The pedagogy I wish to practice builds on a vision that takes in the concrete (the worker, the necessary, the sturdy underpinnings), acknowledges the specificity of race and gender, of paid and unpaid work, *and* evokes the visionary, the possibilities of alternative, economically just realities.

The motto for the college where I teach is "to make a living and to live a life."[15] Dazzled by the technology of solar cars, imaging science, and state-of-the-art computers, it is understandable why many students give the living-a-life part of the motto short shrift. A study of work that is not driven by the requisites of job training offers an opportunity to examine the tensions between life and work and the possibilities for fusion. I have used work as a thematic base for composition courses and have focused on work in literature and not just works *of* literature. I want to elaborate here on how worker consciousness can shape a course that has appeal for technocratic students—"Literature and Technology."

An appropriate course to question the balance of life and work, "Literature and Technology" offers a borderland where competing interests and subjugated knowledges can intersect. I avoid the stance of the humanist opposed to technology; it is unauthentic and beside the point. I ask, instead, for an investigation of the impact of technology on what it means to be a human being. I wish to push beyond the dated "Man versus Machine" dualism and move from the nebulous effects of technology to a more specific interrogation of deskilling, dehumanization, and the technologizing of humanity as slaves, birthing machines, or cyborgs. There are certain questions that always need to permeate the texture of the course: Who has the control? Where is the power? Who is subject? Who is object? Since technology and literary texts are both embedded in historical relations, I begin with readings that raise central questions about literary response to technological change. I surround five or six central texts with historical essays, news articles, journal excerpts, slides, videos, music, enough specific supplementary material to establish a context, a sense of relationality rather than textual isolation. Like photomontage, this literary montage approach offers a kind of aperture to a larger world and the possibility of dialogue with that world. I begin with Hawthorne's "Ethan Brand," Melville's "The Paradise of Bachelors and The Tartarus of Maids" and Leo Marx's *The Machine in the Garden* (1964). These provide a symbolic and literary landscape for raising questions of dislocation and showing the intertextual effect of reading about rich lawyers in juxtaposition with "girl" paper-mill workers. These readings also signal a central concern of the course—whether humans become subjects or objects, agents or victims. The terminology of subjectivity is useful, and students will keep track of those moments in the course when technology or labor transforms a human being into an "it." The garden and the machine juxtaposition in Leo Marx's famous essay exposes a powerful conundrum in American consciousness: a longing for a pastoral, greener America and an adoration for gadgets, for the control that machines promise.[16]

The Education of Henry Adams would be an appropriate next text, but I choose instead *The Lowell Offering: Writings by New England Mill Women, 1840-1845* (Eisler 1980) because I wish to emphasize class and gender in relation to work. This is a good place for students to see female workers as subjects who, although ambivalent about the noise and tedium of factory life, about lives lived "half in sunlight—half in shade" (77), are also proud of their literacy, culture, and passion for knowledge.

Next, to witness the degradation of work and the use of immigrant labor in relation to industrialization, we study Thomas Bell's moving novel *Out of This Furnace* (1976 [1941]). This fictionalized account of three generations of Slovakian steelworkers shows that for the working class, the boundary between work and home is very blurred, as women do laundry and keep boarders because "the job" does not pay men living wages. Often this novel evokes family memories for students: "[I]t compelled me to think of . . . how my grandfather and father [would] go to work very early in the morning and come back tired and hungry. I took this workday experience for granted. . . . This novel opened my mind to exactly how technology dictated life." In a victim-blaming culture, the sources of oppression can be invisible. Bell's novel offered this clarity for another student: "The reason for this inability to move out of these poor conditions is the mills themselves and the management of these mills . . . This is a very disturbing novel."

I contextualize Bell's novel with Lewis Hine's (1977) photographs of Slovakian immigrants as they land in Ellis Island and as they are "Americanized" as steelworkers in Homestead and Pittsburgh. I include technical explanations of Bessemer furnaces, with facts on American immigration policies in relation to industrial growth, and news articles about the displaced steelworkers of the 1980s. I have invited the contemporary photographer Margaret Evans to show slides of her photographs that document what she calls the "deconstruction" of the American steel industry.

I use Charlie Chaplin's wonderful and prophetic *Modern Times* as a transition to a study of the engineer, technology, and literature. This is an appropriate preamble to the satire and irony of Kurt Vonnegut's *Player Piano*. Originally published in 1952, *Player Piano*'s prescient and funny depiction of displaced workers is uncomfortably close to today's newspaper stories. A favorite selection, students enjoy Vonnegut's satire of the corporate world even as they trudge into class perspiring in their job-interview suits.

For a theoretical understanding of what Vonnegut and Chaplin are up to, I draw from Frederick Taylor's *The Principles of Scientific Management*, Karl Marx on "Alienated Labor," C. Wright Mills's "The Idea of Craftmanship," and David Noble's *America by Design* (1987). Cecelia Tichi's *Shifting Gears: Technology, Literature, Culture in Modernist America*

(1987) offers excellent visual documentation as well as acute cultural analysis. Tichi's analysis of the interpenetration of technology and poetry establishes a context for an analysis of technology as subject (Whitman's "To a Locomotive in Winter") and technology as form, what Tichi describes as "the machine-age poetics" of William Carlos Williams (230). This is also a good point at which to introduce working-class women's poetry, particularly Susan Eisenberg's tradeswoman poems (*It's a Good Thing I'm Not Macho*; 1984) and Sue Doro's railroad poetry (*Heart, Home & Hard Hats*; 1986) and selected women's coal-mining songs (*They'll Never Keep Us Down*; 1984).

I ask students to make an intellectual and imaginative leap in the final third of the course during their study of Margaret Atwood's *The Handmaid's Tale* (1987) and Octavia Butler's *Kindred* (1979). Because there are no Bessemer furnaces to light the way, these narratives elicit a more complex understanding of how social relationships are not only impregnated by technology, but are metamorphosed into technology. Atwood's dystopia about the usurption and control of women's bodies, particularly their reproductive capacity, provides a chilling parallel story to *The Lowell Offering*, the corporate "utopia" of 1840. Atwood's "aunts" and Lowell's housemothers are controlling mediators, all serving the "guardians" or corporate owners.

The Handmaid's Tale is a problematic text for many male students. In his paper, Alan writes: "I suspect there is something I didn't get out of his novel. I was extremely impressed with the writing quality and depth . . . but I was left wondering what is Atwood's agenda or mission."[17]

I conclude with a science fiction novel, *Kindred*, written by the African American writer Octavia Butler, and excerpts from Haraway's "A Manifesto for Cyborgs" as a way to examine the curious parallels between slaves and cyborgs. In *Kindred*, time travel, a science fiction cliché, is redefined in the context of slavery—the ultimate exploitation of workers—dehumanization, control, and resistance. Another student said that the "message or warning" in *The Handmaid's Tale* escaped him until he read *Kindred*: "Now . . . I can see that a society existed over 150 years ago with striking similarities to Margaret Atwood's creation. The plantation owners acting much like the Commanders, using their female slave reproductive resources for their own gain." Students had little difficulty with the concept of "technology of slavery," and they were willing to question their assumptions about progress when they realized that improved technology (for example, the cotton gin) actually increased the market for slaves.

I like to conclude by reading from Genesis and Exodus. I remind them that Biblical scholars agree that the Exodus story probably predates the expulsion from the Garden narrative—and that labor should not be studied apart from liberation.

There are many other possibilities for configurations of texts in a "Literature and Technology" course. I may use Marge Piercy's *Woman on the Edge of Time* (1976) or Christa Wolf's *Accident* (1989) the next time I teach this course. Texts that incorporate technology are plentiful; finding material that reveals technology as a force affecting class differences or race and gender oppression is not so easy.

Students choose final projects from a range of topics on technology and culture. I coax them to go beyond technological cheerleading, to problematize and question. Still, I've received a number of praise songs to the automobile from mechanical engineers and paeans to the brave new world of "highways of data" from computer scientists. Others, though, have been more critical and inventive: a paper on artificial intelligence using novels by Robert A. Heinlein and Arthur C. Clarke to argue that "artificial intelligence is by no means an equivalent to the human thought process"; another suggesting that fractals by themselves are not art, but that they can be shaped by artists to create unique images; a good paper on *Walden* that criticized Thoreau's "self-praise" and looked at the possibility of escaping into the woods in the 1990s; another explaining the themes of isolation and dehumanization in the work of sculptor George Segal and the wrapping technique he invented; a witty paper entitled "Star Trek: The Final Paper," in which the author used interviews to examine the appeal of both series (first and second generation) to children and college students; an interesting photo essay on the now defunct, behemoth grain elevators along the Erie Canal in Buffalo, New York; and a brave, feminist analysis of reproductive technology by a student majoring in biomedical technology.

I think that students are excited by the intellectual approach of this course. Dan writes: "I appreciate and like this class because of the multiperspectives I get out of it. Some perspectives are of the past; others are what it could be like in the future. This class has made me sit back and reflect on how technology has shaped my life."

There are complaints about the reading being "too depressing." I agree and sympathize; we all want to divert our eyes, our awareness. Our students have been encouraged to gloss over the unpleasantness of American history with smiley buttons; they are literally *trained* to end every verbal exchange with "have a nice day"; they yearn for closure, for getting on with it without ever identifying "with" or "it." How, then, to see that a little depression is necessary in the struggle for justice?

Who controls work is a question that needs to be raised in literary as well as economic contexts. Whether students find artistry or degradation in their work lives may very well depend on their knowledge of the history and literature of workers. American work literature reveals the underside of American history. If we wish good work for our students, we have to see and teach its complexity. It is not a prepackaged lifestyle; it is not careerism. We need to reclaim it as a primary human concern. We need strategies of resistance to the usurpation and control of work by the military and the corporation.[18] We need to offer our students alternatives to the roles of servant or boss, slave or pharaoh. We need possibilities for good work for ourselves, as well.[19]

Notes

1. Consider Ralph Ellison's allusion to the Book of Daniel in "Battle Royal," the first chapter in *The Invisible Man*, and the need for models on how "to struggle in the camp of the enemy" in practicing a pedagogy of resistance.

2. See Barbara Ann Scott's *Crisis Management in American Higher Education* (1983), especially chapter 8, "The Transformation of the Curriculum," for ways in which universities become handmaidens to corporate interests.

3. One example among many is the anthology entitled *Literature: The Human Experience* (5th ed.), edited by Richard Abcarian and Marvin Klotz (1992). A notable exception is Nicholas K. Bromwell's (1990) article "'The Bloody Hand' of Labor: Work, Class, and Gender in Three Stories by Hawthorne."

4. Many theorists and intellectuals have focused on double consciousness and border perspectives, particularly W.E.B. Du Bois, *The Souls of Black Folks*; Gloria Anzaldúa, *Borderlands=La Frontera* (1987); and bell hooks, *Feminist Theory: From Margin to Center* (1984). In *The Practice of Everyday Life*, Michel de Certeau (1984) sees "marginality" as "no longer limited to minority groups" (xvii). See also Trinh T. Minh-ha, *Woman, Native, Other: Writing Postcoloniality and Feminism* (1989), and Barbara Harlow, *Resistance Literature* (1987), for important theoretical analyses of marginality and culture; see also, Nancy Harstock, *Money, Sex, and Power: Toward a Feminist Materialism* (1983).

5. I felt the rupture in an atomistic way; I had no language or community that could explain or affirm it. One generational difference between the experiences of working-class college students in 1991 as compared with my experience as a college freshman in 1963 is an access to a language that names the experience of rupture—a discourse about otherness, difference, marginality, which provides a way of intellectualizing the distance between school and home. The discourse owes much to the presence of women's studies, ethnic studies, African American studies, and other nontraditional disciplines, but it cannot guarantee, a priori, a genuine challenge to oppressive power structures.

6. Stephen Watt (1992) sees "academic narcissism" as the central problem of the "linguistic left" (A40).

7. Class in America is a knot waiting to be unraveled. Benjamin DeMott (1990) offers this definition: "[C]lass is . . . the inherited accumulation of property and competencies, beliefs, tastes, and manners that determine . . . our socioeconomic lot and our share of civic power" (10).

8. Since "Desert Shield," the 1960s nostalgia has been relegated to fashion and music—both domesticated and depoliticized.

9. See Barbara Ehrenreich, *Fear of Falling* (1990). What percentage of my students are *actually* middle class is difficult to discern (student clothing style is a poor indication); surely, most would identify themselves as middle class.

10. "A Literacy More Urgent than Literature: 1800–1850" appears in an expanded version in John Willinsky, *The Triumph of Literature/The Fate of Literacy* (1991). This paper was presented at the second MLA conference on literacy (September 1990), one of the few academic conferences where there was occasion for interaction among theorists, union representatives, schoolteachers, and workplace literacy teachers.

11. Quoted in the introduction to Lunsford, Moglen, and Slevin (1990, 5).

12. Barbara Christian's "The Race for Theory" (1987; rpt. in Hansen and Philipson 1990) is an important, self-conscious critique of the role of the literary theorist and the interests served by theory.

13. Merod (1987) provides a worthy interrogation of the insularity of academic criticism in the United States. Merod is concerned about the reification of criticism, about the place of critical theory in the world, and about the co-opting and commodification of theory. See also, Cain (1984) and Said (1982).

Why not push Merod's point a bit further and ask under what labor conditions is theory written? What are the models for the structuring of academic work? The strategy of highlighting work as a subject within literary texts not only speaks to the concerns of technocratic students, but also illuminates the hierarchical working conditions within the academy. Consider the privileged conditions of the few and the oppressive situations of the many, and the continuing use of a reserve of adjunct faculty.

14. See "complementary holism" as defined in Albert et al. (1986). For political models for difference and community, see Alperin (1990); Lorde (1984); Reagon (1983); and Bunch (1987).

15. Rochester Institute of Technology originated in 1829 as an Athenaeum and Mechanics Institute. See Gordon (1982).

16. Consider the welcome-home ceremonies for the troops (often portrayed in the media like heroes from WWII movies) returning from "Desert Storm" and the technological pleasures of surgical strikes during the Persian Gulf War. Hurlbert and Bodnar's essay in this volume is especially appropriate in this context.

17. Apropos of Atwood's color-coded division of women's work in *The Handmaid's Tale*, a Penfield, New York high school received a $25,000 grant to conduct a program called "True Colors." The program assigns students to color-coded categories according to their personalities: "Orange students are adventurous, witty, charming . . . blue students are harmonious, enthusiastic, sympathetic, gold students are responsible, loyal, dependable . . . etc." According to the designer, Don Lowry ("[Lowry]" 1991) of California: "[T]he

color-coding is meant to help teachers match their teaching to different learning styles and to help students appreciate diversity and improve their self-esteem" (10E).

18. The question of shaping curricula and managing institutions to suit requirements of the military-industrial complex has surfaced at Rochester Institute of Technology over revelations that President Richard Rose was employed by the CIA while on sabbatical during the Persian Gulf War. See "[Richard Rose]" (1991a; 1991b).

19. I want to thank my colleague Joseph Nassar and my student Andrea Marcussen for their comments on this essay, and my "Literature and Technology" students for permission to quote from their writing.

Works Cited

Abcarian, Richard, and Marvin Klotz, eds. 1992. *Literature: The Human Experience.* 5th ed. New York: St. Martin's.

Adams, Henry. 1980 [1918; 1906]. *The Education of Henry Adams.* Franklin Center, PA: Franklin Library.

Albert, Michael, et al., eds. 1986. *Liberating Theory.* Boston: South End Press.

Alperin, Davida J. 1990. "Social Diversity and the Necessity for Alliances: A Developing Feminist Perspective." In *Bridges of Power: Women's Multicultural Alliances,* edited by Lisa Albrecht and Rose M. Brewer. Philadelphia: New Society Publishers.

Anzaldúa, Gloria. 1987. *Borderlands=La Frontera: The New Mestiza.* San Francisco: Spinsters/Aunt Lute.

Atwood, Margaret. 1987. *The Handmaid's Tale.* New York: Fawcett.

Bell, Thomas. 1976 [1941]. *Out of This Furnace.* Pittsburgh: University of Pittsburgh Press.

Bromwell, Nicholas K. 1990. "'The Bloody Hand' of Labor: Work, Class, and Gender in Three Stories by Hawthorne." *American Quarterly* 42 (December): 542–64.

Bunch, Charlotte. 1987. *Passionate Politics.* New York: St. Martin's.

Butler, Octavia E. 1979. *Kindred.* Boston: Beacon.

Cain, William E. 1984. *The Crisis in Criticism: Theory, Literature, and Reform in English Studies.* Baltimore: Johns Hopkins University Press.

Chaplin, Charles, (dir). 1936. *Modern Times.* 89 min. Entertainment, Inc.

Chittenden, Patricia, and Malcolm Kiniry, gen. eds. 1986. *Making Connections Across the Curriculum: Readings for Analysis.* New York: St. Martin's.

Christian, Barbara. 1987. "The Race for Theory." *Cultural Critique* 6 (Spring): 51–63. Rpt.in Hansen and Philipson, 568–69.

de Certeau, Michel. 1984. *The Practice of Everyday Life.* Translated by Steven Rendell. Berkeley: University of California Press.

DeMott, Benjamin. 1990. *The Imperial Middle: Why Americans Can't Think Straight about Class.* New York: William Morrow.

Doro, Sue. 1986. *Heart, Home & Hard Hats*. Minneapolis: Midwest Villages & Voices.

Du Bois, W.E.B. 1969 [1903]. *The Souls of Black Folks*. New York: Signet.

Ehrenreich, Barbara. 1990. *Fear of Falling: The Inner Life of the Middle Class*. New York: Pantheon.

Eisenberg, Susan. 1984. *It's a Good Thing I'm Not Macho*. Boston: Whetstone.

Eisler, Benita. 1980. *The Lowell Offering: Writings by New England Mill Women (1840–1845)*. New York: Harper & Row.

Ellison, Ralph. 1972 [1952]. *The Invisible Man*. New York: Vintage.

Gordon, Dane R. 1982. *Rochester Institute of Technology: Industrial Development and Educational Innovation in an American City*. New York: Edward Mellen.

Hansen, Karen V., and Ilene J. Philipson, eds. 1990. *Women, Class, and the Feminist Imagination: A Socialist-Feminist Reader*. Philadelphia: Temple University Press.

Haraway, Donna. 1985. "A Manifesto for Cyborgs: Science, Technology, and Socialist Feminism in the Last Quarter." *Socialist Review*, no. 80 (March/April): 65–107. Rpt. in Hansen and Philipson, 580–617.

Harlow, Barbara. 1987. *Resistance Literature*. New York: Methuen.

Hartsock, Nancy C.M. 1983. *Money, Sex and Power: Toward a Feminist Historical Materialism*. New York: Longman.

Hawthorne, Nathaniel. 1937. *The Complete Novels and Selected Tales of Nathaniel Hawthorne*. Edited by Norman Holmes Pearson. New York: Modern Library.

[Hine, Lewis.] 1977. *America and Lewis Hine: Photographs 1904–1940*. Millerton, NY: Aperture.

hooks, bell. 1984. *Feminist Theory: From Margin to Center*. Boston: South End Press.

Hutcheon, Linda. 1989. *The Politics of Postmodernism*. London: Routledge.

Lorde, Audre. 1984. "Age, Race, Class, and Sex: Women Redefining Difference." In *Sister Outsider: Essays and Speeches*. Trumansburg, NY: Crossing Press.

"[Lowry, Don.]" 1991. News feature. The Rochester *Democrat and Chronicle*, 8 May, 10E.

Lunsford, Andrea A., Helene Moglen, and James Slevin, eds. 1990. *The Right to Literacy*. New York: Modern Language Association of America.

Marx, Karl. 1986 [1844]. "Alienated Labor." In Chittenden and Kiniry, 289–93.

Marx, Leo. 1964. *The Machine in the Garden: Technology and the Pastoral Ideal in America*. New York: Oxford University Press.

Melville, Herman. 1968. *Herman Melville: Selected Tales and Poems*. Edited by Richard Chase. New York: Holt, Rinehart and Winston.

Merod, Jim. 1987. *The Political Responsibility of the Critic*. Ithaca: Cornell University Press.

Mills, C. Wright. 1986 [1951]. "The Idea of Craftsmanship." In Chittenden and Kiniry, 301–4.

Minh-ha, Trinh T. 1989. *Woman, Native, Other: Writing Postcoloniality and Feminism*. Bloomington: Indiana University Press.

Noble, David F. 1987. *America by Design: Science, Technology, and the Rise of Corporate Capitalism.* New York: Oxford University Press.

Piercy, Marge. 1976. *Woman on the Edge of Time.* New York: Knopf.

Reagon, Bernice. 1983. "Coalition Politics: Turning the Century." In *Home Girls: A Black Feminist Anthology,* edited by Barbara Smith. New York: Kitchen Table/Women of Color Press.

"[Richard Rose]." 1991a. News feature. The Rochester *Democrat and Chronicle,* 4 June: editorial; 6 June:10A–11A; 13 June: 15A.

———. 1991b. News feature. *The Chronicle of Higher Education,* 5 June: A2.

Said, Edward. 1982. "Opponents, Audiences, Constituencies, and Community." *Critical Inquiry* 9 (September): 1–26.

Scott, Barbara Ann. 1983. *Crisis Management in American Higher Education.* New York: Praeger.

Shloss, Carol. 1987. *In Visible Light: Photography and the American Writer 1840–1940.* New York: Oxford University Press.

Soelle, Dorothee A., with Shirley A. Cloyes. 1984. *To Work and To Love: A Theology of Creation.* Philadelphia: Fortress Press.

Steedman, Carolyn Kay. 1987. *Landscape for a Good Woman: A Story of Two Lives.* New Brunswick, NJ: Rutgers University Press.

Taylor, Frederick Winslow. 1967 [1911]. *The Principles of Scientific Management.* New York: Norton. See also Chittenden and Kiniry, 296–300.

They'll Never Keep Us Down: Women's Coal Mining Songs. 1984. Rounder Records 4012.

Tichi, Cecelia. 1987. *Shifting Gears: Technology, Literature, Culture in Modernist America.* Chapel Hill: University of North Carolina Press.

Vonnegut, Kurt. 1952. *Player Piano.* New York: Avon.

Watt, Stephen. 1992. "Academic Leftists Are Something of a Fraud." *The Chronicle of Higher Education,* 29 April: A40.

Welch, Sharon D. 1990. *A Feminist Ethic of Risk.* Philadelphia: Fortress Press.

Willinsky, John. 1991 [1990]. "A Literacy More Urgent than Literature: 1800–1850." In *The Triumph of Literature/The Fate of Literacy: English in the Secondary School Curriculum.* New York: Teachers College Press.

Wolf, Christa. 1989. *Accident: A Day's News.* Translated by Heike Schwarzbauer and Rick Takvorian. New York: Farrar, Straus & Giroux.

3 The Cultural Work of Teaching Noncanonical Poetry

Cary Nelson
University of Illinois at Urbana-Champaign

I want to ground my remarks about theory and social responsibility in undergraduate teaching within a specific material context—a course in modern poetry that I taught recently. I was returning to the undergraduate literature classroom after several years' absence, having taught mostly courses and seminars in theory. Because I wanted my students to treat critical books and essays as texts, rather than as mere exportable systems of ideas (and because no one else in my department was teaching courses in pure theory at the time), I considered it important to exclude literary texts from my theory courses and to require students to write directly about theory, not to apply it to literature. That was a requirement I maintained for both graduate and undergraduate students. Except for a graduate seminar in contemporary poetry, I thus had not taught literature at all for some time. But now I was writing a book about modern poetry—*Repression and Recovery: Modern American Poetry and the Politics of Cultural Memory, 1910–1945* (1989)[1]—and I did not want the book to be impoverished by lack of contact with student opinions and reactions. Moreover, I had acquired a sense of mission about overturning the modern poetry canon and giving new cultural life to dozens of forgotten poets; it was time to share that mission with our undergraduates. In exchange, they would counteract the hermeticism to which all solitary intellectual projects are subject.

My long sabbatical from literature meant that it was time to begin thinking seriously about what I thought a literature class might do in the late 1980s. In a way, I had no choice. The texts I had used years earlier were either out of print or so narrow in their representations of women and minorities as to be totally alienating. The most obvious new anthologies—such as the current revisions of the *Norton Anthology of Poetry* (1986) or the *Norton Anthology of Modern Poetry* (1988) could hardly have been less generous in their representations of the expanded canon. I no longer really remembered the details of the modern poetry courses I had taught years ago, and I didn't want to think about the effort that would be required to find any of my old syllabi. And indeed literature itself—in a classroom—seemed a foreign and uneasy prospect. Having spent years trying to persuade students who had never read anything *other* than literature in an English class that they ought to stop reading it for a time, I was now required to reverse motion. Little remained of the inertial energy that so often shapes our plans for our literature classes.

But I felt a good deal of motivating energy of other sorts, from convictions about the centrality of theory in literary studies to nearly a decade of frustration with the Reagan-Bush era. A series of contexts— local, national, disciplinary—along with my own research commitments—were coloring what I thought it necessary and appropriate to do. With the Left in retreat across much of the postindustrialized world and with the Right—short of economic collapse—increasingly in control of American institutions, a critical and subversive alternative pedagogy seemed essential. I did not expect to be entirely able to change their lives; I did not imagine this course to be one step toward ushering in a utopia. I did expect, however, to be able to acquaint students with historical perspectives they might not have known beforehand. One way to provide students with models of a more critical relationship to American culture and American political life, I concluded, was simply to acquaint them with the Left literary traditions excluded from their more canonically oriented courses. There is a substantial tradition of progressive resistance to the dominant culture in modern American poetry, and I wanted my students to learn about that tradition and reflect on what it said about their culture and what it might mean in their own lives. Learning about these traditions, I believed, would not only lend Left commitments increased credibility, but also help students disarticulate the elements of the popular common sense that ruled their lives. Though I do not want to exaggerate what can be accomplished in one course, I also do not want to ignore or trivialize what one course can do. Certainly, it is not unusual for one course to help shape several students' intellectual interests for the rest of their careers. Many other students would at least leave the course not only with a very different sense of our literary heritage, but also with a considerably expanded notion of the social functions poetry can serve and with a more self-conscious and critical relation to the discipline of English and perhaps other humanities disciplines as well.

This course, moreover, was part of a pattern of research and teaching commitments that eventually affected quite a few people's lives. I was also teaching graduate seminars in modern poetry, and some of those graduate students were writing dissertations on radical poetry and teaching their own noncanonical undergraduate poetry courses. Other people around the country, meanwhile, were continuing to teach courses in an expanded canon, incorporating research they, I, and others had done. It is worth noting in this context how well-integrated teaching and research in noncanonical literature can be. The forgotten or unpublished poem that I find in a library or an archive one semester can be part of a course syllabus that semester or the next one. My classes, in turn, give me a realistic sense of whether a poem can find a new audience today and what impact it might have. With noncanonical texts, moreover, where little previous scholarship exists, the classroom provides the only forum for detailed dialogue about individual works. Finally, essays like this one give me the opportunity to share the results with still other readers. The cultural work done in the course extends into the work this essay may do. In the light of all of this, the clichés we hear about the inherent conflicts—some would say the complete incompatibility—between research and teaching seem wholly insupportable. At least for those who have the freedom to choose and design their own courses—which not everyone does—research and teaching can be substantially intertwined and more than mutually supportive and corrective.

What I was not particularly interested in doing, I might point out, however, was letting the course be shaped primarily by an effort to honor my students' initial sense of their own needs. I was interested in learning what they hoped to get out of a poetry class, but I was not about to be constrained by it. I had an agenda of discovery and political consciousness-raising for them, an agenda determined by my sense of where the country and the profession were culturally and politically, an agenda shaped by the cultural work I believed was most useful for me to do as a teacher. I was prepared to adjust and redirect my plans as the semester proceeded, especially as I found out which texts and issues did and did not excite them, but even though the class spent most of its time in discussion, the course was clearly shaped by my agenda, not theirs. Some, it turned out, responded enthusiastically; others resisted. A few have since told me or my colleagues that it was one of the two or three best courses they took here; on the other hand, the student who stated in a course evaluation that "if this was to be a left-wing indoctrination course we should have been warned" no doubt captured some other students' views, as well—for they had no choice about going along with the general program, which was a product of the readings I assigned and the topics I raised. Indeed, though it was essential that they talk through the poems and the theoretical issues at stake, this process was important not so much for the virtues of self-articulation, but so that the class could become a theater of contesting interpretations and so that the values I was encouraging could be drawn out of discussion rather than simply be articulated from above.

I realize, of course, that many faculty members are immensely uncomfortable with this sort of unabashed advocacy. The course I am describing, moreover, is in many ways exactly the sort of course the New Right has worked to scandalize. By writing this chapter I may be giving people like Roger Kimball and Dinesh D'Souza notably more substantive evidence than they usually have available to make their case against radical teaching. But I believe there is more to be gained by describing the aims and substance of my teaching practices accurately than by retreating, i.e., by filling and backsliding and denying my interests. In fact, many of my colleagues use the classroom to promote their own values—from religious beliefs to political disengagement to patriotism—while maintaining a mask of disinterested objectivity. I prefer to let my students know where I stand. Like other literature professors, I assign many texts whose values and concerns I share. To some extent, then, the topics we take up in class are promoted by the texts themselves—through poems by women, minorities, and writers on the Left. In a course like mine it is, at least, impossible to argue that I am *imposing* radical politics on the poetry. One can only argue in objection that these poems should not be read, that expanded historical knowledge is of no use if it means lowering the quality of the texts we know.

If the course content was unconventional, however, the format was not. Except for the fact that we did a lot of oral performing of poetry—sometimes individually, sometimes in chorus, and sometimes with the class divided in half and reading successive passages alternately—there was nothing surprising about the classroom structure. Many of these students were students of rather unreflective prosperity, unaware that their privileges were class specific and unaware that education might serve other—and more critical—functions than those associated with facilitating careers. Under the influence of the 1960s and 1970s, some faculty members still believe that simple changes in the classroom structure can revolutionize education by dissolving hierarchies and empowering students to take control of their own education. But that faith in self-determination is actually underwritten by faculty members' confidence in students' basic values. I admired some of my students' values but not others. For some of the students of the 1980s and 1990s, sitting in a circle and taking charge of the class might represent an opportunity to talk about how to invest the money they hoped to earn after graduation. That is less true of a poetry class, to be sure, than of many other subjects, but it is nonetheless fair to say that these students are rather less critically engaged with American culture and their place in it than students were when I began teaching in the midst of the Vietnam War, twenty-some years ago.

As to the poems the students would have chosen to read, those who knew anything about modern poetry knew only the conventional canon. Some of the students—especially women and minority students—were more than ready to read outside the canon, but they would not have been able to name many modern poets to meet that need. Those women who had an interest in feminist poetry knew only the work of a few poets who came to prominence after the Second World War; some knew only Adrienne Rich. Once they had been through the bulk of the course, the students would be able to define their own special interests within noncanonical modern poetry. Even after halfway through the course, they could, with help, design a semester's research project. But the students needed me to guide them toward material and research techniques they had never heard of and issues they had never discussed in the classes they had taken thus far.

As it happens, I was teaching two sections of the course to what turned out to be very different audiences—freshmen and upper-division undergraduates. The differences were at once cheering and depressing. The first-year students were much more open to an unconventional reading list. Most of them saw nothing wrong with a course in which the white male canon occupied less than half their time. Yet these students also knew little or nothing about modern poetry. Many of the students who had been on campus for a few years, however, were quite anxious about the course. Not merely resistant to noncanonical poetry, they were often puzzled and frightened by it. The idea that poetry could be pervaded by social issues rather than by speculations about the imagination and such supposedly transhistorical issues as death and mutability undermined the investments they had made in the study of literature. And they were flatly uncomfortable with the large number of women and minorities in the syllabus. While this pattern made the prospect of teaching beginning students appealing, it offered little reason to be happy about the socialization process in either the department or the university.

Twenty years earlier a theorized classroom had meant, to some degree, an experimental classroom—trying multiple different formats, meeting away from the university, agendas set, in part, by the students. I had taught classes like that in answer to the politics of the day. But these were not the students of twenty years ago. There was a time when

Left teaching meant collaborating with a sense of cultural, political, and educational necessity shared by a majority of the students. Now I was fighting a different action: I was doing resistance teaching in a conservative department under a reactionary government. That meant that I was sometimes working against my students' assumptions, prejudices, and sense of priorities. I had allies among the students, to be sure, including some who were extremely happy to be finally reading poems that had more direct bearing on their lives. But I did not have the kind of Left consensus that was possible in the 1960s and early 1970s, a consensus that made structural changes in the classroom environment both possible and helpful. Although I made certain that all students could air their views and frequently helped articulate positions I disagreed with, it was generally clear where I stood and clear as well that I was politically allied with some students and not others. For some of the students, therefore, I was a figure to resist or reject. I could live with the resulting tensions more easily than I could live with suppressing my values in the classroom, but I nonetheless definitely preferred the class section where more of the students were sympathetic.

As it happened, however, the class composed mostly of first-year students not only had more students open to reading noncanonical poetry, it also had more conservative students who strongly objected to the politics of many of the poems we read. I also much preferred this open rebellion to silent resentment. It made for better debates, and it demonstrated clearly that people bring social and political values to the literature classroom and that those values shape their reading of literary texts. Unfamiliar with the ritualized indirection of literary professionalism, the first-year students simply assumed that all their social investments were at issue in reading poems. Within a few years they would learn to suppress that knowledge—then they would be good literature majors. In the meantime they might learn something useful about the politics of reading and the politics of canonization; they could learn it in part by seeing it in one another's behavior. The older students in the other section were another matter. Most would not admit that their reactions were historically, culturally, and politically grounded. I was never really successful in getting them to see how cultural investments in race, class, and gender affected the way they evaluated poems. In neither class, however, did I have anything like the sort of Left consensus possible during the Vietnam War.

The fact that our culture has changed and thus requires different pedagogical strategies does not, however, render the politics of an earlier moment meaningless. Nor is it a sign of defeat that we have to adapt to different political contexts. The notion that politically relevant teaching will always take the same form does not survive historical analysis and reflection. The attempt—not only by some radical faculty members, but also by faculty members influenced by various traditional humanisms—to impose on all of us one politically correct form of teaching is the tyranny of an empty idealism, not any plausible real-world politics. Even at one moment in history there are likely to be a variety of classroom structures appropriate to different material conditions. Now the content of the course and the cultural purposes I articulated for it seemed far more important than a critique of classroom hierarchy. The students would go through the experience whether they wanted to or not. They would thus be required to write essays about race or gender, essays about poems on working-class experience, whether or not they shared these concerns. They need not come to conclusions I agreed with, they need not even be sympathetic, but they had to take on these issues.

Having encouraged all the students to express themselves as openly as they could, it would hardly have been appropriate for me to penalize them once they did so. Some students, to be sure, made appalling sexist or racist remarks in class. I still remember with embarrassment the day when a basically liberal student was led by a poem written in a black woman's voice to begin generalizing about black people's physique and sexuality. On those occasions, I did my best to wait for others to object before stating my own views. That was not always easy, but it was sometimes rewarding. In the first case above, the students were too embarrassed to speak, so I had to intervene. On the other hand, the student who responded to one of Countee Cullen's concise poems about racism by complaining irrelevantly about "welfare cheats" was resoundingly re-educated by his peers. The poem, they pointed out, was about racism, not about government programs that did not exist when the poem was written. Similarly, a student who reacted to a series of poems about workers being exploited or injured in factories by launching into an attack on unions may not have understood what this connection revealed about him and his culture, but a number of the other students made it clear that they did. On the other hand, all these comments, both those from the left and the right, were valuable examples of the way people read poems from the vantage point of their social positioning. The more professionally acculturated students might have had the same reactions, but they would never admit to them in class.

The problem of how to deal with papers was somewhat different. Since the papers were essentially private communications to me, I did not have to be so concerned with their public impact, but I also lacked the advantage of group re-education. In the end I decided that students should know that I would comment on objectionable remarks in papers but not downgrade people for them. Thus, a witty and outrageously reactionary student knew he could write what he pleased and still get an A in the course as long as his paper was coherent and included the required detailed analyses of individual poems. None of these strategies left me altogether comfortable, but they were the best I could devise. My aim, after all, was to expose students to alternative literary traditions and to explore what kind of work those traditions might do now in our conflicted culture, not to demand a false conformity that would have vanished once the course was over, in any case. Quite apart from the ethical implications of simply trying to impose values on students, the fact is that we cannot do so successfully, anyway. Unlike some faculty members, I do not believe that penalizing students for racism or sexism will cure them of those biases.

I also had a theoretical agenda that directed what I said about our readings. In fact, although the course was called "Modern American Poetry," I'm not sure whether it was really a course in theory or in poetry. The readings we did were all poems, in part because the particular theoretical texts that informed my lectures—such as Ernesto Laclau and Chantal Mouffe's *Hegemony and Socialist Strategy* (1985)—were too difficult for beginning undergraduates and, in part, because teaching them to read contemporary theory would require a course of its own. Contrary, however, to the widespread beliefs of a decade ago, undergraduates *can* read abstract theory, but not every undergraduate can handle the most difficult texts. Certainly, a theory course for juniors and seniors can deal with quite a wide range of recent theoretical texts. I have taught Roland Barthes's *S/Z* (1974) in an undergraduate honors seminar by going through portions of the book sentence by sentence and explicating it, but I have not attempted Derrida's *Of Grammatology* (1976) with the same group. I have also read essays by Michel Foucault, Luce Irigaray, Georges Poulet, Hayden White, and Raymond Williams with undergraduates, but I would not assign them all of Foucault's *The Order of Things* (1971). For this course, moreover, some of the most pertinent work was quite far from literary analysis. Rather than read, say, Stuart Hall on Thatcherism, summarize the history of cultural studies, and then explain how Hall offers a model of discursive politics that can illuminate the history of modern poetry, I chose simply to use his concepts to talk about cultural processes and about the texts we were reading.

Teaching theory only by way of lecture and discussion meant largely betraying my own commitment to critical textuality. Yet in some ways that was less troubling than the realization that the students had no awareness that theoretical concepts and problems come with their own intellectual and political history. Both classes—not only the first-year students but also the juniors and seniors—were inclined to assume that ideas exist in a freely accessible space of contemporaneity. No one ever asked which critics or which disciplines had developed notions such as "relative autonomy" or "rearticulation" that I was using in my lectures. I supplied some of this background because I felt it was irresponsible not to, but I would never have been asked for it. This was also the only area where I consistently felt uneasy about my authority in the classroom, not simply because none of the students felt empowered to resist my intellectual categories, but because none of them imagined that it was necessary or possible to do so. The students were quite willing to criticize my arguments about the profession and about the canon, and they continually offered inventive alternative readings of the poetry we discussed, but they were in no way inclined or prepared to contest the effects of the theoretical concepts I used. That was a limitation in their acculturation which I never overcame.

Nonetheless, a good deal of class time was spent at the blackboard writing down theoretical terms and defining them. Twenty-minute lectures on theoretical issues were frequent, and some entire class periods were spent that way. That the class was generically unstable, a hybrid of theory and literature, seemed to me one of its strengths. Indeed, I think it is fair to say that the theory and the poetry had shifting relations of priority; neither consistently served the other. Sometimes an overview of cultural issues introduced a discussion of poetry; on other occasions, the poems served as sources of theoretical concerns.

Part of what this demonstrates, I think, is that what counts as "theory" and what cultural functions we understand theory to serve vary historically. Throughout the 1950s and 1960s, and into the early 1970s, theory came in discrete units like psychoanalysis, Marxism, or feminism, which could be learned and applied to literary texts. In the course of the 1970s, however, these theories began to define themselves more energetically in relation to one another. At the same time, we began to realize that taking up theory entailed taking up certain writing practices as well. But theory, it seemed, could still be studied without putting intense pressure on the social and political institutions of which it was a part. In the course of the 1980s, however, it became increasingly impossible to teach theory without also reflecting on and theorizing about the social mission of English studies. Consequently, I could not now imagine teaching an introductory literature course which would not also introduce students to current debates in English and to the politics and social positioning of the discipline. I was as concerned to get them thinking about what it meant to study poetry as I was to familiarize them with the poetry itself. From this I hoped that they would begin to be able to understand the social and political meaning of what they learned in other classes and to reflect more generally on the social impact of intellectual work.

The mutual implication or contamination of poetry, theory, and politics was made apparent on the first day. I distributed photocopies of five improbable modern American poems: Mike Quin's "The Glorious Fourth" (1941); Irene Paull's "Ballad of a Lumberjack" (1941); Lucia Trent's "Parade the Narrow Turrets" (1929); Henry Tichenor's version of "Onward, Christian Soldiers" from his *Rhymes of the Revolution* (1914); and Kenneth Fearing's "Dirge" (1935). There is a good chance that none of these texts would open other modern poetry courses; indeed, they would probably fall into a nervous, degenerate academic category that my colleagues call "occasional verse." They are all explicitly political and all satiric, but their form and style vary. Quin's 1941 poem, nine stanzas long, describes a hollow, opportunistic, reactionary politician:

> Senator Screwball would nearly die
> If he couldn't make a speech on the Fourth of July;
> If he couldn't stand up there beside Old Glory
> And blow off his mouth like a damned old tory.

I told the students that they could, if they liked, think of it as a prophetic poem about Dan Quayle. Trent's 1929 poem is an attack on academic escapism: "What do you care if blacks are lynched beneath a withering sky? / What do you care if two men burn to death in a great steel chair"—"Thumb over your well-worn classics with clammy and accurate eyes, / Teach freshman to scan Homer and Horace and look wise." Fearing, in the distinctive frenetic rhythms he adopted during the Great Depression, takes on a modern businessman destroyed by the commodified culture he serves: "O executive type, would you like to drive a floating-power, / knee-action, silk-upholstered six? Wed a Hollywood star?" Tichenor's "Onward, Christian Soldiers" straddles poetry and song in an international economic lesson that is no less pertinent now than it was in 1914:

> Big Business is behind you
> In your fight for kingdom come—
> It is sailing with its cargoes
> Of Gatling guns and rum—
> Just fill the heathen with your creeds
> To keep them out of hell—

And tell them of the shoddy goods
Big
  Business
   Has
    To
     Sell.

Taken together, these poems amount to an irreverent critique of American culture, an uncivil burlesque of the high-modernist canon, and, with Trent's poem, a witty but savage attack on the English profession, a convenient way of making the politics of literary study an unavoidable topic. The poems were also thoroughly accessible, and thus the students formed opinions about them immediately. I announced that we would have a vote to determine which was the poem that seemed most and least "literary" or "poetic." After that, I asked students to discuss the reasons for their votes, having deliberately made no effort to define what I meant by literariness. Some opinions were predictable.

The few students with sensibilities shaped by experimental modernism thought Fearing's poem the most literary. On the other hand, although I expected Irene Paull's "Ballad of a Lumberjack" to rate low, I did not anticipate that it would receive not a single vote. Originally included in a leaflet distributed during the 1937 strike of the Minnesota Timber Workers, its seven stanzas lay out the realities of industrial exploitation:

We told 'em the blankets were crummy
And they said that we like 'em that way.
We told 'em that skunks couldn't smell like our bunks,
But they said that our bunks were okey.

I cast my vote for this orphaned text and prepared to defend it.

Although the students did not quite have a category for "Ballad of a Lumberjack," they were pretty sure it wasn't poetry; it just wasn't respectable enough. So I asked the key question: Would the workers who picked up the leaflet in 1937 have been likely to think it was poetry? There was a moment of genuine surprise, followed by some sputtering, but general agreement developed: they would have. Unwilling to opt for overt snobbery, most had to admit that this poem might have functioned as a poem for that audience; it wouldn't do simply to assert our superiority and exile the poem to some extraliterary category. Nor was the poem quite as simple as they all initially argued it to be. It condensed some fairly complex notions of class difference and rhetorical deception into common-sense language. In combination with the overall spread of votes—which differed in the two sections I was teaching—it became clear that literariness was not self-evidently inherent in poems. It was to a degree a quality the culture invented and reinforced in various, selective ways. I talked for a while about the different kinds of cultural work poems might perform at different times, and I concluded by talking about the canon and about why none of these poems is in it. It would be a course, it was clear, not only about modern poetry but also about the English profession, about key issues in current theoretical debates, and about the varying cultural roles poetry has played in our history. In the end, it was a course in cultural studies, with poetry granted only a relative autonomy, one in which poems were variously reinforced and challenged by other cultural forces. It was also, as discussion about some of the working-class poems made clear, a setting in which students' own cultural heritage and class positioning became more evident, since intimate knowledge about working-class life was hardly universal.

In the light of these five poems, the next poems we discussed, though also largely forgotten, would seem almost conventionally poetic. It was also a strategy I would use in my book: exposure to a series of more bluntly rhetorical political poems would win tolerance for poems where the language was more recognizably and appealingly "literary." We dealt with a series of depression-era poems on working conditions amongst the working class. Included were Edwin Rolfe's "Asbestos" (1933) and Tillie Olsen's "I Want You Women Up North to Know" (1934). If the students had doubts about whether we needed to remember Irene Paull, they had no doubts about the value of remembering these metaphorically inventive poems. Olsen calls on women in the north to recognize

> how those dainty children's dresses you buy
>   at macy's, wannamaker's, gimbels, marshall fields
> are dyed in blood . . .

She asks them to think of women like "Maria Vasquez, spinster, emptiness, emptiness / flaming with dresses for children she can never fondle." Rolfe tells us in a chilling conceit how a dying worker's body becomes his deathbed:

> John's deathbed is a curious affair:
> the posts are made of bone, the spring of nerves,
> the mattress bleeding flesh. Infinite air,
> compressed from dizzy altitudes, now serves
>
> His skullface as a pillow.

The only plausible reasons for eliminating these poems from literary histories and anthologies were ideological. The class began to feel a sense of injustice about the profession's selective memory; it was a feeling I had wanted them to have, but I was still surprised by its intensity. Working-class experience and economic exploitation were apparently not acceptable poetic subjects for the profession. Olsen's poem is based on a letter to *New Masses;* comparing the poem and its source also gave us an opportunity to develop the earlier discussion about literariness.

The students were now involved in looking at the broader range of texts from which the modern poetry canon was selected; they were beginning to be in a position to evaluate and critique the discipline's politics and its sense of its social mission. They were helped by the fact that poems about the dangers of factory life were no longer dated. After years of indifference to reporting Reagan's failure to enforce job safety laws, newspapers were beginning to carry stories about the people being injured and killed in the workplace. These poems thus seemed highly relevant again. And it seemed appropriate that the values they espoused have a place in the sometimes rarified domain of the "poetic."

From there on the syllabus was structured as a dialogue between the canon and its alternatives. In fact, I had ended up assigning the *Norton Anthology of Modern Poetry,* along with my own 300-page, photocopied selection of noncanonical poems, though I also gave them the table of contents of the previous edition of the Norton so they could see how little progress it had made in expanding the canon. Thus it was a course with two texts in explicit competition. About half of the poems we read were well known; the others were not. We were also therefore shuttling back and forth between rereadings of canonical poems and readings of poems that were now out of print. Neither of these commitments, it seems to me, would be sufficient on its own. We need to teach the traditional canon because we cannot otherwise understand either our profession or the place of literature in the dominant culture. The shaping of the exclusionary modern canon is a part of our history that we need to know. But the modern American poetry canon—which now emphasizes Eliot, Pound, Stevens, and Williams—excludes so many important perspectives on race, class, and gender and so many forgotten versions of modernist experimentation that it gives quite a false view of our literary history. And it offers no evidence of the cultural work women and minorities accomplished in poetry in the first half of the century. A wide range of social functions for poetry, along with an incredible variety of poetic forms and styles, are eliminated if we focus only on rereading the narrow postwar cannon. Finally, the modern canon deprives women, minority, and working-class students of the full range of relevant subject positions historically available to them in modern poetry. As a result, the traditional canon distorts and impoverishes the potential meaning of poetry in their lives. It is not, therefore, condescending to argue that women and minorities deserve a chance to see how their particular interests have been taken up in poetry.

In explicitly moving back and forth between canonical and noncanonical poems, always asking why any given poem was or was not canonical, I was to a certain extent also following Gerald Graff's oft-repeated slogan to "teach the conflicts" in the profession. But I was not indulging in any fiction of liberal neutrality; nor was I pretending that all the parties in any conflict are equally empowered. And I was also addressing a number of theoretical issues not being widely debated in literary studies, such as the competitive relations between literature and other discourses and institutions within the culture. We did not treat "poetry" as a secure and preexisting category, but rather as a changing and contested cultural space. We recognized how certain topics, styles, and cultural aims were variously included in or cast out of our notions of "the poetic" at different moments. We looked repeatedly at how poetry won and lost various powers and social functions in the course of the modern period and its critical reconstitution in the decades to follow. And we worked to understand how different groups could simultaneously hold very different notions of what properly constituted poetry's texts and audiences.

The course would not have worked at all, I should point out, if I had been obsessed with the issue of coverage. I decided to leave claims about coverage to paint companies and concern myself more with the course's intellectual aims. That is not to say that people who are concerned with coverage necessarily lack intellectual commitments, though it is to say that a focus on coverage can, at the very least, displace other issues of importance. Sometimes, moreover, people obsessed with coverage use it as a way to avoid dealing with more threatening theoretical and political problems. In the logic of the profession, invocations of coverage give moral cover for a faculty member's anti-intellectualism.

My own sense of what merited time and attention did not, however, always carry the day. Thus, when the students were not interested in a topic, I generally abandoned it. My only complete failure, I think, was my effort to win some sympathy for the more blatantly pro-Soviet revolutionary poems of the early 1930s. The choral classroom readings that worked extraordinarily well for some of the sound poems of the 1920s—turning sound poems by Harry Crosby and Eugene Jolas into ritual incantations—were no help here. Reading 1920s sound poems on their own, students considered them mere nonsense. Reading them in class—sometimes in unison and sometimes in a call-and-response style—they discovered uncanny power and humor in texts that first seemed meaningless. Here, for example, is Jolas's "Mountain Words" (1938) and Crosby's "Pharmacie du Soleil" (1931), the first almost a pure sound poem, the second a list of elements where the names gain poetic force from their sound when read in sequence:

mira ool dara frim
oasta grala drima
os tristomeen.

ala grool in rosa
alsabrume
lorabim
masaloo
blueheart of a

roolata gasta
miralotimbana
allatin

juanilama

---

calcium iron hydrogen sodium nickel
magnesium cobalt silicon aluminum
titanium chromium strontium manganese
vanadium barium carbon scandium yttritium
zirconium molybdenum lanthanum niobium
paladium neodymium copper zinc silver
tin lead erbium potassium iridium
tantalum osmium thorium platinum tungsten
ruthenium uranium

We read Jolas's poem in unison in fairly deep tones and read Crosby's poem by dividing the class in two, with each half reading alternate words in an incantatory contest. As a result, the class grew fond of the poems, but it was still quite a challenge for them to articulate why. On the other hand, choral reading could not save many of the explicitly revolutionary, proletarian poems of the 1930s. I can still remember the dull, flat sounds of thirty-five students unenthusiastically reading the line "All Power to the Soviets!" from Sol Funaroff's "What the Thunder Said: A Fire Sermon." Nor would the revolutionary communist poems of the 1930s be helped now by events that have occurred in Europe and the Soviet Union over the last four years. So I cut my losses and eliminated the rest of these poems from the course.

I was learning, I think, something about the limits of my students' cultural sympathies. In a course devoted exclusively to the 1930s there would, to be sure, have been time for a much more thorough historical grounding in the realities of the Great Depression. We would also have been reading many more depression-era poems. The line "All Power to the Soviets," we might have noted, also appears in Richard Wright's "I am a Red Slogan." That would have given us an opportunity to talk about the role of explicit, preexisting political slogans in 1930s poetry, a discursive element we usually like to think of as having no place in poetry, whatsoever.

The one text where we made some progress with this issue was with Tillie Olsen's 1934 poem "I Want You Women Up North to Know." The bulk of the poem deals with the impossible lives of Mexican American women in Texas who earn, at most, a few dollars a week hand embroidering children's dresses for sale up north. It is not until about two-thirds of the way through the poem that Olsen refers to "a heaven . . . brought to earth in 1917 in Russia." The students talked enthusiastically about the poem by simply avoiding any mention of the offending line. When it did finally come up, the class fell silent, a silence which we were then able to discuss and evaluate.

On the other hand, when students wanted to spend more time with a topic, we adjusted the syllabus accordingly. Thus, when a week on poems about race by white authors stretched to two weeks, something had to go. I looked at the syllabus and decided that Wallace Stevens was expendable. In a moment he disappeared from modernism. I felt a passing sensation of guilt; apparently I was still a pathetic victim of the very ideology I was trying to overturn, but shortly thereafter I experienced a certain bemused pleasure at Stevens's local erasure, and that emotion has happily ruled me since.

It was while teaching poems about race that I felt the strongest sense that I was doing teaching that mattered. We had read work by Angelina Weld Grimké, Countee Cullen, Sterling Brown, Anne Spencer, and Langston Hughes and then moved on to a series of poems by white poets: Sol Funaroff's "Goin Mah Own Road"; Charles Henri Ford's "Plaint"; e. e. cummings's "theys sO alive"; V. J. Jerome's "A Negro Mother to Her Child"; Carl Sandburg's "Nigger," "Mammy," and "Jazz"; Kenneth Patchen's "Nice Day for a Lynching"; Genevieve Taggard's "To the Negro People"; and others. Especially in the 1920s and 1930s, many white poets felt that it was important to write both poems protesting racial injustice and poems sympathetic to black culture.[2] Most remarkable of all is the fact that a surprising number of white poets tried to write poems in black dialect, something it would be difficult to imagine a white poet daring to do, today. Some of these poems I find powerful and effective. In other cases, white poets trying to write positively about black culture ended up repeating offensive stereotypes. But it was sometimes difficult for all of us to agree about whether a poem was or was not racist, a shockingly fundamental matter to be so difficult to resolve. The subtle duplicities of racism in the poems, I believe, gave the students a start at thinking about racism in their own lives, as did the revealing and sometimes heated class discussions.

It was notable that opinions about these poems did not divide predictably along racial lines. The white students, for example, assumed Sandburg's "Nigger" (1916) to be an unredeemably racist poem. But one black student argued that its startling, accusatory, self-assertive conclusion could do important cultural work:

> Brooding and muttering with memories of shackles:
> I am the nigger.
> Look at me.
> I am the nigger.

The epithet which we all found offensive, he argued, was, after all, probably the right word for that moment in history. Nervous, the white students were looking for the quick, politically correct response. The black student called them to more sustained reflection.

What was most striking overall was the students' eagerness to debate the strengths and weaknesses of these poems. In the midst of a racist culture, these poems—especially the ones by white poets—enabled the class to deal openly with issues that they very much needed to discuss. I had assigned the poems in part because I considered it part of my social responsibility to spend classroom time discussing race in America. I wanted the white students in the class to feel the special ethical pressure they would feel only if they heard white poets speaking out against racial injustice. And I wanted the "minority" students in the class to hear white poets engaged in kinds of racially reflective, committed cultural work they might not have imagined possible from members of the dominant culture. For all the students it was a revelation—about the discipline and about American culture—to hear white writers far more intricately and thoughtfully engaged in questions of race sixty years ago than they are in our supposedly more progressive contemporary culture. Sometimes the class came to a consensus about a particular poem. Other times they did not. I made no effort to impose a resolution. This was a case where theories of textual indeterminacy—theories we had often talked about in the course of the semester—had not only the most intractable material support, but also quite powerful and sometimes painful social and emotional consequences. But if these students were going to live in America, then by any sane standard of what matters, they needed to read these poems more than they needed to read T. S. Eliot and Wallace Stevens. That very few of my colleagues would agree with me, in a way, says all one needs to say about the politics of English in America.

Since last teaching this class, my convictions about the centrality of the social mission of English have, if anything, intensified. In an America whose incredibly resistant underlying racism has been steadily strengthened by conservative politicians over the last decade, it has seemed increasingly important to me to get students to talk about race and to write about it in their papers. Again, I have no problem assigning such topics whether or not students would choose to write about them. Yet, the model I used before had only three elements—class discussion, lectures, and individual research papers. But class discussions do not give individual students enough time to work through their feelings and articulate them in detail. And solitary research and writing are not enough to make a difference in students' attitudes, let alone their social practices. So I have now decided to give students small-group research projects to work on, as well. Whenever the mix of students in the class makes it possible, I will structure the groups so as to maximize racial, ethnic, and gender diversity. That is hardly the way the students would sort themselves out; indeed, if time permits, I'll let students choose their own groups for a second project. The first group, however, will be set according to my agenda—to make multiracial intellectual work and multiracial social relations part of the class experience. I believe that this is something the country desperately needs. It is also a socially and politically relevant pedagogy I would challenge the Right to attack, if they dare.

Notes

1. *Repression and Recovery* (Nelson 1989) includes detailed notes and source citations for the poems mentioned in this essay. Those poems quoted in this chapter are also represented with individual citations, below.

2. For an extended analysis of white poets taking up the issue of race, see Aldon Lynn Nielsen's *Reading Race* (1988). Two important anthologies to consult are Langston Hughes and Arna Bontemps's *The Poetry of the Negro* (1949) and Maureen Honey's *Shadowed Dreams* (1989).

I have also taught a unit on race in modern American poetry in which I assign a group of poems by both black poets and white poets without identifying the race of the poet until after we complete part of the discussion. My selections for that assignment were Maxwell Bodenheim, "Negroes"; Kay Boyle, "A Communication to Nancy Cunard"; Sterling Brown, "Scotty Has His Say" and "Slim in Hell"; Witter Bynner, "Defeat"; Hart Crane, "Black Tambourine"; Countee Cullen, "Incident" and "For a Lady I Know"; e. e. cummings, "theys sO alive"; Charles Henri Ford, "Plaint"; Sol Funaroff, "Goin Mah Own Road"; Angelina Weld Grimké, "The Black Finger," "Tenebris," and "[fragment]"; Langston Hughes, ""Ku Klux," "The Negro Speaks of Rivers," "White Shadows," and "Lynching Song"; V. J. Jerome, "A Negro Mother to Her Child"; Stanley Kimmel, "Niggers"; Aqua Lalula, "Lullaby"; Vachel Lindsay, "The Congo"; A. B. Magil, "They Are Ours"; Dorothea Matthews, "The Lynching"; Claude McKay, "Mulatto," "The White City," "The Lynching," and "To the White Fiends"; Kenneth Patchen, "Nice Day for a Lynching"; Carl Sandburg, "Jazz Fantasia" and "Nigger"; Lew Sarett, "Scalp-Dance"; Anne Spencer, "White Things"; Genevieve Taggard, "To the Negro People"; Lucia Trent, "Black Men"; John Wheelwright, "Plantation Drouth"; and Richard Wright, "Obsession."

Works Cited

Allison, Alexander W. 1986. *The Norton Anthology of Poetry*. 3rd ed. Edited by Herbert Barrows et al. New York: W. W. Norton.

Barthes, Roland. 1974. *S/Z*. Translated by Richard Miller. 1st American edition. New York: Hill and Wang.

Crosby, Harry. 1931. "Pharmacie du Soleil." In *Chariot of the Sun*, 23. Paris: Black Sun Press.

Derrida, Jacques. 1976. *Of Grammatology*. Translated by Gayatri Chakravorty Spivak. 1st American edition. Baltimore: Johns Hopkins University Press.

Ellmann, Richard, and Robert O'Clair. 1988. *The Norton Anthology of Modern Poetry*. 2nd ed. New York: W. W. Norton.

Fearing, Kenneth. 1935. "Dirge." In *Poems*, 43–44. New York: Dynamo.

Foucault, Michel. 1971 [1970]. *The Order of Things: An Archaeology of the Human Sciences*. Translation of *Les Mots et les Choses*. New York: Pantheon.

Honey, Maureen, ed. 1989. *Shadowed Dreams: Women's Poetry of the Harlem Renaissance*. New Brunswick, NJ: Rutgers University Press.

Hughes, Langston, and Arna Bontemps, eds. 1949. *The Poetry of the Negro, 1746–1949*. Garden City, NY: Doubleday.

Jolas, Eugene. 1938. "Mountain Words." In *I Have Seen Monsters and Angels*, 164. Paris: Transition.

Laclau, Ernesto, and Chantal Mouffe. 1985. *Hegemony and Socialist Strategy: Toward a Radical Democratic Politics*. Translated by Winston Moore and Paul Cammack. London: Verso.

Nelson, Cary. 1989. *Repression and Recovery: Modern American Poetry and the Politics of Cultural Memory, 1910–1945*. Madison: University of Wisconsin Press.

Nielsen, Aldon Lynn. 1988. *Reading Race: White American Poets and the Racial Discourse in the Twentieth Century*. Athens, GA: University of Georgia Press.

Olsen, Tillie [T. Lerner, pseud.]. 1934. "I Want You Women Up North to Know." *Partisan* 1.4 (March): 4

Quin, Mike [Paul William Ryan]. 1941. "The Glorious Fourth. In *More Dangerous Thoughts*, 91–92. San Francisco: People's World.

Paull, Irene. 1941 [1937]. "Ballad of a Lumberjack." In *We're the People*, 49. Duluth, MN: Midwest Labor.

Rolfe, Edwin. 1993 [1933]. "Asbestos." In *Collected Poems*, edited by Cary Nelson and Jefferson Hendricks, 62. Urbana: University of Illinois Press.

Sandburg, Carl. 1969 [1916]. "Nigger." In *The Complete Poems of Carl Sandburg*, 23–24. San Diego: Harcourt, Brace, Jovanovich.

Tichenor, Henry Mulford. 1914. "Onward, Christian Soldiers." In *Rhymes of the Revolution*, n.p. St. Louis: The National Rip Saw.

Trent, Lucia. 1929. "Parade the Narrow Turrets." In *Children of Fire and Shadow*, 85. Chicago: Robert Packard.

III Feminist Transformations

4 A Room of Whose Own? Lessons from Feminist Classroom Narratives

Paula A. Treichler
University of Illinois at Urbana-Champaign

A Room of One's Own, based on lectures Virginia Woolf gave to women students at Newnham and Girton Colleges in 1928, reflects on women's writing, women's education, and what we might call the conditions of our institutionalization. For all the utopian quotations it is made to yield, the book casts a cold, clear eye on the prospect of equality between the sexes. Its familiarity makes it a good opening metaphor for exploring questions about alternative pedagogies and theory in the feminist classroom; my variant on Woolf's title simply adds a link in the signifying chain constituted within the history of women's studies and feminist theory.[1] Foreshadowing the more explicit politics of Woolf's later writing, *A Room of One's Own* is a book in which awareness of institutional authority casts a shadow on every page: the author repeatedly breaks off her address to her audience because some male figure of authority may be listening in, paying exquisite attention, all the while, to what can be said and heard at given points in history and to the physical and social space of the institution itself.

It is this institutional context which I want to take seriously, here. Certainly there has been progress in the 1960s and 1970s and even the 1980s in opening the academy to diversities of gender, race, class, able-bodiedness, age, sexuality, and material resources; and certainly we have gained insight into the theoretical operation of language, power, and difference. Yet despite progress and insight, it remains difficult to enact, sometimes even to identify, these changes in the conventional university classroom. Continuing reports from women and minority students, for example, suggest not only that their classroom experiences are often different from those of white males, but also that they are unsatisfactory in ways still not recognized within the academy. While orchestrated right-wing attacks on educational equality and "political correctness" fill the headlines, these testimonials by women and

other outsiders are found in more modest venues: government and
institutional status reports, alternative and independent journals and
videos, conferences and conventions. Invisible and inaudible to many,
often anecdotal and experiential, these reports identify as problematic
the curriculum and its epistemological underpinnings, the history of
representation in pedagogy, and the relation of race and gender to
work status and income.[2] They suggest possibilities for change and for
reconceptualizing how classroom interaction might better serve its participants; yet they exist in relative isolation from other analyses of
pedagogical and critical theory and practice and from research on language, gender, and race.

And even these accounts display the immense power of institutions
to naturalize the experiences they are organized to produce. On the one
hand, classrooms offer a space with some independence from the institution and from the world beyond the walls. On the other hand, we do
not cross that threshold and have our entire identities transformed:
much of our social, cultural, ideological, and historical life comes with
us, with its multiple entailments and contradictions. This makes the
classroom experience complex for both students and teachers but also
fruitful for theoretical analysis. There are other questions: If I conclude
that the classroom is not, precisely, a room of my own, then whose room
is it? Who pays the overhead? What does it cost the university to run a
classroom? Who, exactly, pays my salary? Who changes the light bulbs?
What portion of tuition goes to me, to the room, to changing light
bulbs? Whose room is this? What can we do in a classroom? Can we do
anything? Can we say anything? Who will listen? Can we rearrange the
chairs? So what?

To look more closely at these questions and at the relevance of theory
to everyday pedagogical practices, I would like to use a case study
adapted from "real life"—real academic life, at any rate. The setting is
a 1990s undergraduate women's studies classroom at a large research
university in the Midwest—and what happens is this:

Case Study I: Women's Studies 101

Twenty-five students are enrolled this term in Women's Studies
101, the introductory course, of whom sixteen women and four
men are white, four women are black, and one woman is Latina.
The instructor, a woman, has encouraged discussion, and most of
the students participate, although the men do not talk very often.
Carol, one of the black women, is especially articulate and forceful, contributing comments that the instructor considers valuable.
About halfway through the term, the class is assigned to read a
chapter in bell hooks's 1981 book *Ain't I a Woman* entitled "The
Continued Devaluation of Black Womanhood." The two students

randomly assigned to discuss the text are both white women, and what they provide is a synopsis, not a critical analysis. They then suggest in conclusion that racism has diminished on campuses and in the U.S. since the book was written in the early 1980s, especially toward "colored women"; they cite as evidence the fact that recent winners of the Miss America pageant have not been white. Other white students in the class, male and female, then contribute additional evidence to suggest that racism has diminished. The women of color are silent. Just as the instructor is about to challenge the students' optimistic conclusions, Carol speaks up to say she had problems with the presentation and also objects strongly to the direction of the discussion. She cites several recent racist incidents on the campus. She then turns to the women presenters and adds, "Some African American people today would take offense at being called 'colored.'"

During the instructor's office hours that afternoon, the two women presenters come in to say how awkward they felt in talking about something written by a black woman in front of other black women; they felt like intruders and knew they would say something wrong, and sure enough they did; and then they were afraid to respond to Carol because she was so "hostile." A bit later Carol comes in to say she thinks she has been talking too much in the class in general and that it is silencing the other students. Later the instructor describes these events to a male colleague known for his teaching abilities and asks what he would do. He says, "What do you expect in an attitude adjustment course like women's studies?"

Classroom stories like this one have proliferated over the last two decades and are used by students and faculty alike to chart the way through women's studies' sometimes stormy waters. Having read and discussed this particular case study on several occasions, I suggest that at least three narratives emerge (and readers will no doubt think of others). One involves cultural diversity, identity, and the politics of speaking in specific settings; another involves issues of teaching and learning in a "male-dominated" hierarchical environment; and still another concerns feminist theory and its meanings in the classroom. Together, these three narratives—what we might call in shorthand a narrative of identity, a narrative of power, and a pedagogical narrative—form a rich metanarrative about the purposes of a university and whose interests it exists to serve.

"Ain't I a Woman?" A Narrative of Identity

A first narrative—which I'll call "Ain't I a Woman?"—is a social and cultural narrative about the classroom of the 1970s, 1980s, and 1990s in which demographic, legislative, and political changes steadily opened universities and other institutions to "cultural diversity"—creating a student body and campus faculty increasingly and self-consciously heterogeneous in gender, race, ethnicity, age, sexual identification, and physical ability. At the same time, this narrative of diversity has created its own tensions within feminism, a movement that has been grounded in some notion of individual and collective identity.[3]

When we ask, therefore, what is happening in this case study, we evoke familiar themes of difference—difference, power, and contests for meaning. Here we have the archetypal classroom in which difference (a) is supposed not to matter, (b) is to be celebrated, and (c) is to be celebrated only in certain codified ways. And we may not all share these codes. Research on language and gender suggests that girls and boys acquire different cultural rules for interaction. Anthropologists Daniel Maltz and Ruth Borker (1982), for example, argue that women and men bring different cultural patterns to interaction—patterns that grow out of well-established interactional differences between girls and boys. These differences, Maltz and Borker suggest, are likely to create subsequent conflicts in cross-sex communication: (1) women see questions as part of conversational maintenance while men see them as requests for information; (2) women explicitly acknowledge previous utterances and try to connect with them while men have no such role and often ignore previous comments; (3) women interpret aggression as personal, negative, and disruptive while men view it as simply another conventional, organizing structure for conversation; (4) men shift topics quickly while women develop them progressively and shift gradually; (5) women respond to problems by sharing experiences, offering reassurances, and giving support; men hear problems as requests for solutions and respond by giving direction and advice, acting as experts or lecturing their audience. Deborah Tannen's (1986; 1990) best-selling books describe similar differences in a wide variety of cultural and social settings and in many different kinds of relationships; their popularity makes clear that they strike a familiar chord.

Communication across race may be as misleading as communication across gender or culture. The students in the case study seem uncertain about conflict and anger. Is Carol "hostile"? "Angry"? It's possible that she is—certainly, the two white students perceive her as angry and feel awkward and defensive. Yet research like Marjorie Goodwin's (1980) and Marsha Houston's (1985), identifying routine differences in conversational styles of white and black American middle-class women, suggests that many young African American girls get an early verbal training which resembles more what Maltz and Borker describe for boys: learning, among other things, to take conflict and verbal self-defense in stride. Thus, what a white woman perceives as "angry" or as a personal attack may not be that at all, or may simply be "no big deal." Carol asserts herself forcefully in conversation to stake out a clear position; intending to signal neither anger nor personal conflict, she may expect the same. Experiments in social psychology tell us that our interpretations—even our perceptions—in such situations are often unreliable. A crying baby in a videotape is identified by viewers as fearful when they're told it's a girl and angry when they're told it's a boy (Condry and Condry 1976). In his study of collective stereotyping, Warren (1972) analyzed divergent black and white perceptions of a 1969 police raid on a black church in Detroit, where militant black separatists were meeting. A shootout followed and many people were taken into custody, most of whom were released almost immediately by a black judge over the white prosecutor's protests. Warren's inquiry found a divergence of views between white and black people, not only about the event itself, but also about perceived intentions and goals.[4] The individual, in other words, grows up and learns to perceive in a social world.

On the part of the two white presenters, we see considerable anxiety about doing the right thing, comparable to the anxiety of students in the feminist theory classroom to be both politically and theoretically correct.[5] One symptom is the two students' summary of hooks's chapter— faithfully transmitting its content without venturing to comment or critique. Another symptom is the desire to use "correct" terminology: "black women," "women of color," or "African American women" in this context; "homosexual," "gay," or "queer" in some other. Such terms proliferated in the 1970s and 1980s as different voices demanded the right to name themselves, demands which can now be heard. But what Francine Frank and I discovered when we wrote *Language, Gender, and Professional Writing* for the Modern Language Association (1989), a book on sexism in language with recommended nonsexist guidelines, is that these terms will not stay still. Each has a history and exists within a specific field of social relations, and usage entails strategic trade-offs. One distinction we made was between what we called *gender-neutral language*—a formal designation for terms like "firefighter" or "flight attendant" where, in contrast to "fireman" or "stewardess," gender is not formally marked on the word itself—and *nonsexist language*, a social and functional designation. Nonsexist language constitutes a social challenge to institutionalized sexism; its existence and effectiveness must therefore be contextually determined. Gender-neutral language displays no formal gender preference but may *not* function socially to challenge sexism. The term "domestic violence," for example, is gender neutral, unlike "wife-beating," in which the gender of the victim is marked; but in disguising existing male-female power relations, the term does not necessarily challenge sexism. "Chairperson" as a replacement for "chairman" and "chairwoman" is often cited as an example of gender-neutral language that seems also to be nonsexist. But examples of actual usage make clear that the term is not really even gender-neutral, for it is used more often to refer to female chairs than to male chairs, and indeed may even be reserved for feminist chairs. Because language is continually in flux and deployed self-consciously from diverse perspectives, no fixed "hit list" will ever fully succeed— anymore than it has for fascist leaders or, for that matter, conservative language critics who become apoplectic when *everyone* is used as a plural referent for the pronoun "they." Lexical choices need to be made thoughtfully, in other words, and need also to be periodically reevaluated.

Color has no precise equivalent in English, yet, again, the designations are not fixed. And it is perhaps not wholly unreasonable that, amid all the choices, the student in the case study makes a reference to "colored women." The chapter in bell hooks's book quotes historical sources who use the terms "colored women" and "colored people." In *Yearning* (1990), hooks makes clear that this terminology cannot be centrally dictated; to that end, she uses a variety of terms (she has said that she does not care for "women of color"), including "black women," "African-American women," "black folks," and "black women/women of color." Internal debate and historical change of this kind may go unheard by outsiders—that is, by most white people; straight people, likewise, take for granted the existence of names and designations for homosexuals, often oblivious to gay terminology for heterosexuals. The privileged may rarely encounter the rich vocabulary of terms that the less privileged have created to name them: not just "Whitey" and "yuppie" and "straights," but also "breeders," "Miss Anne," "Miss Thing," and "TABs." *This Bridge Called My Back* (Moraga and Anzaldúa 1981) is an eyeopener for white students because of the ways in which it talks about white people and white women. Most revealing, perhaps, is that it does not take whiteness for granted as its fundamental vantage point: white people—evil or good—are not the central figures in these stories.[6]

One important question is what the terms *race* and *racism* signify for different class members, as well as what kinds of facts or evidence might establish whether or not "racism" has increased on campus. Describing the results of extensive interviews with students of many racial and ethnic backgrounds, which were conducted by the Institute for Social Change at the University of California at Berkeley during 1989 and 1990, Troy Duster (1991) writes that

> there is a sharp difference between the ways black and white students feel about racial politics; Asians and Chicanos fall somewhere in between. . . . [White students] may say something offensive without knowing it and get called 'racist,' a word they use to mean prejudging a person because he or she is black. *Why do you call me racist? Hey, I'm willing to talk to you like an ordinary person.*
>
> But when black students use the term, they tend to aim it at a person they see participating in a larger institution that works against black people. *If you're not in favor of affirmative action, that means you're racist.* (64)

Ultimately, perhaps, this narrative could open up to question these designations of identity, what they signify in this classroom, and how they work in the culture at large. It might lead students to discern multiple points of identity as well as contexts in which certain identities might be more salient than others—even, perhaps, the limited utility in some settings of a politics of identity. An older African American woman with children, for example, returning to school after a hiatus, might feel more commonality in the classroom with a comparable white woman than with an African American undergraduate. Finally, there are demographic realities to sort out. In 1968 at the University of California at Berkeley, just over 4 percent of the student population were people of color; today they constitute half the student population. At the University of Illinois at Urbana-Champaign, like many of the midwestern land-grant universities, much of this demographic change will occur in the 1990s.

Does Carol have power? Yes, this is not a dichotomy between the powerful and the powerless: power is not a portfolio that you either carry or do not carry. Does a black woman have a special right to a black woman's voice? The white students seem to think so, yet in the general discussion, they talk easily about "racism." At the same time, Carol feels that she may have silenced the white women and so now proposes to silence herself. Thus whose right to speak is at issue here and is not easily resolved. The politics of speaking encompasses everyone—the white women presenters who feel they have no right to their own voice; the men who are silent when gender is discussed but talkative when race is the issue—probably, again, because they do not feel implicated by the term "race"; the other women of color who are letting Carol speak for them, whether they agree with her or not; even the instructor, whose commitment to women's studies pedagogy (and, possibly, her own discomfort with issues of race) makes her hesitant to break in.

The Bailiff's Shadow

The white students' perception that things are generally all right is fairly typical of "inmates" in institutions and represents what Herbert Marcuse called "happy consciousness." The factors that produce sexism, racism, and other forms of discrimination are disguised, camouflaged, buried; in their place are norms for behavior, assumptions about value and merit, in which those who experience the effects of the system are said to cause its problems. Thus, the women's movement, itself partly the result of a changing labor market and changing household arrangements, is blamed for men losing jobs to women and for the breakup of the nuclear family; black students are blamed for racism, Jews for anti-Semitism. Invoking Woolf directly, a second narrative might thus be called "The Bailiff's Shadow." This is a narrative about teaching and learning within American colleges and universities, institutions that feminists have characterized as "male-dominated." What we usually mean by this is that the university, as an institution, was founded by educated white males for the training and perpetuation of other educated white males—men with independent incomes, men who receive assistance from a wife, a sister, a housekeeper, a servant in the college quarters—to serve the interests of white males. This is a narrative, then, about structural inequities—or, in Woolf's words, about why "women drink water and men drink wine." The male teacher in the case study referred to women's studies as a curriculum in "attitude adjustment"; thus it is a narrative about women's studies and patriarchal rules and whether "attitude adjustment" courses should be required for everyone.

Despite the massive quantity of research on higher education (with its focus on the college sophomore as the experimental animal of choice), we know surprisingly little about actual classroom experience and communication. Data on gender-linked communication in the classroom are even more fragmentary, and most of the work that exists is on middle-class white girls and women in dual-gender settings (coeducational classrooms, for example). The recent trend toward biological and neurological explanations for sex differences is likely to further discourage the study of natural settings.[7] Nevertheless, certain findings emerge consistently enough to suggest some of the main differences between female and male patterns of classroom interaction.[8] What we find is that both male and female students interact more in classes taught by women teachers. Researchers find women's classrooms more discussion oriented; men's are more structured and emphasize the mastery of content. At the college and university levels as well, more interaction occurs in classes taught by women, more student input, more teacher and student questions, more feedback. An important study of sixty college classrooms found more student participation in women teachers' classes regardless of the department, course level, gender ratio, or class size. Women teachers overall were seen as more likeable—but the more they generated class participation, the less competent the students judged them to be in their subject matter. Neither students nor faculty are consistently aware of these systematic gender differences. Virginia Valian (1990) reminds us that perceptions of differences between men and women are most marked in contexts that are traditionally male gendered—for example, women are more likely to be judged incompetent when the subject matter is technical or scientific, less likely when the subject has traditionally been associated with women, like family or childbearing. These findings emphasize that encoding does not necessarily match decoding: in other words, no matter what changes women may make in their own behavior, the ways they are interpreted by others can never be fully controlled.

The persistence of gender stereotypes is chronicled by Valian, who draws upon recent social psychology research to explain why "[w]omen in academia are less successful than men: they make less money, they get promoted more slowly, and they get tenured more slowly" (129). Her assessment is uncompromisingly pessimistic: "Our stereotypes about men and women constitute informal theories about them," and we interpret the data we get in the light of our theories (130). This holds negative consequences for women: "To oversimplify a bit: we see men as deserving their successes, and women as deserving their failures" (132), and these consequences have a cumulative effect: "a man benefits psychologically from his successes"; attributing them to his ability "inoculates him against failure" (135). But when "a woman fails, she and we attribute her failure to lack of ability. A woman will see her current failure as predictive of future failure, because she attributes her failure to a stable uncontrollable cause—lack of ability" (136).[9]

Valian concludes that we must give renewed attention to the challenge of changing expectations and attributions, ours and others'. Presented at a conference on women in the linguistics profession held at Cornell University in June 1989, her analysis was marked by a special urgency for a field which, contending that "women are not a problem," has lagged in recognizing gender issues and feminist scholarship. It was taken for granted at the conference that, as Craige Roberts (1990) argued, discrimination in linguistics "often proceeds without conscious detection, even while it damages the self-confidence and security of the women involved" (184). A number of speakers demonstrated that overall statistical representation of women in linguistics—the usual argument for the profession's complacency—disguises the clustering of women in lower-paid and less-prestigious areas (like foreign language teaching), at lower ranks, in nontenure-track positions, and in departments other than linguistics. The Cornell conference, apart from special sessions held at annual meetings of the Linguistic Society of America, was the first national conference for and about women in linguistics and embodied much of the relief, excitement, and affirmation experienced by women in other fields more than a decade ago.[10] Moreover, recent Ph.D.s, with different resources and fresh insights, were able to recommend a number of excellent, concrete strategies for linguists and other feminist academics.

Margaret Speas (1990), for example, describes the phenomenon of being "first generation mentors"—women who enter positions "as Assistant Professors with no experience at all of what it would be to be female and to serve as a mentor for a graduate student" (196). Noting that one of the mentor's conventional functions is "to introduce and initiate the protege into the customs and demands of academic life," Speas identifies a number of subtle conflicts and difficulties facing the feminist mentor:

> To oversimplify a bit for the sake of example, the successful academic is expected to be objective, competitive and demanding, characteristics which are an extension of the characteristics stereotypically associated with men. Women, on the other hand, are expected to be empathetic, cooperative and nurturing. It is therefore not a straightforward matter to initiate a female student into the world of academia, or even to choose for ourselves the best approach to serving as a mentor. Should I be careful to be aloof and demanding with my students, so that they might observe this behavior in a female professor, and adopt it, at least in part? Or should I be nurturing and encouraging, thus reinforcing female stereotypes, but perhaps providing a balance to the environment fostered by male faculty? At times, we may find that the best we can do is to help students find a means by which they can begin to confront some of these conflicts. (201–2)

Craige Roberts (1990) suggests that women students also form peer-support groups, an experience in graduate school that helped her begin "to see that being a good girl wasn't going to work in this situation, and that taking risks intellectually was necessary to success in the academic environment" (189). Yet she is aware that academic success may involve serious conflicts in values, for example, by slighting students and teaching. Sure enough, she reports, studies of the relationship between success in teaching and in research bear this out:

> One cluster of personality traits was found to relate in opposite ways to research productivity and teaching effectiveness. With some consistency across studies, supportiveness, tolerance, and warmth . . . were associated inversely with research productivity but positively with teaching effectiveness. (192)

For some time, women working in the bailiff's shadow will presumably continue to experience contradictory demands and paradoxical conflicts, both within feminism and in engagements with the larger institution.

Everybody Was Always Talking about Foucault: A Pedagogical Narrative

A third narrative concerns the role of theory in concrete pedagogical settings and actual classroom performance. The phrase about Foucault comes from a female graduate student in a seminar that Cheris Kramarae and I observed in the course of research on women in academic life. We had previously examined interaction in an interdisciplinary feminist theory seminar taught by three female instructors (see Treichler and Kramarae 1983; Treichler 1986); we now looked at interaction in an interdisciplinary graduate seminar in interpretive theory taught by three male instructors (Kramarae and Treichler 1990). Together, the two seminars provide some insight into the classroom experiences of women and men.

To begin, the contemporary academic world, in general, retains the notion of an authorized body of knowledge; relies primarily on classroom-based or laboratory learning; does not stress subjective experience as a legitimate source of knowledge; has a hierarchical structure that stresses individual achievement; and maintains a fairly standardized and accessible set of rules governing classroom behavior and interaction. These rules, which dictate in part that all things flow to and from the teacher, do not seem to have the same meanings and consequences for women and men, nor do women and men seem equally comfortable in the university environment. Especially apparent in graduate courses is what Berenice Carroll (1984) has called "a class system of the intellect" in which not only performance itself, but also interpretation of that performance, accords men a greater advantage—a point I'll return to.

These generalizations certainly held true for the graduate seminar in interpretive theory that we observed. Taught by three male professors with about forty-five students enrolled, the seminar, while different from some graduate seminars in the humanities by virtue of its size and interdisciplinary emphasis, seemed to embody in high relief the features just noted: teacher control of the class structure and the flow of discussion; perception among students that permission to speak depended on specific credentials (including the quality of the contribution, expertise, disciplinary training, and facility with what one female student called "little professor" talk); domination of discussion by a small group composed primarily of male students; little attention to classroom process; and discussion characterized by intellectual challenge and confrontation rather than collaboration. At the end of the semester, we interviewed students and instructors about their classroom experience. Students varied widely in the adjectives they used to describe interaction in the seminar: interesting, amorphous, combative, nice, tense, responsive, productive, useless, paternalistic, supportive, formidable, chaotic, sermonish. Equally diverse were their responses to a specific interaction, a five-minute interchange that we audiotaped in the third or fourth class meeting, in which a female student spoke for the first time: the exchange was tentative on the woman's part, with her ideas not forcefully asserted, yet she persisted for some time, articulating her point in different ways in order to make it understood. Played back some eight weeks later, virtually every student and instructor remembered the exchange, its content, and their appraisal of it. Recalling their thoughts at the time, most men had docketed the interchange according to its content (e.g., "It raised questions of specific interest to me"; "It did not reach any concluding moment"). In contrast, the women chiefly remembered their identification with the speaker's gender and their feelings—frequently of discomfort—as she spoke.

The overwhelming sense among the women was that they had not mastered the language of this classroom, the "theorybabble" that seemed to them a form of language whose mystifying powers were as much social and political as pedagogical. The comment that "Everybody was always talking about Foucault" addressed this problem; its sense of exclusion and intimidation was echoed by most of the other women in the course. Ultimately, the women expressed great ambivalence toward theory: first, they could see that theory functioned in a very seductive and seamless way; second, they perceived that its insights could be extremely useful and *potentially* could open up rather than close off points of dialogue with feminist perspectives. ("Feminist postmodernism," for example, helps get at some of the persistently troubling questions of 1970s feminism—e.g., why all women did not joyfully join in being "liberated" or why "pure liberation" remained in some sense an unfulfillable dream. Certainly, without some notion of fragmented identity and contradictory representation, we cannot begin to understand the many lives that feminism leads today.[11]) Yet third, theory does not function this way in the typical theory seminar; rather, it enables its fluent speakers to evade the important political agenda of the woman's question. And it allows speakers to dismiss or ignore other speakers who do not speak theory.

"Learning to talk about Foucault" is, of course, a metaphor for learning to engage fluently in the specialized language of any field. I should emphasize that I am not arguing "against" specialized language: specialized language and terms accomplish unique intellectual and historical tasks, and learning them is important. What I am interested in is the ease or the pain with which they are learned, the gendered dimension of the learning experience and how it is interpreted by others, and the degree to which both learning and resistance remain themselves untheorized—attributed, again, to the student rather than to the setting. I should also emphasize that "learning to talk about Foucault" is a requisite skill in fields that have not even heard of Foucault. In his autobiographical account of the first year of Harvard Law School, Scott Turow (1977) describes the complex "personal politics of speaking in class." These parallel precisely what we found in our study of the "Foucault" seminar: within the first couple of weeks, three or four students emerge as the regular talkers. Although the regular talkers are usually men, Turow describes one who is a woman:

> Clarissa Morgenstern had come to law school after the dissolution of a brief marriage. She was still only twenty-three or twenty-four but she was a commanding figure—tall, attractive, and dressed each morning in the best from *Vogue*. She spoke in a high-flown, elocutionary style and when called on she would hold the floor for a lengthy statement, not just a one-line answer. . . . (70)

And he captures the oddly confused evaluations of the woman talker that her peers make:

> In general, those people heard from regularly were regarded with a kind of veiled animosity. Many people admired and envied their outspokenness, but for the most part, the regular talkers were treated with an amused disdain.
>
> "I can't stand Clarissa," someone told me one day during the second week. "I can't imagine how I'll live through all year listening to her. The way she carries on, you'd think it was opera."
>
> Stephen repeated to me someone else's remark that Clarissa was "a nice guy off the field, but a terror once she gets between those white lines." (70–71)

I am not sure that there is or that there should be such a thing as "feminist pedagogy" as constituted by a set of practices: chairs in a circle, first names, collaborative agenda setting, and (as much of the literature puts it) collective re-visioning of the production of knowledge. Many women, many feminists, are not comfortable with these practices, particularly when they are sometimes seen to be as expected and institutionally dictated as the most classically delivered "masculine" lecture by a pipe-smoking gentleman scholar in tweeds. In recognition of feminism's paradoxes and contradictions, the ongoing battles over essentialist definitions, and the psychic impasse they periodically engender, a contingent of feminist scholars at the Society for the Humanities at Cornell University in 1989 ironically proposed a conference called "Feminist Theory and How to Dress for It."[12] A lesson from these classroom observations is that language, speaking, teaching, and interaction are all difficult activities that need to draw upon whatever resources are most relevant. A second lesson, perhaps, is that institutions are resourceful about generating new forms of silencing—forms that we ourselves, with our convictions about what is progressive, may help devise and maintain. The bailiff's shadow, in other words, may sometimes be our own.

The usefulness of theory is that it enables us to query our own, everyday pedagogical practices. Discussing postcolonial theory and the classroom, for example, Keya Ginguly (1991) asks how the specificity of the historically recent postcolonial subject can most intelligently be taken into account: Are there ways in which this subject can be strategically presented, represented, understood, undermined, and used in the actual practice of teaching postcolonial theory? How can we adequately theorize the identity, voice, and subject positioning of the instructor (scholar, critic, speaker, graduate student, historical subject)? As she points out, this is in some bald sense a problem for any "amphibious" or bicultural subject called upon to enact a position of privilege and simultaneously to represent (stand in for) the absent nonprivileged Other—to be both master and subaltern. How do we find a way, she asks, of "inserting ourselves into this apparatus of domination and subordination"?[13]

Certainly women's studies has interrogated the paradoxical interplay between domination and subordination inevitably present, even when denied, in the feminist classroom.[14] The question then is therefore to find a way to work with the question of postcolonial *voice*. One way would be to enact theory: to use the very ironies of voice and play with them in the classroom—to play with identities, with historical conventions and cultural expectations, by having "the white male instructor" take a given position and be challenged by "the postcolonial subject," and then turn it around and do it differently, with different roles and different voices, and in line with the kind of historical and contextual specificity Ginguly calls for in understanding the emergence of the postcolonial subject. One might envision being able to orchestrate—with the students' active participation—something of the sort in the Women's Studies 101 case study.

But at this point the wall between the classroom and surrounding institution becomes very thin. Problems of identity and voice come back to the life of the institution itself—to faculty hiring practices, for example, as when our Women's Studies Program at Illinois undertook a job search for someone qualified to teach courses on "Women of Color." Almost at once, as the applications arrived, we encountered what Ginguly calls the "contaminated logic of identity"—this time in the form of the question: Do you have to *be* a woman of color to *teach* "Women of Color"? In the light of current institutional politics and historical conditions, one must on the one hand answer "yes." Yet the meaning of this category is not self-evident, anymore than the category "women" was a decade ago.[15] At other universities, too, there are debates about who counts as a "woman of color," as well as who and what she is supposed to be a "woman of color" *for.*

We can thus identify a theoretical metanarrative about the reality of classroom events, about representation, about the nature of evidence, the nature of signification and signifying, the cultural work of language, agency and power within the classroom, lessons in reading a text, my own agency in constructing this "text." At the same time, the comment that "Everybody was always talking about Foucault" is richly ironic in the sense that it is Foucault, virtually above all others, we would turn to learn why "everybody was always talking about Foucault," to identify the ways in which we speak and are spoken.

More than twenty years ago, psycholinguist Courtney Cazden (1970) called for greater attention to "situation" in assessing the language acquisition skills and social class differences among children: "We must attend not only to the abilities of individuals and how they develop, but to qualities of the situation, or temporary environment, in which those abilities are activated" (294). It sounds so obvious, and yet most of our research, our teaching procedures, and our commonplace pedagogical assumptions about students' abilities continue to focus on students rather than on the interaction between students and their learning environment. When we do look at the interaction, it is not only the students who should be evaluated and subjected to change. A second case study raises explicit questions about the relationship between institutional policies and the classroom. We are still at a large research university but no longer in a feminist classroom:

Case Study II: A Different Drummer

On the first day of an introductory art class, a woman student in the front row is told by the male instructor to stand up so he can judge her potential as a model. She assumes he is joking and just smiles. "What's the problem?" he asks, "Self conscious? You'll never learn to understand painting if you can't loosen up." The male teaching assistant intervenes: "Leave her alone, Jack." The instructor retorts: "Who asked you, asshole?"

The next week another woman student is attempting to interpret a painting. The instructor rolls his eyes toward the ceiling. "Lord," he asks, "How can I be expected to teach art to assholes and philistines?" He turns to the student and says with exaggerated patience, as though speaking to a child: "No, my dear, this is not a painting about a picnic; it is a painting about desire, about the human body and the social conventions that govern it, about the artist as provocateur, and about the nature of the bourgeois soul." He turns to the class at large: "You people have a problem: use your own eyes to look at pictures, not Ronald Reagan's."

Many of the students, particularly the women, find that exchanges of this kind are making them uncomfortable. Finally, as the midterm approaches, two of the women go to see the instructor and ask him to stop making comments about how "uptight" they are. He is not sympathetic. "Do you want to learn about art? Art is *supposed* to make you uncomfortable." The women go see the department head. "Look," he says, "don't take it personally. He even talks to me that way. But he's a topnotch painter and the kind of teacher students remember all their lives. Ignore his little comments and learn what you can." The women find this response unsatisfactory and go visit the dean of the college. "I'm very reluctant to get involved in this," he tells them. "Faculty have complete freedom to do what they want in their classrooms. Anyhow, the guy's an artist and artists march to a different drummer." The women ask whether there is someone they can consult or an office where they can file a formal complaint. "Look," says the dean, "the term's almost over. If I were you I'd take the department head's advice and lighten up."

Questions for discussion included the following:

Do the students in this case have legitimate grounds for concern, or are they overreacting to the instructor's "little comments"?

Does the instructor's behavior fall within most institutions' definition of sexual (or gender) harassment? If so, which specific behaviors constitute harassment?

If the students wish to pursue their complaint, what are their options now? What are their risks?

How might different or changing cultural or disciplinary values be involved in this example?

> Do instructors have "complete freedom to do what they want in their classrooms"?

This case study is designed to explore two competing accounts of contemporary academic life. On the one hand, stories circulate in virtually every discipline about behavior by male instructors that is obnoxious, demeaning, peculiar, sexual, or insulting to individual women or to women as a group. Universities have drafted policies and guidelines prohibiting sexual harassment, including classroom harassment, on the grounds that such behavior creates a workplace unconducive to women's professional performance and intellectual development—and because court decisions have declared an institution's top officers responsible for its workplace atmosphere. On the other hand, as such policies proliferate and come to be increasingly taken for granted, some important distinctions seem in danger of dropping out of the discourse. I'll give just one example, from a daylong seminar on sexual harassment at my own institution which I helped to plan. One motivation for the seminar was a study of University of Illinois students which found that a significant percentage of women students—19 percent of the graduate students, 10 percent of the undergraduates, and 8 percent of professional school students (figures comparable to those from other campuses)—reported having experienced some form of sexual harassment during their tenure at the university (Allen and Okawa 1987). At the seminar, an attorney specializing in sexual harassment cases drew an example from the Illinois survey: a woman undergraduate in an English literature course had reported that when she expressed her doubts in class about the sexual interpretation given to a particular novel, the professor spelled it out for her in such a way that it made her feel stupid and naïve; she found this offensive and felt harassed. Listening to this example and to the attorney's judgment that it constituted sexual harassment, I asked whether it was harassing because the sexual interpretation of the novel made the student feel uncomfortable or because the professor's handling of her response made her feel stupid. "Same difference," said the attorney.

The preceding case study was designed not only to identify the difficulties faced by students who feel sexually harassed, but also to challenge a commonplace confusion of "sexual harassment" with the topics of sex and sexuality, and of "harassment" with attempts to teach ideas that are new and therefore—inevitably—potentially offensive. The case study was originally prepared before the Clarence Thomas confirmation hearing put sexual harassment on the nation's cultural agenda. Yet the Thomas-Hill case does not address the unique conditions of the university classroom; nor, for the most part, do members of the academic community whom I have heard discussing this case. Faculty and students who are at all familiar with the problem of sexual harassment these days usually agree that the instructor's behavior is inappropriate and constitutes sexual harassment, and that the department head and the dean need significant reeducation in university policy. Sexual harassment is illegal, and tenured faculty members have lost their jobs for engaging in it; the instructor (at the least) should have the harassing aspects of his behavior and their prohibited status pointed out to him. Some discussants readily urged that he be summarily suspended from the university.

In the 1960s, when the instructor in this case study presumably came of professional age, classroom practices evolved that were understood as assertions of progressive politics and egalitarianism; personal and sexual student-faculty relationships were sometimes cast in the same anti-authoritarian spirit. But as Anne Bernays's 1989 novel *Professor Romeo* makes clear through its chronological juxtapositions of then and now, academic culture has changed: twenty years of feminist critique combined with antidiscrimination legislation and policies have had a significant impact on the American workplace and campus life. So where have these guys been? They don't have a clue to what's going on and instead dredge up the old chestnut that "artists" deserve special treatment, indulgence, even protection. Their oblivion would not have been out of place on the Senate Judiciary Committee, as it muddled its way through the Clarence Thomas-Anita Hill confrontation.

The case study has generally succeeded in getting discussants to identify the various ways in which the male faculty and administrators behaved badly. But it has failed to get them to discuss what distinguishes sexual harassment from the topics of sex and sexuality or to discuss the ways in which learning may make students feel uncomfortable, even harassed. Indeed, I was absolutely unprepared for the readiness of students, faculty, and administrators alike to deny any distinction between the instructor's behavior toward the students and his interpretation of the painting—their readiness, in other words, to adopt the position of the attorney I quoted above and say "same difference." An important step in cases of potential sexual harassment is to sort out precisely what it is that constitutes harassment. In the "Different Drummer" example, many behaviors are candidates.[16] Yet surely even a temperate defense of academic freedom—that is, a defense that refuses to grant instructors "complete freedom to do what they want in their classrooms"—requires a defense of the instructor's right to present conventional interpretations of what is almost certainly Édouard Manet's celebrated 1863 painting *Le Déjeuner sur l'herbe.*

But what is teaching and what is harassment? Certainly, much of what is taught in classrooms throughout the humanities and social sciences— not to mention law, medicine, the sciences, and women's studies—deals with subject matter and critical analysis that some students will experience as troubling, disconcerting, and offensive. In professional schools, faculty would defend their aggressive *method* of instruction, as well as its content, as vital preparation for participation within the field itself. Law school instructors typically use seating charts to call on students by name, a form of torture familiar through films like *The Paper Chase* and graphically described in Scott Turow's autobiographical book. Here is Turow's account of the first day of class at the hands of a legendary professor of contract law:

> As he went on describing the subjects with which we would soon be dealing—offer, acceptance, interpretation; the list was extensive—I began to think that . . . he would let the hour slip away. No one would be called on and we'd all be safe for one more day. But at six or seven minutes to twelve he returned to the lectern and looked down at the seating chart.
> "Let's see if we can cover a *little* ground today." Perini took a pencil from his pocket and pointed it at the chart. It might as well have been a pistol. Please, no, I thought.
> "Mr. Karlin!" Perini cried sharply.
> Nearby, I heard a tremendous thud. Five or six seats from me a man was scrambling to grab hold of the books that had been piled before him, two or three of which had now hit the floor. That, I was sure, was Karlin who had jolted when he heard his name called. . . . His eyes, as he struggled with his books, were quick with fright, and at once I felt terribly sorry for him and guilty at my own relief. (47)

Theory in the Classroom: Contests for Meaning

No utopian pedagogical forms exist: sometimes the assertion of authority, hierarchy, and propriety brings us as close to utopia as a particular classroom ever will. There are, however, pedagogical practices that enable us to understand how contests for meaning occur and to find ways to make them visible and palpable. In the course of this essay I have discussed a number of examples, approaches, and strategies, designed for a variety of purposes, that seem to me to bear on this effort. I would like to conclude by talking a bit more about these strategies, which, in general, involve the interrogation of institutional structures.[17]

We are in a period of social change in which upheaval, disruption, and fear are coupled with opportunity. In many disciplines, we are standing in the middle of a paradigm shift. Can this be illuminated in the classroom through Bauer and Jarratt's (see chapter 7, this volume) notion of challenging students' "resistance to history" and teaching them to articulate the self in history? But the connection to history, to our own historical positioning, also challenges, I think, the perception that "male" critical theory—postmodernism, deconstruction—is antithetical to feminism. These intellectual developments share an era and its uniquely cataclysmic crises; they also are the result, in part, of postwar changes within the academy which have opened it to a new body of students and faculty and to intellectual questions, as Chris Weedon (1991) puts it in discussing the links between poststructuralist feminist practice, about meaning, subjectivity, and language.

If the classroom and the institution, like the world, are material settings, they can be investigated through material methods. Indeed, one can turn the academy's methods on itself. Does sexism exist or is it a thing of the past? Is racism increasing on campus? Students can, among other things, conduct formal observations of their classrooms (yours and others') and report. But further, as Berry and Patraka (see chapter 6, this volume) suggest, the classroom can serve as a "laboratory of culture," and we can ask how it reproduces or challenges the culture's relations of power. I do something like this in asking students to carry out a microanalysis, my term for a detailed, fine-grained analysis of a tiny portion of the material setting—usually the transcription of five minutes out of an audiotaped or videotaped class, public dialogue, or conversation—and present it in writing and to the class. The goal is to begin with the concrete, the palpable, move to the immediate discursive context, to the structural context, to the institutional context, and so on—rather like Stephen Daedalus's entry in the front of his history book or the Eameses' film *Powers of Ten* (1977)—and then to move back again, bringing the layered contextual identifications back to bear on the transcribed text. What one typically finds is that context is highly determining of interaction; that routine and disruption of routine are equally interesting and fruitful to explore; that transcription of an audiotaped segment of a "real material setting" is anything but transparent and unproblematic; that the microanalysis and macroanalysis not only complement each other but give different students different kinds of material with which to excel; and that interpretations of the text are often strongly contested.

Like the glasses in the science fiction film *They Live* (Carpenter 1988), any theoretical framework reveals realities not hitherto visible. The glasses can be used to see and articulate the rules of everyday life, ideological prescriptions, even the institution's buildings, history, and specific pedagogical practices. Where the protagonist of *They Live* could suddenly see the alien lifeforms who had taken over the planet and the Barbara Kruger-like messages underlying everyday sights and sounds—imperatives like "CONSUME"—at the University of Illinois, we might get a glimpse of the elaborate infrastructure on which a large research university rests and relies. We would not see aliens but rather a large cadre of skilled and unskilled laborers, a hierarchy of jobs and qualifications, a physical plant that exceeds that of a small city in size and complexity. If we brought our glasses to the classroom and asked my earlier question—"Whose room is this?"—we might see messages like "YOU DO NOT TEACH IN A VACUUM" and "YOUR WORK IS SUPPORTED BY AN ELABORATE INFRASTRUCTURE" and even "LIGHT BULBS AREN'T CHEAP." In the old days, the university mostly used eight-foot fluorescent bulbs that required professional installation and servicing and were rarely found outside institutional settings. Now that four-foot bulbs are more common, they need to be protected against theft (for individual home use or for resale) and so are kept in special locked facilities in each building. The only people authorized to change light bulbs (in overhead fixtures or lamps) are skilled and semiskilled workers classified as electricians or—a special designation negotiated with the electricians' union—laborer-electricians (the former make $20–21 per hour, the latter about half that). If a problem arises which the laborer-electrician cannot solve, a call goes out to two electricians assigned all day long to troubleshoot, all over campus, in the "trouble truck." Faculty members who want to change a light bulb in their office must do it in secret—with the door locked and the blinds drawn—or risk being turned in. But the light bulbs are only a tiny portion of the total maintenance costs of the spaces we inhabit. The average maintenance cost for one square foot of classroom space, including an energy component for fuel and light, is estimated at $3.65 per year. This means the annual average upkeep on a thirty-square-foot classroom is about $3,285.[18]

I am not citing these figures to make an argument about worth—to argue, that is, that, on the one hand, our university's infrastructure is outrageously expensive or, on the other hand, that only such a structure ensures conscientious maintenance of a safe physical plant that accommodates 34,000 students, 10,000 bicycles, and so on. My purpose is, rather, to underline the obvious: there is an infrastructure and it has a cost. I also want to observe that, in recent years, research universities have been singled out for attack by congressional oversight committees, conservative critics of higher education, and so on. While one can point to outrageous excesses of expenditure on infrastructure (Stanford's

yacht, for instance), on the whole, I would argue, the resources of
research universities serve as a pretense for a much deeper attack on
what research universities give their faculty and students opportunities
to do: to think, to reflect, to investigate, to mount criticism, and to
create.[19] The problem for critics is not what it costs to change a light
bulb; the problem is what the light is illuminating.

Again, I think self-consciousness is the issue. In the same spirit, one
can experiment with voice, one's own and that of the students, crossing
gender, race, cultural positioning, voice itself (for example, through
such forms as call and response, through experimenting with form as
well as content). Barbara DiBernard and Sheila Reiter (see chapter 5,
this volume) outline the use of *A Feminist Dictionary* (Kramarae and
Treichler 1985) to carry out these crossover dreams. But here, also,
poststructuralist, postmodern, and postcolonial feminisms, as well as
what Dale Bauer and Susan Jarratt call feminist sophistics, can be set to
work in the classroom to explore disorder and diversity as well as
unfamiliar, but ordered, identities. Power is not a portfolio; it is socially
constructed, negotiated, but subject to powerful constraints and may
shift from one context to the next.

No pedagogical form guarantees utopia. Nor is true revolution (in
Thomas Kuhn's sense) readily distinguishable from what Foucault
(1971) describes as "redistributed transformation," in which the elements in a binary pair are assigned new values, but the binary division stays the same.[20] "Alternative pedagogy," "feminist pedagogy,"
and "theory in the classroom" demand that we interrogate the context
within which we work, speak, listen, and teach, holding up each cliché,
each piece of orthodoxy—whether "mainstream" or "alternative"—
and adding a question mark. In general, they require us to attend to the
particulars of the classroom as a material space, as a theater in which
the social, cultural, and intellectual crises of our times are enacted—and
hence a theater in which we can witness and better understand the
crucial contests for meaning that shape the world, the institution, the
classrooms we live in. One might go so far as to say that it is a setting
in which forms of dominance and structures of power relations may
be identified, examined, learned, undermined, mastered, or conceived
differently.

Notes

1. Sandra Gilbert and Susan Gubar's (1979) collection of essays on women
poets, *Shakespeare's Sisters,* is only one of scores of feminist writings that take

their title or theme from Woolf's work. Not all of these references are approving: "Forget the room of one's own," writes Gloria Anzaldúa (1981): "Write in the kitchen, lock yourself up in the bathroom. Write on the bus or the welfare line, on the job or during meals, between sleeping or waking. I write while sitting on the john. No long stretches at the typewriter unless you're wealthy or have a patron—you may not even own a typewriter" (170).

2. Not only do conservative attacks on political correctness obscure real problems on campus, they actually present an alternative vision of campus life that cannot be factually documented. The American Council on Education's 1991 report on the state of the university makes clear that, on most campuses, courses in feminism, multiculturalism, and minority studies remain marginal (El-Khawas 1991). Troy Duster (1991), reporting findings of the Institute for the Study of Social Change at Berkeley, the exception, argues as well that "multiculturalism's critics are selling students short by propagating five key myths": (1) multiculturalism is tearing the campus apart; (2) multiculturalism is diluting our standards; (3) getting rid of affirmative action and other special admissions programs would improve the university; (4) merit and admissions should be based solely on grade point average and SAT scores; and (5) radical professors are setting the campus political agenda. Duster convincingly refutes each myth. See Berman (1992) on the "political correctness" phenomenon.

3. I do not mean to suggest that the pattern of interaction embodied in this case study is novel. Far from it: many of us can remember virtually identical exchanges throughout the 1970s, between straight women and lesbians, or between working-class women and middle-class women, or between male-identified women and woman-identified women, or even between women and men. Discussions of feminist classroom interaction are reviewed in my 1986 essay "Teaching Feminist Theory." Here, I wish to look more at social, structural, and institutional aspects of these interactions in a "postfeminist" era—that is, a period when many assumptions about feminism are taken for granted, even while the term may be repudiated.

4. Warren's 1972 findings on the social nature of divergent perceptions are now supported by a large body of case studies, experimental investigations, and ethnographies. For an overview, see William J. McGuire, "Attitudes and Attitude Change" (233–346), and Walter G. Stephans, "Intergroup Relations," (599–658) in Lindzey and Aronson (1985). See also Duncan (1976). An example of an ethnography of conflict is Jamie Feldman's "Gallo, Montagnier, and the Debate Over HIV: a Narrative Analysis" (1992).

5. Biddy Martin, in an unpublished paper entitled "Theory in the Feminist Classroom," discusses this in some detail with regard to graduate courses in feminist theory. See also the section in my essay "Teaching Feminist Theory" (1986), where I discuss students' various anxieties over reading Julia Kristeva. Long before the issue was joined by conservatives, the notion of "political correctness" was the stuff of satires by feminists and progressives (see Kramarae and Treichler's *A Feminist Dictionary* [1985] for examples). In Armistead Maupin's six-volume *Tales of the City* saga, one recurrent character is a lesbian named DeDe. In *Significant Others* (1987), DeDe is talking with her scrupulously PC lover and refers disparagingly to a third lesbian and her "runty, big-mouthed lover." "DeDe . . ." the PC lesbian begins admonishingly. DeDe replies: "O.K., forget runty. . . . Vertically challenged. How's that? . . ." (125).

Such satiric constructions have shown up more recently in satiric handbooks about how to speak PC and the like.

6. Vito Russo (1981) criticizes a similar tendency in what he calls "gay movies for straight people": though ostensibly about "gay people," the problem always revolves around the straight people for whom the gay person and homosexuality are a problem. As the character of Nick comments in Bill Sherwood's extraordinary film *Parting Glances* (1986): "Straight people are so narcissistic that 99 percent of what you see is about them." See also D'Emilio (1987).

7. A number of recent examples are provided by Thomas Bever (1992), a psychologist who studies the cognitive basis for complex behaviors like language.

8. For a more detailed description and discussion of these findings, see Treichler and Kramarae (1983), Kramarae and Treichler (1990), Lasser (1987), Nelson (1986), Gabriel and Smithson (1990), and Eisenhart and Holland (1992).

9. Valian writes:

> Each time a man succeeds he and we encode a picture of him as competent and effective, and add it to other such pictures. The man's success calls to our mind his other successes, which we have encoded as due to his ability, and consolidates our picture of him as competent.
>
> When a woman succeeds, she and we tend to attribute her success to luck, or to the task's being easy, or to her very high effort, or all three. She has succeeded against expectation, and we find explanations for her success that maintain our theory of male-female differences. Success does not especially redound to a woman's credit, because we do not attribute it to her ability, and therefore we do not build up a picture of her as competent. We have no confidence that she will be successful in the future, because for her to be successful in the future she would have to be lucky again, or have an easy task again, or work very hard again—all very unstable attributes. (131–32).

10. The conference was organized primarily by Professor Alice Davison, with the help of a grant from the National Science Foundation and with the cooperation of the Linguistic Society of America. The proceedings are published in Davison and Eckert (1990).

11. See Treichler (1992) for a discussion and references.

12. Amended immediately, of course, to "Feminist Theories and How to Dress for Them."

13. Ginguly describes a seminar in which a white male graduate student claimed to represent the voice of "the African American woman," and insisted on the unproblematic nature of his right to do so. Theory, he told Ginguly, is a luxury that only those *with* a history can afford, thereby chastising her—"the third world woman"—for elitist theorizing, in contrast to the tasks of textual recovery he implies are more crucial to the material conditions of the subaltern. We witness, she writes,"the spectacle of white men saving brown (and black) women from other brown (and black) women."

14. See, for example, Penley, "Teaching in Your Sleep" (1986); Flynn, "Gender and Reading" (1986); and Baym, "The Feminist Teacher of Literature" (1990).

15. During her term as director of Women's Studies at Cornell a few years ago, Nelly Furman was negotiating with the School of Veterinary Medicine about cross-listing a course on sex differences in animal science. The feminist who had developed the course was going on sabbatical. When the department head indicated that two other women were available to teach the course, Furman tried to explain that a feminist perspective was necessary to make a women's studies listing appropriate. When the department head continued to be puzzled by the distinction between "woman" and "feminist," Furman said, "Let me put it this way: Would you hire a chicken to teach poultry science?" A parallel problem figured in a tenure dispute at Hampshire College in which a Latin American scholar claimed that by using poststructuralist and postcolonial theory in Latin American Studies—rather than more traditional socialist-realist approaches to literature—he was perceived as an inadequate representation of the "Latin American Scholar." Here, it is contemporary critical theory that marks him as alien, as not authentically "Latin American."

16. For example: the instructor's request that the woman student stand up and his statement that he wants to judge her potential as a model; his implication that, in refusing to do so, she has a problem, is self-conscious, needs to "loosen up," and, above all, may never understand painting; his address to the teaching assistant as "asshole"; his response to the woman interpreting the painting, first implying that she (and the class) are "assholes and philistines," then speaking to her as though she were a child and calling her "My dear"; his statement that the class has "a problem," that they are seeing through the eyes of "Ronald Reagan"; and finally his failure to take their discomfort seriously.

17. In a symposium on race, gender, and pedagogy that I participated in at Swarthmore College, Wahneema Lubiano talked illuminatingly about a course in women's literature that she had taught—first, under ideal circumstances at Stanford, and second, under very different circumstances at the University of Texas. Of the first case—a team-taught honors seminar, all women, multicultural-multiethnic students and faculty, lots of potlucks, and great projects— she said, "I had to learn to relinquish my authority as a teacher." In the second case—a kind of "Good Old Boy" nightmare class—she said, "I had to learn to take my authority back."

18. My thanks to Terry W. Ruprecht, assistant vice chancellor for Administrative Affairs and director, Administration of Operations and Maintenance, University of Illinois at Urbana-Champaign, for furnishing this information. Classrooms are different from other kinds of space. For residence halls, the Housing Division adds a 28 percent overhead fee to the cost of an electrician or laborer-electrician, for example.

From the 1990–1993, I have served on the campus Budget Strategies Committee; made up predominantly of faculty, the BSC is charged by the vice chancellor for Academic Affairs and the Campus Senate with advising them on budget savings and reallocations. Although committee members learn more about light bulbs—among other things—than they ever wanted to, service on such a committee is an illuminating and sometimes humbling experience. I highly recommend it.

19. Cary Nelson has made this argument in a number of articles on current campus debates about "political correctness." See, for example, Nelson's "Always Already Cultural Studies" (1991a) and "Canon Fodder" (1991b).

20. For example, in some discussions of feminist pedagogy, a lecture/monologue teaching style comes to be coded as "bad," a collaborative-discussion style as "good," without interrogation of the purposes of both styles and their potential accessibility and usefulness to men and women alike. This point is discussed at length and with sophistication by Patricia Donahue and Ellen Quandahl (1989).

Works Cited

Allen, Deborah, and Judy Bessai Okawa. 1987. "A Counseling Center Looks at Sexual Harassment." *Journal of the National Association for Women Deans, Administrators and Counselors* 20 (Fall): 9–16.

Anzaldúa, Gloria. 1981. "Speaking in Tongues: A Letter to Third World Women Writers." In Moraga and Anzaldúa, 165–74.

Bauer, Dale M., and Susan C. Jarratt. 1994. "Feminist Sophistics: Teaching with an Attitude." [See chapter 7, this volume.]

Baym, Nina. 1990. "The Feminist Teacher of Literature: Feminist or Teacher?" In *Gender in the Classroom: Power and Pedagogy,* edited by Susan L. Gabriel and Isaiah Smithson, 60–77. Urbana: University of Illinois Press.

Berman, Paul, ed. 1992. *Debating P.C.: The Controversy over Political Correctness on College Campuses.* New York: Dell.

Bernays, Anne. 1989. *Professor Romeo.* New York: Weidenfeld and Nicolson.

Berry, Ellen, and Vivian Patraka. 1994. "Local Struggles/Partial Explanations: Producing Feminist Theory in the Classroom." [See chapter 6, this volume.]

Bever, Thomas. 1992. "The Logical and Extrinsic Sources of Modularity." In *Modularity and Constraints in Language Cognition: Volume 25 of the Minnesota Symposia on Child Psychology,* edited by M. Gunnar and M. Maratsos, 179–212. Minneapolis: Erlbaum.

Carpenter, John. 1988. *They Live.* 97 min.

Carroll, Berenice A. 1984. "The Politics of Originality: Women and the Class System of the Intellect." Colloquium paper. Unit for Criticism and Interpretive Theory. University of Illinois at Urbana-Champaign. 10 April.

Cazden, Courtney B. 1970. "The Situation: A Neglected Source of Social Class Differences in Language Use." *Journal of Social Issues* 26(2): 35–60; Rpt. in J. B. Pride and Janet Holmes, eds. 1972. *Sociolinguistics: Selected Readings,* 294–313. Harmondsworth, England: Penguin.

Condry, J., and S. Condry. 1976. "Sex Differences: A Study of the Eye of the Beholder." *Child Development* 7: 812–19.

Davison, Alice, and Penelope Eckert, eds. 1990. *The Cornell Lectures: Women in the Linguistics Profession.* Washington, D.C.: Linguistic Society of America.

D'Emilio, John. 1987. "The Issue of Sexual Preference on College Campuses: Retrospect and Prospect." In *Educating Men and Women Together: Coeduca-*

tion in a Changing World, edited by Carol Lasser, 142–51. Urbana: University of Illinois Press and Oberlin College.

DiBernard, Barbara, and Sheila Reiter. 1994. "Two Women on the Verge of a Contextual Breakthrough: Using *A Feminist Dictionary* in the Literature Classroom." [See chapter 5, this volume.]

Donahue, Patricia, and Ellen Quandahl. 1989. "Reading the Classroom." In *Reclaiming Pedagogy: The Rhetoric of the Classroom,* edited by Patricia Donahue and Ellen Quandahl, 1–16. Carbondale: Southern Illinois University Press.

Duncan, B. L. 1976. "Differential Social Perception and Attribution of Intergroup Violence: Testing the Lower Limits of Stereotyping." *Journal of Personality and Social Psychology* 34: 590–598.

Duster, Troy. 1991. "They're Taking Over! and Other Myths about Race on Campus." *Mother Jones* 16 (September/October): 30–33; 63–64.

Eames, Ray, and Charles Eames. 1977. *Powers of Ten.* 10 min.

Eisenhart, Margaret A., and Dorothy C. Holland. 1992. "Gender Constructs and Career Commitment: The Influence of Peer Culture on Women in College." In *Gender Constructs and Social Issues,* edited by Tony L. Whitehead and Barbara V. Reid, 142–80. Urbana: University of Illinois Press.

El-Khawas, Elaine. 1991. *Campus Trends.* Higher Education Panel Report No. 81. Washington, D.C.: American Council on Education.

Feldman, Jamie. 1992. "Gallo, Montagnier, and the Debate over HIV: A Narrative Analysis." *Camera Obscura* 28: 101–32.

Flynn, Elizabeth A. 1986. "Gender and Reading." In Flynn and Schweickart, 267–88.

———, and Patrocinio P. Schweickart, eds. 1986. *Gender and Reading: Essays on Readers, Texts, and Contexts.* Baltimore: Johns Hopkins University Press.

Foucault, Michel. 1971 [1970]. *The Order of Things: An Archaeology of the Human Sciences.* Translation of *Les Mots es les Choses.* New York: Pantheon.

Frank, Francine Wattman, and Paula A. Treichler. 1989. *Language, Gender, and Professional Writing: Theoretical Approaches and Guidelines for Nonsexist Usage.* New York: Modern Language Association of America.

Gabriel, Susan, and Isaiah Smithson, eds. 1990. *Gender in the Classroom: Power and Pedagogy.* Urbana: University of Illinois Press.

Gilbert, Sandra M., and Susan Gubar, eds. 1979. *Shakespeare's Sisters: Feminist Essays on Women Poets.* Bloomington: Indiana University Press.

Ginguly, Keya. 1991. "Teaching Postcolonial Theory: Theorizing Postcolonial Teaching." Paper presented at the annual meeting of the International Communication Association. Chicago. May 27.

Goodwin, Marjorie H. 1980. "Directive-Response Speech Sequences in Girls' and Boys' Task Activities." In *Women and Language in Literature and Society,* edited by Sally McConnell-Ginet, Ruth Borker, and Nelly Furman, 157–73. New York: Praeger.

Henley, Nancy M., Mykol Hamilton, and Barrie Thorne. 1984. *Womanspeak and Manspeak: Sex Differences and Sexism in Communication, Verbal and Nonverbal.* West Publishing Company.

hooks, bell. 1981. "The Continued Devaluation of Black Womanhood." In *Ain't I a Woman: Black Women and Feminism*, 51–86. Boston: South End.

———. 1990. *Yearning: Race, Gender, and Cultural Politics*. Boston: South End.

Houston [Stanback], Marsha. 1985. "Language and Black Woman's Place: Evidence from the Black Middle Class." In *For Alma Mater: Theory and Practice in Feminist Scholarship*, edited by Paula A. Treichler, Cheris Kramarae, and Beth Stafford, 177–93. Urbana: University of Illinois Press.

Kramarae, Cheris, and Paula A. Treichler, with assistance from Ann Russo. 1985. *A Feminist Dictionary*. London and New York: Pandora.

Kramarae, Cheris, and Paula A. Treichler. 1990. "Power Relationships in the Classroom." In Gabriel and Smithson, 41–59.

Lasser, Carol, ed. 1987. *Educating Men and Women Together: Coeducation in a Changing World*. Urbana: University of Illinois Press in conjunction with Oberlin College.

Lindzey, Gardner, and Elliot Aronson. 1985. *The Handbook of Social Psychology*. Vol. II. 3rd ed. New York: Random House.

Lubiano, Wahneema. 1989. "Pedagogy and Politics." Paper presented at the symposium "Unlearning Not to Speak." Swarthmore College. 18 November.

Maltz, Daniel N., and Ruth Borker. 1982. "A Cultural Approach to Male-Female Miscommunication." In *Language and Social Identity*, edited by John J. Gumperz, 196–216. New York: Cambridge University Press.

Martin, Biddy. "Theory in the Feminist Classroom." Unpublished paper.

Maupin, Armistead. 1987. *Significant Others*. New York: Harper and Row.

McGuire, William J. 1985. "Attitudes and Attitude Change." In Lindzey and Aronson, 233–346.

Moraga, Cherríe, and Gloria Anzaldúa, eds. 1981. *This Bridge Called My Back: Writings by Radical Women of Color*. Watertown, MA: Persephone Press.

Nelson, Cary, ed. 1986. *Theory in the Classroom*. Urbana: University of Illinois Press.

———. 1991a. "Always Already Cultural Studies: Two Conferences and a Manifesto." *Journal of the Midwest Modern Language Association* 24.1 (Spring):24–38.

———. 1991b. "Canon Fodder: An Evening with William Bennett, Lynne Cheney, and Dinesh D'Souza." *Works and Days*, no. 18 (Fall): 39–54.

Penley, Constance. 1986. "Teaching in Your Sleep: Feminism and Psychoanalysis." In Nelson 1986, 129–48.

Roberts, Craige. 1990. "Gender Values and Success in Academia." In Davison and Eckert, 183–95.

Russo, Vito. 1981. *The Celluloid Closet: Homosexuality in the Movies*. New York: Harper & Row.

Sherwood, Bill. 1986. *Parting Glances*. 90 min.

Speas, Margaret. 1990. "First Generation Mentors." In Davison and Eckert, 196–207.

Stephans, Walter G. 1985. "Intergroup Relations." In Lindzey and Aronson, 599–658.

Tannen, Deborah. 1986. *That's Not What I Meant: How Conversational Style Makes or Breaks Relationships*. New York: Morrow.

———. 1990. *You Just Don't Understand: Talk Between the Sexes*. New York: Morrow.

Treichler, Paula A. 1986. "Teaching Feminist Theory." In Nelson 1986, 57–128.

———. 1992. "Beyond *Cosmo*: AIDS, Identity, and Inscriptions of Gender." *Camera Obscura* 28: 21–76.

———, and Cheris Kramarae. 1983. "Women's Talk in the Ivory Tower," *Communication Quarterly* 31.2 (Spring): 118–32.

Turow, Scott. 1977. *One L*. New York: Penguin.

Valian, Virginia. 1990. "Success and Failure: Expectations and Attributions." In Davison and Eckert, 129–41.

Warren, Douglas I. 1972. "Mass Media and Racial Crisis: A Study of the New Bethel Church Incident in Detroit." *Journal of Social Issues* 28: 111–31.

Weedon, Chris. 1991. "Post-Structuralist Feminist Practice." In *Theory, Pedagogy, Politics: Texts for Change*, edited by Donald Morton and Masúd Zavarzedeh, 47–63. Urbana: University of Illinois Press.

Woolf, Virginia. 1929. *A Room of One's Own*. New York: Harcourt, Brace.

5 Two Women on the Verge of a Contextual Breakthrough: Using *A Feminist Dictionary* in the Literature Classroom

Barbara DiBernard
University of Nebraska–Lincoln

Sheila Reiter
Doane College

Barbara: The following dialogue relates our experiences using *A Feminist Dictionary* (*AFD*) in literature classes.[1] My perspective is that of a feminist teacher who has found *AFD* to be a useful tool in bringing feminist theory and practice into alignment in the classroom. Like Bauer and Jarratt in "Feminist Sophistics" and Berry and Patraka in "Local Struggles/Partial Explanations" (chapters 6 and 7, this volume), I view the classroom as a political space. As Florence Howe (1983) writes:

> Teaching is a political act in the broadest context of that word: some person is choosing, for whatever reasons, to teach a set of values, ideas, assumptions, and pieces of information, and in so doing to omit other values, ideas, assumptions, and pieces of information. If all those choices form a pattern excluding half the human race, that is a political act one can hardly help noticing. To omit women entirely makes one kind of political statement; to include women as a target for humor makes another. To include women with seriousness and vision and with some attention to the perspective of women as a hitherto subordinate group is simply another kind of political act. Education is the kind of political act that controls destinies, gives some persons hope for a particular kind of future, and deprives others even of ordinary expectations for work and achievement. And the study of half the human race—the political act we call women's studies—cannot be excluded without obvious consequences to the search for truth. (110)

Like the other authors in the present volume, I believe it is crucial to connect the personal and the public and to connect theory and practice. One of my primary goals as a teacher is to get students to see themselves as agents who are capable of resistance and of personal and social change. In order to facilitate that, we examine hierarchy and power as they operate in the classroom and in the institution (see Bauer and Jarratt, chapter 7, this volume), a process in which *AFD* plays an important part. In addition, I believe that my students and I must practice the "politics of location," as described by Adrienne Rich (1986). Rich contrasts her earlier self, who spoke and wrote of the "common oppression of women" (210), who wrote sentences beginning "women have always," with her located self: "If we have learned anything in these years of late twentieth-century feminism, it's that 'always' blots out what we really need to know: When, where, and under what conditions has the statement been true?" (214) She links location with agency: ". . . I need to understand how a place on the map is also a place in history within which as a woman, a Jew, a lesbian, a feminist I am created and trying to create" (212).

For Rich, this location must begin "with the geography closest in—the body" (212). She is insistent about starting with the material conditions of our lives and returning to them: "Theory—the seeing of patterns, showing the forest as well as the trees—theory can be a dew that rises from the earth and collects in the rain cloud and returns to earth over and over. But if it doesn't smell of the earth, it isn't good for the earth" (213–14).

From Rich, I have learned that helping my students to understand their own locations as well as the "politics of location" should be one of my primary goals as a feminist teacher, one integrally connected with my desire to help them to see themselves as agents. Bauer and Jarratt have, I believe, a similar goal, which they call "the articulation of the self in history" (chapter 7, this volume). *AFD* is one of the most effective resources I have found for moving me and my students toward this goal.

Sheila: I first encountered *A Feminist Dictionary* when it was used as a text in a women's literature class taught by Professor Barbara DiBernard at the University of Nebraska–Lincoln. In that class I witnessed the personal revelations of many students who discovered meanings in *AFD* which reflected their own experience; I knew, therefore, that I wanted to incorporate this useful linguistic tool into my own writing and teaching. The process of exploring pedagogical theories that inform its use neatly insinuated itself into an original research project.

The results of that project, and Barbara's own pedagogical perspective, suggested the following exchange about the use of *AFD*. By the effort's end, we found that the distinction between teacher and student had become quite blurred—*AFD* had facilitated both the eradication of classroom hierarchy and the shared experience of teaching and learning.

The same social conditions that necessitate college programs called "Women's Studies," bizarrely categorized as nontraditional, inspired its editors, Cheris Kramarae and Paula Treichler, to complile *A Feminist Dictionary*, originally published in 1985. One could draw the conclusion that the idea of "women" is somehow, suddenly, new. What is new, indeed, is taking seriously women's experiences and understandings as a form of knowledge. This has become a central tenet of feminism, but its implications have not been obvious or easily acted upon. Bettina Aptheker (1989) writes about how women "needed to learn . . . how to cull a way of knowing from the interpretation of experience" (19). *AFD*, in my experience, helps students to do this.

This is probably not the proper venue for discussing whether *AFD* is, indeed, a dictionary. If its undisguised subjectivity is the stumbling block, the designation stands; a closer look at the standard lexicons in the canon will expose them as considerably less than objective. As the editors of *AFD* observe, "There is no doubt that the 'male' diction-aries, constructed almost entirely by men, with male readers and us-ers in mind, offer useful information about words and about the world. Yet their exclusion of women, together with their pervasive claims to authority, is profoundly disturbing" (*AFD*, 7).[2] If format is the concern, consider this: a dictionary defines words—*AFD* does that, too—but we must always ask the question, whose definitions? *AFD* offers us some heretofore unrepresented perspectives. (Many more remain unheard.) I would suggest that if a discussion about *AFD*'s authenticity as a dic-tionary occupies a class session for a very long time, it may be sympto-matic of a reluctance to deal with the real issues that *AFD* raises, issues of the nature of knowledge and reality.

In their introduction, "Words on a Feminist Dictionary," the editors explain their intention not to "authorize, but to challenge and envision" (*AFD*, 12), that they wish to "elucidate and complicate the terms of feminist discourse" (*AFD*, 4). They clearly see *AFD* as a tool for teach-ing, expecting that one's reading of a citation in *AFD* will "also encour-age a reading of the original source in its entirety" (*AFD*, 4). (The bibliography is seventy-one pages.)

But the editors assure us that this book is only a beginning. Listening for and hearing women's words is, itself, an unconventional task, one that has had no model of scholarship in the traditional sense. Women's words are found in unconventional places, as the editors alert us:

> We must look beneath the surface of orthodoxy. . . . We need to look in such places as gynecological handbooks passed between women for centuries; in women's art; in folklore and oral histories; in graffiti and gossip; in journals; in letters and diaries; in songs, billboards and posters; in the cant and chant of witchcraft and voodoo; in slogans; in parodies and humor; in poetry; in graphics; in comics and symbols; and in the mass of work by "uncanonized" writers whose richness and diversity we are only just beginning to comprehend. (*AFD*, 17)

Here, then, is a compendium of women's words which is well suited for use in the feminist classroom, and here, also, is one way of working with them.

My model is a course in "Twentieth-Century Women Novelists" taught by Barbara DiBernard at the University of Nebraska–Lincoln, a course offered to both upper-division undergraduates and graduate students. A class called "Twentieth-Century Women Novelists" may safely assume students' interest in literature and, perhaps, even in feminism, although the class members' degrees of interest in and knowledge of feminism varied widely. There were thirty-two students enrolled in this particular section. We met for two and a half hours one evening per week, for a fifteen-week semester.

The literature we read dealt with women's most essential experiences, arranged, engagingly, by a life's chronology. In many cases the theme of the work concerned the woman-as-artist. The authors we studied represented women of many colors and cultures (see appendix A, the condensed syllabus). Also, it is important to note the ingredients of this course that may have contributed, in part, to the successful use of *AFD* as a correlative text: an instructor committed to feminism; a course designed around women's literature, representing a wide diversity of women's experiences; and a student-centered classroom.

Several students from this class who were interviewed agreed that the perspectives represented in *AFD* could enhance classes in traditional literature or history.

Barbara: I remember the first time I learned about *A Feminist Dictionary*. A student brought an enlargement of page 433, a promotional poster, to a seminar on "Contemporary Women Writers" that I was teaching. I was astonished by a definition that appeared on the top right-hand side of the reproduction. It read:

STRETCH: The opposite of *SHRINK.* A feminist psychotherapist.

As a feminist, I had been aware, for years, of the patriarchal nature of the English language. I had argued with students and colleagues about the invidiousness of the so-called generic "he" and had begun to realize the ways in which English made women invisible or contributed to their oppression. But this was something new. Here was an opening up of the language to female possibilities. The reverberations of a psychotherapist as one who stretches rather than one who shrinks are still with me.

Almost immediately, I knew that I should use *AFD* in class. The book is truly radical in that it "recognize[s] women as linguistically creative speakers—that is, as originators of spoken or written language forms" (*AFD*, 1). It also confronts directly the issue of power hidden by most dictionaries, a fact unrecognized by my students. In *AFD*'s introduction, the editors write that

> [a]s feminist lexicographers, we do not claim objectivity nor believe that simply by offering a dictionary of "women's words" we can reverse the profound structural inequities of history and culture. The dictionary is also therefore a critique of current and past practices; collectively, the entries provide commentary on the institutionalized processes and politics through which some forms of language are privileged over others—how words get into print, why they go out of print, the politics of bibliography and archival storage, the politics of silence, of speech, of what can be said, of who can speak and who can listen. (3–4)

I teach in a place where few students identify themselves as feminists and most have read very little women's literature. Most women undergraduates at the University of Nebraska walk into my courses saying, "I'm not a feminist, but . . ."—such a familiar phrase by now that it is documented in *AFD*.[3] Some female students will say they believe in equal pay and in equal rights, many that they expect to have families *and* careers, but they have little, if any, sense of the history of feminism or what it stands for. Their images of feminists are media-generated stereotypes of man-hating women who want to force us all to use the same bathrooms. Many women undergraduates firmly assert that they have never been discriminated against. Few understand that feminism encompasses Marxist, radical, socialist, lesbian, and other approaches, that it is a political analysis of the entire social structure.

To take advantage of the breadth of information and points of view in *AFD*, I assigned several words to accompany each reading in my "Survey of Women's Literature" classes—one sophomore level, one senior/graduate level—and a "Twentieth-Century Women Novelists" class—senior/graduate level (see appendices A and B for condensed versions of some syllabi). To be honest, I didn't know exactly what I would do with these words in class. I did make it clear that the words were part of the required reading, and I asked students to comment on them in the reading journals they handed in each class period.

Used in this way in class, *AFD* provided both the literal history and the "historical placement of the feminist rhetor and her students" that Bauer and Jarratt call for as part of their "feminist sophistics" (see chapter 7, this volume). For example, I had us look up "author" in the survey class when we read Anne Bradstreet's "The Prologue" and "The Author to Her Book." Most of the students, especially in the sopho- more-level class, were impatient with and angry at Bradstreet for her seeming disparagement toward her own writing. The *AFD* entry, how- ever, pointed out the long history of the denigration of women writers; suggested the even more difficult situation of women of color; in- formed us that feminist criticism "has called into question the whole process of authoring and evaluating authors and authored works" (*AFD*, 60); and alerted us to the "politics of visibility" which operate even in *AFD*: "[T]he citations or recurrence of some names more than others should be taken as a sign that *our* research procedures, sources, and resources were limited and not that women authors do not exist everywhere" (61). Thus, we had a historical feminist context in which to struggle with our own responses to Bradstreet.

The *AFD* definition of "wife," which in the survey of women writ- ers class we read in conjunction with "To Room Nineteen" and "The Yellow Wallpaper," took us through the word's etymological and social changes from "female human being" to "female attached to a male," as well as to Charlotte Perkins Gilman's succinct "a harem of one." Thus, students whose first reactions to these stories might have been to see the women as outside history, as individually responsible for their own conditions and futures, already had a historicized, politicized context before they came to class.

A journal entry by Tami, one of the students in the course, substan- tiates the way in which *AFD* enriches the literary texts:

> I did something out of routine. I first looked up the assigned words in *A Feminist Dictionary* and then read the novel. I'm sure I would have been impressed with Tillie Olsen's book *Yonnondio* even if I had done the opposite. But having read the various quotes and definitions first, I had instances where I was able to see the words in a new, elaborated upon, or different light. For me, this illuminated the text substantially.
>
> *Yonnondio* was about many different things but in particular the family unit (within society). The most powerful story, though, was that of Anna Holbrook and her daughter Mazie.
>
> The Saunders quote [in *AFD*] about motherhood was especially appropriate to Olsen's work: "It is very hard to disentangle the

positive qualities [of motherhood] from the web of associations
spun by social and economic facts which elevate and restrict our
strength into a static role."

Using this and other quotes from *AFD,* Tami went on to analyze the
social and economic circumstances in which the Holbrooks live and
Anna mothers her family, and to come to an understanding of the novel
which was rich and complex. The definitions took Tami and the rest of
us to the commonly understood meanings of "to mother" and "to
father," to questions of choice, economics, domestic violence, legality,
and responsibility. In this way *AFD* served as a resource for an analysis
of the politics of location in the literature and led to explorations of our
own locations in class discussion and in journal writing.

One's instinctive response to *AFD* is to look up words that are of
personal interest. To encourage and incorporate that personal element
into the class, I devised the "Word of the Day" assignment.

In this assignment, each person takes a turn reporting on a word
which is not assigned for class. My instructions, in part, read:

> Choose any word you want, but preferably one which is related to
> an interest of yours, or whose definition amused, excited, chal-
> lenged, or angered you. You will probably want to compare it to
> one or more "standard" dictionary definitions, if they are avail-
> able. Tell the class why you picked the word, what you learned
> from your investigation, and what you want them to take away
> from your report.

These reports are consistently meaningful, both to the presenter and the
rest of the class. Often, the resulting discussion is extremely rich and
thoughtful, incorporating students' personal experience with the definitions and, frequently, the realization of just how sexist "standard"
dictionaries really are. It is in this assignment that the students' "articulation of the self in history" occurs most clearly.

Women students often enter my classes having never identified
themselves politically as women. Most deny having experienced any
discrimination because they are women; most believe that things are
better now, that women have equality under the law; and they want to
believe that they have been and will continue to be treated fairly. *AFD*
has helped generate the "click" experience for some of these students,
and it has provided all of them with an opportunity to "take account of
their gendered/raced/classed bodies" (see Bauer and Jarratt, chapter 7,
this volume).

A Jewish student used her report to give the female members of her
family, as well as herself, a new feminist historical sense of themselves
as Jewish women:

> Many Friday nights I go to Omaha for dinner. Four generations of women sit around the table. My grandmother, mother, sister (14 years older than me), and myself. When I got *A Feminist Dictionary* I took it home and was thumbing through it at the table. I came across the definition of JAP, or Jewish American Princess, and read it aloud: "Judith who saved the Jewish people; she flirted with the attacking general, drank him under the table; then she and her maid (whose name is not in the story) whacked off his head, stuck it in a picnic basket and escaped back to the Jewish camp. They staked his head high over the gate, so that when his soldiers charged the camp, they were met by their general's bloody head, looming; and ran away as fast as their goyishe little feet could run. Then Judith set her maid free, and all the women danced in her honor. That's a Jewish princess."
>
> Thunderous applause arose from our dinner group. My mother pounded the table and Shabbos wine jumped from the glasses. My sister asked for a copy of the book. For once, a heroic, independent depiction of a Jewish woman.

AFD definitions also shocked white women into a political awareness, for the first time, of what their race means: the definition of "white" states that it is "a political as well as an ethnic category," and Marilyn Frye's quote asserts that "membership in it is not . . . 'fated' or 'natural.' It can be resisted" (*AFD*, 482). For some students, this represents their first awareness that talking about race includes their talking about being white and what it means in their lives. It also, importantly, suggests that white privilege comes about partly through our own assent, but that we can resist it in some ways.

One student who looked up "liberal"—"because being brought up in a devout liberal Democratic family, I have always gotten a warm, familiar, friendly feeling from the word"—was shocked and angered by Kathie Sarachild's quote in *AFD*:

> The liberal fears and opposes clarity and effectiveness because she fears angering the powerful; she does not want to fight. In order to preserve peace, the liberal resists any idea that requires real change in the status quo, in action or theory. (*AFD*, 231)

This student had never realized that a radical critique of liberalism existed. *AFD* did not change her point of view about what constitutes a liberal, but it shocked her into a recognition of a political continuum on which liberalism was not the farthest left, unquestioned position. She had to take responsibility for her "location" in a way that she never had before.

A female student who tries to avoid conflict in her personal life gained insights into the source of her feelings while doing her "Word of the Day" report. In Webster's ninth edition (1986) she found "conflict" thus defined: "1. A fight, battle or war; 2. An antagonistic state or action—mental struggle resulting from incompatible or opposing needs, drives, wants or external or internal demands." As she pointed out in her report, this definition derives "from a male-oriented military and pugilistic perspective," and it made her want to avoid conflict "because only negative results will be achieved; i.e., deaths in warfare, shattered families and homes, etc." In *AFD* she read that conflict is

> [a] needed struggle for growth, inherent in all of life. Conflict is also one of the emotions women—in their work as mothers, daughters, wives, sisters, and general helpmates—are made to feel guilty about experiencing. So we try to disguise it as depression, inadequacy, helplessness and other feelings, and if it seems to threaten the public presentation of sisterhood, we often deny its existence.

This definition helped the student to locate herself as a woman, to understand why, *as a woman*, she avoided conflict and how this fear held her and other women back from standing up for their rights. She concluded:

> As Jean Baker Miller brought to our attention in *AFD*, the maintaining of the status quo is what is holding us back from making real gains for equality, and our inability to initiate conflict is what is keeping us from breaking down the male-dominated status quo.

Another student used her report to explore her fears, worries, and complex feelings about going to medical school. The *AFD* definitions helped her recall an incident that happened many years ago. When she was young girl, a friend's mother had responded to her comment about wanting to be a doctor when she grew up, with the statement that only a very cold-hearted person would want to do such a thing. She had been very angry and upset, but had never been able to understand what her emotions were connected to or why she was so upset. However, after reading *The American Heritage Dictionary*'s definition of "medicine"—which she found lacking in any human element of compassion or caring—and comparing it with the *AFD*'s definition—which included Michelle Harrison's statement that, for her, "doctoring was a form of mothering; the nurturing and healing came from the same energies, from the same center of my self that wanted to mother" (*AFD*, 265)—she acquired a feminist context for her reaction. She concluded her report: "The *AFD*'s definition of 'medicine' supported my belief that I can be a doctor and still acknowledge my womanhood. It also stressed the importance of treating one's patients with respect, regardless of their gender." These students' revelations might not seem earthshaking to longtime feminists, but many of these women were "locating" themselves for the first time, which I believe is their first step in becoming agents in their own learning and in their own lives.

This assignment sparked revelations throughout the students' investigations of the "standard" dictionaries as well as their use of *AFD*. As *AFD* editor Cheris Kramarae (1987) points out, such questioning of the dictionary is a radical act:

> I've checked with hundreds of students; not one has said that dictionary making was even discussed in their classrooms. The dictionary just *is*. No discussion needed. Final word. Grave effects. The discussions [these] students have had are quite revolutionary [because] they are questioning one of the basic, usually unquestioned, texts of our educational system.

Sheila: In almost every case, students chose words that were deeply personal, often self-revealing, for their "Word of the Day" reports. Some students even went beyond "reports" and constructed events: films, videos, other visuals, even food. A man showed women-made films, explained Hollywood's insidious portrayal of women, and talked about the economic realities of women making films. Another student staged a miniworkshop on liberation theory.

It was in the context of the "Word of the Day" that students shared an amazing array of issues. One woman shared the story of struggling to get her disabled sister into and out of a toilet stall labeled "handicapped accessible." A Chinese woman explained the powerful implications that the word "silence" held for her, a word that embodies the virtues of humility and wisdom in her tradition, but that means invisibility for her on a U.S. college campus. One woman passed out chocolate bars and salted peanuts and talked candidly about life two weeks out of every month as experienced by a PMS sufferer. She explored, dubiously, the movement to rename it PME—Pre-Menstrual Energy—wondering if changing the language can really change the reality. A vivacious woman who, until recently, had vehemently denied male oppression of women investigated Jewish history to discover the roots of Orthodox Judaism's roles for women and Jewish female stereotypes, suddenly seeing how others may have seen her or assumed her to be. It was Passover.

Several times a student was confronted directly by the sexism of the "standard" dictionary. Natalie reported that when she looked up the word "contentious,"

> the example my dictionary offered for use in a sentence was from Proverbs 27:15. They went back that far to get this: "Endless drip-

ping on a rainy day—that's what a contentious woman is like."
How totally biased and nasty that is.

Barbara: Another exercise I've used is one I call "New and Needed
Words." Taking a cue from the editors of *AFD*—who know that there
are "Needed Words" and who encourage readers to list quotes and
definitions not included *AFD* on the blank pages at the back of the
book—I asked students to come up with "New Words" and definitions
for them in *AFD* format. With the help of a graduate assistant, I com-
piled these into a book for the class members, and I also sent a copy to
the editors of *AFD* for consideration in future editions. The class response was serious and powerful, showing that these students had
incorporated into their own understanding the importance of what
AFD does and demonstrating, too, that they were language users and
makers.

Judith coined "Matrilegacy" as a response to patriarchal oppression
of women within marriage. Her entry reads:

> A word coined to fill the vacuum left by the term "matrimony."
> According to Webster (*New Collegiate Dictionary*, 1976), matrimony
> is "the union of man and woman as husband and wife: marriage."
> Not objectionable, until compared with patrimony: "an estate in-
> herited from one's heritage" (Webster 1976). Sex-linked words
> (patri = father and matri = mother) reflect history's social arrange-
> ments. In the English legal system, men could receive property
> through inheritance, women through marriage. What does lan-
> guage say about the power in that arrangement? Woman's word
> is not identified with her; man's is. Woman's (implicit) power
> depends on union with a man and must be remade in each gen-
> eration; man's (explicit) power is independent of woman and can
> be passed on to future generations. Woman shares the power of
> marriage and owns no other; man shares the power of marriage
> *and* owns the power of wealth and history. We need a new word
> for providing and receiving value in a society that recognizes
> women's powers. Consider *Matrilegacy*: The heritage provided by
> women, as in knowledge, values, material goods, influence on
> events, love, creative work, examples of lives well lived.

Bill defined "Ca(n)on" as "[a] symbol of the sacred domain of literacy
excellence which displays phallacies in evaluation; the good old boy's
club which often becomes a form of circle-jerk"; while Chris noted the
need for "Prima Don: An egoist; self-centered, temperamental male."

Although I have found *AFD* extremely useful in my women's literature courses, I have also found tremendous resistance to it, which at
times spills over into an anger and resistance to the entire course, or
perhaps, more accurately, focuses the anger and resistance to the course.

Students have been extremely upset over its radical nature, and, unwilling to question the "objectivity" and "truth" of a standard dictionary, they attack *AFD* as being biased. They often hate what they perceive to be its negativity, especially toward men. I remember vividly the angry response to "marriage" the first time I used *AFD* in a sophomore-level class. Although I found several positive definitions of marriage in the long entry, students wrote on and on in their journals about how skewed and negative the definition was, that while marriage might be bad for some people, their parents' marriage was good, and their own current heterosexual relationships and future marriages were and would be very equal and positive. Susanne Bohmer (1989) has analyzed this phenomenon of students' resistance to feminist analyses that students take as unfair generalizations. She states that such resistance is "clearly a way of denying differences and inequalities in our society based on group membership" (55). But this is also the kind of attitude that continued exposure to *AFD* should break down. If the student can locate herself in even one definition, I believe, an irreversible process will have begun.

One student who was the most virulent about *AFD* signed up for another class with me two years after the first, a class in which we were also using *AFD*. She constantly wondered—both in her journal and aloud to me before and after class—how *AFD* could have changed so much, not understanding, of course, that *she* had changed in the interim, not the book. Generously, she shared her responses with me as she went back and read her old journals and compared them with her current responses. Whether *AFD* played a major part in this change, we'll never know, but she had not forgotten it in the interim. Other students reported anxiety about merely carrying *AFD* around with them, while some got into interesting conversations by deliberately leaving it out on their desks at work or on the coffee table at home.

In all of these examples, *AFD* serves as a "counterauthority" in the classroom, to use Bauer and Jarratt's meaning of the term (see chapter 7, this volume). It serves as both an external counterauthority and an internal one. It overtly questions the power relations in the classroom through its definitions (see, for example, "teaching"; "classroom interaction"; "conversation"; "radicalteacher"; "call and response"), and it helps students develop their own counterauthority within their own discourses. The "Word of the Day" reports called consistently for students' stories of their own experiences, stories which they were now able to tell and understand in a social and historical framework. It is no accident, either, that so many students incorporated other voices into their reports. A Jewish woman videotaped a conversation with her grandmother about Yiddish, the mother tongue of her people; the director of a film theater showed one of Barbara Hammer's short films, an exploration of lesbian eroticism; Sheila brought in a local artist to talk about being a woman artist; a student brought in quilts made by her grandmother and her mother; another woman told the story of a friend of hers who had been raped and her anger that we trivialize her experience so easily by the way we use the word "rape" in other contexts. I believe that *AFD*'s use as a counterauthority in the literature classroom moves students toward personal responsibility and action, an awareness of themselves as agents in their own education and in their lives.

Sheila: If I use *AFD* as a teaching tool in future classrooms, I will need to consider, in terms of research and theory in feminist pedagogy, how *AFD*'s quotations work on students' cognitive processes and progress. I do almost no justice, in this discussion, to any of the excellent scholars whose ideas I have appropriated, here. My intention, not unlike *AFD*'s, has been to suggest useful ideas that might inspire a reader to seek out and read these works in their entirety.

My primary sources are a paper by Barrie Thorne (1984), "Rethinking the Way We Teach," and a case study on feminist teaching, undertaken and documented by Frances Maher and Kathleen Dunn (1984), from Wellesley College's Center for Research on Women. To facilitate their study, researchers Maher and Dunn used the model of cognitive functioning devised by Blythe Clinchy and Claire Zimmerman, along with Mary Kay Tetreault's phase theory of curricular integration to analyze their course content.

Maher and Dunn articulated their understanding of the purpose of education in words that provide an excellent starting point for feminist teachers who are considering the use of a text such as *AFD* in their classrooms. Maher and Dunn "assume that the purpose of education is to equip people with the knowledge, both of themselves and of their world, which permits them to make purposeful and active choices" (1). Barrie Thorne addresses the feminist perspective in stating her objective for the student: "To discover that one's experience is not the measure of all things, to come to see white, middle-class, male, and heterosexual assumptions as limited and not the universal, and to explore the experiences of other groups are precious forms of learning" (6). I would add "American" (read "U.S.") to Thorne's series of modifiers and encourage readers to consult Hurlbert and Bodnar's thought-provoking exchange on teaching in time of war, "Collective Pain: Literature, War, and Small Change" (see chapter 11, this volume).

Clinchy and Zimmerman suggest that women college students often enter the learning process in a dualist mode, the belief that a "right answer" to all questions exists somewhere outside themselves and that learning comes from a teacher or a text. Students in this mode often prefer the lecture format "because they are looking for the 'correct' body of information, to learn from the expert" (Maher and Dunn 1984, 6–7). This cognitive mode corresponds to phases one and two of curricular integration, which are the absence of women in the content of courses, and women included, but only as tokens.

In phase three curricula, "women are perceived for the first time *as a group*. . . . Women's experiences are seen as different from those of males and equally valid" (Maher and Dunn 1984, 8). Students who are in the next cognitive stage, multiplism, thrive in phase three curricula. These students begin to hear and use their own personal voices, describing experiences in their own terms, according to their own theories (9). The inherent danger in multiplist thinking is that truths cannot be generalized; everyone has her own, equally valid, point of view.

In phases four and five of curriculum integration, scholarship and curricula become multifocal, allowing the student's experience to be understood in a larger context that embraces class, race, culture, and gender differences (Maher and Dunn 1984, 12). The phase of learning associated with them is contextualism; the student's worldview expands dramatically to embrace ambiguity, and she can begin to see herself as "a knower and a meaning maker—knowledge as an evolving construct" (13–14). The important distinction between multiplism and contextualism is this:

> The multiplist, although full of a sense of self, has trouble separating out or defining specific attributes or qualities of that self, because self-definition (as opposed to self-discovery) depends upon comparison with other people and other personal histories. The contextualist, on the other hand, can see herself as possessed of certain experiences and qualities which she realizes contribute to her particular perspective. She can, then, allow her perspective to broaden and change. (15)

The feminist teacher can create a setting to encourage contextualism, a setting in which students, both men and women, bring their own experience to the concepts presented in course material, where they can begin to comprehend more complicated issues and themselves within them, a context that "legitimizes individual voices and puts them in a larger explanatory context" (16). In such a classroom, *A Feminist Dictionary* becomes a tool of contextualism. It fits well the requirements for phases four and five of curricular integration, the phases that correspond to the development of contextualism in students: "Both employ, according to Tetreault, the same methodology for the construction and validation of knowledge, namely the building of conceptual frameworks and generalizations from the specificity and variety of human experiences, in which the perspectives of all participants, not just the elite few, are encompassed" (Maher and Dunn 1984, 13).

A danger of any theory of cognitive stages lies in wanting to make rigid the edges of those stages, slotting students' progress into categories. Such structures might become more dynamic and truly useful when they are used to encourage critical observations that could generate "the *enactment* of [feminist] theory in the classroom" (emphasis mine) such as Berry and Patraka seek in their essay "Local Struggles/Partial Explanations: Producing Feminist Theory in the Classroom" (see chapter 6, this volume).

Barbara: Clearly *A Feminist Dictionary* is an extremely useful tool in the literature classroom; undoubtedly, teachers of other subjects have found equally valuable ways of using it. I believe, with Sheila, that it can facilitate students' shifts in epistemological positions, including their movement toward becoming "constructed knowers" as described by Belenkey and her colleagues (1986) in *Women's Ways of Knowing.* Constructed knowers "accept the responsibility for evaluating and continually reevaluating their assumptions about knowledge" (139); they also "strive to translate their moral commitments into action" (150). Such knowing thus meets my feminist teaching goals of connecting the personal and the public and seeing ourselves as agents for personal and social change. But like Sheila, I fear the possible danger of using theories to erase differences. What we need to enact as feminists, I believe, is Adrienne Rich's (1986) "politics of location": "Begin with the material. Pick up again the long struggle against lofty and privileged abstraction. Perhaps this is the core of revolutionary process . . ." (213). For me, *AFD* can be a primary tool in this process. To return, then, to where I started: it serves as a "stretch" for all of us.

Notes

1. Kramarae, Cheris, and Paula Treichler, eds. 1985. *A Feminist Dictionary.* Boston: Pandora Press. Although unavailable for a couple of years, *A Feminist Dictionary* was republished in 1992 by Pandora Press in a second edition entitled, *Amazons, Bluestockings, and Crones.*

2. In this discussion, page references for quoted material from *A Feminist Dictionary* will be preceded by the journal abbreviation.

3. Catharine Stimpson notes that the suspicion underlying it "is rooted in the true perception that the Women's Movement is radical and in the false perception that it is monolithic" (*AFD*, 207).

Works Cited

Aptheker, Bettina. 1989. *Tapestries of Life: Women's Work, Women's Consciousness, and the Meaning of Daily Experience.* Amherst: University of Massachusetts Press.

Bauer, Dale M., and Susan C. Jarratt. 1994. "Feminist Sophistics: Teaching with an Attitude." [See chapter 7, this volume.]

Belenky, Mary Field, Blythe McVicker Clinchy, Nancy Rule Goldberger, and Jill Mattuck Tarule. 1986. *Women's Ways of Knowing: The Development of Self, Voice, and Mind.* New York: Basic Books.

Berry, Ellen E., and Vivian Patraka. 1994. "Local Struggles/Partial Explanations: Producing Feminist Theory in the Classroom." [See chapter 6, this volume.]

Bohmer, Susanne K. 1989. "Resistance to Generalizations in the Classroom." *Feminist Teacher* 4(2/3): 53–56.

Howe, Florence. 1983. "Feminist Scholarship: The Extent of the Revolution." In *Learning Our Way: Essays in Feminist Education,* edited by Charlotte Bunch and Sandra Pollack, 98–111. Freedom, CA: Crossing Press.

Hurlbert, C. Mark, and Ann Marie Bodnar. 1994. "Collective Pain: Literature, War, and Small Change." [See chapter 11, this volume].

Kramarae, Cheris. 1987. Letter to Barbara DiBernard. 1 June.

———, and Paula Treichler, eds., with assistance from Ann Russo. 1985. *A Feminist Dictionary.* Boston: Pandora Press.

Maher, Frances, and Kathleen Dunn. 1984. "The Practice of Feminist Teaching: A Case Study of Interactions among Curriculum, Pedagogy, and Female Cognitive Development." Working Paper No. 144. Wellesley, MA: Wellesley College Center for Research on Women.

Rich, Adrienne. 1986. "Notes toward a Politics of Location." In *Blood, Bread, and Poetry: Selected Prose, 1979–1985,* 210–31. New York: Norton.

Thorne, Barrie. 1984. "Rethinking the Way We Teach." In *Feminist Pedagogy and the Learning Climate,* 1–10. Proceedings of the Ninth Annual Great Lakes Colleges Association Women's Studies Conference. 4–7 November 83. Ann Arbor: Great Lakes College Association Women's Studies Program.

Webster's New Collegiate Dictionary. 9th ed. 1986. Springfield, MA: Merriam-Webster.

Appendix A: Readings for Twentieth-Century Women Novelists (including words assigned from *AFD*)

Margaret Atwood, *The Handmaid's Tale.* (From *AFD: money; wife; clothing; technology; technosexism; nature of woman; dress;* and two other relevant words of the student's choice.)

Tillie Olsen, *Yonnondio.* (From *AFD: mother; motherhood; mothering; washing; Mother's Day; father; fathering.*)

Jamaica Kincaid, *Annie John.* (From *AFD: daughter; daughter-right; friend; friendship.*)

Audre Lorde, *Zami.* (From *AFD: lesbian; lesbian continuum; lesbian feminism; lesbianism; race; racism; black; woman-identified woman.*)

Maxine Hong Kingston, *The Woman Warrior.* (From *AFD: guilt; Asian American; silence; International Women's Day.*)

Doris Lessing, *The Summer Before the Dark.* (From *AFD: housewife; housework; marriage; appearance; work; working woman.*)

Paule Marshall, *Praisesong for the Widow.* (From *AFD: widow; widowhood;* plus two other relevant words of the student's choice.)

Margaret Laurence, *The Stone Angel.* (From *AFD: crones; menopause; aging.*)

May Sarton, *As We Are Now.* (From *AFD: grey hairs; Crone's Nest; age; ageism; diary; power; ripening.*)

Anne Cameron, *Daughters of Copper Woman.* (From *AFD: action; medicine woman; Native American literature; menstruation; menstrual strike.*)

Virginia Woolf, *A Room of One's Own;* Joanna Russ, *How to Suppress Women's Writing.* (From *AFD: "Words on a Feminist Dictionary; manglish; laadan; needed words; herstory; art; anonymous; man as false generic.*)

Articles on feminist criticism and pedagogy. (From *AFD: radicalteacher; classroom interaction; conversation; feminism; criticism, literary; novel; quilt; quilting; black feminism; black woman; womanist; ableism.*)

Appendix B: Readings for Survey of Women's Literature (including words assigned from *AFD*)

Unless otherwise noted, all readings are from the following source: Gilbert, Sandra M., and Susan Gubar, eds. 1985. *The Norton Anthology of Literature by Women: The Tradition in English.* New York: Norton.

Amelia Lanier, from *Salve Deus Rex Judaeorum;* Judith Wright, "Eve to Her Daughters"; Stevie Smith, "How Cruel is the Story of Eve"; Muriel Rukeyser, "Myth"; Julian of Norwich, from *A Book of Showings;* readings from Susan E. Browne, Debra Connors, and Nanci Stern, eds., *With the Power of Each Breath: A Disabled Women's Anthology* (Cleis, 1985). (From *AFD: Eve; Pandora; Adam; female; woman; laadan.*)

Anne Bradstreet, "The Prologue," "The Author to Her Book"; Anne Finch, "The Introduction"; Anne Killegrew, "Upon Saying That My Verses Were

Made by Another"; Margaret Atwood, "Spelling"; Virginia Woolf, "Professions for Women"; Florence Nightingale, from *Cassandra*; Anna Wickham, "Dedication of the Cook"; Erica Jong, "Alcestis on the Poetry Circuit." (From *AFD*: l'ecriture feminine; *writing; author; anonymous; words*.)

Virginia Woolf, from *A Room of One's Own*; Adrienne Rich, "When We Dead Awaken"; Alice Walker, "In Search of Our Mothers' Gardens." (From *AFD*: *weaving; art; room of one's own; literature; criticism; virginiawoolf; quilt; quilting*.)

Judy Grahn, from *The Common Women*; Maxine Hong Kingston, "No Name Woman"; readings from *With the Power*. (From *AFD*: *girl; Asian American; name; common woman*.)

Doris Lessing, "To Room Nineteen"; Charlotte Perkins Gilman, "The Yellow Wallpaper." (From *AFD*: *husband; wife; parenthood; should married women work?*)

Margery Kempe, from *The Book of Margery Kempe*; Anne Bradstreet, "A Letter to Her Husband"; Anne Finch, "A Letter to Daphnis"; Fleur Adcock, "Against Coupling"; Aphra Behn, "The Disappointment"; Adrienne Rich, from "Twenty-One Love Poems"; Amy Lowell, "Venus Transiens," "Madonna of the Evening Flowers," "Opal"; readings from *With the Power*. (From *AFD*: *marriage; marital rape; violence against women; love*.)

Zora Neale Hurston, "Sweat"; Susan Glaspell, "Trifles"; Henry Handel Richardson, "Two Hanged Women"; Gertrude Stein, "Ada." (From *AFD*: *woman-identified woman; lesbian; lesbian continuum; lesbianism; dyke; wife battering*.)

Mary Wilkins Freeman, "Old Woman Magoun"; Linda Brent, "Incidents in the Life of a Slave Girl"; readings from *With the Power*. (From *AFD*: *mother; motherhood; mothering*.)

Anzia Yezierska, "The Fat of the Land"; Alice Walker, "Everyday Use"; Meridel LeSueur, "The Annunciation"; Audre Lorde, "Now That I Am Forever with Child," "From the House of Yemanja." (From *AFD*: *child; children*.)

Charlotte Smith, "Thirty-Eight"; Sarah Orne Jewett, "The Town Poor"; Leslie Marmon Silko, "Lullaby"; readings from *With the Power*. (From *AFD*: *ageism; aging; death; Native American literature*.)

Alice James, "Diary"; Audre Lorde, *The Cancer Journals* (Spinsters Ink, 1980); readings from *With the Power*. (From *AFD*: *mastectomy; Amazon; breast; women's health movement*.)

Mary Astell, from *A Serious Proposal to the Ladies*; Margaret Walker, "Lineage"; Maya Angelou, from *I Know Why the Caged Bird Sings*; Judith Wright, "Request to a Year"; Maxine Kumin, "The Envelope"; Ursula LeGuin, "Sur"; Adrienne Rich, "Phantasia for Elvira Shatayev"; Susan Griffin, "I Like to Think of Harriet Tubman"; Sojourner Truth, "Ain't I a Woman?"; readings from *With the Power*. (From *AFD*: *grandmother; gray hairs; wicca; friend; girlfriend; strength; bonding; gynergy; matriarchy*.)

6 Local Struggles/Partial Explanations: Producing Feminist Theory in the Classroom

Ellen E. Berry
Bowling Green State University

Vivian Patraka
Bowling Green State University

In the spring of 1991, we were scheduled to team-teach a course in contemporary feminist theory. We wanted this class not only to be theory centered, but also to serve as an actual site for the production of theory. We were keenly aware of the difference between teaching theory-as-content—a set of critical concepts to be digested—and teaching so as to enable students to produce theory themselves and to interrogate the production of knowledge within particular frameworks. We believed then, as we believe now, that unless we have as our goal the enactment of theory in the classroom, we risk turning it into a commodity that, as such, is easily appropriated by hegemonic discourse. When theory is treated as a formal device or a counter to trade, it loses much of its potential as a radical discourse with the capacity to transform the very place from which dominant discourse is produced.

Instead, we wanted our classroom to function as a "laboratory of culture." Since the classroom occupies an actual space, composed of real people situated within a particular institution, it could, in itself, serve as a laboratory for studying local and specific processes of knowledge production, including the way that knowledge-as-power inscribes itself on subjects. We also conceived the classroom as a laboratory in the experimental sense: a place to invent spaces within theory that have yet

The authors would like to thank Sallie Bingham and the Kentucky Foundation for Women for providing them with uninterrupted time in July 1990 at Hopscotch House, Wolfpen Women Writers' Colony, to work on their project. Earlier versions of this paper were presented as "Local Struggles and Partial Explanations: Producing Feminist Theory in the Classroom," at "The Role of Theory in the Undergraduate Literature Classroom: Curriculum, Pedagogy, Politics" conference at Indiana University of Pennsylvania, in September 1990; and as "Performing Feminist Differences" a "Graduate Studies in English" panel, Southern Atlantic Modern Language Association, in November 1990.

to become spaces in practice, a place of potentials where new models for creating and transforming culture might be generated and tested. Such a perspective helps to redefine the classroom as a new, politicized arena, one that reflects Chantal Mouffe's (1988b) notion of the current "proliferation of political spaces that are radically new and different and which demand that we abandon the idea of [one unique] constitutive space for the construction of the political" (43–44).

Second, we wanted to center the class around theory that is specifically feminist, which first meant distinguishing feminist theoretical perspectives from general poststructuralist maneuvers. This was critical since some poststructuralist theories actively obscure the contributions of feminist theorizing while others subsume it as simply one example within a general radical critique. Feminist theorists frequently do borrow deconstructive strategies to dislodge totalizing structures and master narratives. But they also find utility in building counternarratives and systems of explanation—however provisional—and they share an ongoing commitment to creating and transforming history. As Biddy Martin (1988) notes, there is "a conflict between a fundamentally deconstructive impulse [within feminism] and a need to construct the category woman and to search for truths, authenticity, and universals" (14). In response to this apparent contradiction, she advocates a doubled strategy in which feminism "refuse[s] to be content with fixed ideas or to universalize a revolutionary [feminist] subject" (16), but at the same time allows for a strategic essentializing of the category woman-as-agent as a necessary point of departure for political action.

More generally, we assumed that feminist theorizing involves not only the production of a new set of facts or discourses; it also involves adopting a series of different perspectives that would allow familiar content to be apprehended from alternative directions. In this, our commitment echoed Adrienne Rich's 1971 statement on the project of feminism: "Re-vision—the act of looking back, of seeing with fresh eyes, of entering an old text from a new critical direction—is for women more than a chapter in cultural history: it is an act of survival" (Rich 1979b, 35). Such a revisionary stance involves an ongoing process of dislocation and relocation in which previously acquired knowledge and assumptions are placed in gender-sensitive contexts, and seemingly fixed constructs are opened onto their social, economic, and political determinacies. This process implies the possibility of assuming new subject positions within established knowledge structures and uncovering alternate spaces for the construction of different meanings outside of these established discourses.

The feminist commitment to revision has also occasioned an ongoing process of self-reflection and self-scrutiny which has led to radical shifts within feminist theory itself. And these shifts in feminist theorizing have led, in turn, to necessary modifications in feminist pedagogy to reflect and accommodate changing agendas and perspectives. For example, by the late 1980s, neat categories (e.g., materialist, liberal, and radical or "cultural" feminism) and oppositions (e.g., identity vs. difference) broke down or ceased to be useful. This was occasioned by a poststructuralist questioning of totalizing oppositions and a widespread critique of hegemonic feminism's exclusionary practices, articulated by women of color as well as by lesbians. Such criticisms articulate the need for new pedagogical approaches to feminist theory that are neither totalizing nor marginalizing. In what follows, we offer a theoretical rationale and a methodology for a course that engages issues current within contemporary feminist theory. Our exploration begins with two questions: What now constitutes the subject of feminism, and how might we theorize a feminist subject?

The Subject of F/feminism

We understand F/feminism to be a collective project for social transformation and the reconstruction of knowledge that is composed of different, sometimes conflicting, feminist agendas. A theoretical elaboration of the nature of contemporary F/feminism—our neologism for a collective that is able to preserve the specificity of the different feminisms within it—might begin by historicizing current feminist agendas and debates through a recovery of the specific contexts and circuits of their emergence. Feminists now have a history of sufficient weight to allow us to re-evaluate the nature of earlier feminist goals and strategies and their significance for a contemporary moment. This retrospective impulse—becoming increasingly prevalent in contemporary feminist criticism—is occasioned, in part, by feminism's twenty years of activity on multiple fronts, during which programs for feminist work were being elucidated and enacted both in and outside the academy.

Beyond understanding its retrospective impulse, elaborating the project of contemporary F/feminism also demands incorporating a prospective impulse that seeks ways to modify current understandings and impasses in order to construct new agendas as F/feminism moves toward an uncertain future. This uncertainty can be framed as an identity crisis in contemporary feminism, experienced both externally and internally (Alcoff 1988). On the one hand, during the 1980s, movements for social transformation proved increasingly less effective in the larger political arena of the Reagan/Bush era, a casualty of the wholesale erosion of progressive political agendas which characterized that period. On the other hand, during the same period, feminism achieved what many would consider a stunning victory within the academy; it "came of age" as Jane Gallop (1989) puts it.

Internally, as part of its coming of age, academic feminism has generated more and more powerful and sophisticated theories of female agency and difference. Yet the fact of the differing agendas within feminism—which signal not just ideological differences but power differentials among women as well—has frequently translated into intense conflicts that may threaten the very existence of F/feminism as collectivity. In their introduction to the recent anthology *Conflicts in Feminism,* Marianne Hirsch and Evelyn Fox Keller (1990) characterize the 1980s as a decade "in which the feminist illusion of 'sisterhood' and the 'dream of a common language' gave way to the realities of fractured discourses . . . and a recognition that the dream was in turn sustained, as all such dreams must be, by the illusion of a domain internally free of conflict. . . . [S]truggle and conflict have emerged as the salient marks of contemporary feminism's contestation for the practical as well as the theoretical meanings of feminism" (1).

As a means to reflect the divided, contradicted nature of contemporary feminism and the future possibilities that might be constructed from within these divisions and contradictions, we chose to focus our course around the concepts of "local struggles" and "partial explanations." Implied here is an emphasis on a politics of the local, the fragmentary, the transient, and the incomplete that would analyze and confront power in its specific manifestations, thereby refusing totalizing explanations or strategies of resistance. This is also a postmodern political model of affinities[1] consciously articulated across a range of diverse and shifting feminist agendas that would recognize the existence of struggle as a vital part of this process of articulation.

This commitment to analyze and confront power in its specific, local manifestations has consequences for feminist pedagogy: We set out to explore, even consciously to foreground and manipulate, power relations in the classroom. In this we distinguish between our model and an earlier feminist one where nonhierarchical and nonauthoritarian practices were more unproblematically asserted and shared sisterhood more widely assumed. We wished to retain the utopian possibility of this previous model, but at the same time to problematize notions of nonauthority and noncoercion by exploring the way power inevitably circulates within institutions to constrain the production of discourse and situate subjects in particular ways. Making overt this circulation as it operates across multiple differences within the classroom would, we hoped, allow us to explore those factors that could inhibit accomplishing the earlier feminist goal of nonhierarchical relations among women. Such an analysis could also illuminate the possibly negative potentials existing within the earlier feminist model of shared sisterhood, with its pursuit of consensus and identification, and suggest instead that the feminist classroom might function as a space for the enactment of multiple differences. An emphasis on power relations might also create a context for constructing a politics of location that would allow both teachers and students to recognize the crucial influence of the place from which we speak. It would generate awareness of the fact that we can only produce partial explanations from our particular positions— ones determined by history, ideology, and institutional positioning as well as personal situation.

The Feminist Subject

In the previous section we raised a series of issues that surround the general question, "What is the subject of feminism?" Our illustration follows from the related question "What is a feminist subject?" By "subject," we mean the organization of a space from which to speak, write, act. To clarify this, we first need to focus on the poststructuralist concept of the subject as outlined by Lacan, Derrida, and Foucault, among others: a decentered position constructed in and divided by language, a socially constructed position determined by power relations in discourse, an anti-humanist subject that exhausts a universal belief in self presence. To gender the poststructuralist subject would mean stressing the different ways that women and men have been materially and discursively positioned in relation to power and conceiving gender not as a property of bodies, but as a property of power relations operating through the deployment of various social and political technologies.

But the gendered poststructuralist subject still denies the possibility of agency to women, and it is this possibility that the feminist subject seeks to explore. The feminist subject—as distinct from *Woman*, the representation of an essence, and from *women*, real historical beings and subjects under patriarchy defined by technologies of gender—is an "active construction . . . and a discursively mediated political interpretation of one's history, an embodied, engendered, situated standpoint from which to speak" (de Lauretis 1989, 12). The feminist subject is also a partially theoretical construct, a subject in theory in the process of becoming a subject in history, and thus one who exists both inside and outside current ideologies of gender. This subject moves back and forth between a male representation of gender and what that representation leaves out, moves from the space available in a dominant discourse or a sex gender system to the space not yet representable in it. In an effort to dislocate and transform ideologies of gender, the feminist subject proposes to investigate the terms of a different construction of gender existing in the margins of hegemonic discourse, in local resistances and micropolitical practices. Again, unlike the poststructuralist subject, the feminist subject claims a strategic identity, a position of agency, and a determinate politics. Like the poststructuralist subject, the feminist subject does so through a critique of identity as such, challenging any universal notion of female essence that can be separated from particular cultural, economic, and racial positionings.

The multiple strategic possibilities emerging from this active, self-critical F/feminist subject-in-process are eloquently explored in Trinh T. Minh-ha's essay, "Difference: 'A Special Third World Women's Issue'" (1989). In both its style and content, it reflects an effort to be in dialogue with differences within the self and differences between Third World women and white or hegemonic feminists. This essay makes clear that difference is (1) an aspect of identity (poststructuralist difference); (2) a commitment within feminism (resistance to an essence of feminism, to a static feminist identity); and (3) a difference within feminism based on a recognition of experiential diversity among women and diverse relations to power and privilege. In the following passage, Trinh explores the multiple and shifting meanings of differences in positioning through the manipulation of personal pronouns (*I/i, we, you, me*):

> A critical difference from myself means that I am not i, am within and without i. I/i can be I or i, you and me both involved. We (with capital W) sometimes include(s), other times exclude(s) me. You and I/i are close, we intertwine: you may stand on the other side of the hill once in a while, but you may also be me, while remaining what you are and what I/i am not. The differences made *between* entities comprehended as absolute presences— hence the notions of *pure origin* and *true* self—are an outgrowth of a dualistic system of thought peculiar to the Occident (the "ontotheology" which characterizes Western metaphysics). They should be distinguished from the differences grasped *both between* and *within* entities, each of these being understood as multiple presence. Not One, not two either. "I" is, therefore, not a unified subject, a fixed identity or that solid mass covered with layers of superficialities one has gradually to peel off before one can see its true face. "I" is, itself, *infinite layers*. (26–27)

Trinh T. Minh-ha focuses on a difference within and without. To extend her formulation, the *difference without* refers to continuing differences in the power relations between men and women and thus the collective need to preserve a feminist identity. The *difference within* refers to continuing imbalances in power relations and experience among women and thus the need for preserving feminist differences. It is the tension created between these two concepts of feminist difference that determines the subject of feminism for the nineties. The danger of asserting the need for Feminist identity is that differences will be erased. The danger of asserting an identity politics based on difference is that the possibility of feminist coalitions will be frustrated. Together these dangers establish the need for new political models. A feminist-theory-centered classroom that is a laboratory of cultural production and a place where differences are central can be one site to begin creating these models and exploring this tension.

The Dangers of Difference: Creating Sites
for Productive Tensions

The word *tension* comes from *tensile* which means "capable of being stretched." Neither a static opposition nor a rigid resistance, tensions result when forces are allowed to circulate, to remain in process. As a stress on material produced by the pull of conflicting forces, tension may cause extension, suggesting an opening of boundaries, a breaking out, even a growth beyond original limits. Because this is so, we sought not to resolve tensions but to invent strategies for shaping and articulating them so as to prevent tensions from resolving back into oppositions or resistances.

In working to create sites for productive tensions, we actively tried to encourage an awareness of the contradictions and conflicts existing within various feminist theories and by highlighting several problematic ongoing issues within feminism. These included the nature and value of feminist theory itself; the value and limits of identity politics; the nature of feminist subjectivity and the possibilities of female agency; the compatibilities and potential conflicts between various conceptions of difference; the mystification of essentialism; the limitations of a social constructivist model of gender; the politics of location; and the value of the category "women's experience" to feminist theory. These issues circulated throughout the units in the course.

We began the class with a series of readings on the academic history of feminist criticism, followed by four units on types of feminist theory (materialist feminism, ethnic American feminism, postcolonial feminism, and French feminism). Throughout the opening sessions, we elaborated basic principles and points of commonalty among the individual essays, but we also emphasized their differences so as to disrupt the assumption that categories such as "materialist feminist" are consistent or absolutely distinct in their assumptions from other "types" of feminist theories. Here, and throughout the course, we both categorized and resisted categorizing by allowing articles to "migrate" into arenas in which they might not ordinarily be placed. This deliberate dislocation of easy oppositions or stable categories was reinforced by a final unit that acted as a summary of sorts for the section as a whole: an exploration of the essentialism debate within feminism as analyzed in Diana Fuss's *Essentially Speaking* (1989), a text that illustrates beautifully the importance and the difficulty of such dislocations.

With this groundwork in place, we turned to a variety of other topics including "History/Representation/Performance," "Gendered Bodies, Tech/no?/Bodies," "Pornography, Sexuality, and the Body in Pain," "Feminism and Psychoanalysis," and "Feminism and Postmodernism." In the case of units such as the last two (which could lend themselves easily to rigid oppositions between two terms), we opened up conflicts around feminist uses of male theory through discussion of issues such as (1) the ways in which feminist theory exposes the limitations of these (powerful) discourses of antimastery, and, conversely, the usefulness of these discourses in constructing feminist knowledge or exposing blind spots in feminist models; and (2) the modifications made by feminists in these male paradigms so as to make them more responsive to female needs. In units such as these we, again, tried to provide a range of positions in response to particular debates, using ideological disagreements to prevent them from becoming predictable, overly simplified, or too easily polarized.

Tensions in Theory and Practice

The conflicts represented within feminist theory—tensions that we wanted to explore—also gave rise to more problematic and less predictable ones—a useful reminder of the importance of keeping theory flexible and responsive to the local instance. It is appropriate here to actually describe "the local instance," i.e., the situation and composition of the class. We met once a week from 3:30 to 6:30 p.m. in a smallish room with movable chairs. Several adjacent classrooms were unoccupied, so students working in groups could move in and out of them freely.

We had twenty-three students taking the course for credit and two auditors (we tried to keep auditors to a minimum) in a roughly equal distribution of undergraduates and graduate students. In actual practice, graduate or undergraduate status was less influential in relations among the students than was prior knowledge of and commitment to feminist theory. Of our twenty-five students, twenty-four were female and one was male; two were from China, one from India, and the rest were from the United States, only one of whom was African American. The majority of the class was middle class and heterosexual—one student clearly defined herself in class as lesbian, and a few others wrote from a lesbian standpoint in their writings. We, their teachers, both are white, female, and heterosexual and work in the English department. The students ranged over many disciplines in the humanities, with a few in the social sciences; English was the most well-represented area, including several creative writing majors. There was, at times, a good deal of discomfort among these students over our failure to provide consistent, stable positions in relation to the issues we covered. These expressions of discomfort ranged from the in-class "misunderstandings, factions, discussions at cross purposes, [and] floundering" that characterized Jane Tompkins's (1990) description of her class in "Pedagogy of the Distressed" (659; see also chapter 8, this volume), to office visits with anxious students who needed special encouragement to keep going.

In describing our actual experience of teaching the course, we want to focus on the nature of the multiple tensions operating in the class and to speculate on their causes. Our first site of tension exists between the two terms "feminist" and "theory," between feminism as political movement and theory as an intellectual tradition within Western culture from which women have largely been excluded. Within feminism, this is sometimes expressed as a tension between theory and practice. Such an opposition essentializes and thus limits both feminism and theory: it acts to deny feminism the possibility of being theoretical and acts to prevent theory the possibility of being viewed as a form of activism, an active intervention into the processes of knowledge production. What, for example, does it mean if a student is happy to publicly announce her interest in "doing" feminist theory, but wouldn't be caught dead identifying herself as a feminist shorn of the legitimizing "theory" label? Conversely, what does it mean if a student is secure in her political practice as a feminist, but deeply resistant to theory, which she perceives as an inaccessible discourse of privilege? These are deliberately stated as extremes, but variations of both positions cause tension within and among students in a feminist theory class, and ours was no exception.

None of this is news to writers of feminist theory pedagogy. In 1986, Paula A. Treichler elaborated on this tension in her wide-ranging article "Teaching Feminist Theory," pointing out that the term "feminist theory" itself "is a falsely generic rubric incorporating diverse and sometimes contradictory discursive practices" that "we need not seek to resolve or disguise" (99). What was particular to the situation in 1991, or at least to our class, is that there was more awareness of both the existence and currency of feminist theory amongst students who defined themselves primarily as feminist activists and more activists who had included some "theory" in formulating that activism. This manifested itself in a kind of group commitment to learning and investigating feminist theory, one that could be described as "a willing suspension of disbelief." Most students were willing to situate themselves within "the paradox of women's experience as theory-producers" (1986, 93), to explore the position that Gayatri Spivak (1989) so acutely describes: "As we are engaged in fashioning this discipline [of feminist theory], we realize that we are marrying our passion to an alien, an alienating disciplinary formation. That is the subject position that the passionate feminists in this room occupy: the subject position of producing a mulatto/a—feminism married to critical theory" (207–8).

A second site of tension was created by the contrast between two separate kinds of differences. The first is the feminist theoretical conception of difference, which may refer to (1) differences between—gender asymmetry between men and women and the power differentials it causes; (2) differences within—the poststructuralist difference in which identity is viewed as unstable, dispersed and contradicted; and (3) differences among women according to race, class, affectional preference, etc. These concepts were relatively easy to convey through exploration of essays such as Michele Barrett's "Some Different Meanings of the Concept of 'Difference'" (1989) and Jacques Derrida's "Differance" (1982). In practice, however, differences were hard to locate or point to materially since our student population was fairly homogeneous, if less so than many Bowling Green classes. Differences remained at a theoretical level rather than circulating in personal, material ways in relation to the debates we were studying. In 1986 Paula Treichler queried, "How do we address the issues and concerns raised by women of color, who may themselves be even more excluded from theoretical feminist discourse than from the women's studies curriculum?" (79). While in 1991 there were a considerable number of writings by women of color that fit even the most elite notions of "theoretical feminist discourse," and while we strove to include these and other theorizing pieces by women of color throughout the course—work by hooks, Carby, Spillers, and Collins, for example—it was still the case that difference was "honored" most at the abstract level, where it cost less emotionally and politically, perhaps facilitated by the very sophistication of the articles we included.

Moreover, differences among students in different disciplines and the varying approaches and styles that this created were sometimes more manifest. This helped to produce a second kind of difference that operated very strongly: competitive differences among our students for "mastery" of theory as a discourse of power. Part of this tension arises because feminist theory is being learned in a classroom, i.e., in an institutional setting and for a grade. This is connected to anxiety about taking a position in the "public" arena of the classroom—fear of being wrong, of being on the "incorrect" side of a debate, of admitting perplexity or total incomprehension. It's about the exclusions, rivalries, and ambivalences that come from the desire for some of the "power chic" that mastery of theory bestows and from "the intellectual machismo with which the academy surrounds the study of theory," as Martindale, Shea, and Major (1991, 11) describe it. It's about students' rage at the difficulty of the discourses we were studying—at the same time they were seduced by them and resented it. Initially, we expected their anger to be directed at us, and for the one or two students who came to the class heavily invested in an intellectual posture that our readings and assignments challenged, it was. But more commonly the anger of our students was directed at each other. One student told us privately that she'd never before so disliked other students in a class, her response to what she felt was their higher level of proficiency and its display. Happily, as the course went on, she began to take an active role in discussion; her desire to "claim a space" within the classroom eventually led to her developing strong, well-informed positions in relation to the debates in class. And there was also anger, not openly expressed until our final group project, among students who felt as if they'd had to "go slow" and adopt a posture of apology for their own proficiency and knowledge.

These difficulties are especially apparent when we contrast the classroom dynamic with the more relaxed, supportive atmosphere operating in our ad hoc, off-campus, cultural theory reading group. This group of about twenty regularly attending members is composed of faculty, graduate students, undergraduates, and even interested persons not formally connected to academe. It has met once every three or four weeks in people's homes for the past four years. Some of the students in the theory course were also in this theory group, where they sometimes felt freer to behave more aggressively about their knowledge and their position in response to a theory. What the classroom did provide was the impetus for a more complete working through of concepts and positions in response to a theory. It also exposed students to a more diverse range of responses to the readings. But what the classroom especially lacked was some of the informal group's freedom to be speculative or confused. This tension operated in the classroom however much we sought to demystify theory or to provide the conditions for encouraging speculative thought and intellectual risk taking. Its existence is a forceful reminder of the power of disciplines to co-opt the potential of radical discourses and to limit our ability to reposition ourselves in relation to feminist values. While we certainly continue to believe that theory can give students tools for analyzing the workings of power within institutions and within their own lives, it is important to recognize that, in the classroom, theory frequently operates to reproduce competitive, hierarchical power relations among students—the very power relations that we, as feminists, seek to dismantle.

Although we included quite a bit of group work in class, were we to teach the course again, we would add the structure of ongoing study groups[2] that create the informality of our current reading group. An intriguing model for such groups, suggested to us as a possibility by one of our undergraduates, is based on the Italian feminist concept of *entrustment*. As Teresa de Lauretis (1989) describes it, entrustment refers to a relationship in which one woman "entrusts herself symbolically to another woman, who thus becomes her guide, mentor, or point of reference. . . [It is a] . . . position in a symbolic community that is discovered, invented, and constructed through feminist practices of reference and address" (22; 15). Unlike feminist models in which power differences—viewed as incompatible with women's mutual trust—are ignored or leveled (a model of divestment of power), the entrustment model foregrounds and makes positive use of the inevitable differences in knowledge, power and experience among women. As our student, Julie, put it:

> In any classroom some people are going to have more knowledge or experience in the area being taught than others, and this puts them in a position of power. But that power is not necessarily negative. This is where the entrustment model comes into the picture. Both people involved in the entrustment relationship are aware of the hierarchy and, as I see it, that awareness disrupts the negative potential of the hierarchy. This is of course far more problematic than I am letting on. . . . But I think that power differ-

ences in groups could be manipulated strategically, in time. It is helpful to read theory in a group, and if we expanded the entrustment model into a group mechanism, we could make positive use of the different positionings in relation to theory that exist in our class.

Under the current system, power hierarchies are seemingly inevitable, reproducing themselves not only within individual classrooms, but among disciplines within a single institution, and among institutions ranged according to very diverse resources and privileges. This leads to our fourth tension, one created by our response to the difference between students who have regular access to theory classes and students, at institutions like Bowling Green, who may not get a second opportunity to take a theory course. This situation created a compensatory anxiety for us as teachers: the desire to provide in one semester a comprehensive survey of the most critical, current issues in feminist theory in case the students never got it again. This again raises the paradox of our wanting both to give students access to the power connected to theorizing and to encourage them to critique that power. In "Pedagogy of the Distressed," Jane Tompkins (1990; see also chapter 8, this volume) describes three different models of education: the "banking" system (from Freire 1970), where, according to a coverage model, teachers "deposit" knowledge (653); the performance model, where the teacher is always performing her skill and expertise in front of a class, even when there is much student participation (654); and the model in which teaching becomes "a maternal or coaching activity" (660), where students take real responsibility for the class and exert more control over it. Our compensatory anxiety might have led us to invent a fourth model, the "manic mode," in which two teachers simultaneously try to execute all three of the previously mentioned models. Our investment in this first-time course, our commitment to the students and the course materials as expressed in the elaborateness of our labor, plus the students' own sense of the course's "specialness" at Bowling Green, may have created a kind of identification with and loyalty to us that prevented some open critiquing of the course as it proceeded. And while we reproduced our intensive labor in most of our students, we may also have reproduced some of our own "maniacal tendencies."

Our final tension was created by the presence in the classroom of team teachers rather than a single, coherent, "authoritative" presence. Our students were confronted with the challenge of having to please not one but two people in relation to theory. This was more evident at first, before we both wrote our own separate but compatible (we hope) comments on their paper proposals and papers. As a way to clarify what we mean by team teaching, let us note that we really collaborated on the construction of this course; we also taught the first five classes in tandem, did all the readings for the individually taught classes, and sat together and commented freely in each other's classes. That doesn't mean there weren't tensions between us and within us because of our different histories and agendas in relation to theory and feminism, but these manifested themselves more in private. We probably had too much invested in the course this first time to push the goal of manipulating power relations in the classroom that far.

Strategies for Keeping Tension Productive

Our desire to invent strategies for keeping these multiple tensions productive gave rise to the following series of assignments. We designed them as tools for helping to decrease our students' anxiety about approaching theory and negotiating the tensions that arise in a theory course. We also felt it was important to keep "complicating" these tools, so that students would find it difficult to latch on to one or two strategies and use them as a blueprint to apply uniformly to all our texts. This dual process of providing a range of techniques to increase our students' ability to think theoretically while at the same time undercutting any sense of easy mastery—even undercutting mastery as a goal— helped to reinforce several important notions: that no final stability exists either in defining a feminist theory or a static subject position in relation to it; that having mastery as a goal and an absolute value is itself problematic; and that theory may be appropriated for a variety of uses and effects. Our last assignment, a group project, was designed to bring together the skills and insights gleaned from the previous assignments outside the confines of the two formal papers. In line with our commitment to explore tensions both in theory and in practice, this final project focused on several theoretical models of power relations among women and asked students to engage in a process of negotiating differences and conflict outside a simple model of consensus.

Eleven of our strategies are described below. They begin with assignments focused mainly on creating ways to talk about theory and move on to ones designed to provoke questions concerning the nature, function, and limits of theorizing. Here we are in agreement with Treichler (1986) who asserts that "the feminist theory classroom needs to be a space for self-conscious attention to the nature, scope, traditions, and consequences of theorizing itself" (93). Some of these assignments were given in advance of a particular class; some were completed in groups during class time, and some formed part of a lengthy take-home midterm. Since our class lasted three hours, in a few cases more than one of these strategies occurred in a single class. In most cases, these assignments also served to create a basis for individual student papers—the first, roughly five pages; the second, roughly ten to fifteen. Through this series of assignments, we wanted to created local "situations" in relation to individual readings and evolving class dynamics and "problematics"—areas framed for questioning in particular ways.

1. *Identifying Sources of Difficulty in Reading Feminist Theory.*[3] We provided our students with the following description of four types of difficulties they might be likely to encounter in reading theory and asked them to respond to our early readings by grouping their difficulties in relation to these four categories. Such a categorization strategy had a number of positive effects. First, the categories functioned to announce that theory, as a new genre of sorts, operates within a new set of conventions that require—as any new genre does—alternative reading strategies. When the act of reading theory is approached as the acquisition of a new set of conventions that one learns over time, students are much less likely to become self-deprecating, resentful, or dismissive. Because the categories also allowed students to identify the particular type of difficulty they were having, they were less likely to become overwhelmed when faced with a challenging essay or to see the difficulty as all encompassing and therefore insurmountable. Finally, starting by discussing the difficulties posed by a particular theory allowed the class to move more quickly to the actual issues contained in a given essay. Discussions were thus more focused and substantive. We had intended to use this first strategy for only a few weeks—until students acquired their "theory wings." But it became so popular with the class that we found ourselves using it as a warmup to discussion.

Contingent: Difficulty arises because of unfamiliar and exotic terms, unclear allusions, or even because familiar words are used to refer to new concepts. In part this difficulty arises because theory borrows from a number of different disciplines and is composed of multiple discourses; in part because theory has evolved a discourse all its own. Contingent difficulties can be resolved through familiarity with the terms as one becomes used to seeing them in context.

Modal: Difficulty arises because of resistance by the reader to the text's mode of presentation or its use of unfamiliar terms.

Tactical: Difficulty arises because the writer deliberately uses strategies to dislocate the reader and inhibit a conventional response to the text. An example here would be Irigaray's hysteric's prose or strategy of mimetism.

Paradigmatic: Difficulty arises because the text poses a new ontology, a new paradigm of understanding. This requires a different grasp of phenomena, perhaps an alternate relation between self and text, perhaps a new version of the self altogether. An example is Donna Haraway's "Cyborg" (1990) or Trinh T. Minh-ha's "I/i" as a figure for the split postcolonial subject. This difficulty is insurmountable except through a transformation of understanding into the new mode or paradigm. Feminism itself has been thought of as just such "a shift in perspective," one "far more extraordinary and influential than the shift from theology to humanism of the European Renaissance," in Adrienne Rich's words (1979a, 126).

2. *Characterizing an Author's Standpoint or Speaking Position.* As part of our efforts to encourage students' facility in reading theory, we focused on isolating the assumptions that most explicitly ground or initiate an argument, including especially what is concealed by those assumptions in order that the writer may take up a position. We wanted students to identify the processes by which, in Gayatri Spivak's (1989) words, "you start from an assumption which you must think is whole in order to be able to speak" (211). We first asked them to consider the opening statements of two works by black feminists—bell hooks's 1984 book *Feminist Theory: From Margin to Center* and Patricia Hill Collins's 1989 essay "The Social Construction of Black Feminist Thought." Among other things, hooks and Collins are concerned with developing a specifically Afra-centric epistemology and to specify the way this standpoint acts to critique structures of domination—including those in which white feminists participate in relation to black women. What consequences, we asked, do these differing opening statements have for the rest of the piece? More specifically, how does each writer establish her terrain (where she locates herself, her subject, and her audience) and how do these strategies differ? What is the motivating instance of each piece? How might this relate to the differing times of composition? What other factors, such as primary audience, might influence each author's choice of a standpoint? What might each author be minimizing in order to assume this standpoint? What position is available for you as a reader of this text? What standpoint would you assume in order to talk back to hooks or Collins? What would you be concealing in order to assume this position?

3. *Putting Feminist Theorists into Dialogue.* This exercise used techniques of dialogue—long privileged within feminist theory—with the

aim of opening connections between theorists outside a more familiar model of comparison/contrast, which sometimes leads to the creation of static oppositions between positions. Dialogic strategies would, we hoped, make multiple connections likely and also work to undercut the tendency to regard theoretical voices as monological and authoritative.

To these ends, we asked students to construct a dialogue between two theorists—in which each comments in a variety of ways on the other's ideas—or an interview with the two theorists conducted by the student (the advantage of the latter is that space is held out for the student's own voice). This strategy worked especially well when students put two very different kinds of theoreticians (e.g., Irigaray and hooks; Hartsock and Haraway) in dialogue.

4. *Locating Relationships between Feminist Theory and Activist Practice.* This two-part assignment gave students a chance to situate a theory in relation to an active feminist political practice, testing the efficacy of the former and the assumptions of the latter. The first part of the assignment focused on reading feminist political practice for theoretical assumptions: We provided our students with a copy of "The Women's Bill of Rights"—a fund-raising document put forward by Women for Racial and Economic Equality. We asked them to analyze the theoretical assumptions contained in this bill regarding the nature of women's oppression, the locus of that oppression, the project of feminism as a transformative movement, the nature of the changes sought by it and the likelihood that the proposed strategies would actually bring about effective social change. We wanted students to identify organizing assumptions in this document, but we also wanted them to isolate those material contexts or motivating instances, as we called them, which created the need for the components of this bill. Keeping these material contexts in mind, our students' second assignment was to locate the space available (or not available) within a theory (e.g., Diana Fuss's 1989 book *Essentially Speaking: Feminism, Nature and Difference*) for an active political practice. Although we wanted to avoid promoting reductive criteria that assume theory must always be immediately applicable to a real world context, we also wanted to avoid advocating an approach that removed the need for theory to respond to feminism's material, political commitments. This assignment was, in part, a response to our students' interest in the concept of strategic essentialism and the danger of it becoming too pat a solution for relating theory, practice, and identity politics.

5. *Theorizing Art/Fictionalizing Theory.* This assignment focused on two questions: How does/can a creative work become/be read as a

theoretical text? How can a work of theory be approached in the way that creative texts typically are? We wanted to focus on a number of issues through this exercise: (a) the consequences of a breakdown in the traditional divisions erected between theory and other kinds of textual/visual expressions in the postmodern era; and thus (b) changing conceptions of what theory and art and the functions they perform might be; and (c) the relationship between particular modes of structuring knowledge and larger ideological assumptions.

A. *reading art as theory:* Students chose one of the following texts— the section from Karen Finley's performance piece "The Constant State of Desire," from the film *Mondo New York;* the Madonna videos *Like a Prayer* or *Justify My Love;* Cherríe Moraga's play *Giving Up the Ghost;* and Simone Benmussa's play *The Singular Life of Albert Nobbs*—and discussed the degree to which it might be considered an example of feminist theory or might demonstrate a process of feminist theorizing. We then asked the students to consider whether feminist theory should be evaluated by traditional standards such as consistency and comprehensiveness of explanation, or whether alternative values and standards might be constructed for feminist purposes. This final consideration was part of our ongoing question, "What should a feminist theory do?"

B. *reading theory for tropes:* We gave students the opportunity to clarify the operation of theory by focusing on the use of figurative constructs, or tropes, within an argument—both those used deliberately by theorists—such as Cixous's Medusa, Irigaray's Two Lips, Haraway's Cyborg, and even de Lauretis's Space-Off—and those used by theorists as if they weren't tropes, such as Hartsock's Standpoint. We asked them to trace the function of these organizing figures, to consider the advantages of overtly grounding a theory in a figurative construct, and to reflect on the potential dangers of such a strategy.

This two-part exercise gave many students license to play seriously with theoretical ideas and to pursue, in what felt to them like a less rigid way, the issues raised by our questioning.

6. *Historicizing Positions within Feminist Theory.* We designed this exercise to emphasize the importance of considering the context of production and reception—the history—of particular ideas and debates within feminism. We were interested in having students explore the evolution of debates around issues that had been of longstanding concern to feminists by considering how these issues were revised over time and speculating on what was gained or lost by responses in each decade. In one instance, we drew on readings from the feminist debate

on pornography and sexuality. These ranged from Andrea Dworkin's "Pornography and Grief" (1980) to Linda Williams's *Hard Core* (1989) to an interview by Linda Montano (1989) with performer Annie Sprinkle. First, one of us historicized her own responses to this debate, using anecdotal examples of her positions ranging over a twelve-year period. This mapping of her history and positioning was not chronological and was designed to highlight blind spots, internal contradictions, and changes in position that couldn't completely erase the traces of earlier ones.

We then turned to student responses; in relation to this particular topic, we were especially interested in their noting how material experience and the body, especially the body in pain, is dealt with by various modes of theorizing, from "cultural feminist" to poststructuralist. A focal point of the discussion was commentary on their own positions in relation to incidents of violation and pain described in the readings. How, we asked, do your own bodies respond to these incidents; Is there a difference between this response and how you would position yourselves theoretically in relation to these debates? This last question was a useful strategy for illuminating differences within each student. It also helped prevent a kind of sophisticated denial through which students could potentially divorce themselves not just from particular positions on pornography that were under critique, but from the actual violence against women in which these critiqued positions were grounded.

We further complicated this assignment by using Hortense Spillers's "Mama's Baby, Papa's Maybe: An American Grammar Book" (1987) as an example of the intersection of poststructuralist strategies and questions of race, material history, and pain. This essay relocates dominant feminist notions about gender indeterminacy and the meaning of paternity in light of what such concepts mean historically for African American women and men, so that feminist theory itself must change in response to this experience. Students got an opportunity to explore questions surrounding the category of experience when experience isn't assimilatable to the theory but instead critiques its limitations.

7. Seeking a Resistance Postmodernism in Relation to Feminism. From this emphasis on debates internal to feminism, we moved to external debates, in this case debates surrounding relations between feminism and postmodernism. We used this debate to suggest some of the ideological implications of defining a particular large theoretical term in relation to feminism—from positions that insist feminism has nothing to gain through a relation to "male defined" theory to those that argue that feminism should be considered simply a manifestation of—in this case—a more widespread postmodern cultural condition. After outlining some of the general features associated with postmodernism, we moved to a distinction between a postmodernism of resistance and a postmodernism of reaction. Resistance postmodernism refers to a politically committed postmodern practice aware of the possibilities of local engagements and struggles. It exists in distinction from positions such as Fredric Jameson's or Jean Baudrillard's which hold out little possibility of effective oppositional stances operating within a postmodern culture of late capitalism.

We asked students to evaluate this definition of a resistant postmodernist practice in relation to artworks from the 1970s (e.g., Judy Baca's public mural project "The Great Wall of L.A."; Suzanne Lacy and Leslie Labowitz's political performance art; lesbian art at the L.A. Women's Building) and to artworks such as the "story quilts" done in the late 1980s by African American artist Faith Ringgold, art not typically classified within a postmodern, feminist, visual-art canon (e.g., Mary Kelly, Laurie Simmons, Cindy Sherman, Barbara Kruger, Jenny Holzer and Ida Applebroog—whose works we also showed). Rather than allowing one group of works to simply supplant the others, we wanted to encourage dialogue among the different feminist expressions so that continuities in style and preoccupation and changes over time might be noted. We also asked the questions: If postmodernism can be described as a contemporary cultural condition that is not static and that arises from particular social, historical, and ideological shifts, how many of these works reflect both these shifts and this instability? How many express the breakdown of consensus associated with postmodernism? How many reflect the current crisis in the authority and hegemony of white male ways of knowing and of structuring knowledge? If they do, are there also privileged styles in feminist postmodernism for conveying this, and do these works reflect these modes? Conversely, how might a by-now-codified postmodern mode limit what a feminist artist can express?

8. Evaluating Feminist Strategies for Disruption. As the previous exercise suggests, contemporary feminist work involves struggling over the interpretation of cultural images and working to transform these inherited discourses for progressive ends. This discursive struggle is to be distinguished from more general postmodern strategies of appropriation, bricolage, and discourse piracy, largely because feminism, unlike a more general postmodernism, insists that we specify what kinds of recoding will matter, why, and for whom. Feminism seeks consciously to raise the question of address—of who produces cultural representations and for whom, of who receives them and in what contexts, and to what ends.

This assignment focused on identifying and evaluating the effectiveness of the feminist disruptive strategies that appear in the work of Barbara Kruger. Kruger (1983) conceives her role as a "guerrilla semiologist" with a project to overthrow the positioning power of dominant discourse: those images, clichés, and stereotypes that represent power relations in white, Western, patriarchal culture. In her words, "We loiter outside of trade and speech, and are obliged to steal language. We are very good mimics. We replicate certain words and pictures and watch them stray from or coincide with your fact and fiction" (11). Kruger's work is valuable as feminist theory because it stages—graphically—not only the complex processes by which gender identity is discursively constructed, but also the ways in which this construction has a direct impact on real bodies. In order to assume a gendered position in relation to a Kruger piece, viewers must negotiate among constantly shifting images and discourses, a process of discursive struggle that suggests both the instability and the insistence of gender-specific address. As Nancy Campbell (1988) puts it, "It simultaneously antagonizes and embraces the discourses of dominance and resistance" (58). Composed as it is of "unstable acts of compassion and violence, wholeness and invasion" (60), oscillating between power-identified and power-countering positions, Kruger's work is both intellectually challenging and emotionally unsettling—at least our students found it so. Considering this work proved an effective way to illustrate concepts that, in their abstractness, might otherwise be confusing, such as the discursive construction of gender or de Lauretis's notion of the feminist subject being simultaneously inside and outside of ideology.

9. *Assuming a Position: Personal History, Art, and Theory.* As a follow-up exercise to our work with Kruger, we showed the class two Madonna videos (*Like a Prayer* and *Justify My Love*) and asked students (1) to attempt to view them from a subject position that differed markedly from their own (e.g., a white working-class male, a black female academic, a middle-class lesbian, a gay male dancer, a fortyish heterosexual woman, a fourteen-year-old girl, etc.) and (2) to comment on the effects of this spectatorial dislocation on their own "natural" viewing position. Our hope was to demonstrate the difficulty of imaginatively inhabiting another's subject position and to clarify the difference between "inhabiting" another's subject position and stereotyping the person in the process. The discussion surrounding these issues of identification was quite heated; many students discovered—painfully—that

the more normative (invisible) their own subject position was to them, the more likely the possibility that difference would be perceived stereotypically.

10. Locating Feminist Theories in the Context of Institutional Power. We designed this exercise, which students completed late in the semester, to focus directly on debates concerning the value of theory to feminism. We wanted to construct a situation in which students' personal histories (in this case, in relation to the educational system) and local institutional practices (at our university) were analyzed in relation to a specific theoretical perspective. For this purpose, we used Michel Foucault's theories of how power operates on individual subjects to compel action and how disciplines operate to legitimate some knowledges while at the same time excluding others. The educational system seemed a particularly good site for this encounter between theory and experience: first because it is one of the primary vehicles for the transmission of dominant ideology (according to Althusser), and second because our long-term immersion in the institution provided a common field against which our differing histories could be discussed. Our goal was to encourage reflection on the value and limits of using theory to analyze experience and generate useful models of feminist action and, conversely, the limits of relying too exclusively on experience to construct feminist knowledge and activist agendas. Theory and practice/experience were thus brought into a relation where each would question and destabilize the other. Such a relationship of mutual problematizing is, we feel, one of the hallmarks of contemporary feminism and one of its strengths.

Very generally, our discussion included a brief commentary on central Foucauldian concepts; an elaboration of our educational histories in relation to each other and to Foucault's assertions; reflection on the institutional position of women at Bowling Green (including such factors as the percentage of female faculty, the percentage of institutional resources allocated to women's studies, the number of feminist courses taught per semester, etc); and a discussion of the status of women's studies and feminist theory at other institutions. Here we noted feminism's self-conception as the illegitimate heir of institutional privilege, with a role to delegitimate institutional power. We asked students to contrast this delegitimating function with the ways in which feminism has also legitimated itself institutionally: Which of the feminisms are legitimated institutionally and which are not? Through what mechanisms of inclusion and exclusion? If there is a hierarchy of feminist discourses within institutions, who does it privilege? How would this hierarchy position people who primarily identify themselves as feminist theorists? As feminist activists? As people in Women's Studies?

Students told us this exercise was among the most valuable because it forced them to build linkages between their daily lived experience and the larger structures of domination that tend to remain invisible. Foucault's theories thus became for them forceful tools for rendering visible the workings of institutional power in their lives. This exercise brought home to them our contention—advanced throughout the semester—that feminist theory is an evolving body of knowledge, one that is useful for illuminating women's diverse experiences, one that, far from being abstractly disconnected from these experiences, must be constantly modified in relation to them.

11. Final Group Project: Enacting Feminist Theory/Negotiating Difference: A Group Experiment. We designed our final assignment to function as a culmination of sorts for a class that had explored some of the multiple perspectives and debates circulating in contemporary feminist theory— one that had also encouraged an awareness of the difficulties involved in negotiating differences. We wanted students to engage in a final process of theorizing that would build on and extend the task of evaluating and testing the limits of particular theories. The following five-step group exercise was based on three essays, each of which describes a model for negotiating conflict and power differences among women and constructing lines of affinity across differences: Teresa de Lauretis's "The Essence of the Triangle, or, Taking the Risk of Essentialism Seriously: Feminist Theory in Italy, the U.S., and Britain" (1989); Chantal Mouffe's "Hegemony and New Political Subjects: Toward a New Concept of Democracy" (1988a); and selections from Marianne Hirsch and Evelyn Fox Keller's *Conflicts in Feminism* (1990). Students were assigned to groups of four or five that met several times outside of class, and were to present their results at a final class meeting at one of our homes.

Step one was an exercise in self-location and mapping. Students were asked to position themselves in relation to those categories that operate most frequently in feminist efforts to theorize differences in power, privilege, and experience among women (e.g., race, ethnicity, class, affectional preference), speculating on those that seemed most difficult to consider from their own location. They then discussed with their group the most relevant or significant differences operating within that setting and how these differences manifested themselves.

In step two, students analyzed the model elaborated or implied in each essay and evaluated it according to the question, "What should a feminist theory of power do?" Step three involved choosing a controversial feminist debate and negotiating it in relation to the model set out in one of the essays. The goal here was not to reach easy consensus or resolution of the debate, but to construct a group position that would account for individual differences yet still allow for a group position to be assumed.

In step four, students reflected on the insights gained through this negotiation process and reassessed the value and the limits of the model based on this discussion. They considered such questions as: In what ways did this process demand a change in your location? How might the terms "consensus" and "resolution" be problematized or complicated? What investment did you have in avoiding conflict in your group, and how is this related to your notion of either feminist etiquette or appropriate female behavior? What did you have to "give up" in order to avoid conflict? Or to reach a group position? Did the model offer any opportunities to modify or clarify the process of group negotiation?

Finally, in step five, students designed a fifteen-minute presentation that would demonstrate some aspect of the group's negotiation process or their own response to it. We suggested such strategies as a cognitive map of their personal evolution or the evolution of the group; a dialogue with themselves, with one voice taped; a visual representation; a poem or short essay on, for example, the problems involved in negotiating relations between Feminism and feminisms; a more conventional, short-response paper.

Students produced lively, thoughtful, and imaginative responses to the assignment. One group simulated a meeting designed to negotiate agreement before giving a response to the press on their position in regard to releasing the names of rape victims; one group collaborated on a poster illustrating a variety of sexual images in tandem with writings that vary in position on the issue of pornography; one group produced a set of individual dialogues about power in which each student spoke with herself on tape; one group created a Feminist theory version of the game "Twister," literally engaging the body in being tangled up in feminist theory as they negotiated categories on the game board and each others' bodies. Although there were many remarkable posters, we were most taken with the choice to create performance that so many students made. Both these performances and some of the parodies students created operated as a critical force and a way of letting out emotions that could not be said more formally.

The students also dubbed it "an unqualified success." Their comments included "This project was the highlight of the course, a real learning experience," and "I usually hate group work but this time something really happened. I learned a lot and found out I know more about feminist theory that I thought I did." The success of this and other assignments that asked students to approach theory in an active and interactive way suggest the importance of providing for multiple types of student responses, ones that would include room for testing, speculating, even playing with theory. Early on in the paper, we noted our desire to make the class a laboratory of culture that would function as a theoretical space of not-yet-actualized possibilities in which to conduct experiments in the production of new models of culture, a place of potentials. With this last group project, we felt we'd come close to creating a location for that laboratory, one that could begin to dismantle the opposition between theory and speculative play and begin to create a kind of free space for invention.

Notes

1. For more theorizing on models of affinities, see Haraway (1990) and Mouffe (1988a).

2. For a description of such ongoing study groups, see Treichler (1986, 80–82; 106, *n*19).

3. See Martindale, Shea, and Major (1991) for their conception of the difficulties that come up in response to reading theory. Their four main groups of difficulties include the "[c]onceptual, technical, emotional and political" (10). We found their last two categories especially useful and intriguing.

Works Cited

Alcoff, Linda. 1988. "Cultural Feminism versus Poststructuralism: The Identity Crisis in Feminist Theory." *Signs* 13(3): 405–36.

Barrett, Michele. 1989. "Some Different Meanings of the Concept of 'Difference': Feminist Theory and the Concept of Ideology." In *The Differences Within: Feminism and Critical Theory*, edited by Elizabeth Meese and Alice Parker, 37–48. Amsterdam: John Benjamins.

Benmussa, Simone. 1979. *The Singular Life of Albert Nobbs*. London: John Calder.

Campbell, Nancy D. 1988. "The Oscillating Embrace: Subjection and Interpellation in Barbara Kruger's Art." *Genders* 1: 57–74.

Collins, Patricia Hill. 1989. "The Social Construction of Black Feminist Thought." *Signs* 14(4): 773–45.

de Lauretis, Teresa. 1989. "The Essence of the Triangle, or, Taking the Risk of Essentialism Seriously: Feminist Theory in Italy, the U.S., and Britain." *Differences* 1(2): 3–37.

Derrida, Jacques. 1982. "Differance." In *The Margins of Philosophy*, translated by Alan Bass, 176–202. Chicago: University of Chicago Press.

Dworkin, Andrea. 1980. "Pornography and Grief." In *Take Back the Night: Women on Pornography*, edited by Laura Lederer, 286–92. New York: William Morrow.

Finley, Karen. 1987. "The Constant State of Desire." In *Mondo New York*, directed by Harvey Keith. 83 min. B'Way Films.

Freire, Paulo. 1970. *Pedagogy of the Oppressed*. Translated by Myra Bergman Ramos. New York. Continuum.

Fuss, Diana. 1989. *Essentially Speaking: Feminism, Nature and Difference*. New York: Routledge.

Gallop, Jane. 1989. "Heroic Images: Feminist Criticism, 1972." *American Literary History* 1(3): 612–36.

Haraway, Donna. 1990. "A Manifesto for Cyborgs: Science, Technology, and Socialist Feminism in the 1980s." In *Feminism/Postmodernism*, edited by Linda J. Nicholson, 190–233. New York: Routledge.

Hartsock, Nancy. 1987. "The Feminist Standpoint: Developing the Ground for a Specifically Feminist Historical Materialism." *Feminism and Methodology: Social Science Issues*, edited by Sandra Harding, 157–80. Bloomington: Indiana University Press.

Hirsch, Marianne, and Evelyn Fox Keller. 1990. "Introduction: January 4, 1990." In *Conflicts in Feminism*, 1–5. New York: Routledge.

hooks, bell. 1984. *Feminist Theory: From Margin to Center*. Boston: South End Press. 2-32.

Kruger, Barbara. 1983. *We Won't Play Nature to Your Culture: Works by Barbara Kruger*. London: ICA/Kunsthalle Basel.

Madonna. 1990a. *Like a Prayer*. In *The Immaculate Collection*, photography by Herb Ritts and art direction by Jeri Heiden. 40 min. Warner Reprise Video.

———. 1990b. *Justify My Love*. Jean-Baptiste Mondino (dir.). Warner Reprise Video.

Martin, Biddy. 1988. "Feminism, Criticism, and Foucault." In *Feminism and Foucault: Reflections on Resistance*, edited by Irene Diamond & Lee Quinby, 3–19. Chicago: Northeastern University Press.

Martindale, Kathleen, Susan Shea, and Lana Major. 1991. "Articulating the Difficulties in Teaching/Learning Feminist Cultural Theory." *Radical Teacher* 39: 9–14.

Minh-ha, Trinh T. 1989. "Difference: 'A Special Third World Women Issue.'" In *Woman, Native, Other: Writing Postcoloniality and Feminism*, 79–116. Bloomington: Indiana University Press.

Montano, Linda. 1989. "Summer Saint Camp 1987: With Annie Sprinkle and Veronica Vera." *Drama Review* 33(1): 94–103.

Moraga, Cherríe. 1986. *Giving Up the Ghost: Teatro in Two Acts*. Los Angeles: West End Press.

Mouffe, Chantal. 1988a. "Hegemony and New Political Subjects: Toward a New Concept of Democracy." In *Marxism and the Interpretation of Culture*, edited by Cary Nelson and Lawrence Grossberg, 89–104. Urbana: University of Illinois Press.

———. 1988b. "Radical Democracy: Modern or Postmodern?." In *Universal Abandon?: The Politics of Postmodernism*, edited by Andrew Ross, 31–45. Minneapolis: University of Minnesota Press.

Rich, Adrienne. 1979a. "Toward a Woman-Centered University." In *On Lies, Secrets, and Silence: Selected Prose, 1966–1978*, 125–55. New York: Norton.

———. 1979b. "When We Dead Awaken: Writing as Re-Vision (1971)." In *On Lies, Secrets, and Silence: Selected Prose 1966–1978*, 33–49. New York: Norton.

Spillers, Hortense J. 1987. "Mama's Baby, Papa's Maybe: An American Grammar Book." *Diacritics* 17(2): 64–81.

Spivak, Gayatri Chakravorty. 1989. "A Response to *The Differences Within: Feminism and Critical Theory.*" In *The Differences Within: Feminism and Critical Theory*, edited by Elizabeth Meese and Alice Parker, 207–20. Amsterdam: John Benjamins.

Tompkins, Jane. 1990. "Pedagogy of the Distressed." *College English* 52(6): 653–60. [See also chapter 8, this volume.]

Treichler, Paula A. 1986. "Teaching Feminist Theory." In *Theory in the Classroom*, edited by Cary Nelson, 57–128. Urbana: University of Illinois Press.

Williams, Linda. 1989. *Hard Core: Power, Pleasure, and the "Frenzy of the Visible."* Berkeley: University of California Press.

Appendix: Topic Outline of a Feminist Theory Course

1. The Institutional History of Feminist Criticism
2. Materialist Feminism
3. Ethnic American Feminism
4. Postcolonial Feminism
5. French Feminism
6. Constructing Essentialism/Essentializing Constructionism
7. Feminism and Psychoanalysis
8. History/Representation/Performance
9. Feminism and Postmodernism
10. Postmodernism and Feminist Visual Art
11. Gendered Bodies, Tech/no?/bodies
12. Pornography, Sexuality, and the Body in Pain
13. Institutional Power/ Institutional Critique
14. Negotiating Power Differences/Enacting Models of Affinity

7 Feminist Sophistics: Teaching with an Attitude

Dale M. Bauer
University of Wisconsin–Madison

Susan C. Jarratt
Texas Christian University

Curriculum controversies propelled by the new social movements bring into focus an anxiety about power. In recent years, the popular press has been full of charges that teachers of classes which call into question the social status quo are indoctrinating their students. Such complaints about faculty using their authority as teachers in irresponsible ways have emerged, in part, because of the way power itself is hidden within institutions. Feminist teachers who offer counterhegemonic explanations of the way things are—such as those who teach students to recognize the way knowledge and daily life are based on systems of gender—make students confront the generalized diffusion of bureaucratic and institutional power under which teachers and students operate daily. This epistemic break—from the smooth continuum of knowledge built throughout a legacy of educational experiences within a unified system—forces every student to notice power. Many students resist being wrenched out of the now comfortable paradigm of liberal humanism, with its attendant structures of value and meaning: positivist science, bourgeois individualism, and capitalist progress. The resistance then becomes the object of pedagogical controversy. But those who do make a change and respond to a new explanation of the world demand our attention as well.

The goals of both rhetoric and feminism are change. Feminist sophistics combines the two fields for reflection on processes of change in the classroom and in society, reflection on what it means for a teacher to exercise rhetorical authority toward ends of social transformation. Feminist sophistics brings anxiety about power into sharp focus: the naturalized operation of power, obscured in the day-to-day operations of educational institutions, becomes the subject of the course. When the teacher makes her own political and ethical commitment to social change part of the course, students who have internalized a pedagogical model of education as the transmission of "objective" knowledge may feel an uncomfortable dissonance. Speaking openly about ethics can create for students a painful awareness of the absence of a strong consensus about right and wrong in our huge, diverse social system. But feminist sophistics does not demand that students adopt a politically correct position; in fact, it argues against any fixed agenda in favor of personally grounded and historically located exploration of social identities. For us, teaching feminism "with an attitude" means sharing with students our current commitments, along with the historical contexts within which they were developed, while asking students to engage in similar explorations.

Gerald Graff expresses his concern with power in the classroom by reporting on two equally unsatisfying stances he has adopted toward his classes over the years: over- and underassertion (see chapter 9, this volume). His solution is a call for counterauthority, the breaking apart of the enclosed classroom with its single speaking teacher facing listening students. We believe that our theory and practice of feminist sophistics is another kind of solution to this power dilemma in the classroom. But rather than seeking external mediations of the teacher's single authority, as Graff suggests, we use rhetorical and feminist theories to argue that counterauthority can be developed within students' own discourses. We saw this process taking place when students were led to describe their lives, especially their educational experiences, as socially and historically embedded. We aimed not for "conversion experiences" but for the articulation of the self in history.

Why feminist sophistics? By reading feminism through sophistic rhetoric, we devised a pedagogy linking civic responsibility for public discourse to personal experience. This rhetoric engages difference at the same time that it invites students to trace their own trajectories of growth as they encounter feminist theory. We asked these students to address their cultural locations in response to readings in rhetoric and feminism. What follows is a description of our course and its foundations in sophistic rhetoric, an account of resistances to our pedagogy, and some successful creations of counterauthority through feminist rhetorical attitudes.

Backgrounds

When we conceived of Feminist Sophistics, we imagined a course and a conference (both at Miami University in June 1990) which dealt with the intersections of our disciplines, rhetoric and feminism, and with the histories of both. We wanted to articulate with our students a way of arguing from a feminist rhetorical standpoint. Our speakers for the conference—Patricia Bizzell, Linda Brodkey, Page duBois, and bell hooks— formulated definitions compatible with ours. Bizzell called feminist sophistics a chance to find a "compelling version of rhetorical authority from which to speak on behalf of oppressed groups in spite of the climate of post-modern skepticism, which attempts to render all value assertions nugatory" (7–8). She went on to argue that we need to risk "making fools of ourselves [and to] consider the implications of taking on not only the fool's disregard for social convention . . . but also the fool's embrace of marginal social positions as well" (17). Linda Brodkey defined feminist sophistics as "an attempt to link academic feminism to feminist activism by tracing the history of feminism to a period when rhetoricians, namely, the Sophists took seriously their civic responsibilities as pedagogues" (3). Both Bizzell and Brodkey think of feminist sophistics as furthering a public ethical stance in the academy in contrast to the detached skepticism of postmodern theorizing. They argue for an ethical conception of rhetoric, responsibly directed toward an exploration of difference.

The fifteen students in our graduate seminar that summer eagerly engaged in discussions of contemporary feminist pedagogy. It was their resistance to history, however, that led us to a fuller understanding of what we meant by feminist sophistics. One student wrote in an evaluation that he found the historical readings the least useful.[1] Another student, in her final paper, wrote about her resistance to one of the historically oriented presentations. Not only these two students but others, including conference participants, had trouble making connections between the historical material and their immediate concerns with the way feminists speak and are spoken of, feminism's restructuring of knowledge and classroom practice, and the rhetorical issues involved in feminist pedagogy.

From our perspective, history is vital to the process of addressing these concerns. Given the students' resistance or indifference, we have to ask how history can become an opening into power and classroom politics for students, both graduate and undergraduate. Linking rhetoric to feminism, "Feminist Sophistics" conjures up both "rhetoric" in general and the rhetoric of a particular historical moment: that of the first Sophists of fifth-century B.C.E. Greece. Why choose the Sophists as a theoretical and historical orientation rather than, say, Aristotle? Not because the Sophists themselves were feminists. The literary remains of Protagoras, Gorgias, and the several other lesser known members of this group of traveling public intellectuals present some arguably progressive angles on women, but none advocates enfranchising women as active citizens in the polis. Nor were the Sophists oppressed as a group as were women in Greece. But they were engaged in an intellectual battle with Plato, the terms of which speak to the challenges of contemporary feminisms. Occupying a space of intellectual history and political practice preceding Platonic philosophy, the Sophists were materialists and anthropologists. Drawing on evolutionary theories of human origins and development, they argued for the most diverse range of human potentialities capable of cultivation by society, which they understood to work as a normalizing—that is, ideological—force. Both their political teaching and their discourse practices threatened Plato and later Aristotle with the passion and disorder that accompany radical democracy. We would argue that their pedagogy made possible a critical as well as a reproductive relationship to a rapidly changing social order.

Plato formulated his main themes—metaphysics and oligarchic political rule—in reaction to sophistic rhetoric, structuring the suppression of difference into classical philosophy from the beginning. In fact, the terms under which the heterogeneity of sophistic discourse has been relegated to the margins of knowledge formation throughout Western history since the decline of the Roman Empire have often excluded women from these processes (e.g., on grounds of lack of "rationality"). Perhaps the most powerful example of this suppression, still operative today, is the way seventeenth-century science defined "rhetoric" as external "color" or supplemental "dress." Many still see language as the "warped mirror" through which we seek the clarity of the real. The parallel we develop between sophistic rhetoric and a construction of the "feminine" can be traced to the realm of style, both in language and in its more general reference to gesture, appearance, and dress. Plato and Aristotle condemned the sophistic "style" for a range of features that sketch a profile of an alternative discourse: generic diversity, loose organization, a reliance on narrative, physical pleasure in language production and reception, a holistic psychology of communication, and an emphasis on the aural relation between speaker and listener. These features stand over and against qualities of a philosophic discourse prepared for (though not practiced) by Plato and fully formulated by Aristotle: clear generic distinction, a hierarchy of logical systems with the certainty of first principles and the rigor of dialectic dominating the looser probabilities of rhetoric and poetic, a tight control over the kinds of responses expected, and a visual metaphor of the relationship between the subject who speaks and the object of dis-

course. "Style"—the reductive code for all the former features—is devalued as the absence of substance, a devaluation traceable to the
metaphysical disdain for the body. Both rhetoric and women are trivi-
alized by identification with sensuality, costume, and color—all of
which are supposed to be manipulated in attempts to persuade through
deception. As an emblem of this likeness stands the Greek goddess of
persuasion, Peitho: she is linked with marriage goddesses not for her
domestic skill but because of her seductive powers and trickery (see
Jarratt 1991).

It is no wonder, then, that students object to feminist teachers and
their "style": their gendered bodies and the attention to the material
body, even to clothes or to physical characteristics. The students repeat
in their rejections of history—and of rhetoric—the Platonic division
outlined above. In teaching them to take account of their historically
situated bodies, we argue that a liberatory politics requires a discourse
that locates bodies (ignored or devalued in Platonic metaphysics) in
time, space, and material conditions. The Sophists focused attention on
the real material situations of discourse performance, whether it was
the supreme ideological moment of the annual funeral oration or the
intimate gathering of a group of students around a teacher. A significant
element of these situations was the physical presence of the speaker.
Some suggestive physical images of the Sophists survive: Protagoras
speaking from his bed with young admirers clustered around; Gorgias
performing in radiant purple robes; Hippias showing off his clothes, all
of which he made himself.[2] We read this emphasis not as meretricious
self-aggrandizement (a Platonic reading), but rather as an insistence on
the situatedness of speakers and discursive acts. This attention to the
presence of the speaker, so important to the Sophists, is later theorized
by Aristotle as *ethos*—the creation of a self through discourse in a
moment of connection with a collective, who share practices, places,
and desires. We see in this element of sophistic rhetoric a connection
with the Sophists' historicism. A key difference between the Sophists
and other rhetorical theorists is their historicist vision: an evolutionary
as opposed to a nostalgic or teleological view of historical change (see
Havelock 1957). Indeed, the political rhetoric of the Sophists served as
the primary discourse of social, political, and intellectual change in
fifth-century B.C.E. Greek culture, speaking out in the dramas and
histories as well as in the orations.

In coining "Feminist Sophistics," we recast sophistic "style," not to
reject it in favor of "substance," but rather to redefine it as a conjunction
of the historical specificity of "feminism" as a movement and the self-
conscious placement of gendered (as well as raced/classed/abled) bod-

ies in the classroom. While students are quick to notice bodies, they are less likely to attend to history. Central to our project, then, is the historical placement of the feminist rhetor and her students. And it is precisely students' absence of a historical sense—of an ability to characterize themselves as potential agents within narratives of historical change— that sets limits for many. For undergraduates, this may be connected to an ignorance of recent histories of social change. Some graduate students in composition and rhetoric and some feminist activists—paradoxically, some of those most committed to a politically active pedagogy—look upon history as a detour away from more pressing issues. For them, the study of history is "untimely" in Nietzsche's words (Hollingdale 1983, 60). Nietzsche's categories are to the point: students think of history as antiquarian, a process of preserving and revering the past (72–77). And yet a sense of history is crucial in diagnosing social problems and envisioning a process of transformation. At issue is not the study of historical data for its own sake but toward the development of a historical attitude. In order to have an attitude, a person has to have a position as opposed to remaining undifferentiated. One has to be placed, in space, in time, and in a vision of social order, the last of these making possible "attitude" as an aggressive challenge to social hierarchies.

What does this attitude have to do with history? Consider the colloquial usage, "You're history!" or "That's history!" We take such an expression to mean that something or someone is over, done with, finished. The finality is expressed grammatically here by verb tense (in English, the simple past or the past perfect; in Greek, the aorist)—an expression of the past as a completed act rather than what existence really is: an imperfect tense, moving from the past into the present and future. And for Nietzsche, this position is the very denial of history: "If death at last brings the desired forgetting, by that act it at the same time extinguishes the present and all being and therewith sets the seal on the knowledge that *being is only an uninterrupted has-been*, a thing that lives by negating, consuming and contradicting itself" (Hollingdale 1983, 61; emphasis added).

In fact, this antiquarian view of "history" as a solemn and a quiet storehouse of intellectual furniture is not historical at all; it even gets in the way of developing a historical attitude. Rather, the goal of historical study should be the process Nietzsche describes as negating, consuming, and contradicting, a process we can enact through the connection of singular with collective histories. Placing oneself spatially, temporally, socially creates the possibility for history—for what we call feminist sophistics. Attitude is not identical with a purely confessional mode

of consciousness-raising, nor would we identify it with a kind of composition teaching that uses narratives of student experience as a means
of discovering the true self or a unique voice. Historicizing the self
within the social locates a singular set of experiences as a moving point
in a complex network of intertwined privileges and oppressions.

Reactions to Feminist Sophistics in the Classroom

With this view of a historical attitude in place, we would like to address
student reactions to our feminist sophistics as a classroom practice. We
had some idea of the kinds of resistance that typically surface in student
evaluations of feminist teachers (see Bauer 1990). This comment on a
graduate course taught by a former colleague demonstrates one kind of
response to the feminist teacher: "I would register the same complaint
[about your feminist pedagogy] even if you weren't short, female, and
just about my age" (see Ardis 1992). That the student asserts the importance of the criteria by denying the vividness of the teacher's age, size,
and gender suggests just how much gendered bodies are a part of the
course. The instructor glossed the evaluation as follows: "My student
identified me as [young, short, female untenured vs. male, gray-haired,
and tenured], but then insisted that the distinctions she made didn't
matter. But of course they do. . . ." The student, presumably dissatisfied
with the course, tries to erase gender and age difference, and the historical movement of women into the academy, subsuming them under
a universal standard of judgment. How does a feminist rhetorical
authority enable us to lead our students to take into account our position as bodies in history? Rather than pretending those distinctions
don't matter, as they wouldn't under a humanist paradigm, we need to
teach that differences matter and how they do so.

A second example—from a teaching evaluation someone sent after
considering "The Other 'F' Word" (Bauer 1990)—demonstrates another
kind of resistance to history and difference. The teaching evaluation
from an undergraduate in an English novel course goes as follows:

> This course was different from so many other courses in that it
> was so blatantly and unabashedly ideological, and intolerant. . . .
> In a course [such] as this, there shouldn't be false advertising; this
> was billed as "The History of the English Novel I," and it became
> "Modern Genderism and Jingoism." In spite of these points and
> opinions, I enjoyed the quantity and choice of texts; despite the
> class interpretation, they are interesting in themselves.

Citing the New Critical criteria of texts "being interesting in themselves" without the imposition of ideology or politics, this student

indicts the instructor for her "genderism and jingoism." Although we
cannot debate the actual practices of the teacher in engaging opposing
views, we are interested in the student's equation of "unabashed and
blatant" ideological presentations with intolerance. The student suggests that the expression of an "ideology" is incompatible with classroom tolerance—a universal value. But the student doesn't ask whether
tolerance would include tolerance of race, sex, age, or class prejudice.
The student then separates his/her reading pleasure from the historical
situation of the class, implying that reading those texts would have
yielded the same experience under any conditions. Further, we might
ask what it means that the teacher doesn't live up to the standard of true
advertising. The student suggests that a course in "The History of the
English Novel I" has a commonly understood content, a stable quantity,
which ought to be delivered to the student *qua* consumer. This student's
complaints are based on ethical criteria: tolerance and truth. But when
a student insists on a truth which erases the gendered body or, worse,
exploits it, as does advertising, and a tolerance that can ignore inequities based on social difference, the task of the feminist teacher then
becomes arguing for a different set of ethical standards as criteria for
evaluating educational experiences.

Perhaps it speaks to our own unawareness, but we were surprised
to face similar responses in the graduate seminar: a complaint that
feminist rhetorical authority violates the liberal principal of free dialogue, an ahistorical assumption that the classroom is a place in which
all participants are equally enfranchised to enter open dialogue. We
learned that all things are not equal when students walk through the
classroom door, since the possibility of dialogue is already reduced
insofar as white, middle-class students (of a particular age and educational level) generally feel more comfortable speaking than do marginalized students (see hooks 1991). The student who made this
complaint, identifying himself as a male feminist, criticized the anti-
liberal assumptions of the course, replicating the same move the undergraduate students had in describing the classroom as an ideologically
neutral space. In this case, the male feminist—and there were three
more self-identified but less vocal male feminists in the course—
wanted to maintain the privileged voice of liberalism, despite the fact
that specific voices, as bell hooks argued in the conference, are always
given dominance in the academy. The response suggests a displacement of gender and a denial of the body. Yet displacing gender for
women is neither a privilege nor a possibility. As one of our male
students in "Feminist Sophistics" said, "[As a man,] I am figured into
every cultural equation; my experiences are constructed and validated

for me, my self is discursively satisfying, and to some degree, for any male, the constructed, compulsory self corresponds to what we believe we feel, which is also constructed, of course." In her critique of Diana Fuss's *Essentially Speaking* (1989), hooks (1990) argues that a primary reason for allowing experience in the classroom is to counter the assumptions of a white, middle-class male norm.

Interestingly, this same student who valued open dialogue found "the historical texts least valuable" among the readings. The student's positions were particularly revealing in light of a segment of discussion from the course recorded in one of the logs we had students keep, summarizing each day's work. This discussion occurred on the day we returned to class after the conference, which took place two weeks into the three-week seminar. We were talking about Linda Brodkey's syllabus for a first-year required writing course at the University of Texas at Austin. The course, based on court cases and commentary about the Civil Rights Act of 1964, subsequently became the subject of a national controversy. Much of our time was spent on debating the politics of this course, especially because some students were troubled by its ethics. Would the instructors enter the course with the goal of signing up their students for a particular political position, or would they be teaching engagement—the development of informed opinions or "historical attitudes"—in a process of public discourse? In the discussion that ensued after the talk, Brodkey denied emphatically the former goal, calling it "identity politics," a phrase over which we argued. In the course of offering an alternative definition of the phrase, Dale Bauer used Linda Alcoff's (1988) essay to redefine "identity politics" in terms of coalition building: part of a process of group action based on provisionally held views (what Brodkey called "partial knowledge"). The student's challenge at that juncture was, "How provisional is your feminism?" The thrust of that comment could be summarized as follows: "You're pretending to be open-minded about a belief that you hold deeply and permanently, i.e., foundationally. The reason for your pretense is to defend a particular curriculum through which you hope to win students over to your cause." Bauer responded by reminding this student of her opening talk on feminism, wherein she defined it as a movement historically necessary in the current moment, but one that looks forward to a time when it would be obviated. A student who is, in a particular moment, forgetful of the historical situatedness (and situation) of feminism is also one who finds historical readings least useful. Why does one forget? Nietzsche speaks of the pain of that process of "negating, consuming, contradicting" which the historical attitude demands. In contrast, he defines happiness as "the ability to forget or, expressed in more scholarly fashion, the capacity to feel *unhistorically* during its duration" (Hollingdale 1983, 62; emphasis in original). We would describe this student's accusation as coming out of a philosophical episteme we could trace back to Plato: an ahistorical assumption that beliefs, values, ideas are fixed; a consciousness that forgets the body in history.

What strikes us most about all these students' remarks about feminism is the absence of historical perspective. Sometimes, even when students embrace feminism, they do so without entering into history. We have a concern not only about the resistances to feminism discussed above, but also about its uncritical acceptance as a liberatory rhetoric. Consider the following student's enthusiastic embrace of a new perspective:

> Life before [this instructor's] course was a closed, sheltered, and blindly following existence. (Well sort of). Cultural criticism and especially feminist criticism has not been a part of my perspective in my studies. But [this instructor] awakened me to the stifling foundations on which these schools of thought are based. I appreciated [this instructor's] feminist and cultural outlook. I have been completely sold on these schools, now believing that it is most necessary that as members of society we study the aspects which force other human beings to submit to in suffocating ways.

Though we certainly seek to persuade students to take seriously our practices and the theories undergirding them, we are troubled, here, by the rhetoric of the marketplace—the student is "sold" on feminism—and by the lack of any articulation of the new way of being with her personal history: "Life before . . . was a closed, sheltered and blindly following existence." In teaching a rhetorical feminism, we want to avoid the kind of conversion that moves a student from one blindness to another, from one foundationalism to another; this might be the "indoctrination" which critics on the right fear. The danger arises when the language of liberation simply replaces the dominant language. The new perspective gets figured through the same old economic rhetoric: to be "sold" may show the student's unconscious allegiance to a model of feminism we would subvert. The student sees no negotiation or accommodation with her or his own past position or identity, an identity that seems abandoned for the new, feminist one.

In a sense, we see a repetition compulsion at work: the student quoted here is typical of students who adopt feminism within the space of a semester, seeing it as a liberation of the self (thereby reinforcing liberal individualism) rather than as a linguistic and social orientation toward communal interaction and politics—a rhetoric in the sophistic sense of the word. The danger is that feminism—as it is reflected in some "successful" teaching evaluations (pejoratively known as "conversion narratives")—is mediated by the language of bourgeois individualism. This is feminism without a history, in short, a negation of feminist sophistics.

The solution to this problem does not lie in balance or propriety or moderation within the feminist classroom; rather, we see how feminist rhetoric can be too easily adopted and deployed without exploring personal histories and experiences. To this end, we propose that feminist sophistics can link private and public discourse, making ethics and politics the explicit content of the feminist classroom. Feminism is not just another skeptical philosophy, cynical deconstruction, or ahistorical theory, replacing the liberal humanist principles of free will, open dialogue, truth in advertising, and tolerance of other views. Instead, it posits a complicated vision of the classroom and the society in which both teacher and student are historically located in multiple social positions.

Changing Classroom Practices

We want to make a case for the importance of adopting historical attitudes for transformative work in the feminist classroom. In our course, we ask our students to write themselves into history, creating narratives not in a unique voice, but in a polylogue with past and future selves and others. We also ask students to take a stance—provisional and dialogic—adopting the role of transformative intellectual in culture. To do this means to locate one's raced/classed/gendered body in history. Our request did not take the shape of special assignments—e.g., we didn't explicitly ask students to produce personal narratives. Rather, we incorporated our ideas about historical attitude into our instructions for and commentary on student discussion and writing.

Here we respond to Graff's proposal for counterauthority in the classroom. He sees that authority in terms of structural change: other bodies and voices entering the classroom. Team teaching in itself productively mediated the teacher-student standoff for us. Because we occasionally stressed our differences of opinion and made those differences the subject of discussion, we opened options for the students beyond a simple polar acceptance or rejection of teacher authority. Further, by discussing our histories—coming to feminism, publishing as feminists, working for feminist goals in the department, encountering tensions among women within and outside the academy—we tried to enact the kind of historical positioning we sought to teach our students. We tried to model a self-reflexivity about our own changing sense of historical location and difference. This is a difference, a counterauthority, from within, generated when students confront or recreate their own histories and present locations as social beings. While Graff found himself caught between unacceptable alternatives—either aggressively destabilizing or shoring up the authority of the teacher—we wanted students to internalize conflicts among authoritative voices as part of the dialogic classroom experience. We use Bakhtin's terms to emphasize the way active engagement with language in the classroom shapes the consciousness of the participants. We understand the shared linguistic experience not in terms of communication—the delivery of message from one, or even two, subjects to others—but rather in terms of a collective activity through which we are all constantly engaged in processes of semiotic and social transformation. Instead of conversion, we hoped to see dialogic reflection in our students' writing and oral responses.

We began this transformation by asking the students to respond to any one of bell hooks's essays in *Talking Back* (1989). Using the Bakhtinian emphasis on the internalization of voices and heteroglossic potential, we asked the students to write in their own voices (plural, not singular) as students, scholars, and teachers and generated what became a heated debate about the kinds of pedagogy she advocated. The following are examples of the students' meditations:

> Yes, bell hooks' writing is an effective blend of the personal and the theoretical, of the political and the intellectual. Her writing is lucid and confrontational. It is these aspects which invite one to actively engage oneself in dialogue with her assumptions. Yet, the beginning of her essay ["feminism: a transformational politic"] troubled this reader. Why am I, the dreaded privileged white female, divorced from making any change in the world, or for understanding the complexity of domination within sex, class, and race? Indeed, it is this very struggle with the text which makes the work effective. This perplexed reader found the latter tone of the essay to be more inclusive. . . .

This student demonstrates her discomfort with hooks's feminism through the range of voices she produces. Leery of throwing herself into dialogue with hooks, she writes about "one" who can do so: "one" actively "engages oneself in dialogue with her." The resisting self, troubled by transformational politics, is styled "this reader," keeping the critical distance taught as part of bourgeois liberal discourse. We see a dramatic confrontation with a social position when she takes responsibility for her race and class through the personal pronoun "I," even though this "I" has no agency and is "divorced" from understanding. She can admit to being affected only by removing herself as subject: ". . . it is this very struggle. . . ." As she is let into the essay, the reader becomes, more sympathetically, the "perplexed reader." The multiple voices in this response present a fascinating display of Bakhtinian internalized struggle for authority.

Another student rejected the controlled voice of academic discourse for an engaged, personal response:

> "The master's tools will never dismantle the master's house." Thanks, Audre [Lorde], I'm glad you said it. And thanks bell for showing us that, yes Virginia, there really is a feminist discourse that is both academic and accessible. hooks calls into question the big "Why?" Why am I studying feminist theory and perhaps more importantly, what am I going to do about it? This week we've done a lot of "engaging in academic discourse" about stuff like feminist theories, ideologies, pedagologies, homoglossia, sparagmogentilia, phallocenthrillia, (ad nauseam) and along comes bell hooks who rattles our cage and says—hey how is this jazz at all applicable, at all accessible? In truth hooks says, ". . . how can we transform others if our habits of being reinforce and perpetuate domination . . . elitism . . . learning the white man's ways . . ." Good question. And for me anyway, it is yet another inquiry into the seemingly endless depths of my (and perhaps many other students?) patriarchially-based academic ego. Regurgitation.

This student engages easily in dialogue with black feminists hooks and Lorde, aligning herself with them over against another self: her "patriarchially-based academic ego." But even though she playfully ridicules this position, she suggests its significance by referring to its "seemingly endless depths." She ironically distances herself from that identity by bracketing out the phrase "engaging in academic discourse" and defines it with playful variations on the authoritative language of theory, but she then suggests parenthetically a bond with other students who share that location. (In fact, she was the only student who did not finish the course, although her performance in the class was perhaps the most lively and engaged. By the end of the semester, she rejected the idea of a formal paper, seeing it as just another example of "sparagmos"—the dismembering of the individual.)

A third example of dialogic counterauthority came in the following response to hooks's "pedagogy and political commitment"—from the same student who objected to the practice of rhetorical authority in our class:

Hmmm. Bell hooks says that Paulo Freire "speaks as a white man
of privilege who stands and acts in solidarity with oppressed and
exploited groups. (Darn—that's not me.) About herself, hooks
says, "as a black woman from a working-class background, I stand
and act as a member of an oppressed, exploited group, who has
managed to acquire a degree of privilege . . . [teaching] within the
walls of universities peopled largely by privileged white students
and a few non-white students." (Nope, that's not me either.) So
Freire and hooks both offer subject-position credentials which
prove the legitimacy of their radical pedagogies, credentials that
I—as a privileged white male teaching mostly privileged, mostly
white students—lack.

This student certainly locates his textual interlocutors and himself
in gender, race, and class categories, but he works from a theory of
authentic subjectivity that "legitimates" only those in oppressed positions, rejecting the Bakhtinian/Freirean notion that one can internalize
and "speak for" the oppressed through dialogic understanding. By
insisting on "subject position creditials," he makes himself a victim of
his white, male privilege and outside—or beyond—change. His own
voice remains safely within parentheses, dividing off "what's me" from
"what's not me," in a response that denies the goal of dialogue—to
internalize and *speak with* someone else textually. Only the thoughtful
"Hmmmm" holds out some hope! If we were to have worked closely
with these texts with our students, we might have pointed out to this
student the potential for alignment in his text: Freire is "white," male,
and privileged, according to hooks; hooks teaches in a mostly white
university, like our student. Here we see the elements of personal location but without a well-developed interplay of voices or sense of the
possibilities for change. We might have argued that the context for
dialogue is everywhere, unless one insists on the monolith of power
and privilege.

Our hopes for the operation of dialogic counterauthority were realized most fully in the case of another student who responded at first
with resistance to the history section of the course. An Argentine earning a Ph.D. in educational leadership, this student strongly resisted
reading Plato's *Phaedrus*. She asked why we needed to return to that
oppressive philosophical tradition, especially since we had spent some
time talking about the Sophists and their egalitarian rhetoric. But she
was impressed with Page duBois's feminist critique of Plato in *Sowing
the Body*. Having been introduced to a feminist mode of reading, this
student was willing to reexamine the tradition, i.e., to read with a new
attitude. Her shift in position had to do with more than duBois's persuasive analysis of the dialogue, however—it emerged from a recon-

struction of a personal history within the recent turbulent history of her country. In class discussion, she explored the conditions under which she encountered classical philosophy as an undergraduate. Attending the University of Comahue in 1977, she studied under a dean who had been put in his academic position by a military triumvirate which had seized the government from Perón in 1976. Because the universities in Argentina are nationally controlled, the administrations, deans, and faculty are all replaced when major changes in government occur. This junta was particularly attuned to the ideological force of education, to school as an ideological state apparatus. In her final paper, she analyzed the situation as follows:

> In terms of my personal experience, this approach [duBois' read-
> ing of the *Phaedrus*] was especially meaningful in terms of recall-
> ing how the whole program of my career as a college student was
> structured in 1977 (after the Coup d'etat in 1976) around philoso-
> phy—five required courses of philosophy centered around Plato's
> dialogues and Werner Jaeger's *Paideia*—where a clear sense of
> hierarchy, the privileged knowledge or truth of an elitist few in
> opposition to the sophists, the avowal for an authoritarian form
> of government, and the total disempowerment of women were
> legitimized.

Our student, engaged in a study of critical pedagogy driven by her commitment to liberation theology and to feminism, initially associated any reading of Plato with the politics of dictatorship. But through a reflection on her own history and changing public contexts, she was able to reassess the significance of a feminist critical reading of the classical tradition: one that opened a space for what Plato omits, sup-presses, silences in his construction of philosophy. Our Argentine stu-dent's resolution of her resistance suggests a more general solution to the pedagogical problem with history: a fusion of feminist politics of location with investment in personal/social narrative.

Conclusion

What we've outlined above is a way of teaching a political history— rhetorical and feminist—which draws on our own knowledge in these disciplines but also invites the students to a heteroglossic approach of their own. Bakhtin's term *heteroglossia* (defined as "another's speech in another's language, serving to express authorial intentions but in a refracted way" [1981, 324]) is appropriate here since it suggests how authority is not only internalized but also challenged by one's personal history in dealing with authority. In the cases discussed above, we've seen resistance and denial of other voices, voices in tension, and, lastly, revaluation through a polylogue of personal/historical voices. In our class, we aimed to negotiate authority in the classroom but without manipulating it. We did what the Sophists did as transformative intellectuals: showed students how the collective process of negotiation (see Graff, chapter 9, this volume) was part of our and their continuing encounter with histories, both public and private. Feminist dialogics becomes a feminist sophistics when the dialogue is centered on persuasive power, not to enhance the personal authority of the teacher (as in some views of the Sophists), but to work at understanding the processes by which linguistic and social power work.

As sophists we care about both power and style, but our aim is not the cultivation of "political correctness." We side with Kenneth Burke (1941), who writes that the process we advocate "would . . . violate current pieties, break down current categories, and thereby 'outrage good taste.' But 'good taste' has become *inert*" (947; emphasis in original). Burke turns the PC argument back on its spokespersons, demanding an active redefinition of our work as teachers. We offer feminist sophistics in the way Kenneth Burke proposed literature as "equipment for living," asking students to take an active role in an ongoing historical process of sociological criticism within and outside the classroom.

Notes

1. In our three-week seminar, we assigned Plato's *Phaedrus* and Page duBois's reading of that dialogue in *Sowing the Body* (1988).

2. See Sprague (1972). Some of the evidence for the Sophists' physicality comes from Plato (e.g., *Protagoras*). It might be argued that Plato, in fact, is the sensualist, as does Walter Pater in "Plato and Platonism" (Bloom 1974, 224–40). Certainly, his dialogues, not only the ones about the Sophists, are filled with sexual suggestiveness. But our reading suggests that the tension between the dramatic and dialogic Plato and his metaphysical theories (often contained within the myths like the reincarnation cycles in *Phaedrus*) can be read as a struggle to suppress the materiality on which the Sophists insisted.

Works Cited

Alcoff, Linda. 1988. "Cultural Feminism versus Poststructuralism: The Identity Crisis in Feminist Theory." *Signs* 13: 405–36.
Ardis, Ann. 1992. "Presence of Mind, Presence of Body: Embodying Positionality in the Classroom." *Hypatia* 7.2 (Spring): 167–76.

Bakhtin, M. M. 1981. *The Dialogic Imagination. Four Essays by M. M. Bakhtin.* Edited by Michael Holquist. Translated by Caryl Emerson and Michael Holquist. Austin: University of Texas Press.

Bauer, Dale. 1990. "The Other 'F' Word: The Feminist in the Classroom." *College English* 52: 385–96.

Bizzell, Patricia. 1990. *"The Praise of Folly,* The Woman Rhetor, and Post-Modern Skepticism." Paper presented at the Feminist Sophistics Conference. Miami University. June 22.

———. 1992. *"The Praise of Folly,* The Woman Rhetor, and Post-Modern Skepticism." *Rhetoric Society Quarterly* 22: 7–17. Reprint of Bizzell (1990).

Bloom, Harold, ed. 1974. "Plato and Platonism." In *Selected Writings of Walter Pater,* 224–40. New York: New American Library.

Brodkey, Linda. 1990. "Toward a Feminist Rhetoric of Difference." Paper delivered at the Feminist Sophistics Conference. Miami University. June 21.

Burke, Kenneth. 1941. "Literature as Equipment for Living." In *The Philosophy of Literary Form: Studies in Symbolic Action.* Baton Rouge: Louisiana State University Press.

duBois, Page. 1988. *Sowing the Body: Psychoanalysis and Ancient Representations of Women.* Chicago: University of Chicago Press.

Fuss, Diana. 1989. Essentially Speaking: Feminism, Nature and Difference. New York: Routledge.

Graff, Gerald. 1994. "A Pedagogy of Counterauthority, or the Bully/Wimp Syndrome." [See chapter 9, this volume.]

Havelock, Eric A. 1957. *The Liberal Temper in Greek Politics.* New Haven: Yale University Press.

Hollingdale, R. J., trans. 1983. "On the Uses and Disadvantages of History for Life" by Friedrich Nietzsche. In *Untimely Meditations.* New York: Cambridge University Press.

hooks, bell. 1989. *Talking Back: Thinking Feminist, Thinking Black.* Boston: South End Press.

———. 1990. "Is There a Place for Experience in the Classroom?" Paper presented at the Feminist Sophistics Conference. Miami University. June 22.

———. 1991. "Essentialism and Experience." *American Literary History* 3.1 (Spring): 172–83. A revised version of hooks (1990).

Jarratt, Susan C. 1991. *Rereading the Sophists: Classical Rhetoric Refigured.* Carbondale: Southern Illinois University Press.

———. 1992. "Rhetorical Power: What Really Happens in Politicized Classrooms." *ADE Bulletin* 102 (Fall): 34–39.

Sprague, Rosamond Kent, ed. 1972. *The Older Sophists: A Complete Translation by Several Hands of the Fragments in Die Fragmente der Vorsokratiker.* Edited by Diels-Kranz and published by Weidmann Verlag. Columbia, SC: University of South Carolina Press.

IV Negotiating Authority and Difference: Radical, Oppositional, and Collectivist Pedagogies

8 Pedagogy of the Distressed

Jane Tompkins
Duke University

Fear is what prevents the flowering of the mind.
                              —J. Krishnamurti, *On Education*

I

As professors of English we are always one way or another talking about what we think is wrong with the world and to a lesser extent about what we'd like to see changed. Whether we seek gender equality, or economic justice, or simply believe in the power and beauty of great literature, we preach some gospel or other. We do this indirectly, but always. What I have to say is very simple and comes directly off this point: our practice in the classroom doesn't often come very close to instantiating the values we preach.

I was led to think about the distance between what we do as teachers and what we say we believe in by Paulo Freire's *Pedagogy of the Oppressed* (1970), whose great theme is that you cannot have a revolution unless education becomes a practice of freedom. That is, to the extent that the teaching situation reflects the power relations currently in force, which are assumed to be oppressive and authoritarian, to that extent will the students themselves, when they come to power, reproduce that situation in another form. He argues that if political revolution is to succeed, pedagogy must first enact that very unalienated condition which the revolution presumably exists to usher in. Now the situation that currently pertains in the classroom, according to Freire, can best be understood through the analogy of banking. "In the banking concept of education," he writes, "knowledge is a gift bestowed by

Reprinted with permission from *College English* 52.6 (October 1990): 653–60.

those who consider themselves knowledgeable upon those whom they consider to know nothing. . . . Education thus becomes an act of depositing, in which the students are the depositories and the teacher is the depositor. Instead of communicating, the teacher issues communiques and makes deposits which the students patiently receive, memorize, and repeat" (58).

I don't think that this is the model we have to contend with in the United States today, at least not in higher education, at least not for the most part. We have class discussion, we have oral reports, we have student participation of various kinds—students often choose their own paper topics, suggest additional readings, propose issues for discussion. As far as most of us are concerned, the banking model is obsolete. But what we do have is something no less coercive, no less destructive of creativity and self-motivated learning, and that is something I'll call the performance model.

I became aware of this phenomenon some four or five years ago when I was teaching a combined graduate-undergraduate course at Columbia University. Why the realization came to me then, I can't explain. I remember walking down the empty hall to class (always a little bit late) and thinking to myself, "I have to remember to find out what they want, what they need, and not worry about whether what I've prepared is good enough or ever gets said at all." Whereas, for my entire teaching life, I had always thought that what I was doing was helping my students to understand the material we were studying— Melville or deconstruction or whatever—I had finally realized that what I was actually concerned with and focused on most of the time were three things: (a) to show the students how smart I was, (b) to show them how knowledgeable I was, and (c) to show them how well-prepared I was for class. I had been putting on a performance whose true goal was not to help the students learn but to perform before them in such a way that they would have a good opinion of me. I think that this essentially, and more than anything else, is what we teach our students: how to perform within an institutional academic setting in such a way that they will be thought highly of by their colleagues and instructors.

What is behind this model? How did it come to be that our main goal as academicians turned out to be performance? I think the answer to the question is fairly complicated, but here is one way to go. Each person comes into a professional situation dragging along behind her a long bag full of desires, fears, expectations, needs, resentments—the list goes on. But the main component is fear. Fear is the driving force behind the performance model. Fear of being shown up for what you are—a fraud, stupid, ignorant, a clod, a dolt, a sap, a weakling, someone who can't cut the mustard. In graduate school, especially, fear is prevalent. Thinking about these things, I became aware recently that my own fear of being shown up for what I really am must transmit itself to my students, and insofar as I was afraid to be exposed, they too would be afraid.

Such fear is no doubt fostered by the way our institution is organized, but it is rooted in childhood. Many, perhaps most people, who go into academic life are people who as children were good performers at home and in school. That meant that as children they/we successfully imitated the behavior of adults before we were in fact ready to do so. Having covered over our true childish selves, we have ever since been afraid of being revealed as the unruly beings we actually are. Fear of exposure, of being found out, does not have its basis in any real inadequacies either of knowledge or intelligence on our part, but rather, in the performance model itself which, in separating our behavior from what we really felt, created a kind of false self. (This notion of the false self comes from Alice Miller's *The Drama of the Gifted Child* [1983]). We became so good at imitating the behavior of our elders, such expert practitioners at imitating whatever style, stance, or attitude seemed most likely to succeed in the adult world from which we so desperately sought approval, that we came to be split into two parts: the real backstage self who didn't know anything and the performing self who got others to believe in its expertise and accomplishments. This pattern of seeking approval has extended itself into our practice as teachers. Still seeking approval from our peers and from our students, we exemplify a model of performance which our students succeed in emulating, thus passing the model down to future generations. Ironically, as teachers we are still performing for the teachers who taught us.

There is one other kind of fear that I want to mention here, institutional in its origin, and that is the fear of pedagogy itself as a focus of our attention. We have been indoctrinated from the very start, at least I was, to look down on pedagogy as a subject matter and to deride colleges of education. I was taught to see them as a sort of natural repository for the unsmart, the people who scored in the 50th percentile on their tests and couldn't make it into the higher realms to which I had so fortunately been admitted.

I remember quite vividly my introduction to this point of view. It was in an anteroom at Swarthmore College while waiting to be interviewed by a committee representing the Woodrow Wilson Foundation. While I sat there in a state of abject terror, I overheard a conversation between two young men also hoping to convince the committee's greybeards to find them worthy of a fellowship. One of them said to the other—I no longer remember his exact words—that thinking about teaching was the lowest of the low and that anyone who occupied himself with it was hopelessly beyond the pale and just didn't belong in higher education. I'll never forget my surprise and dismay at hearing this opinion which had never occurred to me before, for I had previously thought (coming from a family of teachers) that teaching was an important part of what any college professor would do. As things turned out, I subsequently embraced the view I overheard and held it as my own for some thirty years; or rather, this view embraced me, for my antipedagogical indoctrination went on pretty steadily throughout graduate school.

Now obviously, despite all this, I must have given some thought over the years to what went on in my classroom. One cannot be a total somnambulist and still survive, though I think a lot of people, myself included, have come pretty close. But I paid attention only when forced to because things weren't going well, and even then I felt I was doing something vaguely illegitimate. I used to wonder by what mysterious process others managed their classes, since no one I knew had been trained to do it and no one ever talked, really talked, about what they did. Oh, there were plenty of success stories and the predictable remarks about a discussion that had been like pulling teeth, but never anything about how it really felt to be up there day after day.

In this respect, teaching was exactly like sex for me—something you weren't supposed to talk about or focus on in any way but that you were supposed to be able to do properly when the time came. And the analogy doesn't end there. Teaching, like sex, is something you do alone, although you're always with another person/other people when you do it; it's hard to talk about to the other while you're doing it, especially if you've been taught not to think about it from an early age. And people rarely talk about what the experience is really like for them, partly because, in whatever subculture it is I belong to, there's no vocabulary for articulating the experience and no institutionalized format for doing so.

But there is one thing people do sometimes talk about in relation to teaching, and they do this now more frequently than in the past. They talk about using teaching as a vehicle for social change. We tell ourselves that we need to teach our students to think critically so that they can detect the manipulations of advertising, analyze the fallacious rhetoric of politicians, expose the ideology of popular TV shows, resist the stereotypes of class, race, and gender; or depending on where you're coming from, hold the line against secular humanism and stop canon-busting before it goes too far.

But I have come to think more and more that what really matters as far as our own beliefs and projects for change are concerned is not so much what we talk about in class as what we do. I have come to think that teaching and learning are not a preparation for anything but are the thing itself. There is a Catch-22 in the assumption that what you say in class or what you write for publication is the real vehicle for change. For if you speak and write only so that other people will hear and read and repeat your ideas to other people who will repeat them, maybe, to other people, but not so that they will do something, then what good are your words?

I've come to realize that the classroom is a microcosm of the world; it is the chance we have to practice whatever ideals we may cherish. The kind of classroom situation one creates is the acid test of what it is one really stands for. And I wonder, in the case of college professors, if performing their competence in front of other people is all that that amounts to in the end.

II

I've now made an awkward lunge in the direction of creating a different world in the classes I teach. It wasn't virtue or principle that led me to this but brute necessity caused by lack of planning. A year ago last fall, because I knew I wouldn't have time to prepare my classes in the usual way, I borrowed a new teaching method from a colleague and discovered, almost by accident, a way to make teaching more enjoyable and less anxiety-producing.

More enjoyment and less anxiety do not sound like very high-minded goals. In fact, they are self-centered. My upbringing taught me never to declare that anything I did was self-centered, especially not if it had to do with an activity like teaching, which is supposed to be altruistic. But I had discovered that under the guise of serving students, I was being self-centered anyway, always worrying about what people thought of me. So I tried something else for a change.

What the method boils down to is this: the students are responsible for presenting the material to the class for most of the semester. I make up the syllabus in advance, explain it in detail at the beginning of the course, and try to give most of my major ideas away. (This is hard; holding on to one's ideas in case one should need them to fill some gap later on is bred in the bone after twenty-odd years in the classroom). The students sign up for two topics that interest them, and they work with whoever else has signed up for their topic; anywhere from two to four people will be in charge on any given day. On the first round of reports the groups meet with me outside of class to discuss their ideas and strategies of presentation. I give plenty of feedback in written form, but no grades.

I find that my classes are better. The students have more to say in every class, more students take part in the discussions, students talk more to each other and less to me, and the intensity and quality of their engagement with the course materials is higher than usual. Because I don't have the burden of responsibility for how things are going to go every time, I can contribute when I feel I really have something to say. I concentrate better on what is being said, on who is talking, and on how the class is going—how things feel in the class.

The upshot is that I do less work and enjoy class more. But I feel guilty about this, partly because somewhere along the way I got the idea that only back-breaking work should produce good results. I struggle not to feel guilty at teaching in a way that is pleasurable to me and free from fear because part of what I now try to do as a teacher conveys a sense of the way I think life ought to be. This means, among other things, offering a course that is not a rat race, either for me or for the students. I no longer believe that piling on the work is a good in itself or that it proves seriousness and dedication. The point is not to make people suffer. The trial-by-fire model that graduate schools set is a bad one for the classroom. Education is not a preparation for war; the university is not a boot camp.

Still, there is the question of whether, in shifting the burden of performance onto the students, I'm not making them do work I'm too lazy to do myself, sending them off on a journey with inadequate supplies, telling them to go fishing without a rod or bait, demanding that they play the Kreutzer Sonata before they can do a scale. It's true that in some cases the students don't deal with the material as well as I could, but that is exactly why they need to do it. It's not important for me to polish my skills, but they do need to develop theirs and to find a voice.

When the same person is doing the presenting all the time, inevitably one line of approach to the materials is going to dominate. But when it's not the teacher who is always calling the shots, the interests of the individual students have a chance to emerge. You find out what they want to focus on, think is important, believe in. Several points of view get to be enunciated from the position of designated speaker: students get practice in presenting material in a way that is interesting and intelligible to other people; the variety keeps the class entertained and passes responsibility around so that even the quietest students have to contribute and end up feeling better about themselves.

Almost every class I've conducted in this way has had its own intellectual center of gravity. A cluster of issues, or sometimes a single problem, keeps on coming up; the students develop a vocabulary and a common set of references for discussing it. This gives the class a sense of identity, a coherence as much social as intellectual.

But I want not so much to make a pitch for this method, which, after all, is not that new, as to relay what I have learned from these experiences.

Last spring I taught a course on a subject I had been wanting to explore but knew little about: the subject was emotion. The course was offered under the rubric "Feminist Theory in the Humanities," one of three core courses in a women's studies graduate certificate program newly launched at my university. I'd gotten the idea for this course from a brilliant lecture Alison Jaggar had given entitled "Love and Knowledge." Jaggar argued that since reason, in Western epistemology, had traditionally been stipulated as the faculty by which we know what we know, and since women, in Western culture, are required to be the bearers of emotion, women were automatically delegitimized as sources of knowledge, their epistemic authority cut off from the start.

Using this idea as my inspiration, I decided we would look at the way emotion had been dealt with in the West—in philosophy, psychology, anthropology, literature and literary criticism, and religious studies (this was an interdisciplinary course both in subject matter and in enrollment). We ended by looking at examples of feminist writing that integrated emotion and ideation both in substance and in form.

This was the most amazing course I've ever taught, or rather the most amazing course I've never taught, because each class was taught by the students. Since I had no expertise in any of the areas we were dealing with except the literary, there was no way I could be responsible for presenting the material every time. So, having put together a syllabus by hook or by crook, I distributed responsibility for class presentations in the way I've just outlined. I encouraged the students to be creative in their modes of presentation, and, since this was a course in emotion, encouraged people to be free in expressing their feelings and to talk about their own experiences whenever they seemed relevant. One of the points of the course was, in practice, to break down the barrier between public discourse and private feeling, between knowledge and experience.

You see, I wanted to be iconoclastic. I wanted to change the way it was legitimate to behave inside academic institutions. I wanted to make it okay to get shrill now and then, to wave your hands around, to cry in class, to do things in relation to the subject at hand other than just talking in an expository or adversarial way about it. I wanted never to lose sight of the fleshly, desiring selves who were engaged in discussing hegemony or ideology or whatever it happened to be; I wanted to get the ideas that were "out there," the knowledge that was piled up impersonally on shelves, into relation with the people who were producing and consuming it. I wanted to get "out there" and "in here" together; to forge a connection between whatever we were talking about in class and what went on in the lives of the individual members. This was a graduate course, and the main point, for me, was for the students, as a result of the course, to feel some deeper connection between what they were working on professionally and who they were, the real concerns of their lives.

This may sound utopian. Or it may sound child-like. But I did and do believe that unless there is some such connection, the work is an empty labor which will end by killing the organism that engages in it.

The course was in some respects a nightmare. There were days when people went at each other so destructively that students cried after class or got migraine headaches (I started getting migraines after every class before long). There were huge misunderstandings, factions, discussions at cross-purposes, floundering, a sense of incoherence, everything that one might have feared. There were days when I decided I had literally opened Pandora's box and that we would all have been better off conducting business as usual. One day I myself was on the verge of tears as I spoke.

But this was also the most exciting class I've ever been in. I never knew what was going to happen. Apart from a series of stunning self-revelations, wonderful readings added to the reading list by the students, and reports whose trajectory came as a total surprise, we were led, as a class, by various reporting groups into role-playing, picture drawing, and even on one occasion into participating in a religious ceremony.

I learned from this class that every student in every class one "teaches" is a live volcano, or, as James Taylor puts it in his song, "a churnin' urn o' burnin' funk." There is no one thing that follows from this discovery, but for me it has meant that I can never teach in the old way again—by which I mean that I can never fool myself into believing that what I have to say is ultimately more important to the students than what they think and feel. I know now that each student is a walking field of energy teeming with agendas. Knowing this, I can conduct my classes so as to tap into that energy field and elicit some of the agendas.

Which brings me, in conclusion, to my current rules of thumb, reminders of what I've learned that keep me pointed in the right direction:

- Trust the students. Years of habit get in the way, years of taking all the responsibility for the class on yourself. You have to believe that the students will come through and not be constantly stepping into the breach. The point is for the students to become engaged, take responsibility, feel their own power and ability, not for you, one more time, to prove you've got the right stuff.

- Talk to the class about the class. For mnemonic purposes, we might call this the "good sex directive." Do this at the beginning of the course to get yourself and the students used to it. Make it no big deal, just a normal part of day-to-day business, and keep it up, so that anything that's making you or other people unhappy can be addressed before it gets too big or too late to deal with.

- Less is more. It's better to underassign than to overassign. Resist the temptation to pile on work. Work is not a virtue in and of itself. Quality of attention is what you're aiming at, not burnout.

- Offer what you have. Don't waste time worrying that your thoughts aren't good enough. A structure for people to use in organizing their thoughts, to oppose, to get their teeth into is what's needed. Not *War and Peace.*

- Don't be afraid to try new things. This is a hard one for me. I'm always afraid a new idea will flop. So it flops. At least it provides variety and keeps things moving. I call this the Shirley MacLaine Principle: if you want to get the fruit from the tree, you have to go out on a limb.

- Let go. Don't hang on to what's just happened, good or bad. In some situations you probably can't tell which is which anyway, so let things happen and go on from there. Don't cling to the course, to the students, to your own ideas. There's more where they all came from. (A corollary to this rule is: you can't do it all. The whole point of this approach is that the teacher doesn't do everything.)

Gay Hendricks writes in *The Centered Teacher* (1981):

> It is easy, if we view teaching as a one-way street, to fall into the trap of doing more than 50% of the work in the classroom. If we see teachers as having the answers and the students as having the questions we invite an imbalance in the relationship which can only cause a drain on teachers' energy. It is important to have a relationship with students which generates energy for *all* concerned rather than drains it. (27)

Teaching is a service occupation, but it can only work if you discover, at a certain point, how to make teaching serve you. Staying alive in the classroom and avoiding burnout means finding out what you need from teaching at any particular time. I went from teaching as performance to teaching as a maternal or coaching activity because I wanted to remove myself from center stage and get out of the students' way, to pay more attention to them and less to myself. On an ideological plane, then, you might say I made the move in order to democratize the classroom. But on a practical plane I did it because I was tired. Sometimes, I used to think of my teaching self as the character played by Jane Fonda in a movie about a couple who had entered a dance marathon to earn money during the Great Depression; it was called *They Shoot Horses, Don't They?* In moving from the performance to the coaching model, I was seeking rest.

I'm not suggesting that other teachers should adopt this particular method. There are a million ways to teach. (Nor do I think the method is suitable only for graduate students or students in elite institutions: Freire worked with illiterate peasants). What I'm suggesting are two things. First, what we do in the classroom is our politics. No matter what we may say about Third World this or feminist that, our actions and our interactions with our students week-in week-out prove what we are for and what we are against in the long run. There is no substitute for practice. Second, the politics of the classroom begins with the teacher's treatment of and regard for him- or herself. A kinder, more sensitive attitude toward one's own needs as a human being, in place of a desperate striving to meet professional and institutional standards of arguable merit, can bring greater sensitivity to the needs of students and a more sympathetic understanding of their positions, both as workers in the academy and as people in the world at large.

Works Cited

Freire, Paulo. 1970. *Pedagogy of the Oppressed.* Translated by Myra Bergman Ramos. New York: Continuum.

Hendricks, Gay. 1981. *The Centered Teacher.* Englewood Cliffs, NJ: Prentice-Hall.

Jaggar, Alison M. 1989. "Love and Knowledge: Emotion in Feminist Epistemology." In *Gender/Body/Knowledge: Feminist Reconstructions of Being and Knowing,* edited by Alison M. Jaggar and Susan R. Bordo. New Brunswick: Rutgers University Press.

Miller, Alice. 1983. *The Drama of the Gifted Child.* New York: Basic Books.

9 A Pedagogy of Counterauthority, or the Bully/Wimp Syndrome

Gerald Graff
University of Chicago

In a recent, widely discussed essay entitled "Pedagogy of the Distressed," Jane Tompkins (1990; see chapter 8, this volume) presents a vivid account of a paradox acutely felt by many teachers, me included. This is the discovery that the very intellectual aggressiveness that has qualified you to teach and earned you your status in the professional world often stifles, inhibits, or intimidates your students. Tompkins writes with special vividness about how the pressure exerted on her by the academic profession to be a brilliant intellectual "performer" works against her when she enters the classroom, widening the distance between her and her students and preventing a genuine exchange.

Tompkins's delineation of the problem is more convincing to me, however, than her way of dealing with it. Her remedy for excessive pedagogical self-assertion, in effect, is to efface herself, or at least to reduce her professional role in her class. After putting together her course syllabus (it was a graduate course, according to Tompkins), Tompkins "distributed responsibility for class presentations" to the students and removed herself from the spotlight. This enabled her to go "from teaching as a performance to teaching as a maternal or coaching activity. . . ." The point, she says, was "to remove myself from center stage and get out of the students' way, to pay more attention to them and less to myself" (658–60).

Though Tompkins's solution is attractive up to a point, it seems hardly an ideal one in the long run. I believe I would feel cheated were I to take the class Tompkins describes, and I believe students *should* feel cheated (though Duke University graduate students are no doubt more prepared to have the intellectual burden of a course shifted to them than most undergraduates). Certainly, had I read Tompkins's *Sensational Designs* before entering the course, I would want the class to be an extension of that book's stimulating ideas and would feel frustrated and disappointed were Tompkins to get herself out of the way. What is the point of taking a course from Tompkins and not some other instructor if Tompkins suppresses the very traits that have made her distinctive as an intellectual?

Something seems amiss when a person of such powerful intelligence as Tompkins feels she has to suppress this power in order to avoid suppressing her students. We go through a hard process of struggle to create an intellectual identity for ourselves in our professional and publishing careers—why, then, should we have to hide that identity when we teach? In Tompkins's case, some of the motivation seems to come from her feeling that asserting her intellectual identity in her teaching would be acceding to a kind of narcissistic masculinism. This, I take it, is why she describes her self-effacing teaching style as a "maternal" one. It is true that aggressive intellect has too often been seen as a male province, but to surrender the realm of rationality to males, leaving emotion and sentiment to be monopolized by women, seems a self-defeating response to the problem.

Nevertheless, the problem is a real one, and Tompkins's essay would not have provoked the stir it has if it did not strike a chord with many teachers. I, for one, feel I have been wrestling unsuccessfully with the problem my whole teaching career. When I first came out of graduate school and started teaching literature, I was confident of my ideas—a version of Yvor Winters's moralistic attack on modernism and the New Criticism—and eager to push them in my classes. I took up strong positions, identified myself with a cause, and stated my views "up front," leaving students in no doubt as to where I stood. Not surprisingly, I soon discovered that the effect of this polemical onslaught was to make my students all too compliant and docile. The more aggressive I became, the more passively I was received. Like the class in a famous *Doonesbury* comic strip, my students dutifully copied down my most outrageous pronouncements, and however much I assured them that conformity to my views was not a prerequisite for a good grade in the course, they acted as if they thought it was.

Naturally, I took little satisfaction in an acquiescence that derived less from the cogency of my ideas than from my students' willingness to defer to whatever their teacher "wants." This deference made me feel uncomfortably authoritarian—and it was not just that this was the 1960s, a bad decade to feel authoritarian in. Soon I found myself lecturing less, encouraging more discussion, and affecting a less assertive style. I restrained or overqualified my opinions, and I contrived to feign uncertainty even when I did not feel any. Curbing my tendency to overcontrol the discussion, I bent over backwards to encourage students to express their own reactions.

With this change, my students usually put down their pens and warmed up, a more relaxed atmosphere ensued, and my anxieties let up for the moment. But it was not long before they were replaced by another set of anxieties, for I could not help feeling a sense of unreality about my now supposedly more democratic and student-centered classroom: Were these class discussions genuine, or were my students still ritualistically giving me what they supposed I wanted, only in a more oblique way than before? And what about the intellectual level of the discussion? It was not hard to get my students to talk, but was this the kind of talk the subject demanded? Were my students making progress in grasping the subject matter, or was I simply enabling them—and myself—to feel good by letting them express themselves?

For that matter, was I even enabling them to feel good? I noticed that the less I controlled the class discussion, the more restless some students became even as others became more animated. While one half of the class welcomed open-ended discussion and eagerly plunged in, the other half hung back bored or confused, or simply stopped attending. I imagined this latter group thinking: "I'm paying exorbitant tuition fees in order to learn something from the professors, not to listen to my classmates grope in the dark." This attitude can easily be dismissed as a manifestation of the "banking" view of education whose poverty has been so eloquently pointed out by Paulo Freire (1970) and his followers. But when our students (or their parents) are banking upwards of ten to twenty thousand dollars a year in tuition and costs, their concerns about the substance of what they are learning, or even about its crude market value, are not unreasonable. In any case, reflections of this kind would sooner or later cause me to lose patience with my equivocating persona and drive me back to self-assertion. At that point, the half of the class that had rebelled against the discussion emphasis would come to life, while the half which had flourished under it would become visibly alienated.

Over my teaching career I have found myself repeating this assertion/retreat cycle often, sometimes during the same class period or even the same sentence. When I assert myself aggressively, I feel as if I am imposing my authority on students, turning them into passive receivers of intellectual bank deposits. But when I hold back I feel I am defaulting on my responsibilities, and I wonder what I am doing teaching at all. Pardon the sexist language, but in the one case I feel like a bully, in the other like a wimp.

I know that I am far from alone in experiencing the bully/wimp syndrome. In fact, I want to argue here that the bully/wimp syndrome derives ultimately from a problem of authority inherent in all teaching.

The problem remains an unresolved legacy of the educational experiments of the 1960s, and before that of the progressive education tradition. In the 1960s, many teachers sought to overcome the "bully" aspect of teaching by declaring that they were not teachers so much as "resource persons" or "facilitators," less concerned with inculcating intellectual content than with helping students get in touch with their own needs and feelings. The results were rarely inspiring, however, for it turned out that few students were equipped to take over the burden of authority from the teacher, and those who were equipped to do so were precisely the ones who were least in need of being taught. The lesson that was learned—or should have been learned—from the 1960s is that the removal of the teacher's authority, or of authority structures such as grades and requirements, does nothing in itself to help students to mature intellectually and become independent of their teachers.

Then, too, another lesson that should have been learned from the 1960s is that it is not so simple for teachers to retreat from authority, for the institutional structures they work in invest them with authority even when they try to renounce it. As John Trimbur (1985) has argued, "teachers cannot be simply facilitators, because such a role ignores the institutional context and the authority it ascribes to the teacher." Trimbur concludes that instead of attempting to deny our membership in the academic discourse community, we should "recognize the teacher's role as a representative" of that community "in order to help students understand and demystify [its] workings and structures of power . . ." (105). Instead of vainly pretending to surrender institutional power, teachers should help students acquire a share of it.

Surrendering authority is possible, after all, only for those who have already attained mastery within an intellectual discourse community. Such a surrender itself requires the sort of sophistication about abstractions like "authority" that sets the teacher apart from and above students. This is why the device of announcing to students that "there will be no answers in this class, only questions," usually does more to intensify than to quell student anxiety. The suspension of "answers" actually reduces students' degree of classroom control, since it deprives them of one of the few guideposts they bring to a class without giving them anything to take its place. Teachers have the luxury to suspend answers, since they already control the discourse of questioning that replaces the suspended answers. In effect, the questioning mode becomes a new kind of answer, and for students yet another rarefied and intimidating academic discourse.

This is but one instance of how the most "progressive" and "liberatory" classroom methods can seem as authoritarian to students as the traditional ones. The point is especially easy to overlook today amid the violent contentions of the so-called culture war, where there is a tendency to get so drawn into defending one list of books and ideas against an opposing one that we forget that, for many students, it is the life of books and ideas *as such* that is the problem, regardless which side is drawing up the reading list. For such struggling students, replacing a traditional discourse of answers with a nontraditional discourse of questioning can easily seem like the same old stuff in a new package.

In our legitimate eagerness to bring nontraditional outlooks to students, it is easy to overlook the fact that the very distinction between the "traditional" and "nontraditional" is not readily perceptible to some of them. This fact was brought home to me recently in teaching an undergraduate course in which we read a range of critics on opposing sides of the canon conflict. I noticed that some students had difficulty seeing much difference between radicals like Terry Eagleton and conservatives like Allan Bloom. For these students, Eagleton and Bloom were simply two professors speaking a very different language from their own about problems they have difficulty regarding as problems. Though the intellectual distance separating an Eagleton and a Bloom may seem immense to us, as it would seem to Eagleton and Bloom themselves, to these students it was insignificant. The very issues that make it possible for Eagleton and Bloom to clash so dramatically constitute a bond that puts them in another world from these students, the alien world of intellectual authority.

The Freirean "transformative intellectual" addresses the problem by conceiving the classroom as a "dialogue" rather than an instrument for the "banking" of traditional information. To students who are not convinced they want their consciousness transformed, however, the Freirean classroom can be as coercive as any traditional one. Freire (1970) and his followers repeatedly insist that the "thematics" of "libertarian education" must "come from the people" being taught (116), that if liberation is imposed from the top it is not libertarian education at all but just another form of "banking." If some of "the people" in a class, however, decide that liberation for them means becoming free-market conservatives—a possibility never taken up by Freire, so far as I know—such a result evidently would not count as libertarian education. Insofar as the Freirean dialogue assumes that the needs of the students naturally coincide with the outlook of radical politics, the outcome of the dialogue is predetermined in a way that will seem coercive to the many students of conservative leaning who populate American schools and colleges.

The moral of all this for me—and here is one more lesson that should have been learned from the 1960s but that progressive teachers still often resist—is that however much we attempt to turn education into an egalitarian dialogue, the superior intellectual authority of the teacher is a given that cannot be sloughed off. That is, there is an *unavoidable inequality* built into the teacher-student relationship, if only because once teachers and students are regarded as intellectual equals there is no longer any reason for the teachers to teach the students. To be sure, the teacher-student relation is constructed differently in different societies and eras. Nevertheless, I take it as a postulate that, in order to be meaningful, the distinction between teachers and students requires an assumption of hierarchy, an assumption that the teacher possesses some knowledge, competence, or skill that the student lacks.

On the other hand, radical teachers since the 1960s have made an important contribution (or have reclaimed it from the progressive tradition) in insisting that authentic education necessarily aims at *the destruction of this inequality* between teacher and student. The paradoxical goal of teaching is to render the teacher unnecessary, to obviate the authority of the teacher as students eventually become authorities themselves. In this respect, the conception of teaching and learning as a dialogue between equals has an important regulative role.

By definition, however, this self-extinguishing aim of teaching comes only at a later stage of the process (though sooner in some cases than in others), and until that stage is reached, the teacher must provide a model of intellectual authority that the student can internalize. When the process works, students gradually identify with their teacher's authority until they can appropriate it and turn it to their own purposes, perhaps even against the teacher. This is only another way of reasserting the progressive maxim that genuine learning has to be an active process, not a passive reception of information or skills.

All this has been recognized by the more thoughtful progressive teachers, who seek not to renounce their classroom authority but to *problematize* it, to call their own authority into question without abandoning or surrendering it. This double-edged position is difficult to maintain, however, for its components tend to work against one another. This is the problem that motivates Tompkins, and the problem I described myself, above, as struggling with: my classroom authority has been either too strong or too weak to be internalized by my students. When I assert myself, my authority is not internalized but passively submitted to. But when I weaken my authority, it is still not internalized because there is nothing to internalize. My struggle to reconcile these positions by shifting back and forth between them—the bully/wimp alternation—only tends to confuse my students.

How, then, can teachers problematize their own pedagogical authority while retaining enough of it to give students something to identify with and a reason for being students? Self-problematizing gestures on the part of the teacher are no solution, since these gestures unavoidably presuppose the authority they appear to give up. Of course, some teachers handle the problem better than others, and many no doubt handle it better than I do. But I want to propose here that no amount of classroom agility on the part of an individual teacher can satisfactorily resolve this problem. Teachers cannot overcome the bully/wimp syndrome by themselves—they need help from their colleagues.

To be more specific, I want to argue that the problem of classroom authority cannot be satisfactorily resolved as long as the standard unit of teaching is the self-contained, autonomous course, that is, the course without any structural link with other courses. It is the structure of autonomous courses, not any particular pedagogical style or strategy, that inevitably keeps students dependent on their teachers, regardless of how traditional or progressive a course may be in content or form.

Let me underscore the point: no matter how democratic, dialogical, and open your classroom is, no matter how much you problematize your own authority and decenter the dominant ideological structures, your students will still remain intellectually dependent on *you*, if only because there is no one else present to depend on, and most students will not yet be in a position to be intellectually independent without help—they would not be students if they were. The autonomous course, I am suggesting, inevitably keeps students dependent on teachers, irrespective of what is taught in it and how it is taught.

To put it another way, in order to displace their own authority, teachers need a *counterauthority* in their classrooms. Until students have achieved a measure of intellectual authority in the subject matter of a course, the only person likely to be capable of becoming a counterauthority for a given teacher is another teacher. In other words, what my classroom needs is someone who can stand up to me, something few of my students are yet able to do and something they are unlikely to learn to do without models of how to do it. I cannot serve as a model of how to stand up to myself—I need someone else to do it.

Here, it seems to me, is where Jane Tompkins goes astray after presenting a superb account of the problem. Tompkins correctly sees that it is her very virtuosity as a performer that silences her students. But she fails to see that getting "out of the students' way" is neither a happy alternative nor the only one available to teachers. Had Tompkins had another colleague (or colleagues) in her classroom to act as a counterauthority, or had her class been connected to another class whose assumptions (and pedagogical style) challenged hers, Tompkins's aggressiveness would have been counteracted without her having to get herself out of the way, and her students would not have been denied the model of intellectual authority—and of intellectual debate—that they need. This option does not occur to Tompkins because she assumes that teaching is inevitably a solo performance, something teachers do in isolation from their colleagues. She therefore does not see that it is not the narcissistic ethos of the academic profession that forces teaching to become an egotistical performance, but the isolation of the traditional course.

What I have called the bully/wimp syndrome, then, seems to me to be rooted finally in the isolated conditions which we have been accustomed to regarding as normal and inevitable in teaching. This is why the problem cannot be solved by the usual progressive devices such as encouraging more discussion, replacing rows of bolted desks with a roundtable, or even making the individual classroom more collaborative (as writers like Trimbur recommend), though collaborative learning does seem a step in the right direction. If we hope to empower students, we need to move beyond the privatized concern with individual pedagogical practices and look more closely at how those practices are collectively structured.

Indeed, the very use of the expression "the classroom," when what is referred to is the entire educational process, betrays a habit of thinking of teaching as something we naturally do by ourselves, with no relation to our colleagues. Our fondness for "the classroom" as an idealized image betrays the tendency to equate education with *teaching*, as if the whole process were merely the sum total of a series of unrelated classroom experiences. This reduction of education to an aggregate of individual teaching practices ignores the interrelations and conflicts of the messages conveyed by different courses. It obscures the operation of the curriculum as a system and blinds us to the way the curriculum effaces the dialogical, interdependent nature of intellectual work.

The result of such a curriculum is to make it difficult for students to recognize the terms of the academic "discourse communities" that they are expected to join. Thanks to composition and rhetoric theorists like Trimbur, Ken Bruffee, Elaine Maimon, Patricia Bizzell, and others,[1] we are increasingly aware that academic learning involves a process of socialization into a complex and often clashing set of discourse communities. It follows that an effective curriculum would need to give coherent representation to the various discourse communities of the school or the university. A disconnected curriculum cuts out the dialogues between different teachers, courses, and disciplines and erases the linkages that enable students to recognize a discourse community *as* a community.

The unspoken faith underlying the autonomous "classroom" is that students will learn to enter into academic conversations by being exposed to a series of individual professorial voices and internalizing them by osmosis. But since the conversation itself is only partially and fragmentarily represented, what students experience is not a conversation at all but a series of monologues. An integrated curriculum, by contrast, by taking the conversation itself as its structuring principle, would figure to enable students to see the different courses and disciplines *as* a conversation and thereby take the next step and enter it. In short, an integrated curriculum would promise to have a better chance to initiate students into the academic discourse community than a set of autonomous courses, precisely because it would constitute itself as a community.

For most teachers, of course, such a community is not a realistic option given the exigencies of the teaching situation. The beleaguered composition teacher, anxious about what to do on Monday morning with a group of recalcitrant freshmen, does not have the luxury to worry about anything so lofty as restructuring the curriculum—something not within the power of individual teachers to bring about in any case. If we automatically tend to visualize teaching as something that goes on in the enclosure of "the classroom," this has a lot to do with the fact that, in the bureaucratic institutions most of us work in, our own courses seem to us to be the only arena over which we can imagine exercising control.

Then, too, progressive teachers—especially those who equate all forms of institutionalization or organization with "totalizing" coercion—are especially prone to idealize the privacy of the classroom as a sanctuary in which they can radicalize their students without being subject to the panoptic gaze of authority. If the curriculum relegates these teachers to a marginal position, they find marginality preferable to being co-opted. Unfortunately, the very isolation that seemingly increases the teacher's control also stringently circumscribes that control, constricting his or her range of experience while preventing teachers from achieving collective solidarity or helping one another in their teaching.

Furthermore, the fragmentation of isolated classrooms intensifies the difficulty teachers have in making themselves clear to students. It is a commonplace that one of the factors that makes teaching difficult—especially in subjects like English, which do not possess a clear identity among nonprofessionals ("Oh, you teach English? Guess I better watch my grammar!")—is the absence of reference points that can be taken for granted. One does not know what one's students already know, and one cannot assume that they share any particular context or piece of information. Though complaints about curricular fragmentation are common enough, we do not see that "the classroom" idea is itself a powerful source of fragmentation, contributing to the difficulty teachers have in clarifying their views and in overcoming student alienation.

"But I don't need my colleagues to help me make my position clear," some teachers will protest. "I tell my students where I'm coming from 'up front' at the start of my classes. I announce frankly, 'I'll be teaching this course from a Marxist [or feminist] perspective.' My students always know where I'm coming from." The problem with this approach is not simply that, despite such assurances, students will inevitably be unsure how far it will really be permissible to challenge the instructor's declared viewpoint. There is also the fact that the drama of intellectual (and political) self-identification is impoverished when the teacher's self-identification occurs in isolation.

Consider what often happens in professional meetings and symposia when someone prefaces a comment with a self-characterization such as, "I'm a Marxist." In my experience, anyway, such a comment often draws a response like, "You call yourself a Marxist, but you sound like just a bourgeois liberal to me." (Alternatively, "You call it Marxism, but to me it sounds like Stalinism.") Though our students may question our positions, it rarely occurs to them to question the validity of our claim to represent those positions. Students are socialized to accept their teachers' self-identifications at face value—how could a teacher who avows a Marxist or feminist label be *wrong* about what he or she claims to be representing? Being socialized into an intellectual community, however, means recognizing that a claim to represent this or that *ism* is as contestable as any other claim. To assume that students need not bother with such conflicts over self-representations is to assume that students are not part of our intellectual community anyway. If students never see professorial self-identifications being challenged—something that initially only other teachers are likely to be able to do—it will be hard for them to mature to the stage of challenging them themselves. Here is just one way in which the privatized classroom promotes a rigidified conception of authority, one in which speaking subjects are assumed to be in possession of their own positions and where positions are not seen as negotiable and changeable.

I have written widely elsewhere about the depoliticizing evasion of conflict that results when the walls of "the classroom" protect teachers from the different perspectives of their colleagues (see Graff 1992). As critics both on the left and the right have often noted, there is something deceptive about a pluralism in which deeply conflicting ideologies and methods seem to coexist peacefully only because there is no arena in which they confront one another. The curriculum is free to become as radical as it pleases in the "cultural studies" sector while in other sectors remaining as traditional as ever, and the contradiction does need to be acknowledged or even noticed.

Even if such conditions preserve an uneasy peace and quiet—and this seems less and less the case—their educational consequences are harmful. A literature student today typically moves from one course in which it is taken for granted as uncontroversial that the established canon is an unquestioned heritage, to another course in which it is taken for granted as uncontroversial that the canon is a social construction with profoundly political motivations and effects. The only ones who are in a position to challenge either set of assumptions articulately, or even to point out that they are assumptions, are outside the room, in the office or classroom down the hall or across the quad. No wonder both teachers and students often feel as if they operate in an unreal, hothouse atmosphere, when courses are screened from the unpredictability of real-world debate in which the turn taken by the discussion cannot be safely controlled.

When I read a version of the present paper at the Indiana conference, it was assumed that my arguments would be accountable to peer criticism, and in fact they were stringently criticized. Yet when I enter my classroom this accountability somehow ends. The quality of my teaching may be evaluated, but my particular ideas are usually immune to criticism, as if they were my private affair. Since students enjoy no such protection, they become the site of the increasingly violent ideological contentions represented by the faculty, while lacking the faculty's power over the vocabularies in which those contentions are played out. It is hardly surprising if students protect themselves in their own way by compartmentalizing the conflicts, giving each teacher whatever he or she seems to want even when it is contradictory. After all, if the university cares so little about such contradictions that it refuses to address them, why should students take them seriously?

But why would a more collective structuring of teaching figure to change any of this? Instead of students being intimidated by a single teacher, would they not be even more intimidated by a phalanx of teachers acting in concert? This can certainly happen, and it is likely to happen unless considerable forethought is given to pitching the discussion in a way that starts with where the students are, that remains sensitive to when they lose interest, and that assigns them active roles in the discussion to prevent their lapsing into passive spectatorship. However, such self-scrutiny about the terms of academic discussions and their relevance or lack of relevance to the students' interests seems likely to be more readily sustainable the more collaborative and integrated the teaching process becomes. Key questions about why students should care about particular debates among the faculty would more readily surface as an explicit and continuing theme of discussion instead of being swept under the rug. For it is usually far easier for another teacher than for a student to interrupt and ask, "Excuse me, but what's the relevance of what you are saying? Why should anybody care about that?"

In a classroom routine that included such counterauthoritative voices, teachers would actually be able to be more aggressive in adopting "advocacy" positions with less danger of bullying their students. Questions of authority would themselves tend more easily to become part of the explicit object of study instead of being tacitly presupposed or suppressed. Such a setting, I think, would ultimately go further in empowering students than "transformative" pedagogies that do not have to answer to the conflicting pedagogies down the hall and across the quad, and that consequently figure to be as coercive as traditional pedagogies when they are structurally protected from dissenting voices. In this respect, teachers who open their courses to a dialogue with others are doing something more deeply radical and democratic, making a more fundamental challenge to traditional academic structure, than those whose message may in content be more dramatically oppositional.

Collaborative teaching in fact is becoming an increasingly popular pedagogical trend. A recently published book entitled *Learning Communities*, by Faith Gabelnick, Jean MacGregor, Roberta Matthews, and Barbara Leigh Smith (1990), usefully lays out the pedagogical and administrative rationale of these programs, which have come to be called "learning communities." Gabelnick and her co-authors define a learning community as a curricular structure that links different courses and often different disciplines around a common theme. The book describes a number of reputedly successful programs, across a whole spectrum from community colleges to research universities, exploding the myth that curricular integration is possible only in small liberal arts colleges. Thus courses in literature, philosophy, and science are linked under the theme of "Technology, Morality, and Culture." Or courses in economics, art, and sociology are linked under the theme of "The Arts in the

Culture of Capitalism." Insofar as questions of gender cut across all disciplinary boundaries, it is not surprising that women's studies programs have lent themselves especially well to learning community pedagogies, and the book lists a number of these programs as valuable models. The point of the learning community is to structure the interplay of courses in a way that enables students to become active participants in professional intellectual discourses rather than passive spectators.

One effect of bringing different fields, disciplines, and discourse communities into conjunction in the learning community is that disciplinary boundaries are displaced without being effaced, something that would result in administrative and conceptual chaos. The starting point is the established disciplines and courses, but these are put into a dialogue that enables established categories to be questioned or defended within the dialogue itself. Contests between disciplinary and interdisciplinary approaches become part of the object of study, as the terms structuring the program become a regular part of its concerns. Thus a more theoretically self-conscious discussion emerges, since major theoretical conflicts no longer fall into the cracks between disconnected courses. Like a postmodern building, a curriculum organized as a learning community foregrounds the constructed nature of its own principles and categories.

The authors of *Learning Communities* do not mention any programs in which recent controversies over the humanities canon and the politics of literature and criticism have become the theme of a learning community. But these would seem to be obvious themes to be exploited by a college, division, or department that wishes to integrate some portion of its curriculum. Given the nature of the conflict, there is hardly a course in the humanities today that does not constitute a polemical statement about the conventional canon and the politicization of literature. Even those teachers who refuse to enter the debate and claim they prefer to "just teach the books" are making their own kind of move in the debate, one that the learning community enables students to "read" as a significant choice and to compare with other options.

Needless to say, foregrounding conflicts in this fashion assumes a faculty democratically representative of the diversity of American culture, and one in which democratic rhetorical conditions prevail. If the more heterodox faculty (including the untenured) are not represented, or if they feel unable to speak frankly without fear of retribution from senior faculty or administrators, no true dialogue is possible, just as it is not possible if there is fear of admitting to politically incorrect views. Where the conditions exist for a genuine staging of central conflicts, however, and I think such conditions do exist at many campuses today, a curriculum organized dialogically seems to me more likely to generate political awareness across the student body—if not a monolithic or predictable kind of awareness—than a curriculum containing numerous politically enlightened courses whose teachers preach to the converted (or to the intimidated) in the safety of their private classrooms.

A practical model of how to use our conflicts and differences to put our courses into dialogue is already at hand in our professional symposia and conferences, which take place regularly on our campuses but are rarely utilized in the instructional process itself. In fact, the increasingly rich extracurricular culture of lectures, discussions, readings, performances, and symposia that go on daily at any campus tends to *compete with* the formal curriculum, often forcing us to choose between events that closely converge in their concerns but clash in the schedule (or that we do not even find out about until too late). Events that have the potential to provide a clarifying and energizing context for our courses go to waste, or else their potential is realized only for the handful of students who have the time and initiative to attend. Imagine a department, division, or college (or a subgroup of faculty within any of these units) deciding to suspend classes for a week, say, and hold a symposium around a theme like "The Politics of Knowledge," in which several courses come together, having chosen one or two common readings to focus the discussion. Instead of holding classes as usual, instructors and students would participate in the symposium, which would be designed to clarify major issues and controversies bearing on the subject. The event would then serve as a reference point for future discussions when the classes reconvene separately as usual.[2]

Such a strategy need not be a surrender to vulgar notions of contemporary "relevance," for a focus on present conflicts would figure to generate discussion of where those conflicts came from—the fact, for example, that earlier prototypes of the present canon conflict in literature were theological and ecclesiastical. Teaching the conflicts, in other words, entails teaching history, and for the same reason, teaching politics. Nothing is more likely to bring the political differences of teachers and their subjects out into the open than a dialogue in which those differences were kept continuously in view instead of being marginalized, as they now are, in the curriculum's radical ghetto. An open dialogue on campus in which political questions are central would ultimately be a more radical departure from the traditional norm than the establishment of oppositional enclaves.

When I delivered this paper at the Indiana conference, a feminist in the audience commented in the discussion period afterward that she for one had never had to worry about her students' being intimidated by her authority: for her as a young woman, the problem was to establish *any* authority in her classroom. Since she had little power, the possibility of her being a "bully" did not arise. She added that making conflict into an organizing principle as I was recommending might end up as just another version of the traditional male model of agonistic competition and confrontation. My response was to point out that what she had just done—calling attention to problems that I had ignored or swept under the rug—was precisely what I want to incorporate into our day-to-day teaching. It cannot happen, however, when we teach in isolation from our colleagues.

Notes

1. In addition to these writers, see the important work on discourse communities by such writers as David Bartholomae, Andrea Lunsford, Lisa Ede, and John Schilb. A useful overview is provided by Lunsford and Ede's *Singular Texts/Plural Authors* (1990).

2. I develop further this idea of "cross-course conferences" in the final chapter of *Beyond the Culture Wars*, where I also discuss a number of other recent integration experiments. Since then, the University of Arizona English department has instituted a regular series of student-run conferences in its composition program.

Works Cited

Freire, Paulo. 1970. *Pedagogy of the Oppressed*. Translated by Myra Bergman Ramos. New York: Continuum.

Gabelnick, Faith, Jean MacGregor, Roberta Matthews, and Barbara Leigh Smith. 1990. *Learning Communities: Creating Connections among Students, Faculty, and Disciplines*. San Francisco: Jossey-Bass.

Graff, Gerald. 1992. *Beyond the Culture Wars: How Teaching the Conflicts Can Revitalize American Education*. New York: W. W. Norton.

Lunsford, Andrea, and Lisa Ede. 1990. *Singular Texts/Plural Authors: Perspectives on Collaborative Writing*. Carbondale: Southern Illinois University Press.

Tompkins, Jane. 1985. *Sensational Designs: The Cultural Work of American Fiction, 1790–1860*. New York: Oxford University Press.

———. 1990. "Pedagogy of the Distressed." *College English* 52.6 (October): 653–60. [See also chapter 8, this volume.]

Trimbur, John. 1985. "Collaborative Learning and Teaching Writing." In *Perspectives on Research and Scholarship in Composition*, edited by Ben W. McClelland and Timothy R. Donovan, 87–109. New York: Modern Language Association of America.

10 The Teacher's Authority: Negotiating Difference in the Classroom

Patricia Bizzell
College of the Holy Cross

The teacher's authority to set the classroom agenda has become problematic ever since we academics began to question whether this task could be performed with so-called scholarly objectivity. That is, we now question whether decisions on what to teach and how to teach it can be made solely on the basis of value-neutral disciplinary expertise. Our questions have arisen in noticing, for example, that particular social groups have been systematically privileged—or excluded—in the construction of reading lists; that particular gender- or race-based styles of language use have been preferred—or censored—in the classroom; and so on.

These questions have foregrounded the idea that seemingly objective decisions on what to teach and how to teach it are deeply informed by the teacher's values, which, in turn, the teacher has learned from his or her own education in cultural values, education both in and out of school that includes cultural attitudes about gender, race, and social class. In short, we have come to see the classroom not as value neutral, but as value positive.

Responses from academics to this value-positive view of the classroom have been mixed. Many have reacted with alarm and with calls to somehow regain the purity of the old value-neutral venue. Often, these reactions evince particular horror at the thought of the teacher deliberately setting an agenda and, as these critics would say, imposing it on students. Other teachers have responded to the value-positive view by accepting it, by treating the value-positive condition of the classroom as inevitable, and by going on to discuss pedagogical options within a value-positive climate—these options, of course, frankly informed by the values of those who propound them.

Here, I would like to offer a brief consideration of some of the issues involved in this debate over the teacher's classroom authority, by presenting myself as a member of the latter group, those who accept the value-positive condition, and by discussing criticism of my work from members of the former group, those who seek a return to value-neutral purity.

In my recent work, most notably in my essay "Beyond Anti-Foundationalism to Rhetorical Authority" (1990), I have been attempting to define a pedagogy of persuasion, which would operate by what I call "rhetorical authority." My commitment to this theoretical problem arises out of my postmodern conviction that value-neutral teaching is not possible, combined with my ethical conviction—a conviction, that is, derived from my own learned and affirmed values—that value-neutral teaching is not desirable.

Hence, for example, in the "Beyond Anti-Foundationalism" essay, I take James Berlin to task for teaching a composition course designed to promote critique of sexism and exploitative labor-management relations while at the same time disavowing any intent to change his students' values. I argue that he does want to persuade his students to values of sexual equality and left-oriented labor relations and that he ought to admit this.

Furthermore, I argue, it would actually be more respectful of students' values to admit this because the admission invites engagement with the teacher's beliefs instead of the silent accommodation to them that characterizes, in my view, the supposedly value-neutral classroom. I argue that the values-avowing teacher is saved from being a propagandist by the extent to which he or she must draw on values shared with the students in order to be persuasive. I suggest that typically this kind of engagement will take the form of the teacher pointing out contradictions among the students' values, e.g., between pro-sexism and pro-equal human rights.

I locate the basis for this kind of negotiation among values in feminist theories developed from analysis of the personal as political, especially the "positionality" defined by Linda Alcoff (1988; see also Diana Fuss 1989). Key here is the values proponent's willingness to take personal responsibility for his or her values but at the same time to recognize their provisionality in changing historical circumstances and their openness to revision by debate. Indeed, I critique Alcoff for not being sufficiently aware of the collective nature of values formation. This provisionality and openness comprise avenues whereby the values-avowing teacher can be changed by persuasion emanating from his or her students. The class becomes an ongoing exercise in collectively formulating and revising consensus on values. Such discussion about values, I contend, is just as essential to the process of learning to do rhetoric—my main business in the classroom—as it is itself a rhetorical process.

In spite of the fact that the very point of my work here is to disestab-
lish the teacher as a propagandist, it is, apparently, my call for persuasion in the classroom and for the exercise of rhetorical authority
by not only the students, but also the teacher, that has caused me to
be attacked. Maxine Hairston, in her essay "Diversity, Ideology, and
Teaching Writing" (1992), says I am one of those "self-styled radical
teachers" (187) who "use the classroom as platforms for their own
political views" (188). According to Sandra Stotsky, in her essay "Writing as Moral and Civic Thinking" (1992), I think that my "personal
values on social and political issues should be privileged over those of
[my] students" and that their "critical distance from [my] professional
skill and expertise should be eliminated" (797). Let me now look in
some detail at this critique.

Hairston argues for value-neutral teaching. She suggests that the
only alternative to this kind of teaching is teaching in which the teacher
propagandizes for his or her personal political agenda. While Hairston
correctly identifies me as one who believes that value-neutral teaching
is impossible, she is not correct in saying that I endorse teachers'
"us[ing] the classrooms as platforms for *their own* political views," or
taking license "to promote *any* ideology" (188; emphasis added).

A more correct statement of my views would be to say that while I
do endorse teaching that promotes particular values, not claiming to be
ideologically neutral, I do not believe that these values are simply those
that the teacher prefers. Rather, I think that these values should be those
that are cherished in the society whose culture the educator is paid to
reproduce. I think, then, that there is a third alternative not mentioned
by Hairston, neither the teacher as conduit of ideas nor the teacher as
propagandist: namely, the teacher as acculturator or persuader.

I have argued (in the "Beyond Anti-Foundationalism" essay, which
Hairston cites) that the teacher-as-acculturator gains the authority to
promote particular values *only* when those values are consensually
endorsed by the society in which the teacher is working. The teacher's
authority, then, does not come from "intellectual intimidation" (188), as
Hairston fears from the teacher-as-propagandist, but rather from the
teacher's fellow citizens, including the students, who delegate to the
teacher the authority to transmit cultural treasures. This is a sort of
republican theory of teaching, we might say, with the teacher as duly
designated representative of the society.

One obvious problem with this teacher-as-acculturator model, however, is that it cannot function in a society without consensually endorsed values. If there is no consensus, there is no way to authorize the
teacher to persuade for a particular values content. Hairston, with her

emphasis on American "diversity" in her essay, perhaps wishes to convey an image of the United States as just such a society lacking in values consensus. She might say that given our lack of consensus, the only principled course is value-neutral teaching (if that were possible). Perhaps, too, this is why Sandra Stotsky argues that teaching writing as moral and civic thinking should mean only teaching students to adhere to such conventions as to define key terms, to present all sides of an issue, and to avoid stereotypes (see Stotsky 1992, 799). She too emphasizes American diversity in her characterization of the United States as a "multi-religious society" (806).

I would argue, however, that one of the misconceptions on which this view of diversity rests has to do with the nature of social consensus over values. It does seem to me that there is no total and uniform consensus over values in the United States. I certainly agree with—and celebrate—the characterization of the United States as diverse. But I think consensus is only very rarely total and uniform. What is more usual in societies, I think, is that the cultural heritage of values is a mixed bag. I think it is not unusual for societies to treasure and convey values that are conflicting or even contradictory.

Hence, one of the traditional functions of teachers-as-acculturators, as I read the history of education, has been to attempt to sort among the values and to promote those that in their judgment seemed most suited to the times. The teacher-as-acculturator, then, does not merely transmit the cultural heritage, but also selects and shapes it. One could argue that the authority to do this shaping, too, is delegated to educators by their fellow citizens. And usually, too, doing this shaping is accompanied by debates with other educators over just how the process should proceed. Current debates over so-called "political correctness" in the classroom can be understood as debates over what values from the American cultural archives most need to be foregrounded in these times.

The particular values that I would endorse in my teaching promote democratic participation in public life, toleration and appreciation of difference, and special efforts to remove conditions of inequality that prevent participation and appreciation. Certainly these are not the only values in the American cultural archive, and other educators might wish to argue with me about whether these are the values that most need to be highlighted now. But I would contend that the values for which I argue are not made up out of whole cloth by me. I inherited them; and my struggle is to pass them along to students.

Moreover, I think the debate over what values need to be reproduced should continue, not only among professional educators, but among other citizens as well, and particularly among students. The classroom in which I promote my values is not a site of monologue: on the contrary, students' objections to the values I promote, and the alternative values they propose, must be taken as seriously as their attempts to frame arguments in agreement with the values with which I align myself. This is the pedagogy of persuasion, not coercion. In this pedagogy, I feel authorized to attempt to persuade students to try on the inherited values, while at the same time the students also exercise persuasion, on me and their peers, where they see changes being needed in the cultural consensus. My students do not seem to be as malleable or as awe-struck by my professorial position as are the students that Hairston and Stotsky want to protect (see Janangelo 1992). Indeed, I can give specific examples of matters on which they have changed my mind.

In some small way these collaborative classroom practices might be seen as modeling the practices of a participatory democracy, fostering civic virtue among the students, as much as direct teaching of civic virtue values content might do.

I realize, however, that Hairston might object to the very idea of teaching to encourage civic virtue. Such a goal, after all, is much more congenial to teachers who see themselves as acculturators and persuaders, as I do, than to teachers who see themselves as the stewards of neutral truth. That Hairston sees herself this way, I infer from her contention that "all academic traditions" maintain that the university must be "a forum for the free exchange of ideas" (188). Thus, she neglects such histories of education as Bruce Kimball's, which argues that the characterization of the university as a place for the free exchange of ideas is itself value-positive, and typical of only one strand of Western thought about education, the strand Kimball assigns to thinkers he calls "philosophers," a strand that has been dominant only since the late nineteenth century. Kimball identifies at least one other strand, which he attaches to thinkers he calls "orators," who have argued since classical times that education may and must transmit the values its supporting culture endorses most highly.

I also infer Hairston's value-positive preference for value neutrality from her apparent preference for the writing course that teaches "nothing but" writing. This appears to mean that only mechanics, coherence, and process issues can be discussed. That is, we could say to a student, "You need one more example here to make this argument about killing all homosexuals really convincing"; but we could not ask the student to consider whether an argument for killing all homosexuals was not contradictory to other values the student might hold, such as that all human beings are created equal and endowed with unalienable rights to life, liberty, and the pursuit of happiness. Stotsky seems to leave herself in the same position with respect to the kill-all-homosexuals argument; indeed, she would not even want to invoke the Declaration of Independence against it, as she believes that "collectively determined moral thinking on social and political issues," of which the Declaration is presumably an example, is "a major source of [the] corruption" of "the common good" (797).

I suspect, however, that for Hairston, what is most controversial about my position is not that I openly avow that my teaching is value-positive; rather, I think she may be most offended by my calling for an inspection of the heretofor largely neglected *content* of writing courses, what the students are reading and writing *about*, and my saying that we should use this content to promote particular kinds of negotiations over values, rather than simply seeking, for instance, to analyze essays as models of so-called "effective" introductions, "vivid" descriptions, or "well-organized" arguments. My renewed attention to what might be called the literary content of the writing course is, indeed, subversion of the composition curriculum in some circles.

The selection of materials now for the typical composition course might almost be called defiantly random. It has tended to begin from the teacher's choice of a topic she thinks her students will want to write about, such as "childhood," and then the collection of readings on this topic selected because they are moving; because they present varied ethnic, social-class, and gender perspectives; because they are the teacher's personal favorites; and so on (see my 1991 essay, "Power, Authority, and Critical Pedagogy"). I think, instead, that we should choose course material that centers around some moment in American history when different groups were contending for the right to interpret what was going on. Text choices could then be what Mary Louise Pratt (1991) has called "literature of the contact zone," texts in which the language users are specifically trying to negotiate difference, to cross or blur socially constructed boundaries, to communicate across them, etc.

Moreover, the investigation of texts negotiating difference should not proceed simply in order to catalog the various aesthetic and rhetorical strategies generated in dialogue, for the purpose of aiding students in interpreting and modeling them. To these worthy exercises I would add an explicit goal to help students and teachers become more competent citizens of a multicultural democracy, which would mean that they would have to be willing to negotiate difference themselves. They would not be allowed to remain within one comfortable enclave, whether defined as privileged or victimized.

Of course, I can never know to what degree the values I promote reflect an American consensus. I am trying to suggest that it is only in the process of seeking agreement on values that consensus can be formed; and consensus kept alive by a rhetorical process is always provisional, always regarded as open to change. This, of course, means that on my own account, above, my authority as a teacher-as-acculturator is provisional, shifting, and changing. But I agree to this deal; this is one reason, indeed, that I advocate a pedagogy of persuasion. This pedagogy is intended to be part of this rhetorical process of negotiation over values.

All this checking, of course, will do me no good if Hairston and Stotsky are correct in thinking that there are no values Americans can agree on. But I hope that there is still some kind of national will to live by the values I want to promote, in spite of the clamor of separatism and hatred of difference coming from so many groups these days. Perhaps the new emphasis on multicultural education can be seen as an expression of this will, an attempt to refresh the inclusiveness of democratic values. I hope so , if for no other reason than that I cannot resolve myself into a singular special-interest-group identity. My "self" is complex, contradictory, and changing. Therefore I want to believe that my multiplicity can be voiced, that Americans as a group valorize the negotiation of difference.

I realize that what I express here is merely a hope, one for the possibilities of dialogue and of collective action which could make some inherited American values more likely of embodiment in our social order than they have been up to now. But I, for one, especially after Los Angeles, cannot enter the pedagogical situation without hope.

Works Cited

Alcoff, Linda. 1988. "Cultural Feminism versus Post-Structuralism: The Identity Crisis in Feminist Theory." *Signs* 13: 405–36.

Bizzell, Patricia. 1990. "Beyond Anti-Foundationalism to Rhetorical Authority: Problems Defining 'Cultural Literacy.'" *College English* 52: 661–75.

———. 1991. "Power, Authority, and Critical Pedagogy." *Journal of Basic Writing* 10 (Fall): 54–70.

Fuss, Diana. 1989. *Essentially Speaking: Feminism, Nature, and Difference.* New York: Routledge.

Hairston, Maxine. 1992. "Diversity, Ideology, and Teaching Writing." *College Composition and Communication* 43: 179–93.

Janangelo, Joseph. 1992. "Pedagogy of the Rich and Famous: Stories of a Class(room) Struggle Near Beverly Hills." *Iowa English Bulletin*: 87–96.

Kimball, Bruce A. 1986. *Orators and Philosophers: A History of the Idea of Liberal Education*. New York: Teachers College Press.

Pratt, Mary Louise. 1991. "Arts of the Contact Zone." *Profession '91*, 33–40. New York: Modern Language Society of America.

Stotsky, Sandra. 1992. "Writing as Moral and Civic Thinking." *College English* 54: 794–808.

11 Collective Pain: Literature, War, and Small Change

C. Mark Hurlbert
Indiana University of Pennsylvania

Ann Marie Bodnar
West Mifflin, Pennsylvania

I. Mark and Ann

We began this article on February 24, 1991, the first day of the Allied land attack on Iraqi forces in Kuwait and southern Iraq. We were trying to concentrate as we wrote, but like millions of people around the world, we felt drawn to our TV sets to keep up with CNN's coverage of the war and, like a handful of people, to peace demonstrations in the city of Pittsburgh and at Indiana University of Pennsylvania.

We were convinced that our country's actions were wrong, but we weren't entirely sure about what we could do about them. So, we kept teaching, studying, talking, reading, and writing—trying to understand. We, an English professor and an undergraduate student, each tried to focus our activities toward learning about this war and, in the specific context of this article, how its approach generated an atmosphere of often intangible fear and tension in a literature classroom we and other students shared in the fall of 1990, the time America drifted further and further toward armed conflict with Iraq. We hope that by telling our story about what we did and felt and said on the eve of this war, we will be better able to learn how to teach and study in protest to the next war.

II. Mark

One day in June, 1990, just weeks before the Iraqi invasion of Kuwait, I was browsing in the Borders bookstore near Pittsburgh. I was picking books for EN 121, "Humanities Literature," an introductory course for non-English majors that I would be teaching in the fall. One of the books I discovered was *The Graywolf Annual Six: Stories from the Rest of the World* (Walker 1989). As I looked it over, I thought, here is a collection of literature from other nations that my students will enjoy and that they need to read. Because it is interesting, it will encourage my students to become, as one of the stated departmental goals for EN 121 suggests, 'lifelong readers' of literature, and because it is an international collection, it will help students to consider the relation of their lives to the lives of people living, as the title suggests, in the *Rest of the World*.

I teach at Indiana University of Pennsylvania, a state institution in western Pennsylvania. Many of my students are from Pittsburgh and Philadelphia. Some are people of color. And some are not Christians. But the majority of them are from rural areas and small towns. They are often first-generation college students. They are often the daughters and sons of the working and lower middle classes, of miners, laid-off steel workers, and small-town, white-collar employees. They are generally from families who hold to "traditional" American values: loyalty, family, hospitality, belief in Jesus, in America, in the value of competition, in hard work, and in seeing a job through to the end, as well as the importance of knowing when talk should end and action should begin. The pervasive *ethos* of the students who come from IUP's neighboring areas seems to be one that the Ford Motor Company sells—in order, obviously, to sell cars. In a television advertisement, Ford explains to us that western Pennsylvanians hold native sons like Joe Montana—and, yes, only white sons are named—as heroes because western Pennsylvanians have a commitment to achievement and quality. In it, we see western PA students demonstrating their devotion to the American team spirit by participating in school sports—or cheering for those who do. Life is complete within the carefully scripted confines of this commercial. It has family, football, and Fords. It does not include any reason for developing one's understanding of the world beyond the safety of the neighboring hills and homes. It does not supply a reason for reading a book like *The Graywolf Annual Six: Stories from the Rest of the World*.

So, in the fall of 1990, as war with Iraq began to seem inevitable, I was assigning the fiction by Iraqi and other Arab writers in *Stories from the Rest of the World* in order to encourage my students to explore the meanings of their lives in relation to the lives of people in the Middle East. In keeping with my usual practice, I asked the students to write, in their notebooks, their immediate responses to whichever of the stories interested them or about which they had questions. These responses would become the starting place for further class writing and discussion.

Far and away most of the students wrote about "From Behind the Veil," by Dhu'l Nun Ayyoub (1989). This story is about a young woman, Siham, the young man who is infatuated with her, Ihsan, and the traditions of their country, Iraq. Ihsan, and particularly Siham, strain against the traditions of courtship and dress that constrict their behavior and, at the same time, they revel in the social roles that traditional behaviors and dress offer them. They are children of the present, defining their roles as they are caught between the past and the future and in the contradictions such time warps create. One student, Mary, wrote that she could identify with Siham, who is "faced with one of the problems that many teenagers face—whether to hold on to tradition (obey parents) or conform with peers." Another student, Carol, saw that her strategies for gaining social power paralleled Siham's own use of the veil. She described how she herself uses "masks"—"pretenses"— with other people so that she will be able to hide the feelings of insecurity she endures in social situations.

Another story by an Iraqi writer, "Clocks Like Horses," by Mohammed Khudayyir (1989), is a story of a man who visits an old watchmaker to get his antique pocket watch repaired. For me, it is a delicately woven tale, consisting of the narrator's careful attending to the physical details of his world and the stories of the watchmaker, and exploring, along the way, the nature of time and our place within it. But many of the students wrote that they really didn't understand or enjoy "Clocks Like Horses." Some thought it was just a simple story. Some said that "nothing happens in the story." And some said they couldn't understand it because they didn't understand the culture that produced it—I would find out more about this as the semester progressed.

After the students had interpreted and discussed these stories and others, I asked them to describe, in their notebooks, what they had made of the connection between what they had been reading and talking about and what was going on in the Persian Gulf.

Some of the students wrote that these stories show how all people are the same "wherever they are," so war is irrational. Some said that they indeed feel tremendous prejudice against Arabs but that reading these stories helped them "to stop and think" about their prejudices. Some claimed that while they feel great prejudice against Iraqis, this hatred did not affect their reading of the stories. A very few admitted that they weren't keeping up with events in the Middle East and therefore didn't have an opinion about the impending war (one student even mistook Iraqis for Iranians in her journal writing). One said that he thought that "in this class, we all look too deep" into what we read and into the cultures of the authors. One said that she currently has friends in the army and did not want to think about the Middle East situation because to do so causes her to worry. And some even wrote that these stories showed them that the view that all Arabs are cruel, greedy, religious fanatics is a false one. One complained that Americans "are looking at all Arabs as an ominous 'thing' that must be fought." And some expressed gratitude that they were finally getting at least a small introduction to Arab culture. But as one student put it, "I now have a greater sympathy for those involved in the Iraq conflict, but I still have an American attitude and I don't want my friends or family suffering. Therefore, if we must take action against Iraq to end this conflict, then I believe it is the right thing."

At the conclusion of this in-class writing, I asked the students to share their notebooks with their colleagues and to write responses to one another. When one student, John, accused Americans of being culturally illiterate, Stephen wrote the following response:

> I believe you are right. We Americans are swayed by the media and big business, but we have the responsibility to look for the true image of other cultures. We must not accept what we are told and question and find out the true story.
>
> But, I am a little biased because I am in the Army. I begin my active duty in January, and there is a good chance that I will end up in Saudi Arabia. I do not have a distorted view of the Iraqi people, just their leader. What he has done is inexcusable. And, contrary to many Americans, I believe that we are not over there just because of the oil. Yes, it is a big part, but we are also there to try and restore the Kuwaiti government. I don't know if you feel we should be there or not. I would just like to say that if you like to drive your car, or buy new clothes, enjoy any comfort in this country, then we need to protect our interests in the Middle East.

As I reread Stephen's entry, I can't help but admire his skepticism about the stories told to him by business and government. But I also wonder why he doesn't articulate what I see as an incongruity between his call for greater understanding of other cultures and the "bias" he has because he is "in the Army." Why doesn't he ask, I wonder, whether oil and "comfort" are, possibly, among the reasons for American interest in the Persian Gulf, or from deploring the fact that few Americans enjoy the comforts of big oil profits? How does one suggest to him that discovering "the true story" about another culture, as if there ever were one such story, might lead him to critique American foreign and domestic policy more forcefully? In broader terms, how does—or should—a teacher ask a student to recognize incongruities that would, potentially, shake the student's deepest convictions? And what of the teacher's convictions? How does a teacher ensure that his or her pedagogy is designed in such a way that the incongruities that he or she is living are also available for discussion and change? And how does one manage to do all of this when one is faced with the deep irrationality of an imminent war?

I don't have the answers to these questions. But since I became a professor here at IUP in 1986, I have been trying to develop pedagogies which foster collectivist-like social relations through collaborative reading, writing, and evaluation activities (Hurlbert 1989; 1991). My goal is to join with students in critiquing the competitive social relations that many students and teachers enact, the prejudiced thinking that many of us do, the harmful actions that many of us take, and the oppressive culture in which all of us live. To accomplish this in "Humanities Literature," I assign readings in contemporary writings that dramatize how American conceptions about gender, aging, sexuality, and race affect the ways in which all of us treat other people.

But in the fall of 1990, I felt a growing frustration with my own inability to do anything significant on my students' behalf. What is the good, I kept asking myself, of my politically oriented pedagogy, when my country continues to behave in what I believe to be politically irresponsible ways? All educators, I suppose, sometimes feel uncertainty about the effectiveness of their teaching. But the fall semester brought new and different and deeply disturbing misgivings for me. In light of the events in the Persian Gulf, I felt, more then ever, an obligation both to speak my politics and to intervene, in ethical ways, in the "intersubjective space" of my classroom (Benjamin 1986). For me, the events of intersubjectivity, the everyday classroom experiences, are moments in which students and teachers think and act to liberate or oppress and, when the pedagogy is working, to understand how and why they do. The goal, as utopian as it sounds, is to extend liberatory impulses and initiatives and to transform oppressive ones.

As the fall of 1990 progressed, I heard small numbers of women and men in my classroom voicing unpopular opinions about war with Iraq. I saw that I had to create a classroom in which they wouldn't be silenced by those students who were calling for war—especially as their call for peace was, I believed, potentially liberating. At the same time, I also needed to create a classroom in which the students arguing for war wouldn't be alienated. If that were to happen, the class would be a failure. No communication would transpire. No one would be changed.

I also felt great anxiety—and I know that many, many teachers around the country were feeling something similar, even if they were describing it in other ways—because each day that my students talked about war with Iraq was another day in which the insanity of war came closer. I felt that my classroom was suddenly opening up, unfolding itself, and extending, as untenable as it may sound, far beyond the confines of Indiana University of Pennsylvania. The context of my teaching seemed to grow beyond my ability to see it. In the context of international affairs, each of my student's actions took on unnaturally large implications. The threat of war made me hypersensitive, constantly looking for the significance of every word and gesture. My pedagogy, I thought, suddenly had to become—if it ever could—influential in national—even global—spaces. I kept asking myself if I weren't overreacting, and the answer I kept coming back to was "yes—and no." The time before the war with Iraq was a tense one, a compressed one in which, for those of us opposed to the war, Washington and Baghdad both failed to offer responsible leadership. As both countries' administrations rushed forward along what seemed to be irrational paths, it seemed necessary to scream as loudly as possible that our governments were failing us. As war approached, I became more and more angry and frantic and determined that my students and I needed new ways for interpreting the political realities of our country and world and for taking actions based on these understandings—and all in one semester.

I suppose that some people might say that it is not my job to meddle in the lives my students lead outside my classroom. And to some extent, they might be right. I'm not trained as a therapist or group counselor. But in a troubled world, teachers can't avoid responding to—perhaps intervening in—the events influencing the pains, needs, and, even, as James Berlin (1991) has demonstrated, the subjectivities of students. Trying to isolate one's self from one's students is one of the surest ways to shut down genuine dialogue. In his study of ethics and the evaluation of human actions, Garrett Thomson (1987) reminds readers of some deceptively simple and important points: that one way to evaluate the ethics of an action is to determine the extent to which it attends to the needs of another and improves the quality of the other's life. Thomson argues that not taking an appropriate action in the presence of a person in need is to harm them and to act unethically. We teachers cannot, in this perspective, turn our backs to the blindnesses and silences that society forces on our students—and on each other.

III. Ann

I saw Stephen one night during an intermission of a campus performance by comedian George Carlin. We said hello, and since I knew that he would be graduating at the end of the semester, I asked him what his plans were. He said that he would be starting four years of active duty in the army. I thought of the impending war. I felt shocked and sickened with fear. I thought, "He doesn't deserve to die."

I didn't hide my emotions very well, and Stephen began to justify why war may be the only answer in the Persian Gulf. "Hussein," he said, "must be stopped. He is too explosive. If he gains control of the oil wealth in that area, our domestic freedoms may be in jeopardy."

I was taken by the compassion in Stephen's voice. This man believed what he was saying. I thought, just for a moment, "If only I could hate him. If only he were just some damn warmonger." But I knew he wasn't.

I remembered how I was in a group with Stephen and Bill, a fraternity brother,[1] when we wrote about David Leavitt's short story, "Territory" (1991). Stephen wrote: "I just can't understand why someone would want to be lovers with a person of the same sex. Homosexuals don't really bother me. I would just like to understand why."

I wrote a long entry back to him. Part of it read: "I think that trying to understand why a person is what they are isn't the issue. I think the issue is respecting people as people and in the case of homosexuals, respecting them for being different from society's norms and for finding love in the people that they do. Maybe this will help in your understanding of why."

Just by Stephen's response I could tell that he was interested in what I had to say. He was open to different perspectives. I never got the feeling that he was a violent person. Bill, however, was absolute in his attitudes. I remember that I also read his entry on "Territory," and he said, flatly, that homosexuality was wrong—and disgusting:

> I hated this story and found it to be repulsive. I'm sorry to say that I hate people like that. The reason why is that I [am] homophobic and it [homosexuality] goes against all that society stands for and goes against the basic laws and values.
>   That's all I am going to say on this subject. I will keep my ideas to myself. Personally I resent Mark making us or me read this.

Bill didn't want to be challenged. What he believed, he believed was right, and he would use aggression, I think, to defend his thinking. He seemed to enjoy putting down people in class who disagreed with him. I also wrote a long response in his notebook, concluding with:

> My concern is that you don't use your dislike for homosexuals to oppress them. Let's face it, you will probably end up being in a position of power one day. You could very easily end up discriminating against homosexuals rather than dealing with them as human beings.

I think you didn't give the story a chance. It wasn't merely about a homosexual male, it was about a family: a mother who was overbearing and a son who, in turn, was insecure, and a father who was never there. Maybe you'll be able to one day reread it with this in mind.

Ann

I learned from this exchange. I could see how Stephen respects people even though they may have different attitudes. He sets an example for how to listen to others, as he shows in the response he wrote in Bill's notebook:

> Bill—I agree with Ann. People tend to hate homosexuals because they do not understand them. We are afraid of what we do not understand. Homophobes tend to hate homosexuals because they have some of the same feelings and they are scared to deal with these feelings. Try to have an open view and not worry about people's sexual preferences. Sex and sexual preference is too over-stressed in this country. We need to focus more on people's attitudes and what they contribute to society.

Stephen

Talking with Stephen is different from talking with Bill. Bill scares me. He is not tolerant of others or open to the opinions of others. He makes me want to fight back. And I'm afraid of those times when I oppressively force my views on others, rather than working to maintain an open dialogue. I'm afraid that out of frustration and a lack of energy I'll lapse into a state of intolerance and impatience that is similar, in some ways, to Bill's. I'm afraid, ultimately, of the consequences of such behavior.

IV. Mark

Once, when I was teaching another section of "Humanities Literature," a colleague suggested that, in keeping with the collectivist impulse of my course, I ought to have students select literature for the class. So, half way through the fall 1990 semester, I asked the students to discuss, first in small groups, and then as a whole class, what novel they would like to read (my plan was to have them create a short list, discuss it, and then vote for the one that we would all read). This process took several days. In small groups, the students came up with selections and synopses of novels from popular literature such as works by Stephen King and Sidney Sheldon; books of movies they knew: *Flatliners, Flowers in the Attic,* and *Lord of the Flies;* and books they studied in high school:

Catcher in the Rye and *Lord of the Flies,* again. Ann suggested *The Bluest Eye* by Toni Morrison, and another student, Kim, suggested Marge Piercy's *Woman on the Edge of Time.*

To begin the whole-class discussion that followed this initial list making, I explained how I pick literature for this course. I explained how I want the reading to reflect American society so that we might, to some degree, understand it and work to improve it. I described how I try for a balance in gender, race, and sexual orientation in my curriculum, and I asked them if they should consider the same criteria in picking their novels.

Bill answered, "Why should we care about the color of an author? I mean, why can't we just read a book for enjoyment?"

Pam, who once announced during a class discussion of *Brown Silk and Magenta Sunsets* that she was not prejudiced, added, "Yeah. I'm sick of always reading things by blacks. Let's just read something we want to read."

At that point Ann said, "But I think the issue is that literature by women and people of color has been excluded from university and high school curricula for a long time."

The class discussed Ann's point for fifteen or so minutes. A couple of students agreed with her, but most argued that the length of the book and the fun they would have reading it should be the primary criteria for their selection. When Ann added a further dissenting opinion, Pam turned to a male friend sitting next to her and laughed.

After class, Ann came into my office. She was upset.

"Sometimes I just don't understand other students," she said. "I'm a sociology major. I think we should be reading literature by women and people of color in college. I know the others don't agree with me. Sometimes I think I should just keep my mouth shut in my classes. Maybe I'm the one who's wrong."

I was surprised. The day's class discussion had been intense, even (as I explain below), at times, hurtful, but Ann struck me as a someone who would speak for change even in the face of resistance. I wondered what I could say to her. That I'm thankful that she is in the class? That she says things that I agree with, that I think *need* to be said? Should I tell her that she has more of a chance of influencing her colleagues' thinking in class discussion than I, a teacher, do? And is it ethical of me to let her speak for my positions in class discussions? Is that what I'm doing? Am I using her? Would telling her that her thinking is socially responsible be tantamount to choosing sides in class? And aren't the sides already chosen? Would it somehow undermine the rights of other students in the class to say what is on their minds if I tell Ann that I agree with *her*—even if some of what the others say is naïve at best and racist and sexist at worst? Is my desire to protect all of my students' right to speak becoming a denial of my own social responsibility? I thought for too long.

"No advice?" she asked.

"No advice." Though I quickly added, "But it seems to me that you have a good mind. You ought to speak it."

Every one of the students expressed sadness about that class in their notebooks. Yes, I was aware of the tension in the room. The students seemed to split into cliques—groups who supported the suggestion of one person over another as much as supporting the idea of reading one book over another. Worse, the students demonstrated a lack of respect for each other—something they rarely did. Despite my admonitions, they interrupted each other. They made faces at the suggestions of books and supporting arguments made on behalf of them. The class had become something ugly. They had split into factions—teams—and each was determined to win at all and any cost. When Sidney Sheldon's book *The Windmills of the Gods* (1987) was finally picked, its supporters' faces and body language expressed smug satisfaction, while other individuals and groups expressed disappointment—even exhaustion. Everyone was glad that the "battle" was over, but I was afraid that we were all, somehow, losers.

And I was not alone. The students expressed profound disappointment when they wrote notebook entries after voting on *Windmills*. How, they asked again and again, could there ever be peace in the world if they couldn't even pick a book peacefully? Why, they wondered, were they so unwilling to listen to each other, to respect each other's opinions? And why, some of them asked, was the class as a whole so willing to pick a book because they thought it would be easy? I asked myself questions, too. Why, for instance, did the students avoid books that would make them think about cultural biases just when government and the media seemed to be promoting war with Iraq? And what would it cost them—not to mention the people of Iraq—if they avoided challenges to the industrially and governmentally managed visions of themselves and their culture that they are bombarded with every day? How, I asked myself, could I allow them to pick a Sidney Sheldon novel and miss the chance to read something that might cause us all to study the oppressions in which we take part and which, I believe, hurt us all? Yet to not allow them to choose the Sidney Sheldon novel would violate the students' right to choose reading materials. How was I to negotiate this dilemma? (For more on my response to my students' reading, see section VI, below.) And how was I ever going to keep this divided group in constructive dialogue? One student, Sarah, pointed out how deep the gulf in the classroom ran:

> We got into quite an argument. There's a few frat boys in the corner who will probably never grow up. [But t]here are some people in the class who are very intelligent. And I wouldn't mind sitting around with them in a coffee shop discussing theology, philosophy, politics, and human nature. They seem like very good thinkers (they're mostly women for some reason, too).

After the class picked *Windmills of the Gods* and wrote and shared their notebook entries with each other in small groups, I asked the students to discuss, as a whole class, why they had chosen it. Its proponents basically reiterated their opening arguments. They said it was light reading and that they were entitled to some fun.

"Besides," Bill added, "everything we read doesn't have to be about politics and discrimination. Not everyone wants to read that stuff all the time. You see, Mark," he said as he turned in his seat toward me, "we don't need a revolution in America."

As I paused to think about how to respond to Bill, I realized that we only had a minute and a half left in the period. Do I demonstrate to Bill, I thought,—*and in a minute and a half*—where he and I disagree and where we might agree? Do I try to explain the deep division between what I think he means by the word "revolution" and what I mean by it? Do I run the risk of losing Bill, someone who resists critical examination of his thinking—someone who has the potential to do great harm to others? No. In this situation I have to trust the value of a full semester of dialogue. The class was ending.

I could see pain on Ann's face.[2]

V. Ann

I remember that class, too. It's as if it's been burned into my memory.

A discussion began about the literature we chose to read and the significance of literature to culture. Literature—as Mark's course seemed to be saying—could be used as a means of creating social change. Mark said, during this discussion, that in one paper written for the class, two students—a European student and I—had made the point that in some areas of the world a revolution—a political movement toward social change—could be started with a poem. In some countries poetry and literature still have that power. The discussion moved from this to how education meant something different for the students of the People's Republic of China who were involved in the pro-democracy movement than what it does for the students in our classroom. Education, like poetry, could move the students of Tiananmen Square to work to change their country in dramatic ways. It was at this point that Bill said, "You see, Mark, we don't need a revolution in America."

After class I made the following entry in my notebook:

> I'm discouraged, upset and in fear of the future. I can't believe Bill said today in class that we don't need a revolution. I was ready to explode when I heard this. How can someone say such a thing so mechanically? I was going to say something in response . . . but I refrained because I had such a surge of negative energy, such hate. I have to admit I was disappointed in the class's response, and also in Mark's. It is really frustrating because I thought Mark would kick into the radical politics, but he didn't. What is the role of the instructor? Merely to pacify the masses or to challenge them? Which is it? Why didn't Mark inject some challenging politics? Most of my fellow classmates have probably never heard of the Green movement. It's not fair. I feel that I'm not fulfilled, that there is still part of me that needs more. I'm scared because the entire university system appears to be falling apart in the sense that universities are becoming high-tech havens rather than places for obtaining higher knowledge. I read Bowles and Gintis's book, *Schooling in Capitalist America* [1976], last year. In it, they explain how with the demand for more education, the quality of education is deteriorating. This is in part what they refer to when they talk about the credential society that we live in.

As I reread my journal and look back on that class, I can feel again the sting and frustration I felt that day. How do I convince people that there is a need for a revolution in America? I believe that a nontraditional form of "revolution," one that doesn't use weapons and violence, is possible. I see it as a massive movement to alleviate social injustice. In a sense, a "revolution" is occurring every day. For instance, every time a teacher goes into a class and challenges students, small but significant gains are made, gains that lead, maybe, to larger ones. Education is one key to this revolution. The problem is that the truths that I am talking about aren't taught in our traditional history, literature, or philosophy courses. They are the ideas that bring to light the realities of white, male oppression.

When I first began to study sociology, I was caught up in the persuasive rhetoric of professors who talked about the need for a radical revolution that would transform society. But this traditional notion of "revolution" is too abstract and unrealistic for me to work toward on a daily basis. So now a new idea of revolution guides my living. Rooted in the radical ideology of Marxist professors, it focuses on the evolution or transformation of an individual's mind so that he or she will take action for creative change whenever that individual sees social injustice. In this perspective, a revolution continues to happen every day that people struggle against oppression and social injustice.

The amount of time our class spent picking a novel to read was symbolic of the intensity of the struggle among people with opposing viewpoints about oppression and injustice. For instance, I supported the suggestion that we read Marge Piercy's *Woman on the Edge of Time* (1976), but others didn't. In fact, one student, Jason, said that he had read the book for another class and found it confusing. I think, however, that some of the students rejected it because it was written by a woman about a Latina.

VI. Mark

Yes, Ann's memory of how the class's discussion moved from literature to revolution to education and to the roles each plays in the others is right. I remember that Bill's comment at the end of it, that we don't need a revolution in America, just floored me.[3]

But I had other shocks that semester, such as when I heard the class's response to *Windmills of the Gods*, a book I thought of as a fairly typical spy and romance thriller about how a cloyingly wholesome political science professor from America's heartland, Mary Ashley, becomes the monumentally successful ambassador to Romania.

We read *Windmills* near the end of the semester, and, quite frankly, I expected the students to critique its suspense and romance plot for its predictability and its mass media version of political intrigue for its shallowness. But most of them did neither. Sharon wondered if the cloak and dagger politics, spying, and murder in *Windmills* were a reality. Margaret believed they were, and proceeded from this position to criticize our government loudly: "I believe that this [intrigue] does go on, more than what we know, which isn't much. I think our whole government *sucks*. It cheats us, lies to us, and keeps things from us that we have a right to know." Another student, Carol, even saw Angel, the infamous assassin in the novel who turns out to be a woman instead of, as we are led to believe, a man, as a mark of feminist ideology: "The mean, cruel, merciless, intelligent, cunning assassin is portrayed in a lot of other books and movies as being a man. Why can't it be a fat, ugly woman?" Several students even argued, as Barbara did, that the character of Mary Ashley marks a feminist breakthrough: "I also found it refreshing to see a woman in power. It's a shame more women are not put in these positions of power and prestige."

Now I can't claim to know exactly how the students arrived at these interpretations of *Windmills of the Gods*. But I do know that I suffered a critical blindness about the value of these readings. I completely missed the point that a Sidney Sheldon novel was itself an important artifact from which much could be learned about culture. I failed to see that my students could take a book like *Windmills of the Gods* and replicate the acts of cultural interpretation and political critique that we had been doing all semester with texts such as Bharati Mukherjee's "The Management of Grief" (1990), a story of how a Canadian Indian woman suffers the grief of losing her family to political terrorism, or Tim O'Brien's "The Things They Carried" (1990), a story made up almost entirely of lists that give a sense of the soldiers' experiences in Vietnam. My students had discovered, with little or no help from me, how mass-media literature contains sources for critical thought. One student, Diana, a poor cousin of a "Reagan Kid" (see Janet Zandy's chapter in this volume), even connected American actions in the Persian Gulf with American agendas elsewhere in the world: "Our government is so corrupt that when we blame other countries of something, we are just as guilty as they are, but we keep it hidden better than they do."

Perhaps the students were aided in their reading, as strange as it sounds, by the impending war. Perhaps the tension they felt from the coming of war was leading them to politicize their reading and to attend to the larger cultural implications of this book. And why not? Every night the news was full of Iraqi and American political rhetoric. But why hadn't I done as my students had? I watched the same news and read the same book, but I hadn't reached any sort of critical understanding of culture as a result of reading *Windmills*. All I had done was reiterate predictable complaints about silly media fantasy. But my error went deeper than that. Instead of being pleased that my students were making social critique as a result of reading a popular novel—instead of being happy that they were teaching me how to read—I wondered how, after nearly a whole semester's work, they could misinterpret *Windmills of the Gods* so badly. Why weren't they more critical of it? Why were they trying to make something out of nothing? (I wonder how they read my silences in class. At least they didn't abandon their readings to suit my response.) I violated, in other words, principles which I want to guide my teaching: respect for the students' right to interpret, to make meaning—and their right to enjoy reading. (There is, after all, no good pedagogical reason to censure the pleasure of reading. The problem is that students like Bill, who had argued for *Windmills* because it would be fun to read, and I weren't able to accommodate each other's choices, each other's joys. I think that too much went unsaid among Bill and other students and me. Because of the compressed time of the university schedule, but also because of the tension of prewar time, certain statements were just too personal, too complicated, and too volatile to share if we were to live together and learn anything from each other.)

I think the answer for my own critical blindness lies in the tensions of the semester (and because misreading a class is always possible). With the war looming large, it was entirely possible to feel that there was no time for mistakes—for misinterpretation. Precisely because I was working within the irrationality of a time in which war was quickly approaching, I could not bear to think that my students were being duped, yet again, *and in my class*, by the popular media. I was distracted from the events of my classroom by world events, and the price was that I didn't teach as well as I could have. Now, in retrospect, I know that the study of any literary artifact is also a study of culture. I can even ask if the peace movement I supported was as much a cultural artifact, an effect created by popular media news coverage, as the reasons for going to war in the first place—but not in the fall of 1990, or in the spring that followed. The irrationality of the time had, in other words, fully invaded my thinking.

Of course, not all of the students arrived at such a positive interpretation of *Windmills of the Gods*. A few students, such as Kathy, read it this way:

> [I]t left no room for thought at the end, except for one: So what? It was an empty feeling for me as a reader. My mind didn't race with the thousands of questions that I usually get after reading something like "The Management of Grief" or "The Things They Carried." When I read them I asked why did the author write this piece? What special symbolism does it hold? Why did I feel anger, hurt, and depression after reading this? None of these questions came to mind after reading Sheldon.
>
> I think [this] reading has shown me how blind I've been to my own reading. My views have broadened not in just what I read, but in how I read as well. When I read contemporary literature, I can learn about the author, his/her style, his/her ideas, but also about myself, society, and the world. This is scary. It causes me to think about my life. When we read some of the poetry, such as "Three Mile Island" [by Maureen Owen], I learned about Three Mile Island. I had no idea what this was about until I started talking with others in this class. How blind a life we all lead. And I seem to be right in the mainstream of this. I'm not up on current affairs in the world. I've always thought, "I can't change the world, so why bother worrying about it?" Well, now I look at what I read, and I can see how I've buried myself in fantasy. I've always read mysteries, science fiction, and romance novels—maybe now its time to wake up and read some of the more meaningful things.

As I read Kathy's response, I heard an accurate description of a discomfort that many of my students and I were beginning to feel, no matter whether we enjoyed the book or not. In a world bent on violence, we could no longer afford such luxuries as uncritiqued actions or high-toned academic thinking. We had reached a time when we each needed to find that literature—and why should it be the same literature for all of us—that would help us see "how blind a life we all lead."

Despite the disagreements over the selection and interpretation of *Windmills of the Gods,*—or the other arguments we had—the students of "Humanities Literature" learned to live with each other. Certainly, one reason they got along was that they spent so much time working together. There were forty-seven of them, sitting twice a week in this large circle, looking at and listening to each other. Their confidence in each other grew as they developed honest, yet considerate, ways for talking about contemporary literature and the society it represents. In addition, most of them shared the same fears about speaking in any class, let alone one this size. Commiseration, in this case, bred respect. They were also constantly reading and responding in each other's notebooks, becoming active in each other's learning. This brought them closer to each other as they learned to expect suggestions from their peers that would push them to do better work. I also hope that the model of behavior that I try to set for them in class also had a positive effect: I try to listen. I try not to interrupt. When I respond in a discussion, it is with the intention of making sure that everyone's point of view—even those with whom I disagree—is carefully weighed. In addition, the students knew that they weren't in competition for grades in this class. I used no curves when grading, and papers could be written collaboratively, in small groups, or by the whole class and for a shared grade (more on this, below). It is also fair to say that they liked the class, and this helped them, in many cases, to develop a fondness for each other. As one student wrote in her notebook: "Sometimes, no matter how down I feel, just seeing someone from this class on the street can brighten up my whole day." But certainly, the impending war, again, supplied another, particularly powerful reason for their learning to live together. While they were not united in their levels of commitment to going to war with Iraq, all of the students were, to some degree, suffering. By the end of the semester, it seemed that everyone was writing or talking about someone they knew in the Persian Gulf. The war was fast becoming something no one could avoid, something that, like it or not, we were all in together.

The Soviet theorist Fyodor Vasilyuk provides a way of understanding just how much my students and I were—and still are—at risk. Vasilyuk (1988) explains how the problems that each of us faces in our local and international lives can counteract the creative nature of our experiences. For instance, we can lose the "psychological possibility" (195) for action in a world that overwhelms us with either difficulty or ease (95–172). In either case, we may fail to face that which makes a situation "critical," that is, what requires our creative efforts toward a solution. When this happens, Vasilyuk argues, we fail, as peculiar as it sounds, to experience. We fail to work for solutions to mundane and world problems, and we fail to construct the "new selves" necessary for life in the new circumstances or worlds we imagine and work for (164). Experience can lead us, in other words, to produce a future, rather than to merely repeat the past or endure the present, the people we were or are. But in order for it to do so means, in the specific case of my students and me, that we face the ways in which the impending war affected our lives and the lives of others around the world. And while my students felt as powerless as I did to stop a war that seemed inevitable—it was, after all, "George Bush's war"—they seemed to realize, if not to some common degree or with complete unanimity, that they had to begin to rebuild America by starting with their own lives. Perhaps they felt that if they worked to address prejudices in themselves, the world would somehow decide not to go to war.

Or so it seems to me. For the final paper of the semester, the students created a plan for writing a "book," a project that helped them to deal with one of the chief factors that makes their experiences critical—their own stereotyping and prejudices toward others. After much productive discussion, the students followed up on a suggestion that one of them made early on, that they interpret photographs of people on city streets—which Stephen volunteered to take in downtown Pittsburgh—and then analyze their interpretations. In this way, they argued, they might discover what "predispositions"—a term that one of them introduced to the class and that all of us began to use—they bring to the act of interpretation.

I liked the idea.

"What," I asked, to see whether the students had critiqued their own plan, "does interpreting a photograph have to do with interpreting literature?"

David immediately said, "When we read, we create images from written text. Here we are creating written text from images. We are turning the reading process around."

Perhaps, I thought, by doing this project we will learn something about how we interpret the world. Perhaps we will also learn how the interpretation we all do in every moment of our lives sets up the social relations we enact with others. Perhaps we will think about the kind of social relations we *want* to enact and *need* to enact in a troubled world. And perhaps my students and I will remember what we learned in this class before we act to harm others.

The students proceeded to organize each chapter of the book *You Can't Judge a Book by Its Cover* around a photograph. They divided themselves into groups (mostly of four) and chose one photograph to study. Then, every student wrote part one, an "interpretation" of the subject or person of the photograph (usually a first-impression description of the subject, followed by imaginative projections such as the subject's occupation, values, future, etc.), and part two, a critical reading of the stereotypes and other predispositions that he or she exhibited in part one. Then, the students exchanged their writing with one other person in his or her group and wrote part three, a critical response to the other student's first two sections.

One of the photographs was of a young African American male standing on a street corner wearing a baseball cap, jacket, blue jeans, and sneakers. One student—and all of the students contributed their work anonymously to the book—wrote in part one that, on first impression, "I figured . . . he is waiting for someone to approach him to buy drugs. . . . If he is selling drugs, it's because he's been laid off from his job at the garage for over a year now." In part two, this student examined his/her narrative and suggested that the prejudice he/she exhibited was probably the result of growing up in a small town, where there were "few blacks . . . So naturally the usual jokes were passed around, and I fell into the usual small-town prejudice trap." This "prejudice trap" also caused this student to create confused, racist, and sexist readings of the literature for the course. Writing about P. J. Gibson's *Brown Silk and Magenta Sunsets* (1986), whose main character, an African American named Lena, achieves material affluence by the end of the play, this same student wrote:

> I found myself returning once again to my stereotypes. First of all, I couldn't picture Lena as a black woman. She was rich, eccentric, a white woman, I thought. I did find a contradiction in my thoughts, though, because the thing that made me see Lena as black was how she ran after Roland and abandoned her child. Then the thing that made me see her as white was also this. It seemed more like something a white woman would do—abandon her child. Black women are usually depicted as very child oriented. They want to protect their "babies." Another stereotype perhaps? A media influence maybe?

Another stereotype? Well, yes. But at least this student is questioning the discourses he/she creates in the world. Or, as this student wrote about the effects of this class:

> After I have completed [reading a] piece of work, I look at how it makes me feel. In doing so, I examine my thoughts more closely and many of my biases and stereotypes become evident. I ask myself, "What makes you feel this way and why? Is it fair of you to make this kind of judgment?"

These may be good questions to ask, but they did not prove to be enough. As one of this student's colleagues wrote in his/her part-three reading of the other student's work: "The writer's assessment of [his/her] stereotypes is fairly accurate. But that does not excuse them." Clearly, the students were holding themselves to a high set of standards, and they were learning the centrality of critical thinking in any attempt to live up to these standards.

But perhaps the greatest lesson the students were learning was that we—they and me—have to *do* something with critical thinking. Thinking critically about our experiences, to borrow again from Fyodor Vasilyuk, restores the psychological possibility for action, and the possibility for action carries with it the social responsibility to act. Or, as one student wrote in his/her part two: "Before this class, I took a lot for granted; now I question 'why?' I must also go a step further and try to change those beliefs that are wrong."

VII. Ann

At first I was disappointed with the idea of our class book. I thought it was an inappropriate, unsophisticated project for a college literature course. I thought, "What about a more scholarly endeavor?"

In retrospect, however, I think it was meaningful for me and my peers. Many of us learned about our personal prejudices. Many of us also learned that working collectively within an open dialogue is beneficial to all involved and is a much more humane and empowering experience than the competitiveness that we are constantly taught in other classes.

This experience of working together to produce this work typified a major theme of the course, but I didn't quite understand the complexity of this until I read an article entitled "Critical Thinking: Strategy for Diversity," by Edwina Battle Vold (1989), for a sociology of education course I was taking. In this article, Vold claims that nurturing dialogue in a classroom leads to critical thinking: "Learning to deal with perceptions and to conduct serious discussions about beliefs and different behaviors is best developed in a climate where open dialogue is encouraged" (126). Unfortunately, teachers and students often stifle this kind of interchange because one's values can end up being challenged in the wrong ways. But our class book provided us with an opportunity to question our beliefs and actions by using knowledge developed by the class itself. In this way, we could challenge each other in positive ways and start to create new beliefs and actions.

VIII. Mark

The final exam was one of the most moving experiences of my teaching career. The semester was over, and on campus, people's excitement about Christmas break was combined with anxiety about a war that seemed inevitable. In fact, I can read the level of my own emotions in the following essay question that I wrote for the exam. Reading it now, I cringe at how crudely fashioned it is; at the same time, I recognize that through it, I spoke to my students with directness and authenticity. As it turned out, most of the students opted to respond to it, even though they could have picked others:

> Everyday, at some point during the class, I consciously felt that I was teaching against the backdrop of an impending war between our country and the country of Iraq. This made me nervous, tense, and anxious. I felt that somehow I had to teach against this war. (But I should also tell you that I didn't pick the stories we read by Iraqi and other Arab writers for this reason. My book selection was made before August 2 and Iraq's invasion of Kuwait.)
>
> As I told you, I could lose friends on both sides. (I can imagine students of mine meeting each other from different sides of the war, each determined to kill the other. I know that the size of the armies and the desert would make such a meeting nearly impossible, but I, like all of you, have deep reasons for worrying.) Were you also thinking about the threat of war during this class and your reading of the Iraqi and Arab writers? If so, how did your thinking affect your reading? Did you feel the nervousness I talked about? Did you feel anger for the people of Iraq? If so, how did your anger affect your reading? Did you feel a need to speak out for or against this war in your notebooks and in class? Has the reading for this class affected your current thinking? If so, how? If not, why?

Their answers to this essay question varied greatly. A few students, like Cheryl, wrote in a way which suggests that "Humanities Literature" hadn't encouraged her to compare her present suffering to that which she or others might endure in a time of war:

> I never gave the idea of war much thought other than in English class. All these feelings surfaced in class, and I feel that I drew back in class discussions in fear of saying something to upset myself. My girlfriend was married recently & shortly after, her

husband was activated— not even enough time for a honeymoon.
This whole ordeal has affected so many lives already that maybe
it is time to start battling it out.

It would, I suppose, be easy to condemn Cheryl for failing to value
the lives of American service people and Iraqi citizens over her girlfriend's honeymoon, but that would be a useless gesture. Such condem-
nation wouldn't foster dialogue or recognize the values of Cheryl's
culture. Rather, I would like to ask her: "What is the meaning of a
honeymoon compared to the meaning of your girlfriend's husband's
life? Or to the lives of thousands of Iraqi citizens?" But I *can't* ask Cheryl
these questions. Sadly, this was a case of a semester coming to a close
just when I was finding the right questions to ask and the right students
to ask them of. Posing and hearing the right questions at the right
times—especially in a class of forty-seven students and in the middle of
an even fuller teaching load—often seems an impossible task. And so
students like Cheryl pass through our classrooms and our lives.

And there was George. I wish we had had an opportunity to talk
about the meaning of his "willingness to fight an enemy" he didn't
"know anything about":

> Since I am in the Army Reserves, the possibility of going to the
> Gulf was always on my mind. In the beginning of the semester I
> really didn't worry about it too much. About a month ago I started
> watching the news every day to keep informed. My best friend
> was activated two weeks ago. It seems now that it is only a matter
> of time before me and my other friends will be called to active
> duty. I have become so nervous now that every time the phone
> rings I think it is going to be my company commander.
> I don't think, if given the chance, that I would have spoken out
> against this war. I don't have strong feelings either way about the
> war. I guess that what I'm most concerned about is my willingness
> to fight an enemy that I don't know anything about.

As I reread these finals, it seemed that many of Ann's colleagues
were beginning to feel the need for making arguments that were at least
similar to ones that she had been making all along. On his exam, Martin
confessed that, at the beginning of the semester, he had "wanted to be
Rambo and destroy them" [the Iraqis], but that he now realized that he
hadn't been "thinking rationally."

Another student, John, wrote:

> As I was reading *Stories from the Rest of the World*, I kept won-
> dering if my friends [in the army] would be alive by the end of the
> story. I thought that one of the [Iraqi] authors could be the one to
> end one of my friends' lives.
> After reading "From Behind the Veil" one would get the im-
> pression of innocence [in the characters]. However, my mind

made me think that the innocence that was depicted is not real. I guess this probably distorted some of the meaning I got from the story.

Certainly, John was thinking about how life beyond the classroom is connected to what we read in profound ways. He was also thinking about how hard it is to change the predispositions influencing our reading and actions. But perhaps most importantly, he was learning that there are options to war: "At first I thought we should blow the shit out of Iraq . . . but now I can't feel hatred at all. We need to fight for World Peace, not war."

And then there was Judy, who realized even more directly than most how critical thinking leads one out of the hatred that is part of the American character:

> Our country is turning into a country of Iraqi haters. It's good that at this time we've been exposed to writings by Iraqi and other Arab writers. I will go home this week to my small, rural town where everyone thinks we should blow up Iraq—it's such a small country—the people aren't worth anything. It's not true. I've never thought of myself as an Anti-war peace demonstrator—but deep down a little part of me is. I feel for the people on both sides of this thing. It's been beneficial (I think) for many of us to read these stories. Hopefully now, and as the crisis blossoms, we won't have or feel the predispositions and stereotypes that the media/country is presenting to us.

As for Stephen, who was about to begin active duty as a 2nd lieutenant, he said the same things at the end of the semester that he did at the beginning. His commitment to the military line is deep. His belief in America right or wrong is strong:

> The possibility of war in the Middle East did not affect my reading. Actually my reading affected my thinking of the people. My belief was that all Arabs were fanatics. They would do anything for their cause, even die for it. But after reading the stories I can see that not every Arab is a fanatic. They are feeling, emotional people also. They are not barbarians.
> I am all for a peaceful solution of the problem. But I am willing to fight also. The people who are against the war need to understand that if Iraq could control most of the oil in the world they would not have it as good as they do now. Saddam is nervous now about getting into a war with the U.S. He would even be more nervous if he knew that all Americans were behind the government and are for the use of force in the Gulf.

Despite what he wrote, I knew Stephen to be a quiet, decent man. This is what troubles me. How do quiet, decent men reach the point where they say, "But I am willing to fight . . ."?

IX. Ann

I said good-bye to Stephen at the final. I wished him luck, but it seemed superficial. I just wasn't sure what to say to him, so I asked him where he would be stationed.

He said it would be overseas and seemed excited at the prospect that he might get more money with an overseas commission. We hugged each other and he left and I returned to the exam. That Stephen had mentioned the "money" he would make weighed heavily on my mind. I assume that money was one reason he enlisted in the first place. Stephen was another victim of an insane system.

X. Mark and Ann

The war with Iraq ended with massive Iraqi casualties, few Allied casualties, and General Schwarzkopf as a national hero. War was *in* again. The American public still seemed to view the war as a sporting event that the U.S. won handily. HBO and CBS, to name only two media giants, televised special musical tributes to the troops. The same corporations that avoided connecting themselves to the war effort when they were uncertain about how American public opinion would respond quickly associated themselves with the "new patriotism." Even financially troubled New York City held the largest parade in history to honor the soldiers. War looked safe and noble, possible to do and win. War appeared, as paradoxical as *this* sounds, to be a viable alternative for ending world conflicts.

Ann: Once, when we were talking in his office, Mark said that people seem to be in a lot of pain which they try to avoid. The pain, he said, stems from the fact that we are living in a democracy that is failing us. I see what he meant. We don't get the things that American society guarantees, even though we are taught to believe that we do. I think that many people know this, but they ignore it. I saw my classmates avoiding this pain. On numerous occasions, Pam objected to reading material by African Americans. In fact, when we were picking a novel to read, Pam said that she didn't want to read something that would confuse her or make her think too much—that would cause her, as she said, "to bust her brain." Thinking about this, I wonder what right anyone has to cause someone like Pam to confront her pain. I come from the school of thought which says that if you want to make significant change, people need to be made uncomfortable, to feel pain, first.

For example, they may have to feel the pain that a racist act causes before they will feel compelled to stop repeating it. But I am beginning to wonder if we are capable of really facing the pain we both cause and suffer.

Mark: I can't stop thinking about the final exams. Kathy connected a news report she saw on TV about the psychological problems faced by Vietnam vets with the problems faced by Henry in Louise Erdrich's "The Red Convertible" (1991). Making this connection helped her to appreciate the meaning of her life by moving her to look for patterns and larger truths. Kathy took, in other words, an important step in developing the "personally grounded historical attitude" that Dale M. Bauer and Susan C. Jarratt describe (see chapter 7, this volume). Kathy wrote, "I'm living in a time period others will be studying about in the future. My children will be questioning me about Kuwait just as I question my parents and grandparents about the wars they lived through." By placing herself within history, Kathy is recognizing the critical nature of her experiences.

And then there was Karen's exam, with its haunting ending: "Something must be done soon, and I would be willing to be active in any type of student protest that would happen on campus. I will also consider writing to the government. HELP—DO YOU HAVE ANY SUGGESTIONS for students to show they care about our situation in the Middle East?" These were the last words she wrote for our class.

On her final, Ann wrote, "There seems to be this overriding veil that people wear most of their lives. I can't help but think of the short story by Dhu'l Nun Ayyoub, 'From Behind the Veil' (1989). The type of veil Americans wear is one that shields out the pain and injustices of our society."

And I can't help but think of Frank, a student who tore the pages dealing with Arab writers out of his notebook (I quote it verbatim) before he handed it in to me to read, one of the only students who chose not to write about the war on the final. Consider one notebook entry he did not tear out. It deals with David Leavitt's short story "Territory" (1991): "Territory. The territory stirred up a lot of my feelings. I hate gays; first I don't see how anybody could be gay, but this fag in the story was brave because he had enough nerve to bring his lover home to meet his mother, that was the only thing that was brave about that guy. I also didn't like the part where they almost got caught screwing. I hated this story; sorry but I did. I don't have anything to write." How is any teacher going to reach Frank in fifteen weeks and in a class of forty-seven students?

On her final, Ann also wrote that, as a peace activist on our campus, she needs to remember that "the beauty and challenge of starting a movement is figuring out a way to tap as many people as possible" in order to get them actively involved.

Ann: Karen asked for help on the final exam. My first reaction upon hearing this was one of excitement. There was a group of students on campus who formed a group that protested America's involvement in the Middle East and eventually the war. There were numerous activities that we, the group, did. The prevailing focus was to teach peace. (We are currently planning to set up a campus peace center that will work to prevent other wars from occurring in the future.) Then I had to stop my excitement. The group's intentions were appropriate—but they were also *necessary.* And they are small. The Persian Gulf crisis is only a small part of the picture. To really help may mean changing a life-style—attempting to live a life with vision and *commitment* to change. The excitement wears off. Our plans for the peace center won't be accomplished easily. I can't help but feel overwhelmed. Helping to change things shouldn't be so painful.

Throughout my "Humanities Literature" experience, I was tor-mented by the idea that I am an "elitist" or a "snob." All too often I would get frustrated by what I thought was the narrow-mindedness of my fellow classmates (to some degree they *were* narrow-minded). It was so easy, so safe for me to disregard what my peers were saying. In that sense, I was narrow-minded, too. I never took the time to try to figure out why my classmates thought as they did, even though I took a tremendous amount of time analyzing myself. It was all too easy for me to think that I am correct for thinking as I do. I do still believe that I am an "elitist," in a sense, because I believe my politics are correct for me and the world—if we are to have a humane world. At the same time, however, this makes me feel guilty, because, I ask myself, "What right do I have to force my beliefs on others?" I guess the question I have to answer is how do I hold the views I do without oppressing others? I realize that I don't have to be antagonistic to communicate a point. I can explain my perspective as a choice. I don't have to force my thinking on someone else—and I don't want the "system" to force ideas on me. I didn't get truths in this class in ways that I expected or even wanted, but I did get "prepped" for being a "facilitator of change." I didn't "get" radical politics, but I did gain skills that help me be more humane and understanding. My idea of "revolution" has been altered. I no longer look for quick change.

Mark: As I took part in peace demonstrations and saw the counterde-monstrations, I, like others of my generation, felt again the painful confusions of the Vietnam years. There was, too, the tension caused by anonymous telephone calls, with their implied threats against my fam-ily, that I received after attending a demonstration that was filmed by several of Pittsburgh's TV stations. And there was the feeling of per-sonal responsibility for what my country was doing, for the global space to which my classroom was connected. And there was the frus-tration I tried to keep to myself—the brew of tensions I felt when some of my students—and I'm embarrassed that I thought this way—didn't agree with me about America's role in the Gulf. No doubt these stu-dents saw me as being on "the other side." I didn't want them also to see me as another enemy to be faced, as someone they no longer wished to talk and listen to (and I certainly didn't want to think of them in those terms, either). So, I found myself struggling with how to maintain my commitment to democratic teaching methods while, at the same time, maintaining my commitment to speak out against the impending war whenever I could. In reality, I wanted to sway as many of my students as possible from their readiness to support the sending of American troops into combat.

In fact, I have to face the fact that in the fall of 1990 my teaching did not accurately reflect the principles that I thought guided it. I pretended to a democratic and dialogic pedagogy, but the reality was that, even though I tried to offer all of my students equal opportunity for speaking their minds in my classroom, I was not completely open to having my own thinking changed. Looking back, I probably would have been relieved if someone had made me see why the impending war was just, but I also recognize that I would have resisted that argument in any number of ways. I might have said that there is no just cause for killing another human being, or that we Americans have no right arming Middle Eastern war machines and then staking out a moral high ground for ourselves. No, I wasn't open to changing my mind. As Washington's pro-war rhetoric increased, I became more and more convinced that my stand on the war was correct.

If I ask myself how I read the experience of "Humanities Literature" today, I would have to say that it mostly troubles me. For one thing, I can write and talk about this most recent American war as if it were already a historical event of the past. As I reread some of this article, I cringe at some of the emotions I felt, as if they were part of some time buried deep within the anonymity of a personal past—as if all of this is something that happened then and that I am writing about now. This worries me. If the raw power of the events and death of the most recent war are already to become part of the past, part of the abstraction of war, then I don't see how we will avoid another war. I know that each and every American can't walk around each and every day feeling the issue of war as intensely as he or she might have when America was actually going to war or was at war. But I think that the resistance to war that I and others felt in 1990 and 1991 is not as focused now that the war is in the past and not in our every waking thought. I honestly fear that we Americans are already condemned to a next war. This may not be an original thought, but I trust that many educators teach with it, to lesser and greater degrees, buried within them everyday.

I also see EN 121 as an example of how hard it is to teach about—let alone endure the reality of—any charged social issue. Looking back, I know I was careful not to use my power as teacher to silence those students with whom I disagreed. But I'm not certain—in light of how I thought and felt at the time—about the ethics, let alone the possibility, of my being able to open my own mind to change about the deaths of thousands of Americans, allies, and Iraqis. I hope, of course, that my pedagogy promotes democracy, collaboration, dialogue, and even collectivism, but none of these principles means that I should leave my subjectivity outside the doors of my classroom. Henry Giroux (1992) has written convincingly that we English teachers—all teachers—need to become moral voices in our classrooms and communities. I agree. But I'm not sure how teachers should teach in a time—or after a time—of a social issue as emotionally charged as war. There are no easy answers. Knowing that didn't make the painful reality of fall 1990 any easier to endure.

Perhaps what worries me most about fall 1990—and I don't think that I'm giving in to an uncritical cynicism—is that even though my students and I participated in a time when we could have *dramatically* realized the costs of personal comforts and local prejudices, we didn't. It seems that the tensions surrounding events in the Persian Gulf, America, Pittsburgh, and at Indiana University of Pennsylvania, even the seemingly trivial act of picking a novel for the class to read, marked a crack in the American *ethos* that my students and I live each day. A fissure opened, and we were divided over our willingness to face the pains others must endure so that we might be comfortable, the pains we are willing to inflict on others to ensure our way of life. Then, as quickly as it opened, this crack in the American *ethos* closed and "healed," and we went back to the sleep between wars that makes war possible. It was a critical time, but it was so full of confusion and propaganda that we lost an important opportunity to learn all we could about local, national, and world politics; economics and cultures; and the forces that drive America and the world toward war. We lost, in other words, a chance to become united in a call for change, in a determination that things would finally be different.

But if I look for hope in all of this, I find some. Perhaps the demand my students made in *You Can't Judge a Book by Its Cover* for all people to control their prejudices was the best they could do in fifteen weeks and from within the government's pro-war media blitz. Perhaps *You Can't Judge a Book by Its Cover* can even be read as a collective declaration of the fact that most of my students were no longer willing to tolerate prejudice and violence in their world. If so, it wasn't enough. It didn't stop the slaughter of thousands of human beings.

Mark and Ann: What do we want English teachers to know and think and do? As we see it, English teachers—all teachers—can work to transform our classrooms—meaning teachers' and students' classrooms—into sites in which and *from* which we keep reading and writing and telling stories against war and other oppressions. Classrooms can be more than places where students learn *about* literature. Literature classrooms can be places in which to begin a lifelong process of creatively acting—not just making and consuming—responses to the literature of the world, responses that keep us vigilant to the possibility of war. In literature classrooms, students and teachers can begin to understand how they live their local lives in connection with national and international events. Knowing this, maybe they can influence both for peace.

Learning literature, then, is learning to come to terms with our collective needs and pains and how they foster local and world violence, but not with the goal of learning to live with an oppressive and all-too-present status quo. Learning literature is learning that we must change the world—however small the changes we make may be. Learning literature is learning to act to correct those elements which make our experiences critical.

None of this is easy. But English teachers have a unique opportunity to help students examine, not just what they think, but *how* they think. It's time to look the American *ethos* that the media sells us in the face. It's time to reject the resentments and the suspicions we must endure to be the Americans we are "supposed" to be. It's time to rewrite the designs on others that America entertains. It's time for English teachers to help students question how the American character's hatreds and fears lead to war and consume our capability to love. It is possible, in other words, to question how the narrative of the American character prepares us for war. And it may very well be that collective investigation and intervention is our only means of stopping it. Alone, we go on suffering. As one student, Patrick, wrote on his final, "No law, ordinance or treaty can end the war which goes on in one's head. It would be great if it did, but it doesn't."[4]

Notes

1. *Mark and Ann:* We do not wish to condemn fraternity brothers in this article. We speak only of what happened in this class.

2. *Mark:* A reader might try to infer which students I "liked best" or which ones got the A's and F's. It can't be done. For instance, "Humanities Literature" was the second class that Bill took with me. He could have chosen any one of my sixty-five colleagues. In addition, following the lead of Mary H. Beaven (1977), I create ways for students to self- and peer-evaluate their work, and I take these evaluations into serious account as I assign grades (and students have class procedures for questioning the grades I assign). I do not grade students on their political beliefs.

While writing this chapter, I have learned about the challenges that writing narratives about a classroom poses. Ann and I have chosen to write a narrative because we feel that the traditional constraints of academic discourse would not allow us means for recreating the human element of our course. A sense of our collective humanity was what was most missing from the official rhetorics of Washington and Baghdad in the fall of 1990.

Ann and I have talked about the responsibility we feel to get our story right. Yet we aren't trained as writers of fiction or literary nonfiction. We have tried to represent the reality of EN 121 in as much of its complexity as possible, but even in doing so, it feels very possible to get the reality of "Humanities Literature" pitifully wrong. We have written a narrative for political and ethical reasons, but the form problematizes these same political and ethical objectives.

3. *Mark:* Precisely because Ann's memory of this incident was different from my own, I wish that I had been able to include more of my students in the writing of this chapter, particularly Stephen, Pam, and Bill. But, of course, not every one of our students would have had the commitment—why should they?—to seeing a chapter through the years it takes to get into print. What's more, our students often graduate—and even go to war—before we finish the narratives in which they appear. I can't help but think, though, that if it were possible to include Stephen, Pam, and Bill in the writing of this account, the article would come closer to achieving collectivist ideals—which is, perhaps, just what Bill wouldn't want to achieve. Still, working with Ann has confirmed my belief that students should be heard as well as seen in the academic writing in which they appear.

4. *Mark:* All of the students in this article gave me permission to quote from their work. I have changed their names and edited their writing where necessary.

Works Cited

Ayyoub, Dhu'l Nun. 1989. "From Behind the Veil." Translated by S. Al-Bazzazz. In Walker, 97–103.

Bauer, Dale M., and Susan C. Jarratt. 1994. "Feminist Sophistics: Teaching with an Attitude." [See chapter 7, this volume.]

Beaven, Mary H. 1977. "Individualized Goal Setting, Self-Evaluation, and Peer Evaluation." In *Evaluating Writing: Describing, Measuring, Judging,* edited by Charles R. Cooper and Lee Odell, 135–56. Urbana: National Council of Teachers of English.

Benjamin, Jessica. 1986. "A Desire of One's Own: Psychoanalytic Feminism and Intersubjective Space." In *Feminist Studies/Critical Studies,* edited by Teresa de Laurentis, 78–101. *Theories of Contemporary Culture, Vol. VIII.* Bloomington: Indiana University Press.

Berlin, James A. 1991. "Composition and Cultural Studies." In *Composition and Resistance,* edited by C. Mark Hurlbert and Michael Blitz, 47–54. Portsmouth, NH: Boynton/Cook-Heinemann.

Bowles, Samuel, and Herbert Gintis. 1976. *Schooling in Capitalist America: Educational Reform and the Contradictions of Economic Life.* New York: Basic Books.

Charters, Ann, ed. 1991. *The Story and Its Writer: An Introduction to Short Fiction.* 3rd ed. Boston: Bedford.

Erdrich, Louise. 1991. "The Red Convertible." In Charters, 417–24.

Gibson, P. J. 1986. *Brown Silk and Magenta Sunsets.* In Wilkerson, 425–505.

Giroux, Henry A. 1992. "Textual Authority and the Role of Teachers as Public Intellectuals." In *Social Issues in the English Classroom,* edited by C. Mark Hurlbert and Samuel Totten, 304–21. Urbana: National Council of Teachers of English.

Hurlbert, C. Mark. 1989. "Toward Collectivist Composition: Transforming Social Relations through Classroom Practices." *The Writing Instructor* 8.4 (Summer): 166–76.

———. 1991. "The Walls We Don't See: Toward Collectivist Pedagogies as Political Struggle." In *Practicing Theory in Introductory College Literature Courses,* edited by James M. Cahalan and David B. Downing, 131–48. Urbana: National Council of Teachers of English.

Jackson, Elaine. 1986. *Paper Dolls.* In Wilkerson, 349–426.

Khudayyir, Mohammed. 1989. "Clocks Like Horses." Translated by Denys Johnson-Davies. In Walker, 134–47.

Leavitt, David. 1991. "Territory." In Charters, 825–41.

Mukherjee, Bharati. 1990. "The Management of Grief." In Ravenel, 333–50.

O'Brien, Tim. 1990. "The Things They Carried." In Ravenel, 271–89.

Owen, Maureen. 1987. "Three Mile Island." In *American Poetry Since 1970: Up Late,* edited by Andrei Codrescu, 19. New York: Four Walls/Eight Windows.

Piercy, Marge. 1976. *Woman on the Edge of Time.* New York: Knopf.

Ravenel, Shannon, ed. 1990. *The Best American Short Stories of the Eighties.* Boston: Houghton-Mifflin.

Sheldon, Sidney. 1987. *The Windmills of the Gods.* New York: Warner.

Thomson, Garrett. 1987. *Needs.* International Library of Philosophy. Edited by Ted Honderich. London: Routledge and Kegan Paul.

Vasilyuk, Fyodor. 1988. *The Psychology of Experience.* Moscow: Progress.

Vold, Edwina Battle. 1989. "Critical Thinking: Strategy for Diversity." In *Education and the American Dream: Conservatives, Liberals, and Radicals Debate the Future of Education,* edited by Harvey Holtz, et al., 124–33. *Critical Studies in Education.* Granby, MA: Bergin & Garvey.

Walker, Scott, ed. 1989. *The Graywolf Annual Six: Stories from the Rest of the World.* The Graywolf Short Fiction Series. Saint Paul, MN: Graywolf.

Wilkerson, Margaret B., ed. 1986. *Nine Plays by Black Women.* New York: New American Library.

Zandy, Janet. 1994. "Human Labor and Literature: A Pedagogy from a Working-Class Perspective." [See chapter 2, this volume.]

V Toward Cultural and Rhetorical Studies

12 The Role of Rhetorical Theory, Cultural Theory, and Creative Writing in Developing a First-Year Curriculum in English

Alan Kennedy, Christine M. Neuwirth,
Kris Straub, and David Kaufer
Carnegie Mellon University

What we describe here is both the process and the results to date of our attempts to think through some of the relations between "theory" and pedagogy, especially as they relate to the question of a foundational class in English for the first year of college.[1] The concern with the first-year experience in English falls within a long and distinguished tradition at Carnegie Mellon—including but not exhausted by names such as Gladys Schmidt, Erwin Steinberg, Richard Young, Peggy Knapp, Lois Fowler, Gary Waller, Kathy McCormick, and Linda Flower—that has affirmed both the import of theory to curriculum development and curriculum development to theory in matters of the first-year course. Crossing many generations and theoretical orientations, the CMU tradition, collectively, has approached reading and writing as complex, multitiered concepts requiring elaboration at cultural, institutional, social, and cognitive levels. Taking our turn in this tradition, we had the daunting task of trying to add to as well as assimilate many powerful voices that had preceded our own.

Perhaps more than in previous formulations of the first-year course, ours depends on the organizational theory underlying an English department. If the first-year course engages students in practices of literacy and is intended to be a broad introduction to the discipline, then it stands to reason that students, in the first year, should learn to become reflective in the many literate practices occupying the site of English departments. At the same time, English departments are themselves seldom strategically organized to encode the many diverse and tacit literate practices they encapsulate into a corpus of knowledge which is explicit, linear, and structured enough to be called a curriculum. The problem with the first-year course, we reasoned, is in part a problem of organization. The blueprint of a first-year curriculum required, we thus concluded, an organizational history and diagnosis, to which we now turn.

Our department is not focused on a comfortable global coherence that some English departments have found, and continue to find, in the project of "covering" the history and development of English literature. If we look for a model of "coherence" in our department, we look first to the history of our institutional construction and position. For example, the institutional histories of our faculty are diverse. While a number of faculty have Ph.D.s in literary subjects, many of this number have migrated from the study of canonical texts. A second portion of faculty, primarily in the rhetoric program, were trained in communication, education, rhetoric, and linguistics. Finally, about another third of our faculty, in the creative writing program, took the M.F.A.

Our particular history includes a program in literary studies in the New Critical tradition dating back to the 1940s. A program in creative writing was set up about twenty years ago and still continues to play a crucial role in our undergraduate curricula. In the late 1970s the department instituted a program in rhetoric, and the first of our Ph.D. programs granted a doctorate in rhetoric. Carnegie Mellon became well-known for empirical research into the processes of reading and writing, with a particular emphasis on composition research. Without losing this edge, the interests of the rhetoric faculty have expanded and diversified to include work in collaborative planning and writing, the history of rhetoric and writing, reading, linguistics, writing in nonacademic settings and computer-based tools for reading and writing. This broadened base of rhetorical studies at CMU has become increasingly valuable, and visible, to the department at large, especially with the most recent expansion into the area of "cultural studies." Over the last half dozen years, an undergraduate major in "Literary and Cultural Studies" and a doctoral program in "Literary and Cultural Theory" have been put in place. Focusing on our histories and our local resources made it possible for us to engage in constructive debate about curricular directions, more than would be the case were our history more homogeneously centered around a coverage model of literature. Departments with literature at their core have tended to marginalize rhetoric and composition ("poetics" had won the battle over rhetoric in the nineteenth century, and earlier), and also to regard creative writing as an unsuitable academic subject for a university department of English. In our circumstances, it is possible to describe these programs with the image of a triangle (see figure 1). Each program meets with the other at the corner, each begins where another leaves off, each has its own terrain, its own assumptions about what it means to be "literate," and is yet connected to and reliant on the others. If any one, or any other pedagogical imperative, occupied the center, then all the others would be marginalized with reference to it. With none dominating the center, each aids the others in constructing alternative uses of literacy.

Because we look to our histories, we find it all but impossible to think that it is our task to build a curriculum from the top down, paying no attention to our particular context. It may be that the day has passed for such universalist attempts at curriculum construction. We are clearly in a time of transformation, tension, debate, conflict, while in the energetic pursuit of a model for English studies that might restore an urgently needed sense of purpose to the "humanities."

Our image of the first-year curriculum was designed to feature literate practices underlying each prong of this triad. Given the image of our triad, and our historical diversity, it seemed essential to devise an introductory class that best represented what the discipline, represented broadly, could be about. This goal took the shape of an insistence that what we needed was "one class." It was not always clear to us just what this meant, though the reference stuck. And while we have never elaborated to our own satisfaction all that is at stake in the "one-course" motif, it has much to do, superficially at least, with an effort to blur organizational and intellectual boundaries while pursuing points of local coherence across boundaries. In an environment where the various subcultures of our department pursue their own specialized frameworks toward language and literacy, establishing points of local coherence across the subcultures, it seems to us, can engender a reflective understanding of (and perhaps respect for) the various specialized ways literacy gets practiced in a department of English. Making these points of coherence a packageable part of our first-year curriculum, presentable in a single course or course concept, seemed the least we could do for our first-year students—and for ourselves.

Even within our own department, we are not the first voices to endorse the imperative that can easily be identified with—or confused for—the slogan "teach the conflicts" of an English department. Despite the fact that Gerald Graff (1992) has already written one version of the story, many of our faculty have adopted a second career trying to "synthesize" the English department—not a surprising result, especially in a department where the coverage model has been jettisoned and nothing nearly so simple nor comfortable has come to stand in its place. Nonetheless, not all attempts at synthesis are equally cogent or compelling, and we have resorted to the "one-course" terminology to try to distill our synthetic effort from what previous efforts have been, or at least from what we have perceived them to be. Unlike some

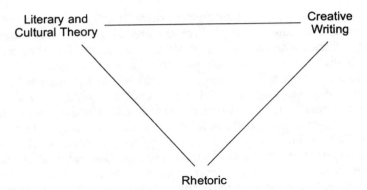

Fig. 1. The paradigm of English department programs at Carnegie Mellon.

previous efforts at synthesis (including, perhaps, Graff's), we see no incompatibility between exploring local coherence across subspecialties within English and respecting the specialized focus of different programs within the department. The search for local coherence is not a search for ultimate coherence, or consensus for that matter. The effort to blur boundaries need not diminish the level of specialization within the department, but should add to the reflexiveness that makes one a more thoughtful and self-critical specialist. We oppose the idea that the "teach the conflicts" slogan should turn the business of the English department into only one privileged specialty (i.e., Graff's specialty). Such a turn would clearly create a prejudice against the work of an empirical researcher, a poet, or a cultural critic specializing in the third world, none of whom wants to have to study English departments in order to thrive in one. It would also create an unfair bias for persons who make the "conflicts" their personal specialty or who seek a metaperspective on the perspectives of the English department—so-called "bridge" people. Gary Waller, our former head, used to regularly endorse the need for our department to hire a "bridge" person, one whose knowledge spanned the multiple cultures of the department. While the call seemed understandable and reasonable-sounding then, it seems to us, in retrospect, to have been ill-founded. Lacking a global grasp of the field (which we claim to be all but impossible, even for a polymath, given the diversity and levels of specialization that now mark English studies), the "bridge" person is lucky to have the depth required to pass muster within a single specialty culture. And if the "bridge" is hired only to establish some points of coherence with multiple specialty groups, then the "bridge" has achieved only what we think it appropriate for any reflective member of an English department to achieve. Because the first-year course, in our design, becomes a working laboratory for establishing coherence across specialities, the one-course strategy at the first-year level militates against the structural inequalities that create a market for "bridge" people. Such a strategy symbolically—and, in actuality, insofar as symbolic organization can influence real organization—attenuates unproductive conflicts because it asks persons from different specialties to collaborate to "present" the work of English with no beginning bias of where the center lies.

It is harder, we have come to think, to execute the same democracy of assumptions in a multiple-course, first-year program, that is, in a program where two courses cannot collapse into one or were not originally designed from a common base in which they might do so. The reason is that a single course (or course design) can occupy a unique history in an institution with a unique set of clients and expectations. At times, the distinctive historical baggage inherited by two courses can dictate how they are institutionally perceived, even when the course contents have long evolved to invalidate those perceptions. A good example of how these institutional mechanisms can work at cross-purposes with course content is evident in the two first-year classes preceding the course design discussed here: "Strategies for Writing" and "Reading Texts."[2] Both classes could claim sophisticated pedagogical constructions, complex conceptual formulations and successful implementations, if we can define "successful" as satisfying a broad range of clients across the university. Their relative success as independent courses was not the problem. The problem, we came to realize, was their perceived independence and the institutional prejudice that hung on this perception of independence.

For example, despite the claims that the "Strategies for Writing" class was the equal of the "Reading Texts" class in teaching skills of reading and writing, it was nevertheless the case that the institution perceived these courses differently and (with the tacit compliance of the English department) assigned a completely different institutional status to these courses. Students with an AP above 2 or an SAT above 580 were exempted from the "writing course." Many exemptees were then routed into the "reading course." The writing course had no special status within the College of Humanities and Social Sciences. The reading course was a "disciplinary" requirement for all majors in the college. Through these structural inequalities, the message was unmistakable that the writing course was to be treated as "remedial" while the reading course held "disciplinary" standing. Small wonder that, despite the department's protestations to the contrary, some of our "clients" around the campus continued to insist that one class was "better" for their students than the other (e.g., the writing course was better for the developmental student in need of "basic skills") and that the reading course was designed to challenge the superior student in a manner unknown to the writing course. What made the whole exercise of apparent choice between the two courses even more dubious was an invidious fact: far more salient than the differences in educational experiences these courses provided was the sobering fact that, in view of "Strategies" occupying the perceived center of "remedial" education in English for the entire university community, it drew its population from the bottom 48 percent of the incoming first-year class. Our SAT cutoff point for exemption had no deep rationale to it. It was purely an administrative necessity: we needed to reduce the number of students to that number which we could adequately handle in our classrooms. Other departments and colleges on campus might well have believed that we had some reason for believing in the academic meaning of a particular SAT cutoff point. They were mistaken. As we began to realize, we had been sending another kind of unfortunate message across campus. We were saying, in effect, that we had deliberately designed a class—the writing class—for the lower half of the student body. We were apparently quite happy to send the best students off to take other classes (including the reading class). It now strikes some of us as odd that we should have done that.

While our resources are not likely to expand to the point of enabling us to subscribe the entire first-year class (some 1,250 students as of 1991) into our first-year English program, we did institute two policy goals that begin to address these resource problems over the short and long term. The first goal, already implemented, is to eliminate any discrepancy in entry criteria for the writing and the reading course. Satisfying this goal offers little comfort and, regrettably, has caused some confusion to the students on campus who are truly in need of remedial help and who were misinformed (through their advisor in engineering or whatever) that they would get that help all along in the writing course. In the end, however, truly remedial students are better served, it seems, by providing support services (e.g., tutoring, writing labs) specifically designed to address their problems rather than by letting certain courses become stigmatized as "remedial" (as "Strategies" had become), even when remediation is not their intent. (We are in the process, incidentally, of trying to develop these support services.) The second goal is to gradually increase the percentage of first-year students enrolled in one or both of the first-year offerings. While we cannot teach all first-year students, we can at least set the goal to teach more. As mentioned above, we now admit some 48 percent of the first-year class into first-year English courses (except those who take "Reading Texts" as a college requirement). We are currently considering targets—and expansions in our budgeting—that would, over a five-year period, increase our capacity to something on the order of 65 percent of the first-year class.

It stands to reason that the ultimate success of these administrative goals hinges, in no small way, on the intellectual goal of implementing a one-course concept for the first year—for if the university community is to understand what we mean them to understand about literacy, rather than letting them rely on their own ingrained images, we need to build a first-year concept that makes the various literacies introduced sufficiently "integrated" to resist decomposition by stereotype. This is the basic rationale and advantage, we believe, of the one-course design for the first year. A one-course concept is a single course or set of courses where coherence has been established across otherwise diverse assumptions and frameworks. Coherence in this setting refers to conceptual frameworks, vocabularies, and goals that can be explicitly shared and reinforced within or across courses. Because the local coherence within a one-course concept is *coordinated* and *reinforced* across courses, the strengths of each course are more likely to be perceived by first-year students as complementary rather than competitive. The danger of local coherence in a multicourse concept is that, even if the literacies taught manage to escape institutional stereotyping, the differences across courses can sometimes render the appearance that these same literacies are competitively positioned. The local coherence of one course, in other words, can compete with and work to "nullify" or "offset" the territorial coherence sought by another.

"Strategies" and "Reading Texts" are good examples of intrinsically coherent courses whose coherence was nonetheless institutionally perceived as being competitive with one another. This competition made it possible to perpetuate institutional stereotypes about the courses which neither deserved. While both courses gave a sophisticated accounting of "writing," "reading," "context," and "culture" in their local course designs, each course retained sufficiently competitive frameworks and vocabularies (problem solving in the case of "Strategies"; poststructuralist reading theory in the case of "Reading Texts") to make students and the TAs who taught sections of them believe they were investing in very different—even diametrically opposed—ideologies of literacy when teaching one or another course. Despite "Reading Texts"' treatment of writing, for example, its classification as a serious writing course was undermined by the more dominant problem-solving treatment of writing given in "Strategies." Instead of a production-based focus on writing, a focus on the design and implementation of the written arti- fact itself, "Reading Texts" offered what one might call an ideologically based focus—asking students to delve into, and write about, the often hidden assumptions of ideology that underly the production of read- ings and texts. Instead of the more dominant agent-based focus on writing, treating the author as an individual cognitive agent, "Reading Texts" tended to shift ground between a culture-determined and an agent-determined focus on literate production. The culturally deter- mined focus of the "Reading Texts" course is evident in statements such as the following from the *Reading Texts* textbook: "All readers bring values, prejudices, and assumptions acquired from their social and cultural backgrounds to their readings—and these to a large extent determine the ways they develop their readings of texts" (McCormick, Waller, and Flower 1987, 14). In this focus, a reader's response to (and eventual writing about) a text is determined by the match (or mis- match) of ideological elements in the writer's historical repertoire and those elicited from the text. Within the culture-based focus of *Reading Texts*, the observation that readers bring their history to their interpre- tive tasks reflected the history of a culture more than a reader's per- sonal history: "Our fundamental point is that the beliefs you have as a person affect you as a reader: reading is not something you do inde- pendent of your historical situation" (McCormick, Waller, and Flower 1987, 23). The culture-based focus of reading in *Reading Texts* made clear that the terms of interpretation were posited as lying beyond the agent's personal history, in the culture at large, and disproportionately dictated by the culture's "dominant ideology," the ideology setting the bounds for what readers are most likely to mistake for their "natural" responses.

However, from time to time, this culturally determined focus of reading in *Reading Texts* shifted ground to a more strongly formulated agent-based focus. Despite the fact that the dominant culture dispro- portionately influences reading, *Reading Texts* nonetheless held out the promise that the ideological tracing of literate production can work to increase the cognitive reflectiveness of the reader: "Perhaps the most persuasive of the reasons for reading literature . . . is to make readers look at themselves, their society, and their history in fresh, stimulating, and sometimes disturbing ways" (McCormick, Waller, and Flower 1987, 23) The reflectiveness accrued from this agentive focus toward literate behavior was also evident in the constructive image of literacy promul- gated by *Reading Texts*, as embodied in the construct of the "strong reader":

> A strong reading of a text is a clearly articulated reading that self-consciously goes "against the grain" of a text. A strong reading is *not* a misreading. Nor is it perverse or imperceptive. It can only develop if a reader is aware of the dominant text strategies and chooses, for various reasons, be they literary or cultural, to read the text differently. You can recognize that a text may want you to respond in a given manner, but you may *choose* to use your cultural awareness to resist that prescribed way of reading. You become thereby a strong independent reader. This kind of reading is one we wish very much to encourage—where you define a particular perspective on a text, develop it persuasively, and articulate its implications. (McCormick, Waller, and Flower 1987, 28; emphasis in the original)

Needless to say, the cultural and agentive foci of literate behavior in the "Reading Texts" course are not easily reconcilable images of literacy. If our inheritance determines how we read, the mechanism by which we "overcome" it needs a careful elaboration that is not forthcoming in the first edition of *Reading Texts*.[3] Such a mechanism would need to chart the transformations by which the (social) processes of cultural determination and cultural ownership influence and in turn are influenced by the (cognitive) process of enhanced personal reflectiveness that are supposed to accrue as readers attend to the ideological sources of literate production. The challenge of formulating such a mechanism is that the social process of ideological determination, if true, should tend to dampen rather than enhance the reader's cognitive sensitivity even to the possibility of interpretive range and depth. Yet within the agent-focus of *Reading Texts*, an individual reader is allowed, seemingly through a sheer act of will, to profoundly subvert (at least resist) the complex social forces that constructed him or her as a reader in the first place: "You may deliberately try to read like someone else, from perspectives other than your own seemingly natural one, say from a feminist, a political, or a fundamentalist position. In that way you learn what it is like to read from a particular perspective different from your own" (McCormick, Waller, and Flower 1987). Yet there seems nothing in *Reading Texts* theory of ideology (under the current formulation) that confers any efficacy on the power of individual reflection and resistance.

On the other hand, despite the "Strategies for Reading" treatment of context and culture, its classification as a serious cultural course was undermined by the more dominant postmodern treatment of culture provided by "Reading Texts." The rhetorical theory behind "Strategies for Writing" was a sophisticated problem-solving, process approach to writing. It required students to learn how to analyze complex situations and produce writing solutions to problems of communication. Looking at the research about just what people who write do when they write produced a lot of useful information for a pedagogy of writing:

> If we looked at composing as a psychologist might, we would find that it has much in common with the problem-solving processes people use every day when they are planning a trip, taking an exam, making a decision, or trying to make a diplomatic request. The general research on problem solving in the past twenty years has discovered a great deal about the special strategies of expert problem solvers in various fields, including master chess players, inventors, successful scientists, business managers, and artists. (Flower 1985, 2)

"Strategies for Writing" had one tremendous advantage over other possible formulations for a writing class. Since the problem-solving approach is of central importance at Carnegie Mellon, we were able to gain a ready level of community acceptance by having our first-year class focus on learning to write as a matter of problem solving. The other strength of the class was its concentration on process before product. The problem-solving approach, students discovered, "is really a frame of mind or an attitude. . . . As a problem solver your first concern is not with the finished product—with fitting into a format or convention, with following the rules of grammar, or even with producing a polished style. Instead your attention is squarely focused on your own goals as a writer, on what you want to do and say" (Flower 1985, 3). The advantages of such an approach have been made clear a number of times and need not be stressed here. What is relevant to note, for our purposes, is that while "Strategies," like "Reading Texts," treated elements of "reflection" as well as "production" in literate behavior, "Reading Texts" offered an image of "literacy" that subordinated production to reflection (about production), and this image, in turn, encouraged the false and pernicious impression (among clients of both courses) that "Strategies" (with a less hierarchical treatment of reflection and production) was basically concerned *only* with production, was basically just a "skills" course, disengaged from context and culture.

In essence, we found in "Strategies" and "Reading Texts" a first-year course architecture whose parts were clearly superior to the whole. While maintaining sophisticated views of literacy in their own respects, the views of literacy promoted by each were not reconciled, or even commonly accommodated, as a two-semester, first-year experience. As a result, "Reading Texts" retained the reputation of a "real" course that didn't teach skills; "Strategies" retained the reputation of a "writing" course that taught only that skill. The content of each course belied the institutional stereotype; nevertheless, there was not enough coordination across the courses to refute it.

We hope that we've laid out some of the premises we think are at issue in deciding on a one-course concept design for the first year. The evidence for this design must be forthcoming in the details of its implementation. We do not claim to have achieved a one-course design—we only claim to have made substantial progress in that direction. Before we proceed further into the details of our first-year design, we need to issue two important caveats. First, we must distinguish between a one-course concept and the specific implementations of that concept as they arise in various course designs. The one-course conception presented in this paper reflects only one of a multitude of possible designs. Since the coordinators of the new first-year curriculum (currently Straub and Neuwirth) serve only a three-year term, it is important that the high-level decision making and planning that go into a one-course design be replicable, even if the specific details of a specific implementation are not. What we report on here are the implementation details of a one-course design featuring the interplay of "argument" and "interpretation" and two courses, "Argument and Interpretation" (A&I) and "Interpretation and Argument" (I&A), spun from that design. While it would be nice to report the unparalleled success (on whatever criteria) of these courses, they have, as this paper is being drafted, yet to be in place even for a semester, and so such a report is premature at best.[4] Accordingly, our focus in this paper—and the burden of the argument we want to accept—is not the promise of our proposed implementation but rather how the details of the implementation furnish evidence for the larger promise of a one-course design for the first year. Second, any one-course design is no better than its implementation, and any implementation is bound to carry biases that are not necessarily generalizable to the one-course design strategy itself. For example, our current coordinators are specialists in rhetorical theory (Neuwirth) and cultural theory (Straub). They have worked actively with members of the creative writing program to bring creative writing into the first-year experience. Nonetheless, the input of creative writing would (and will) probably look much different when a member of the creative writing program takes on a coordinating and not simply a consulting role.

Our own thinking about the details of a one-course concept began to crystallize in our mutual disagreement with a position voiced by Maxine Hairston in an "Opinion" piece in *The Chronicle of Higher Education* (Hairston 1991). Hairston has argued that students write best about those things that they are interested in. She argues that writing courses "should not focus on politically charged issues," and positions herself in opposition to the contested class at the University of Texas at Austin, English 306. Her position, we all came to believe, begs a number of issues. It depends, for instance, on some subjective estimation of what a "political" issue is, as opposed to a "nonpolitical" one. It requires some ability to discriminate when an issue is "charged" and when one is not. Perhaps a degree of chargedness is to be measured by the extent to which it is getting current coverage in the popular press? One can understand why Hairston might want to separate substance from the craft of writing: she is possibly anxious to protect the discipline of writing instruction, which has fought to achieve some degree of respectability, from inroads of mere topicality. That claim, if it is one she would make, would be at odds with her belief that "students develop best as writers when they are allowed to write on something they care about." That claim identifies an ability to improve one's writing with a predisposition to the topicality of the issue being addressed—if topicality can be taken to mean that the subject has a personal investment in the issue. Hairston insists that "Having them write about other people's ideas doesn't work well." To be sure, it certainly doesn't when teachers turn the course into a reading course, as often happens (we have seen writing courses based on "readings" turn into essentially literature courses). Also, we have seen students debilitated by being required to write about a charged issue (e.g., abortion) with which they have had some sort of traumatic emotional experience.

What is really at issue in Hairston's claim, however, is the issue of who owns ideas. Are there ideas that are not those of "other" people? Are there ideas that are exclusively one's own, and that one therefore takes a greater interest in and therefore writes better about? Does such a claim entail the belief that writing about ideas is not a way of acquiring those ideas? That I have to be in possession of an idea and claim it as uniquely my own before I can write well about it? Such a separation between writing and thinking processes seems to be at odds with what a lot of thinkers about the issue would believe. Hairston's position seems to be based on a simple notion of "interest." If students are interested, they will write better. How, though, to lead them into a development of new interests? How to get them to "take" an interest or to understand that they already take one, and so it is in their "interest" to learn to read and write with at least a minimum level of cultural understanding? A pedagogy that does not take developmental change into account, that cannot claim to be attempting to help students engage in a change of thinking, probably does not really deserve at all to be called a responsible mode of teaching.

In our own planning, then, we wanted students to be engaged in a process of writing that involves learning, and a process of dealing with topical issues (or issues of "interest") in a way that entails writing. Our early discussions quickly focused on issues of argumentation and interpretation. We felt that our students did not, by the time they came to graduate, really show sufficient abilities in argumentation. They could, most of them, write well enough, express themselves verbally well enough, but too often these expressions were limited to issues of self-expression. They could not be counted on to develop a well-argued presentation of a position to which they felt committed, and at the same time explain how that position depended on a complex process of interpretation. Related to the deficiencies in interpretive analysis, it seemed to us, was a low level of ability to understand, both sympathetically and critically, positions other than one's own. And since the process of interpretation and understanding positions other than one's own is crucial to developing an argument, we felt we had fallen into a useful circular discussion that might yield some results.

Clearly it's nothing new to be thinking that argumentation should be the basis of a first-year class. There are many anthologies continuing to flood the market which are designed to engage students in the process of argument. They have differing levels of adequacy, but it seems to us that too many of them simply give students numerous examples of argumentative prose, criticize them, and then encourage the student to get engaged in the argument. Such a product-based approach seems to assume that the mere topicality of an issue and certain argument structures will somehow magically empower students to argue. Fortunately for us, in our rhetoric program we already had a strong research interest (in the work of Flower and Spivey) on hybrid reading/writing tasks. Further, in our curriculum we have had a class, "Reading and Writing Arguments," that could inform aspects of a one-course design. The class has a sequential program, elaborated in *Arguing from Sources: Exploring Issues through Reading and Writing* (Kaufer, Geisler, and Neuwirth 1989). Two of the authors of that text were teaching the class (Kaufer and Neuwirth), and one of them is the co-designer of our newly planned pair of classes (Neuwirth, teamed with Straub). The class, as given recently, has focussed on issues of literacy. Students are given eight to fifteen essays dealing with literacy. They are not asked to do "research" to find essays themselves, and to that extent we are not planning to teach students how to do a "research paper." Our view is that searching is a complex skill, dependent on having a knowledge base for one's subject. It is possible for an amateur to amass a long list of possible titles, just by doing a computer keyword or title search. But the process of selecting from that list is an expert task. It would take too much valuable time away from learning the writing processes in first-year classes, we believe, to engage students in a high-level expert task, early on.

The subject of "literacy" is clearly a topical one, but in the English class, it has another advantage of being reflexive. There is a certain intuitive topicality to the issue, and students seem not unwilling to invest in the issue once they have signed up for the class. They do need to be told how, as potential future leaders of the community, they need to be informed about issues of reading and writing (they may be facing problems engendered by illiteracy in the companies they work for, etc.); and told that, if they have children, they may want to know about how reading/writing is taught in the schools and which methods are preferable. And, of course, they need to be shown throughout the semester the importance of the *disciplinary knowledges* they are learning to the acquisition of writing *skill* (an understanding of the relationship between power and communication, between world and representation, how metaphors affect the way we see problems, etc.). It is also necessary to sell the idea that they should all be reading/writing on the same topic: if they write on the same topic, they are able to give more intelligent comments, more like those which an expert reviewer would give (e.g., "You neglected H's argument, here"); we are better able to help them achieve a contribution (and to judge that something they do *is* one). Thus, we construe literacy broadly to include the relationship between theory, interpretation, and data; between knowledge and power; and to include also the processes of reading/writing and the teaching of writing. All of these elements are part of the disciplinary knowledge that students need in order to acquire reading/writing skills.

So far so good, if the class is (as it was) primarily a class designed by our rhetoric group. What would it look like if we wanted to meld with it the concerns of a cultural studies program? That question led us to confront a prior one, discussed to a greater extent, below: What are the concerns of cultural studies—at least, what are the concerns of cultural studies that we would most want to embody in an introductory class that has to do double duty as both a disciplinary introduction and also as a service class to our campus? One of the simplest keys to understanding our approach to cultural studies is to notice how often in our departmental discussions a central question recurred: "Who benefits?" In our attempts to understand the nature of cultural production and reception, we found ourselves asking, "Who benefits?" to get our analysis underway. So it seemed natural to ask that issues of literacy in the class address themselves to issues of power, especially issues of unequal power distribution when access to the apparati of literacy are considered across lines of race, class, gender, and other forms of culturally constituted difference. So as we took a first step in planning a newly coordinated class, we made it a point to insist that issues of power not be forgotten.

Our insistence did not, however, take the form of instituting a shared thematic between I&A and A&I. Issues of diversity, difference, and power had to be integral to the very grain of the courses, not simply folded in as thematic objects of study. Hence, different thematic issues were chosen for each (about which we will have more to say, later), and a common methodology was sought that could accommodate both rhetorical and cultural approaches to teaching argumentation and interpretation. Instead of assuming that cultural studies would supply a "content" to be methodologically processed by the rhetorical machinery of argumentation, we sought out ways in which an awareness of power and difference emerges from the two courses' shared methodology of argumentation.

The strength of the method set forth in *Arguing from Sources* is the ease with which it is conceived as a process as well as a series of products. Students learn a process of thought as well as how to produce certain kinds of papers. Since it is defined as a method of cognition that leads to textual building blocks rather than models of surface text, the process of argumentation described below works as a method of interpretation—a reading practice—that is adaptable to thinking about meaning as culturally and individually produced. The methods of summary, synthesis, and analysis drawn from "Reading and Writing Arguments" provide a framework, an organizing principle, for teaching students in both I&A and A&I how the individual cognitive nature of reading and writing can also be represented in terms of cultural difference and power distribution.

The class in "Reading and Writing Arguments" proceeds in several clear pedagogical stages. First students are taught about summary. They are given one essay on the issue and asked to produce a summary. What students have to learn in this section is that summary differs from mere repetition or précis. Summary, it turns out, is a way of transforming a text; it is an action taken on a text. Summary tells us as much about the summarizer as about the summarized; it is a theory of the text, an appropriation of it. For example, one of the things we ask students to do is to include a hypothesis about the problem case "underlying" the text. In the text we choose for summary, the problem case may be implicit and students must infer it. They succeed to the extent that their hypothesis can account for the data of the text. Thus, in producing the summary, students become aware (we hope) about the fact that they are using an *interpretive theory* (problem-solution schemata) to make inferences about the text (even the decision of what is important and not important to include in the summary is usually guided by an implicit theory). A different theory (e.g., narrative schemata) might focus their attention in other ways and "lead" them to construct a different representation. Some of the valuable vocabulary associated with summarizing is caught in the opening paragraph of the text *Arguing from Sources* (Kaufer, Geisler, and Neuwirth 1989):

> Throughout history, explorers have relied on incomplete maps of uncharted territories. Columbus started with maps portraying the New World as India. Lewis and Clark started their westward expedition with poorly specified maps of the Missouri River. To make their journeys, explorers go through four phases: (1) they consult the maps of others; (2) they explore similarities and differences among maps; (3) they make the journey themselves; (4) they return to design a new map. The exploration process involves designing and redesigning structures in order to accommodate what is learned from new explorations.
>
> What is true for exploring physical territories is also true for exploring issues. Like physical exploration, the composition of argument involves the structuring and restructuring of maps through an issue—not physical maps but mental maps. Authors are constantly designing and redesigning their mental maps of an issue in order to make their exploration as rich, productive, and up-to-date as possible. (2)

As students learn the details of the procedure for producing a summary, they can be introduced to the idea of map making. It can be put to them that constructing a summary, making an argument, is like making a map and is related, in the same metaphor, to occupying a position. We tell students that the reason for summarizing, for representing a representation, is that it becomes an important building block for developing one's own representation. Lest the vocabulary of argumentation seem too agonistic, it can be explained that a map is a representation, just as an argument is. An argument can work toward the establishing of justified belief, but it remains only an argument and need not claim to be the final word on any issue. Students can begin to understand that their summary, or map, of any single text is in fact, therefore, a representation of a representation. They need not think that the whole exercise is merely subjective, which they will not when they have worked through the processes of arguing, and equally they need not conclude that every good argument is of necessity the final and winning argument. They can come to learn that many more travelers will have to construct maps before a territory can be thought to be known. And if they know anything of maps and representations, they can be persuaded that the argumentative process of constructing our world together is one worth carrying out indefinitely.

With such a vocabulary, one is already speaking a language that people in cultural studies can readily appropriate. It needs to be remembered that the language of mental representations belongs to cognitive science, and cultural studies people might not necessarily be comfortable with a language that does not foreground socially constituted relations. On the other hand, there is no reason to assume that all uses of terms need to be totally congruent. So while cognitive scientists might on some occasions focus on the personal nature of mental representations, and their relation to individual behavior, cultural studies creates other "occasions" in which this emphasis is difficult if not impossible. It is nonetheless the case that representations can overlap and so can become the basis for cultural knowledge and social interaction. Generally speaking, a representation is a "cultural" representation when it can make some claim to belong to a general or shared culture. So television advertisements can be thought of as cultural representations, in part because of their deliberate constructedness, and in part because of their distribution in a powerful medium. Students, when they enter the realm of argumentation, and begin to take positions on public, topical issues, can begin to see themselves, therefore, as entering into a world of cultural representation. Because their argumentation will have been carefully constructed, because they will have learned that one cannot merely say anything and have it pass as argument, and because they will have entered some kind of public space where "interests" are at stake, it makes sense to suggest to them that their arguments are representations, or maps of the world. They might come, then, to see that the validity and value of their maps require some kind of public scrutiny—it is not enough for them merely to have expressed themselves. They might also come to see that making a contribution to an ongoing conversation is one way of carrying out a responsible task of an intellectual citizenry.

They might. But then again, they might not. A modicum of humility moves us to admit that the links between the individual and the cultural are not automatically made by this use of rhetorical methodology. As our colleague Kathleen McCormick points out, students will often cling tenaciously to the ideologies of individualism that push them to co-opt the political as personal and to deny the connections between their "own" beliefs and the workings of race, class, gender, sexual orientation, age, etc., as the cultural means by which beliefs are constructed (McCormick, Waller, and Flower 1987). We do not see any quick fixes for this problem, but we are trying to avoid compounding it by insisting that students leave the course indoctrinated by a value system determined in advance. A pedagogical insistence that students relinquish their notions of individualism for socially grounded theories of agency and ideology may, as McCormick suggests, instantiate a new ideology of objectivity, a new insistence on the "correct" version of reality to be learned. The methodology of argumentation demands that students learn a process of accountability to themselves and others for the versions of reality they embrace. As a methodology it certainly is bound to theory—we are not claiming a theory-less method of reading or writing. Its limits, as a means of promulgating more progressive ideas or as an impetus to social change, lie in the communities to which students find themselves accountable. Perhaps we can hope, at best, for students to experience a productive tension between individual cognition and social process, personal beliefs, and ideology.

But that jumps a long way ahead. Summary is the first stage of producing an argument, but it deals only with a single text. Students must then begin trying to understand how a range of authors take differing or intersecting positions on related issues; this is the "synthesis" stage. Students are asked to read several more essays, and to begin attempting to isolate the key issues, and to note how authors relate to these issues. In this process, students are constructing an organization of the community opinion; the organization of opinion is not there waiting for students to *discover* it—they must build it, and it is possible to build several different ones. Different ones highlight different aspects of the conversation. The organization they build *does* need to have a certain sort of relationship to the authors' positions, which we ask students to be "faithful" to. For example, if students build an organization of views on the question "What is writing?" they might construe Barth in the following way: "While Barth doesn't answer this question directly, he seems to think of writing as an activity reserved for a talented few. For instance, when he talks about the value of a writing course, he suggests that only a few will be writers but all will benefit by achieving better appreciation of what the talented few produce." That is, we ask them to make explicit their inferences and evidence for inferences. What they then do is to begin constructing a "synthesis tree." They are asked to decide intuitively where the community splits on what seems to them to be the central issue. Effectively, based on their summaries and synthesis, they see their authors as beginning to fall into two "camps." Inside each of the two major "splits" in the conversation, they will locate further minor splits. Building this "tree" is a way of building a representation of the issue.

When students have constructed a representation of the major issue, and understand how a community of authors divides on the issue(s), they are then ready to explore the issue in depth through "analysis," the third stage of developing a position. "The purpose of analysis is to explore your issue in enough depth to allow you to arrive at a position of your own or, at the very least, conclusions that you can develop into a position" (Kaufer, Geisler, and Neuwirth 1989, 178). Exploration can take many forms, of course, but it will likely include a focus on problem cases, and an attempt by the individual students to come up with problem cases from their own experiences. Students will have learned that "authors see an issue through problem cases that cause tension. Something about these cases leaves the author in a state of restlessness, dissatisfaction, or frustration." Students are asked to look into their own experience for an event that is a problem case related to the issue they are exploring. They will have developed a database of possible problem cases from their attempts at summary and synthesis. They can attempt to personalize these problem cases: "For each entry in your list, tell or write a story that makes you the victim of the frustration." Such a task allows students to draw on personal experience as much as they want—or it allows them to invent from their personal resources something that will have the force of a personal story. They are not being called on to indulge in personal reminiscence, since the experience they narrate will always be conceived as a "case of" something. They are being asked to employ personal resources, not merely to indulge themselves. We ask them to write the story in a way that will convince other people that the problem they are describing exists and has significance (e.g., it is widespread, it has negative consequences in terms of shared values, etc.). That is, we ask our students to make an "existence/significance argument"—to find all the available means of persuasion (from their experience and from the readings) to persuade someone that the problem exists and is important.

In a related way, they need not get into personal issues if for any reason they are shy about the issue. They can simply adopt the first-person narrative style and make up a "troublesome narrative." With some kind of personal fix on the issue, students can begin to explore possible solutions to the problem case they are dealing with. Some students, of course, pick problems that come from their experience with the readings themselves. For example, one student picked the following problem: "The authors in the community were identifying isolated problems in the teaching of writing but failing to relate them to an underlying cause, namely, inadequate definitions of writing." They are encouraged to work toward developing a solution that is a result of the way they are beginning to see themselves traveling through the issue at hand. They are explicitly not encouraged to take sides or to rely on some one authority or another. Such an approach, relying on an authority, is dismissed as "off the rack" shopping for solutions, instead of being seen as a way of producing a personal position statement. If an "off the rack" solution exists for the problem, then it's not a problem (their existence proof fails). When they encounter such a situation, they must either refine their statement of the problem case, so that their readers can see that the "off the rack" solution does not fit, or else build a different problem case. At the end of the analysis section, students won't yet, of course, have developed a full-blown position.

> Having thoroughly explored the issue, you are now ready to see what your commitments look like against the context of your exploration. You're ready to draw some conclusions about the issue. By "conclusions," we don't mean anything as careful and elaborate as a line of argument. . . . Instead, we mean statements that are likely to lead you—after further exploration, testing, and revision—to ideas that you can eventually refine into an original position, line of argument, and finally an original essay or contribution. (Kaufer, Geisler, and Neuwirth 1989, 209)

Ultimately, then, students are led into constructing their own arguments. Clearly, this is not a process that can be carried through in a short period of time. It is not the kind of class in argument that one can give if one is interested only in "correcting" mistakes in students' attempts to produce a well-argued position; a considerable investment of teaching time is required for such a pedagogy to work. Such a class offers a way of teaching students to write arguments instead of merely assuming that they will know what to do if asked to do it without detailed instruction. The teaching of writing in English classes cannot be a matter of correction rather than instruction; therefore, it is a critical task for members of English departments to work together to develop a detailed pedagogy. If, as we think is the case, the pedagogical system of our argument and interpretation class reflects the actual practice of writers, then it seems to us the appropriate pedagogy for teaching our students to become actively engaged as writers.

As we indicated above, we have plans to institute two first-year classes—each being the mirror image of the other. The methodology drawn from "Reading and Writing Arguments" drives both courses, but while the emphasis in A&I is on the first term, I&A focuses primarily, but not exclusively, on interpretive practices. We have already described the thematic focus of A&I on issues of literacy. It remains for us briefly to describe the focusing theme of I&A and to explain a bit as to how the argumentation methodology will be adapted to a course that emphasizes how people organize and articulate meanings in specific communities.

Let us repeat that we do not intend to have our two classes break down into one that is more oriented to writing, while the other is more oriented to literary and/or cultural studies. Nevertheless, there will be relative weights given to the two classes, given the two major programs that will contribute to their design. In each of the classes, writing will be taught and not merely assigned. And writing will be taught according to the principles we have just outlined, which are intended to lead students into understanding the complexities of holding positions. Because the I&A class is intended to originate more from the literary and cultural studies side of our resources, it seemed fair to ask ourselves somewhat stringently just what cultural studies is or does. Given that cultural studies is an emergent discipline, it was not easy for us to come up with a definitive answer. We put the question to ourselves in a way that might seem inhospitable to people who do literary or cultural studies: "What skills does cultural studies require and teach?" Given that the humanities disciplines have traditionally defined themselves against such questions of utility, we had given ourselves something of a problem. However, as we discussed the pedagogy of the A&I class, it seemed clear to us that the emergent field of cultural studies differed, at least as we had begun to practice it, from the more traditional approaches to literary studies that have been common in English departments. Part of the inheritance of literary studies in our times is that of the literary icon, or the well-wrought urn, the self-contained aesthetic object, an object that might well tease us out of thought "as doth eternity." Although the argument would be too lengthy to rehearse here, perhaps it can be taken as a given that the heritage of the old New Critical approach to texts was ahistorical. Cultural studies, on the other hand, insists that texts, and cultural objects in general, are situated in time and place. They occupy "positions," that is to say, and from those positions make various claims on our attention. Once cultural productions are conceived as positional, they can be thought of as taking or representing some kind of action. Kenneth Burke thought of texts as "dancing an attitude," and thought of attitudes as "incipient actions." A "cultural studies" approach to cultural productions and receptions needs to pay attention to the way in which texts belong to historical contexts and to related political, economic, and social contexts. Perhaps what still needs more theoretical consideration is the problem of just how it is that such situated productions actually do dance out their attitudes, or incipient actions, when they come into relation with new reading situations. The question, then, of the "use" of cultural productions in differing situations—the ways in which cultural productions are used, appropriated, made use of—demands further theoretical attention.

For the purpose of trying to construct a curriculum that makes use both of cultural theory, rhetorical theory, and creative writing,[5] however, it is perhaps already enough to notice that cultural objects can be described as occupying positions, as presenting or making representations, as, in sum, making some kind of argumentative claim on us. Clearly, such argumentative claims will often tend to be only implicit claims; the nature of art, after all, is still in many cases to disguise artfulness. Even in those advertisements that are self-consciously self-reflective, there is often a blatant dissimulation of artfulness. The commercial depicting "ordinary people" who are "spontaneously" singing the Pepsi song might be an example. There may be no better way of handling the issue of ideology in cultural studies than by thinking of it as a matter of implicit argumentation; and to think of one way of resisting ideology as the production of a counterideological argument, or position.[6] It may be that the cultural studies class, "Interpretation and Argument," will work best if it introduces students into some practical work with the theoretical issues surrounding interpretation. Clearly, it would not make sense to introduce first-year students directly to hermeneutical theory. But those in charge of constructing the curriculum should have a grasp of hermeneutics and semiotics, and should attempt to introduce texts and objects and exercises into the classroom which engage students in tasks of summary and synthesis and which lead them to recognize that a representation of something should not be taken as the only representation or as the thing in itself. They should learn, at some level, that representations are often representations of representation. There is a large range of texts etc. that can serve such functions, some of which are briefly discussed, below. The work that is done with such texts should have as its concern the need to develop in students a consideration of how viewpoints differ depending on the situation and positioning of the observer or agent. Students, that is to say, would be led into an understanding not only of the nature of representations, but also of difference. At the end of the day, or the class, one would hope that students with a growing understanding of differences, positions, and the way that representations work would be able to work toward the production of their own argumentative positionings without having to surrender their understanding that others may well differ from them. So the production of argument need not develop into a matter of entrenched defensiveness, or agonistic conflict. Such a pedagogy holds out the promise that we can begin to discuss systematic, and falsifiable, curricula that carry out our educational responsibilities to society by making it possible for students to enter the world productively, creatively, and critically.

In keeping with the premise that I&A should mirror rather than oppose or even "supplement" A&I, our thinking about this new course thus far holds in common with A&I the goal of teaching students the integral connections between the two terms "argument" and "interpretation." Students will be taught to conceive of texts (including their own productions) as constituting various intersecting or opposing sites or positionalities on a "map" of discursive possibilities. Our pedagogical theory rejects Hairston's static model of students as prepackaged, self-contained bundles of interests, incapable of writing outside of personal perimeters. On the other hand, we take seriously the notion that students need a knowledge base in order to take meaningful positions; showing students what a Marxist or feminist reader might look like and asking them to imitate that reader does not adequately account for the complex, incremental process by which writers acquire and shape their positions and opinions. Our solution to the problem of how students acquire new knowledge and learn to write from the positions made possible by that knowledge is based on what we have learned from rhetorical theories of argumentation about the socially mediated nature of knowledge, and from cultural studies about the role that representation plays in creating that knowledge. We hope to accomplish the pedagogical task of giving students access to a knowledge base and teaching them how to speak in relation to the discourses that produce it by introducing them to thematically organized textual "units" that include a variety of voices, genres, and media. These will make up a discursive "map" of possible statements or articulations on a particular issue that has both social and individual ramifications. The writing tasks that students will be assigned will draw on the methods of summary, synthesis, and narration to help students place themselves in relation to other positions on the discursive territory constituted by the texts that form the reading material for the class. "Finding" one's self on this terrain is more than a matter of responding to a range of texts; our experience leads us to believe that it will bring students to construct for themselves the differences among a variety of texts (including their own and their classmates') and the assumptions about power and authority upon which these differences are discursively based.

The methodology of argumentation gives students access to an orderly (albeit artificially organized and highly simplified) version of what experienced readers do in a far more complex and intuitive way when they create meanings from texts. Summary imposes demands that students make their responses answerable to the text in that they are asked to produce evidence for their readings. It also puts pressure on students to be responsible to a reader for whom they are trying to perform a service as well as to persuade: the hypothetical reader who hasn't read the text being summarized. Synthesis asks students to articulate relations between texts, to bring them into a conversation with each other and to convey that conversation to a hypothetical reader. As we have said, it also pushes them to think about positionality through the metaphor of mapping. Analysis also comes into play, but in a rather specialized way. What we wish to emphasize when we teach students how to analyze is a two-fold process by which they find and assess their own positions on a topic and by doing so learn to evaluate the strengths and weaknesses of other positions specifically as they relate to their own. Hopefully, this process of relating different "texts" to each other (a process for which synthesis prepares) can be dialectical, allowing for rethinkings of their own as well as others' positions. Narrative is, as we have suggested, important to this process, and the course will focus in part on how stories—their own and others'—make arguments. The stories they will be asked to write will, then, forge links between their personal experience (broadly defined, as we suggest above) and the experiences encoded in the stories and expository arguments that they are reading. As Greg Sarris argues, storytelling can help students fill the gap between their individual beliefs and ideology, and analysis gives us a specific method, tied to a concrete task, to help students do this work.

As we write, this course is still in the process of being designed, but we can say a few tentative words about its reading materials, its writing tasks, and the relationship we envision between the two. We hope constructively to confuse the distinction between course "content" and "writing skills." It may be helpful to detail some information about the nature of the course's reading and writing tasks before we go on to explain how these two often falsely dichotomized parts of the English curriculum are related in our thinking about what would be most useful for incoming students.

At this point, we are in the process of assembling a two-sided unit that will invite consideration and investigation of how the human body is represented in a variety of print and media texts. One half of the unit will focus on the idealization and standardization of the body, while the other will contain materials concerned with representing differences and similarities between well and ill bodies. The former might contain, for instance, articles on the representation of women in modern advertising, Tony Morrison's novel *The Bluest Eye*; articles on the representation of male athletes, and films such as *Pumping Iron* and *Pumping Iron II: The Women*. A unit on well and ill bodies could include Frances Burney's eighteenth-century mastectomy journals, Judith Williamson's and Simon Watney's work on how AIDS is represented in the popular press, a historical analysis of hermaphroditism as a medically defined "disorder," and the memoirs of Herculine Barbin, a nineteenth-century French hermaphrodite. The texts will be chosen as much for their differences as for their similar themes. The primary goal in selecting them is to induce in students an awareness of how representation creates and regulates differences in even so fundamental a material issue as the body and how it is valued and perceived.

The notion of the body was not chosen randomly nor innocently. As Peter McClaren (1991) argues, the academy typically suppresses bodily experience (except as it erupts in athletic programs, a carefully contained and specifically encoded articulation). By doing so, it ignores one of the primary means by which cultural differences are expressed and experienced. Feminist scholars (Suleiman, Gallop, Jacobus, Keller, and Shuttleworth, Epstein and Straub) have been pointing out the socially constructed nature of bodily experience for years, and in choosing this topic we felt a productive contradiction between the highly cultural and also highly individual nature of the body. While we see the appropriateness of this topic, we do not wish it to limit the horizon of possibilities for the course's future. Our long-range intention is to produce a flexible repertoire of such units that will help to foreground the issue of representation. A unit on how the family is discursively reproduced, for instance, or on representations of labor would allow similar opportunities for teaching how difference and power are constituted through signs. We hope that these units can be produced in such a way as to allow additions and subtractions as well as choice of units by individual instructors.

The goal, then, is not somehow to hand on to students an abstracted set of "writing skills" with which they are asked to master the course's "content." Rather, we hope that students will learn that "content" is produced through representation, that the "tools" are the house they build, and vice versa. These representations include—but by no means privilege—their own summaries, syntheses, and "troublesome narratives." We are less anxious that students learn a repertoire of writing tools or ideological positions than that they learn how writing, like other forms of representation, is an act that necessarily brings writers into relation with each other and that this relation is implicitly or explicitly one of the means by which power is created and deployed.

Clearly, we have work ahead of us. We believe however that the task of constructing a "one-course" design curriculum in English is one that is long overdue. The relative absence of theoretically grounded attempts to think through the nature of the discipline could well be part of the malaise of the humanities. If the new "theory" of literary and cultural studies does have anything profound to offer by way of changing our lives in the academy and in society at large, then it is clearly time for it to make serious attempts to move to instantiate its claims. Our contention here is that a one-course design curriculum can be very practical, that it can have an explicit and committed agenda, and that it can remain open to correction in the ongoing process of learning how it is that we should carry on the task of teaching. Our further claim is that there is a constructive alliance between cultural theory, rhetorical theory, and creative writing, an alliance that has hardly ever been tapped into, let alone fully exploited.

Notes

1. Kennedy coordinated contributions and wrote the first draft of much of the essay; Kaufer rewrote substantial portions of the whole piece; Straub and Neuwirth contributed specific passages dealing with the two planned, new classes. We all collaborated throughout so as to establish full joint authorship and ownership.

2. Our discussion of the class "Reading Texts" that follows draws on the very successful and widely used text of the same name, which grew out of the class (see McCormick, Waller, and Flower 1987). This text was one of the first attempts to elaborate a "new" theoretical pedagogy for teaching English. We recognize the wide influence it has had and the work it did in making issues of ideology and reader/text interaction part of the current climate of discussion.

3. McCormick and Waller have acknowledged the underspecification of this mechanism and intend to elaborate it in a second edition of *Reading Texts*.

4. The classes have now had a full year in our curriculum. They were presented to the university community under a general rubric: "76-100/101: An Introduction to English Studies: Argument and Interpretation." The two classes were listed separately as "76-100: Argument," and "76-101: Interpretation."

5. There really isn't room here to develop the ways in which creative writing could and should be incorporated in general university writing classes. Our curriculum has made only modest steps toward incorporation and that is specifically with reference to instruction in writing narrative. Modest as this step is, it at least signals that our creative writing faculty have a central role to play in our first-year writing curriculum and tells our students something important about how we, as a department, view writing. At present, discussions of the college-level required curriculum include discussion of a category of classes (sometimes referred to as "making and knowing," sometimes as "producing and reflecting") from which students must take at least one class. The category will specifically include creative writing classes (as well as others from our other programs). We believe this will signal an important decision to position creative writing at the center of a liberal arts curriculum and not exile it to the peripheries. To generalize the importance of creative writing in writing instruction in general, one would need to insist that students learn something of particular importance when they learn to reflect on their own practices. Perhaps the way to develop the point would be to say that in creative writing classes, students learn something in a unique way about producing discourse in particular genres. Since the world is made up of generic discourses, such learning is of direct relevance to students' literate entrance into the public world.

6. This claim would seem to be in line with the argument developed by Voloshinov (1986).

Works Cited

Barth, John. 1985. "Writing: Can It Be Taught?" *New York Times Book Review*, 90.1 (16 June): 3.

Flower, Linda. 1985. *Problem-Solving Strategies for Writing*. 2nd ed. San Diego: Harcourt, Brace, Jovanovich.

———, et al. 1990. *Reading to Write: Exploring a Cognitive and Social Process*. New York: Oxford University Press.

Graff, Gerald. 1992. *Beyond the Culture Wars: How Teaching the Conflicts Can Revitalize American Education*. New York: W. W. Norton.

Hairston, Maxine. "Opinion." 1991. *The Chronicle of Higher Education*, 23 January: B1–B3.

Kaufer, David S., Cheryl Geisler, and Christine M. Neuwirth. 1989. *Arguing from Sources: Exploring Issues through Reading and Writing*. San Diego: Harcourt, Brace, Jovanovich.

McClaren, Peter L. 1991. "Schooling the Postmodern Body: Critical Pedagogy and the Politics of Enfleshment." In *Postmodernism, Feminism, and Cultural Politics: Redrawing Educational Boundaries*, edited by Henry A. Giroux, 144–78. Albany: State University of New York Press.

McCormick, Kathleen, Gary Waller, with Linda Flower. 1987. *Reading Texts: Reading, Responding, Writing*. Lexington, MA: D.C. Heath.

Myers, Greg. 1991. "Lexical Cohesion and Specialized Knowledge in Science and Popular Science Texts." *Discourse Processes 1991:* 1–26.

Spivey, Nancy. 1990. "Transforming Texts: Constructive Processes in Reading and Writing." *Written Communication* 7: 256–87.

————, and J.R. King. 1989. "Readers as Writers: Composing from Sources." *Reading Research Quarterly* 24: 7–26.

Voloshinov, V. N. 1986. *Marxism and the Philosophy of Language.* Translated by Ladislav Matejka and I. R. Titunik. Cambridge, MA: Harvard University Press.

13 Transforming the Academy: A Black Feminist Perspective

Beverly Guy-Sheftall
Spelman College

In a compelling essay describing her own revolutionary pedagogy, feminist theorist and professor bell hooks (1989) invokes Miss Annie Mae Moore, her favorite high school teacher, who embodies the idea of the teacher as subversive and whom hooks reverentially calls her "pedagogical guardian." Miss Moore was

> passionate in her teaching, confident that her work in life was a pedagogy of liberation, one that would address and confront our realities as black children growing up within a white supremacist culture. Miss Moore knew that if we were to be fully self-realized, then her work, and the work of all our progressive teachers, was not to teach us solely the knowledge in books, but to teach us an oppositional world view—different from that of our exploiters and oppressors, a world view that would enable us to see ourselves not through lens of racism or racist stereotypes but one that would enable us to focus clearly and succinctly, to look at ourselves, at the world around us, critically, analytically. . . . (49)

In his introduction to Paulo Freire's *Pedagogy of the Oppressed* (1970), which delineates the concept of "education as the practice of freedom," Richard Shaull, hooks reminds us, offers a concise definition of revolutionary pedagogy, to which Miss Moore might have exclaimed "amen":

> Education either functions as an instrument which is used to facilitate the integration of the younger generation into the logic of the present system and bring about conformity to it, or it becomes the practice of freedom, the means by which men and women deal critically and creatively with reality and discover how to participate in the transformation of their world. (50)

There have been two major problems in the American academy which I have struggled against in my own teaching over the past

---

This essay appeared in an earlier, abbreviated form as "Practicing What You Preach." *Liberal Education*, 77.1 (January/February 1991): 27–29.

twenty-one years. The first is a fundamental assumption for the contributors to this volume: much of what goes on in educational institutions reinforces the problematic and erroneous notion that the normative human experience is Western, European American, white, male, Christian, middle-class, and heterosexual. A deep sense of alienation is likely to plague students whose own identities are different from what they've been led to believe is the norm by the texts which they are required to read and the Eurocentric values which they are encouraged to embrace. Students who represent this norm, and they are fast becoming a minority in many educational settings, have difficulty seeing the world and their place in it differently. In short, as Anne Balsamo and Michael Greer put it (see chapter 14, this volume), one of our central pedagogical problems is that "individuals are differently situated in a variety of networks of domination and oppression that are, for many white, middle-class students and teachers, naturalized and therefore invisible." Second, because students have not been encouraged to feel connected to what they are required to learn—they are led to believe that education is an objective, purely rational endeavor—it is no surprise that students feel unattached to the world of real human beings and therefore disinclined to want to change the conditions under which many people live throughout the world.[1] In their collaborative essay, C. Mark Hurlbert and Ann Bodnar (chapter 11, this volume) poignantly describe the conflictual relations between traditional educational expectations and social activism. The central question they pose is how can literature classes become "places in which to begin a lifelong process of creatively acting . . . [to] change the world." Likewise, in my own thinking about our dilemmas as progressive educators and in reflecting as well upon my own professional career as a scholar/activist, I find that certain related questions keep intruding:

1. Can the university be a site for serious, transformative work?
2. Can one be truly "oppositional" or "subversive" as a university professor within one of the most hierarchical institutions within our society?
3. Can we teach in ways which do not reinforce structures of domination, racism, sexism, or class exploitation?
4. How can we use our power as teachers in ways that are not coercive, punitive, controlling?
5. Can we undue the "miseducation"[2] that most students have been subjected to by the time we get them in our college classes?

6. Can we undo our own "miseducation" since most of us are also victims of patriarchal, racist, sexist ways of knowing and teaching?

Are we willing to endure the anger and frustration, and even hostility, at times, of students and other faculty when we overturn, challenge, their most cherished ways of seeing the world and themselves? For example, despite what most students have been taught since the beginning of their formal schooling in the United States, Christopher Columbus did not "discover" this country in 1492; in fact, he invaded indigenous peoples' land and set in motion a process of decimation, even of genocide from American Indians' point of view. How radical it would be for all of us to teach in such a way that all of our children would know who the real criminals and thieves have been throughout history; one can get a hint at such answers by going to museums and seeing artifacts which belong to someone else. How refreshing it would be to know who the real victims have been throughout history and most important what has been stolen and by whom. How radical it would be to simply tell the truth, for example, which would, of course, begin with admissions in our own country about the annihilation of native peoples, their culture, and ways of life.

I want to turn now to what I attempt to do in my own classes at Spelman College, where I have been teaching since 1971, as a way of illustrating how we might begin to think about transforming our classrooms and our pedagogies and therefore the academy itself.[3] My own classroom innovations are linked to a major curriculum development project in women's studies which was initiated by the Women's Research and Resource Center in 1983 and funded for four years by the Ford Foundation. The project addressed the need for a gender- and race-balanced core curriculum at Spelman which would be sensitive to the particular experiences of women of African descent throughout the world. Specifically, ten core courses and/or introductory courses in the humanities and social science disciplines were targeted for revision. This project propelled Spelman to the forefront of curriculum development efforts in women's studies on historically black college campuses; we also became the site for the first "mainstreaming" project in women's studies on a black college campus.

My own teaching strategies were impacted as well. On the first day of class I am very open and explicit about what it is that I am trying to accomplish. As Cary Nelson (chapter 3, this volume) explains with respect to his teaching a contemporary American poetry class, he had "an agenda determined by my sense of where the country and the profession were culturally and politically, an agenda shaped by the cultural work I believed was must useful for me to do as a teacher." Likewise, I don't present myself as politically neutral, void of a value system and biases.[4] I indicate that much of what I think and believe and value is not consistent with the dominant culture's belief system, especially as it relates to race and gender. I acknowledge that I don't know everything—that I am always, hopefully, in the process of growth, self-evaluation. I indicate that I'm not the same teacher that I was ten or fifteen years ago, thank goodness! I also indicate that I am not the ultimate authority in the class.

On the first day of a particular class, "Introduction to Women's Studies," which I presently co-teach with Spelman's president, Johnnetta Cole, I (we) assign a group of autobiographical texts by non-Western women or women within our own culture who would be considered "other," and indicate that the students will become "experts" on the cultures from which these texts emerged; in subsequent classroom discussions on the varieties of female experience, the students will provide insights they've gleaned from their assigned texts and their reading (histories, ethnographic studies, sociological literature, etc.) about these cultures as we discuss questions of race, class, ethnicity, and gender. We chose autobiographies or autobiographical novels, in some cases, because these genres place women at the center of their own experience and provide "an occasion for viewing the individual in relation to those others with whom she shares emotional, philosophical, and spiritual affinities, as well as political realities" (Braxton 1989, 9). These texts, which are supplemented by secondary material on the culture from which these life stories emerge, include Beverly Hungry Wolf (Blackfoot), *The Ways of My Grandmothers* (1980); Helen Sekaquaptewa (Hopi), *Me and Mine: The Life Story of Helen Sekaquaptewa, as told to Louise Udall* (1969); Winnie Mandela (South Africa), *Part of My Soul Went With Him* (1985); Rigoberta Menchu, *I, Rigoberta Menchu, An Indian Woman in Guatemala* (1984); Tsitsi Dangarembga (Zimbabwe), *Nervous Conditions* (1988); Kamala Markandaya (India), *Nectar in a Sieve* (1954); Nafissatou Diallo (Senegal), *A Dakar Childhood* (1982); Ellen Kuzwayo (South Africa), *Call Me Woman* (1985); Maxine Hong Kingston (Chinese American), *The Woman Warrior* (1976).

On the first day, I (we) also introduce myself to the class and have the students introduce themselves so that they will know that who they are as particular human beings is significant in terms of what transpires in the classroom. I say to them, the majority of whom are black women, that what they have experienced already is more representative of the lived experience of the world's population (people of color and women) than what they've read about in most of their classes—the experiences of a small group of Western white men. In solidarity with the other feminist perspectives represented in this book, a significant component of my "oppositional" pedagogy is to decenter Eurocentric, male models and experience, and to critique the process by which we come to believe that whiteness and maleness are the most valuable commodities which humans can possess.[5] Where one begins is very important. I would begin, for example, in world literature classes where human civilization began—not with the Greek classics, *The Iliad* and *The Odyssey*, but with texts such as *Sundiata*, an epic from Mali, and *The Book of the Dead* (Egypt) from ancient Africa.[6] Spelman students are frequently shocked to learn that the cultural and intellectual heritage of the West is traceable to ancient African civilizations. Writing assignments would include comparisons of the epic tradition in different cultural contexts.[7]

In the "Introduction to Women's Studies" class, I begin not with the experiences of middle-class, Western, white women, but with the experiences of many Third World women of color who are still agricultural workers, food producers, hard workers, and whose very survival (themselves, their families, their kin group) depends on, for example, their ability to locate water and find firewood. In this regard, I show, during the first two class periods, filmstrips on women in cross-cultural perspective, specifically women in sub-Saharan Africa, India, and China.

A second major pedagogical strategy is making central to my students' learning the idea that knowledge is also experiential. Thus, by extending Ellen Berry and Vivian Patraka's (chapter 6, this volume) notion of the classroom as a "laboratory of culture," we can acknowledge that we learn not just by reading books, doing library research, but by getting outside the parameters of conventional classroom instruction. A major assignment, for example, in "Introduction to Women's Studies," is the requirement that students choose a site where gender/race/class issues are played out; students are required to visit their chosen sites not just as objective, unconnected participant observers, but as workers, volunteers, if you will, and do a final paper and oral report. It is hoped that what students have learned about the complexity of the human experience from their reading of literary texts (autobiographies and autobiographical novels) will be useful as they embark upon the "real world" evident in their chosen sites outside the university. What follows is the poignant introduction to a student's final paper on her experience at a battered women's shelter, which underscores in a profound manner the connections students are able to make between themselves and the persons being "studied" with this particular approach to the assignment:

> The shelter is an enormous gray Victorian house. I entered cautiously, unsure of what awaited me. I looked for cots lined up against a wall. There were none. After I sat there a while watching the women milling about, entering and exiting their bedrooms, tidying the living rooms, cooking food, talking, laughing, and watching television, I realized that I had slipped into a tiny community unawares.
>
> "Are you new here?" asked a little boy who could not have been more than six birthdays.
>
> "No, stupid," returned a little woman at age eleven. "She works here."
>
> The little boy in his faded overalls and runover shoes voiced the most startling of all of the observations I made during the hours spent volunteering at the Council on Battered Women: there are no obvious distinctions between me and the women who ran for their lives to the safety of the shelter. I often traveled unnoticed among these women about whom there are so many societal assumptions.

The papers should also demonstrate a synthesis of the students' reading of secondary sources about particular issues (domestic violence if it's a battered women's shelter; alternative education if it's a private school for African Americans); the insights they've gained on site; and analyses (from history, sociology, anthropology, and psychology, for example) of the concepts and theories (such as the relationship between patriarchy and male violence against women) they've learned in class and from reading assignments about culture/race/class/gender. What I (we) hoped, as well, was that students would be able to see something of themselves within the communities they experienced. The conclusion to the preceding paper demonstrated just that:

> On the corner of the street I visited there is a large house filled with women and their children who have everything in common with any other women and children you might know. The kids like to play Nintendo and eat cookies just like my nieces and nephews. The women are sometimes in good moods, sometimes in bad moods, like all other women. Like the rest of the world, they want to be happy and want their children to be happy, and safe. And just like all of us, they have felt the sting of patriarchy. The only difference is that for them, it is not just a figure of speech.

I am convinced, from what students tell us and from what they write, that teaching in these new ways (being very conscious about what we teach and why we teach what we teach)—which bell hooks (1989) describes for herself as adopting a revolutionary feminist pedagogy—

holds the potential for real change in our students. Some concrete examples from my own classroom can illustrate this point. The class I co-taught with President Cole in 1989 was an unusual one for Spelman College, the oldest and one of only two liberal arts colleges for black women in the U.S. There was a lone white student from Agnes Scott (a predominantly white women's college on the other side of Atlanta) who admitted on the first day that she was very nervous and had not had the experience of being a racial minority in a classroom; there were two students from Morehouse (a historically black men's college across the street from Spelman, with whom we share a similar history) who were also nervous and huddled close to Cole and me on the first day, feeling somewhat more safe, I presume. Within three weeks, one of the Morehouse men (who died tragically, following a fraternity hazing incident during the course of the class) was talking openly about his new ideas about being a good father, especially as it related to raising a daughter, which he admitted he now preferred to raising a son. His friend talked honestly about violent behavior in his relations with his sister and why it was necessary to reconceptualize notions of masculinity. He chose as his site Men Against Violence, a self-help, all-male group organized for the purpose of understanding and struggling against their own patterns of violent behavior. The student from Agnes Scott decided to spend a semester as an intern in Washington, D.C., working on minority issues and wrote back to us after the last Governor's election in Georgia that her own grandfather had voted for Andy Young! This was astounding, she asserted, because he had, in fact, been the person who literally, in his role as jailer, locked up Martin Luther King, Jr., during his early imprisonment in Georgia.

I am convinced that what happens in this women's studies class (which we teach yearly) is suitable, even critical, for students everywhere, irrespective of their race, ethnicity, or gender. Students leave this Afrocentric, woman-centered class knowing more about themselves and the world in which they live, but also feeling connected to the people about whom they studied and among whom they worked. At the end of her paper about a homeless shelter, a student mused:

> What separates me from a homeless pregnant girl in the street? What is the fundamental difference between my mother and the women addicted to crack standing in line everyday between 10:00 a.m. and noon for food? Is the difference money? Education? While I do this study and go back and forth to my warm room, looking forward to Christmas at home, I ask myself what makes me different. I realize I am asking the wrong question. What makes us all the same? We look at these statistics and we try to

isolate these people from society, but we can't do that. Everyone is part of society; you can not exclude according to circumstance.

Another student alluded to feelings of hopelessness and the difficulty of "letting go":

One day I walked into the shelter and felt like crying. I saw Levinda, Karen's little girl and she was in the corner crying. I asked her what she was crying about and she said that in school that day the kids were making fun of her, saying that she lived in the homeless place. She also said that they made fun of her because she didn't have barrets [sic] in her hair like the other girls. Levinda said that she asked Karen for some barrets, and she told her that she couldn't afford them. After I left the shelter that evening I went to the drugstore and I bought Levinda barrets . . . I felt so good about myself once I gave her the barrets and I braided her hair and put them on her. That night I went home and I thought about it, and it all seemed so insignificant. Buying Levinda barrets couldn't make her situation go away and it really bothered me. . . . I don't think anything has ever affected me the way Cascade House did, because it made the problem real for me. Initially, I saw the homeless as statistics, and really thought of it as drunk men on the side of the street corner, who I felt should get their "act" together. I think I could relate better when I saw that it was women and children along with the men who were suffering. . . . It was the first time that I researched something and felt as if I couldn't let go. . . . I stopped by to say good-bye to Levinda and her mother and I felt as if I was abandoning them. . . . When I left Cascade House that day I left a part of me there.

Finally, we have tremendous power as teachers and administrators to help students rethink and challenge their own socialization with respect to racism, sexism, heterosexism, to name only a few "isms" which hurt all of us. Despite our sense of powerlessness when it comes to overcoming the awesome problems which confront us, we can help to influence the direction in which this country will move as we approach the twenty-first century. At the end of the feminist theory class I taught at Spelman this academic year, a male student from Morehouse commented upon how the course had "changed" him in some ways:

I can definitely say that some of my attitudes on gender were stereotypical and therefore problematic. I think this was due primarily to my lack of knowledge . . . as well as to some underlying misconceptions I had about what it means to be male and what it means to be female. . . . [T]hough female oppression exists, I hadn't recognized its importance in the struggle of African people. Moreover, my readings of the various texts have made a considerable impact on the way I view myself, females in general, and my relationships with females. If nothing else, the texts have prompted intense introspection and forced me to ask very challenging questions including: (1) Is marriage a viable option? (2) Must the African female's struggle be separate from that of the total liberation of African people, and (3) Must I now reevaluate what it means to be male in order to understand female sexuality?

White students certainly need an inclusive curriculum and "oppositional" pedagogy as much as "ethnic" students do. We must not lose sight of the ultimate purpose of "revolutionary" pedagogies, and that is educating students who will work to make this planet a better place for all humans to live. Working with an advocacy agency for women of color with AIDS (Sisterlove), a student of ours confronted her homophobia and the need to embrace difference:

> While at the office working, I had the opportunity to speak with feminists, lesbians, homosexuals and other men involved in the fight against AIDS. At first, I was nervous about being in the room, but soon after, I loosened up. We had interesting discussions about our differing sexualities and practices.... At the conference on December 1, 1990, World AIDS Day, I no longer concerned myself with who was or wasn't straight. As the Rev. Jesse Jackson said, "[W]e all were bonded by the common thread, making up one large quilt."

If we are to really change our classroom practices in ways compatible with what the contributors to this volume have variously described, we must prepare students for a world in which non-Western peoples of color and women are the world's majority. Our collective human survival and the freedom and dignity in which some of us can live will depend, in large part, on our commitment as educators to help eradicate poverty, racism, sexism, and other forms of domination which various groups continue to experience globally. We must not, as so many of us have argued, continue to teach only "the canon," which has consistently excluded or devalued the experiences of many groups of people. We must discontinue the harmful practice of educating many students away from themselves. We must disrupt the practice of "miseducating" the majority of our students. Sensitivity to issues of race, ethnicity, gender, and class would begin the process of "multicultural literacy" and rid us of the ignorance in which we have basked so blissfully and arrogantly for decades. In opposition to E. D. Hirsch's call of "cultural literacy", we must create educational environments which will produce multicultural literates:

> Multicultural literacy is the ability to function effectively in a nation and world made up of peoples from diverse cultures, races, and groups.... [It] helps individuals to respond effectively

to diversity by recognizing the interconnected nature of our society. (Banks and Banks 1989, 5)

We must also heed the words of bell hooks (1989), who makes a compelling argument for the need to transform ourselves into different teachers, armed with "radical and subversive" feminist strategies which are capable of forging a new world desperately in need of emerging:

> We must learn from one another, sharing ideas and pedagogical strategies.... We must be willing to ... challenge, change, and create new approaches. We must be willing to restore the spirit of risk—to be fast, wild, to be able to take hold, turn around, transform. (54)

Notes

1. I am indebted to sociologist Margaret Anderson for her insights on curriculum transformation as it relates to women and people of color. See especially "Denying Difference: The Continuing Basis of Exclusion in the Classroom" (1987).

2. I am indebted to Carter G. Woodson's classic work *The Mis-education of the Negro* (1933) for many of my ideas about the need for curriculum transformation in the liberal arts. See also Elizabeth Kamarck Minnich's *Transforming Knowledge* (1990) for a contemporary discussion of the "dominant meaning system" which renders invisible the experience of groups other than white, European American men.

3. For a more detailed discussion of my role in curriculum transformation at Spelman College, see Beverly Guy-Sheftall's "Transforming the Academy: The Case of Spelman College" in James and Busia's *Theorizing Black Feminisms* (in press). See also Bell-Scott, Guy-Sheftall, and Royster's "The Promise and Challenge of Black Women's Studies: A Report from the Spelman Conference, May 25–26, 1990" (1991). For a history of the college, see Guy-Sheftall and Stewart's *Spelman: A Centennial Celebration* (1981).

4. We are indebted to the black studies movement of the 1960s for its arguments about the political and nonobjective nature of the curriculum taught in institutions of higher education since the beginning. Minnich (1990) argues some years later that "the *root* problem" is that "at the beginning of the dominant Western tradition, a particular group of privileged men took themselves to be the *inclusive* term or kind, the *norm*, and the *ideal* for all . . ." (2). A considerable body of literature on feminist pedagogy is now beginning to emerge. It includes the work of Frinde Maher and Barbara Omolade.

5. See Elsa Barkley Brown's brilliany essay "African-American Women's Quilting" (1989) for a discussion of her own pedagogy and her concept of "pivoting the center" rather than "de-centering" in her approach to teaching. See also bell hooks's *Feminist Theory: From Margin to Center* (1984) and Chela Sandoval's "U.S. Third World Feminism" (1991).

6. See Molefi Kete Asante's *Kemet, Afrocentricity and Knowledge* (1990) for a discussion of the writing systems of classical African civilizations in the Nile Valley and of the Greeks, to whom he refers as "intellectual children of the Africans" (4). See Chinweizu, Onwuchekwa Jemie, and Ihechukwu Madubuike's *Toward the Decolonization of African Literature* (1983) for a discussion of African oral narratives or epics such as *The Mwindo Epic, Sundiata, Monzon and the King of Kore,* and *Kambili;* see also Martin Bernal's *Black Athena* (1987) for a stunning analysis of the origins of "Western civilization" in the East African Rift Valley.

7. See Beverly Guy-Sheftall's "Women"s Studies at Spelman College: Reminiscences from the Director" (1986) for a discussion of curriculum reform in the core at Spelman College during the 1980s.

Works Cited

Anderson, Margaret. 1987. "Denying Differences: The Continuing Basis for Exclusion in the Classroom." The Research Clearinghouse and Curriculum Integration Project. Center for Research on Women. Memphis State University.

Asante, Molefi Kete. 1990. *Kemet, Afrocentricity, and Knowledge.* Trenton, NJ: Africa World Press.

Balsamo, Anne, and Michael Greer. 1994. "Cultural Studies, Literary Studies, and Pedagogy: The Undergraduate Literature Course." [See chapter 14, this volume.]

Banks, Cherry A. McGee, and James A. Banks. 1989. "Teaching for Multicultural Literacy." *Louisiana Social Studies Journal,* 16 (Fall): 5.

Bell-Scott, Patricia, Beverly Guy-Sheftall, and Jacqueline Jones Royster. 1991. "The Promise and Challenge of Black Women's Studies: A Report from the Spelman Conference, May 25–26, 1990." *NWSA Journal,* 3 (Spring): 281–88.

Bernal, Martin. 1987. *Black Athena: The Afroasiatic Roots of Classical Civilization.* Vol. 1. New Brunswick: Rutgers University Press.

Berry, Ellen E., and Vivian Patraka. 1994. "Local Struggles/Partial Explanations: Producing Feminist Theory in the Classroom." [See chapter 6, this volume.]

Braxton, Joanne M. 1989. *Black Women Writing Autobiography.* Philadelphia: Temple University Press.

Brown, Elsa Barkley. 1989. "African-American Women's Quilting: A Framework for Conceptualizing and Teaching African-American Women's History." *Signs,* 14 (Summer): 921–29.

Chinweizu, Onwuchekwa Jemie, and Ihechukwu Madubuike. 1983. *Toward the Decolonization of African Literature.* Vol. 1. Washington, D.C. Howard University Press.

Dangarembga, Tsitsi. 1988. *Nervous Conditions.* London: Women's Press.

Diallo, Nafissatou. 1982. *A Dakar Childhood.* Translated by Dorothy S. Blair. Harlow, Essex: Longman.

Freire, Paulo. 1970. *Pedagogy of the Oppressed*. Translated by Myra Bergman Ramos. New York: Continuum.

Guy-Sheftall, Beverly. 1986. "Women's Studies at Spelman College: Reminiscences from the Director." *Women's Studies International Forum*, 9: 151–155.

———. (In press). "Transforming the Academy: The Case of Spelman College." In *Theorizing Black Feminisms*, edited by Stanlie James and Abena Busia. New York: Routledge.

———, and Jo Moore Stewart. 1981. *Spelman: A Centennial Celebration*. Delmar.

hooks, bell. 1984. *Feminist Theory: From Margin to Center*, Boston: South End Press.

———. 1989. *Talking Back: Thinking Feminist, Thinking Black*. Boston: South End Press.

Hungry Wolf, Beverly. 1980. *The Ways of My Grandmothers*. New York: Morrow.

Hurlbert, C. Mark, and Ann Marie Bodnar. 1994. "Collective Pain: Literature, War, and Small Change." [See chapter 11, this volume.]

Kingston, Maxine Hong. 1976. *The Woman Warrior: Memoirs of a Girlhood among Ghosts*. New York: Knopf.

Kuzwayo, Ellen. 1985. *Call Me Woman*. London: Women's Press.

Mandela, Winnie. 1985. *Part of My Soul Went with Him*. New York: Norton.

Markandaya, Kamala (pseud.). 1954. *Nectar in a Sieve*. New York: J. Day.

Menchu, Rigoberta. 1984. *I, Rigoberta Menchu: An Indian Woman in Guatemala*. Translated by Ann Wright. London: Verso.

Minnich, Elizabeth Kamarck. 1990. *Transforming Knowledge*. Philadelphia: Temple University Press.

Nelson, Cary. 1994. "The Cultural Work of Teaching Noncanonical Poetry." [See chapter 3, this volume.]

Sandoval, Chela. 1991. "U.S. Third World Feminism: The Theory and Method of Oppositional Consciousness in the Postmodern World." *Genders*, 10 (Spring): 1–24.

Sekaquaptewa, Helen. 1969. *Me and Mine: The Life Story of Helen Sekaquaptewa, as Told to Louise Udall*. Tucson: University of Arizona Press.

Woodson Carter G. 1933. *The Mis-Education of the Negro*. Washington: Associated Publishers.

14 Cultural Studies, Literary Studies, and Pedagogy: The Undergraduate Literature Course

Anne Balsamo
Georgia Institute of Technology

Michael Greer
Illinois State University

"Cultural studies," in Richard Johnson's (1986) words, "has been formed in a two-sided and highly contradictory relationship between academic knowledges and political aspirations" (277). Perhaps nowhere is this tension more pronounced than in the relationship between the political and pedagogical aspirations of cultural studies and the academic knowledges embodied in the undergraduate literature curriculum. Cultural studies may be said, in part, to begin with a class-based critique of literature and the literary canon, and many cultural studies scholars today are rightly suspicious of English departments' moves to colonize and incorporate cultural studies within existing disciplinary and curricular frameworks.[1] At the same time, however, it does appear that cultural studies is finding an academic home of sorts—in the United States, at least—within English departments, and that we will need to find ways of teaching cultural studies in relation to literary studies without sacrificing or eliding the contradictions inherent in this necessary and historically contingent institutional compromise.

Teaching cultural studies in a literature department implicates one in a number of intersecting activities and projects which extend well beyond the spaces of the individual course or classroom. Radical critiques and revisions of the Anglo American literary canon, while perhaps the most highly visible of these projects, are only part of the institutional

The authors would like to thank several colleagues at Illinois State University who helped in the process of shaping this essay. Deborah Wilson read an early draft and offered helpful suggestions. Charles B. Harris provided valuable information on the institutional history of the "Women and Literature" course, as well as significant departmental support for their projects. Ron Strickland organized a faculty teaching improvement seminar on cultural diversity in May 1991, in which a number of ideas in this essay were first formulated and refined through collective discussion.

intervention that must accompany changes in classroom practices. Canon revision itself by no means signifies a commitment to cultural studies; nor does the simple adoption of popular cultural texts as objects of study alongside literary texts. If the constitutive tensions between cultural studies and literary studies are to be productively brought to bear on the production of knowledge in the English department, we will need to critique, revise, and expand the undergraduate curriculum; assert the linkages between interpretation and everyday social life; argue for a vision of "culture" in terms of what E. P. Thompson (1963) called a whole way of struggle (in which literature itself is at times quite marginal); engage the terrain of "the popular" in all of its manifestations—in addition to redefining our pedagogical practices and our role(s) in the classroom.

This essay is written as a series of reflections on specific experiences: it grows out of discussions we had with our colleagues and students, the responses we have gotten to our promotion of cultural studies in committee meetings and faculty teaching workshops, and, most notably, the practices and struggles of teaching as they have taken place in and around the undergraduate literature classroom. The essay was written during the 1990–91 academic year, while we were both teaching in the English department at Illinois State University at Normal.[2] In part, this essay may be read as our joint response to our colleagues in the profession of literary studies who have posed the question of what it means "to do cultural studies" in a literature class. We are not advancing a single model for the importation of cultural studies, but we do want to chronicle some of the specific strategies we have employed and the problems—both practical and theoretical—we have encountered along the way. Our main premise is that cultural studies is most usefully seen as a displacement of "literature" and an interruption of the established practices of the teaching of literature. Cultural studies can never by smoothly integrated into existing literature programs without ceasing to become cultural studies. It is, rather, a way of making trouble, of posing unanswerable and bothersome questions about the institutionalized discourses of literary study.

Politically, the name "cultural studies" is most visibly connected to a small number of programs which, like Carnegie Mellon's or Syracuse's, have reconstituted their departmental and curricular frameworks to explicitly foreground literary *and* cultural studies. Our essay is, however, most specifically directed toward another audience: those, who, like ourselves, have a desire to teach cultural studies but who find ourselves working in rather more traditionally defined programs. Short of radically reshaping the discipline of literary studies—which is always more than a matter of rewriting the undergraduate catalog—we are left to work out a series of specific interventions, strategies, and practices by which to displace literature and the literary within the literature classroom itself. We perceive our project, therefore, as a way of using cultural studies to *rearticulate* literature and the literary—to link "literature" to a different set of intellectual and historical discourses, and to "speak" (articulate) "literature" differently.[3]

Our essay, focused on specific classroom practices and experiences, represents only part of the larger project of "doing" cultural studies in an English department. We have, however, attempted to situate our specific discussions within a variety of institutional histories, in order to highlight some of the necessary connections between individual classroom activities and the disciplinary frameworks which shape them. Ultimately, of course, classroom practice is inseparable from other disciplinary and institutional structures and debates, and it is our belief that the work of pedagogy must extend beyond the classroom to include the committee meeting, the curriculum debate, and the disciplinary structuring of knowledge itself. If we are to remain in some sense faithful to the intellectual, institutional, and political histories of cultural studies, we will thus need to foreground what Richard Johnson (1986) calls "the main tension" between the academic knowledges of the English department and the political imperatives of cultural studies.

The remainder of our essay is focused on two courses we have been involved in teaching recently. The first section, written by Anne Balsamo, concerns a course on "Women and Literature," a course generally populated by nonmajors from other departments and programs. The second outlines Michael Greer's "Literary Analysis" course, a required course for English majors. We have attempted in each case to remain as close as possible to the details of our actual teaching practices, informed by the belief that pedagogical "theory" is, in fact, inseparable from the practice of teaching. Writing about the everyday details of teaching, we have found, is in itself a difficult challenge, as well as a risk, for we therein make our classroom discourses available to others in all their sometimes mundane specificity. Taken together, the two sections constitute a collaborative and altogether provisional intervention on behalf of cultural studies.

"Women and Literature": The Institutional Context

As originally proposed, "Women and Literature" was designed "to explore through literature the meaning of being a woman." When it was approved for inclusion in the English department curriculum in 1974, it replaced an experimental course called "Men vs. Women" and was intended to serve as one of the core requirements in the women's studies minor. Writing in 1974, the authors of the course proposal were a bit skeptical about the future of the course, predicting that it might draw at least twenty-five students each semester from all areas of the university. At this juncture, the institution had not imagined a fully developed women's studies program and had certainly not anticipated the increase in interest in women's studies that developed throughout the decades of the 1970s and 1980s.

In 1979, the school adopted a revised set of general education requirements that were identified as the University Studies Program; the 100-level "Women and Literature" course was one of the first proposed by the English department to serve as an option in the University Studies humanities requirement. Although the women's studies program more broadly remained underdeveloped—in terms of curricular offerings, full-time faculty lines, and funding—this move dramatically increased the number of sections of "Women and Literature" offered each semester, from two per semester in 1974 to as many as eight by 1982. Student demand for the course remained consistently high, and the only impediment to increasing the number of sections to satisfy this demand was the lack of qualified faculty to teach what is considered to be a specialized course. By 1989, six out of seven sections of this 100-level course were taught by temporary faculty. In trying to piece together the history of the organization on this 100-level course, I have often come up empty-handed, partly because the course has often been taught by temporary faculty members who have passed through on their way to somewhere else, and partly because, as Cynthia Huff (director of Women's Studies at Illinois State since 1989) explains, the files on women's studies courses are, more generally, sketchy and incomplete. It appears that the 100-level course traditionally has been organized according to a modified "coverage model," where the reading materials are drawn from different genres and from different historical periods to provide an overview of the literary expressions of "the feminine experience." The broad objective for this course, as stated in the course proposal written in 1973–74, is "to explore through imaginative literature the meaning of being female in a male-dominated society." The official description of the course in the university catalog, which has changed little since 1974, restates this objective: "A study of the female experience in imaginative literature; short stories, novels, poetry, and drama with emphasis on women writers of the twentieth century."[4]

This unremarkable institutional history has, in part, undermined my penchant for polemic: women's literature has had a place in this curriculum for fifteen years. Nevertheless, until I began teaching this course I did not fully appreciate the paradoxical position of women's literature vis-a-vis the literature society discussions taking place in cultural studies. But when a sympathetic colleague argued that we should jettison the "Women and Literature" course, along with other "litero-centric" courses, in an attempt to disrupt the ideological work of teaching literature, I argued more forcefully than I ever thought I would for the importance of literature. To call for the decentering of literature is an understandable move when the literature being "decentered" has enjoyed the benefits of high cultural status; but, in the case of, say, working-class poetry, women's writing, slave narratives, and other forms of devalued, marginalized writing, the first move must be to get this writing recognized as worthy of the kind of critical attention afforded a "properly literary" work. The point is to use women's writing as a testament to the consequences of cultural evaluation whereby a select body of writing is institutionalized as worthy of study and anointed with the value-laden designation of "literature," and to suggest the incredible range and complexity of cultural work that has been disregarded and actively suppressed through the process.

When I inherited two sections of this course, I took it as an opportunity to transform a literature-based course that would still contribute to the broad representational objectives of the "Women and Literature" course proposal, but would be organized in keeping with my political and theoretical commitments to cultural studies. The description I offer below weaves together the story of two sections of "Women and Literature": among the students in the one section were seventeen white women and three black women, five white men and one black man; the second section had twenty-five white women students. The narrative I elaborate below offers one way to organize a more detailed description of the course; others are possible. In elaborating the core topics covered in class discussions, I hope to illustrate the specific influence of feminist cultural studies on the revision of this "Women and Literature" course.[5]

The course builds on the stated goals and objectives of the English major by contributing to the development of critical reading and writing skills; it departs from the structure of such a major by moving away from a discipline-based understanding of reading and writing as ahistorical "means of understanding" to one that elaborates those skills as culturally and historically determined discursive practices.[6] I selected three key phrases from the course proposal and catalog description to organize my reconstruction of the course: (1) the meaning of the term "literature"; (2) the notion of "female experience"; and (3) the structure of life in a male-dominated society. To begin with, I was interested in involving the students in a discussion of a contemporary issue in the field of literary studies by having them examine the relationship between the "literary" and the "nonliterary" as a socially constructed distinction involving reading practices, textual effects, discipline conventions, and cultural evaluation.

The study of literature in this course was framed as the study of a discursive formation that constantly undergoes revision through contestations about its cultural purpose. Reading and writing assignments, group projects, and discussion sessions were designed to reinforce the notion of culture as a fertile field of struggle and change. I was concerned to work against a reflection model of culture that would suggest, for example, that nineteenth-century short stories reflected the actual conditions of women's lives at that time; rather, I wanted to examine literature as part of the cultural apparatus that shapes women's lives and as a discursive medium through which women rethink the contradictions and tensions of their gendered identities. In this sense, literature is understood as only one of several expressive media of gender acculturation. To understand more clearly how these media influence, and in part determine, the production of gendered identities, the course included a section on language and the social conditions of knowledge and power. The second half of the course begins with an examination of the material conditions of women's writing and works outward to consider women's position in various networks of power and domination: racism, colonialism, heterosexism. Building on discussions about the position of women in these networks of relations, the final section of the course theoretically addresses the tensions between notions of agency and of identity by investigating how gendered practices and identity are overdetermined by social and historical forces, on the one hand, and yet form the basis of creative discursive strategies (including reading and writing) of resistance and expression, on the other.

Forms of Acculturation

From the beginning, the broad topic of the "Women in Literature" course was focused on forms of gender acculturation, to explore the different *discursive* mechanisms through which "appropriate" gender identities are constructed and disciplined. In a traditional sense, women's "literature" was a starting point, but from there the course moved between literary texts and other forms of textual expression not usually designated and valorized by the term: here, I am referring specifically to the inclusion of such *popular* cultural textual forms as film, television, music videos, graphic arts, photography, and comic novels, but also other forms of women's writing such as institutional criticism, collectivist manifestos, and dialogues between women about pedagogy, art, and the material conditions of women's creativity. Taken together, the course materials demonstrate that despite active attempts to suppress women's engagement with literature and other creative activities, women were, and continue to be, prolific artists, writers, image makers, illustrationists, musicians, essayists, and poets, who critically participate in the business of producing, reproducing, and transforming American culture. But the main objective wasn't simply to orchestrate a multimedia parade of cultural artifacts, but rather to analyze the central role of culture in the production of gendered subjects.

In an attempt to lay the foundation for my later elaboration of a model of the discursive production of subjectivity, I began by suggesting that men and women are actively socialized to assume stereotypical gendered roles when they read certain works of literature. At first, few students volunteered support for this proposition, although one woman begrudgingly admitted that her notions of heterosexual romance were influenced by the drama of *Wuthering Heights*: "Sometimes I think there is something wrong with me—I would love the heat of a grand passion, but all I can ever get is a Bic lighter flame." Her contribution to class discussion provided the opening for other students to talk ironically about the persistence of traditional myths of femininity, masculinity, and heterosexuality. For example, in one discussion about Jewett's "The White Heron," another young white woman readily admitted that the myth about women being somehow "closer to nature" was getting on her nerves. Her reaction, we learned, was based on her experiences in a corporate internship in which she was assigned a position in personnel working on "benefits" communication, rather than a position in systems programming, working on a technical manual. These discussions established a foundation for our collective analysis of other forms of cultural texts in two ways: the short stories narrate several gender mythologies that are still widely circulated and inscribed within contemporary culture; additionally, students constructed a working notion of "acculturation" to name the process whereby people learn to reproduce dominant narratives of gender identity.

The feminist cultural theory that serves as the deep background for the course includes work by British feminist cultural scholars, who, in different ways, have theoretically elaborated the cultural determinations of gendered subjects.[7] In this work the emphasis on "the popular" is not constituted as a fashionable gesture toward relevance, but rather reflects the theoretical and political importance of everyday life as a cultural arena where identities are constructed, and sometimes transformed, even as they are determined by broader social, economic, and historical forces. At different points throughout the semester, I lectured on the history of popular texts to describe the changes in language, narratives, and social relations in which those texts are implicated. Throughout the semester, students considered other forms of gender acculturation, including Hollywood representations of femininity and masculinity, female comic book superheroes, and magazine gender advertisements.

Language and the Conditions of Knowledge

In this section of the course, my aim was to challenge the often unexamined understanding that language is a transparent medium of expression, and, relatedly, to explore the connection between language and power. The background readings for these sessions range from those that consider specific word usage, such as the essay by Francine Frank and Paula Treichler (1989) on the use of the generic "man," to those that deconstruct culturally significant texts. One essay by Judith Williamson (1986), for example, elaborates the semiotic strategy of image advertisements whereby woman is constructed as the "great Other in the psychology of patriarchal capitalist culture" (110). Other essays on black language and bilingual life serve to introduce the topic of race as a framework for understanding the relationship between discourse and power.[8] The point here is twofold: to describe the relationship between language and reality and to illustrate the semiotic production of cultural meaning.

Each week during this section of the course, students were asked to contribute a popular media example that illustrated a gender or race bias; not only does this assignment encourage them to actively engage their common culture—a process I no longer assume happens naturally—it also directs their attention to the specific language used to construct cultural meaning. Several students brought in editorials from the student newspaper; one in particular ignited class discussion.[9] The headline read, "Watch Out, Big Sister May be Watching You," and the editorial began by ridiculing the efforts of one feminist scholar to rewrite familiar fairy tales to reflect nonsexist relationships. Using this as an opening, the editorial went on to denounce those feminists who want to include "substandard" writing by women and minorities in the canon of "Western Literature." The response to the fairy tale project was divided along gender lines; comments from male students indicated that they believed that revising fairy tales was a waste of time; female students, on the other hand, several of whom were mothers with small children, were more willing to defend the importance of such a project. But the issue that particularly animated students was the editorial's opinion that the "rewriters" (of the canon) were replacing "classic authors" with "substandard" ones: "To fill the void left by George Orwell and Herman Melville, the professors are scraping the bottom of the literary barrel to find enough women and minority writers." This explicitly antifeminist editorial was useful in demonstrating quite pointedly the magnitude of resistance to revisionist thinking about language and culture. Furthermore, the editorial illuminated the close interconnection between the classroom and the media world, where the social relations of one public arena directly infiltrate the structure of the other. This editorial offered one local articulation of the discourse on "political correctness" that continues to preoccupy the popular media. The discussion became an occasion to describe the process of institutionalization whereby certain knowledges are legitimated and validated through the disciplinary effects of curriculum construction, which in turn, led us to discuss the process of canon formation as cultural evaluation.[10]

Probably one of the more important essays students read is Bernice Sandler's "The Classroom Climate: A Chilly One for Women" (1982). As an example of institutional criticism, this essay presents a detailed analysis of the academic situations that effectively discipline and silence women's contributions to intellectual exchange, in the classroom, the research laboratory, the faculty conference room, and elsewhere. I asked students to reflect on their language use in this and other classes and to consider, for example, the classroom conditions that encourage them or discourage them from contributing to class discussion. In response, students begin to analyze their relationships to various academic classroom discourses. As a matter of course, these discussions usually include an awkward but explicit conversation about the power relations in our own classroom. Even though I am susceptible to bouts of uncertainty and lapses of confidence in my cultural "authority," I know that that authority is institutionally substantiated and that as long as our educational interactions take place in the context of the academy, the power relations are overdetermined in my favor.

Critical Frameworks: Racism, Ethnocentrism, and Identity Politics

The class continued the analysis of the different valuation of men's and women's contributions to cultural and social life that were initiated in the women and language section in reading discussions of Virginia

Woolf's essay *A Room of One's Own* (1989 [1929].[11] At this point, I asked students to elaborate Woolf's analysis of the material conditions of women's writing in which she promotes the understanding of litera-ture, not as "a repository of timeless truths concerning an eternal hu-man nature," but rather as a cultural production, in which certain forms of expression, interpretations, and indeed, constructions of the world, are differently valued than others.[12] Woolf's preoccupation with the material conditions of the creation of women's art provides an opening for us to turn back and interrogate *her* text for its classist, racist, and ethnocentric biases.

Positioned symbolically at the center of the course, a unit on critical frameworks includes a three-day session on racism, ethnocentrism, and heterosexism.[13] A lecture on black feminist criticism is followed by a class session in which I present a lecture on the structured organization of racism, U.S. imperialism, and other forms of systemic bias, including those based on class, religion, sexuality, physical ability, and ethnic identity.[14] The long-range purpose of presenting this structural outline of the major social and discursive systems of power, domination, and oppression is to complicate the notion of "experience" as a sufficient basis for critical analysis. The more immediate point is to demonstrate how individuals are differently situated in a variety of networks of domination and oppression that are, for many white, middle-class stu-dents and teachers, naturalized and therefore invisible. Earlier, white female students may have begun to understand the connection be-tween personal experience and the patriarchal discipline of women's writing or language use; at this point, they begin to grapple with their position of privilege in a racist system. I situated this talk in the con-text of the articles on "political correctness" in which I explained that, in contrast to the way those articles parodied feminist and antiracist perspectives, those critical frameworks, in fact, elaborate how "politi-cal correctness" is a utopian fiction; there is *no* position of innocence from which one could claim to be "politically correct." On the con-trary, for feminists, one of the most potent lessons of the 1980s is the understanding that in living in the U.S., we are all implicated in net-works of domination and exploitation that we persistently refuse to acknowledge.

For the third day of this unit on critical frameworks, students read two essays from the journal *Heresies: The Issue is Racism,* one describing the mechanisms of day-to-day racism (Cross, Klein, Smith, and Smith 1982), and the second, which deals with the issue of teaching about racism (Shaw and Wicker 1982).[15] Not only do these articles focus our attention on everyday life by directly addressing the dynamics of day-to-day racism, they demonstrate, in describing concrete exercises that can be adapted for classroom use, the importance of developing teaching practices for unlearning racism. Many of the students in my classes were education majors, so in requiring them to read an essay on teaching about racism, I was contributing to their acquisition of nonracist professional skills. Further, in response to the essay about teaching practices, I could elaborate my own pedagogical commitments that govern the staging of this course. The class sessions on racism actually included three sections: a large-group discussion of definitions of racism, dyadic exchange about personal experiences of racism, and a written response about the process of teaching about racism.[16] Not surprisingly, such explicit discussion—about racism, homophobia, and other forms of systemic violence—are often uncomfortable, for me no less than for the students. Often I was indirectly forced to admit my uneasiness and to confront the consequences of my own classroom practices in teaching about racism as a white woman working with twenty-five white female students (during one semester) or with a class that included twenty-two white students and only four black students (another semester), and no Hispanic American or Asian American students. When a student expressed a strong racist belief that was based on a personal story, I knew that I had to respond critically to the racism. I also described the impasse I find myself in, between the desire to recognize the power of personal narratives, on the one hand, and the commitment to challenge racist, homophobic, or classist beliefs, on the other. These discussions are often difficult, and there are no guarantees that they change attitudes or behaviors, but I think they are worthwhile for many reasons, not the least of which is that in staging these discussions, I am compelled to elaborate my pedagogical commitments as well as my complicity with ideological myths and systems of domination.

The Popular Cultural Determinations of Identity

Although the media examples I use vary from semester to semester, reflecting the constant flow and change of popular icons, I usually require students to view the film *Mildred Pierce* (1945). I work through an analysis of the film that considers the representation of Mildred in two different, symbolic, filmic worlds: the domestic melodrama and film noir. Here students are offered an opportunity to seriously engage not only a different form of cultural text, but also different and difficult material on psychoanalysis, feminist film theory, and the politics of representation.

An assignment during this section of the course asks students to produce an autobiography of sorts that describes their individuated consumption of popular texts. The intent is to encourage students to think about how they construct their own identities in terms of signs, symbols, and commodities that circulate as part of the economy of popular culture. Specifically, I ask students to reflect on the forms of popular culture that they enjoy and to describe the gender, race, and class identities promoted in this popular culture. I explicitly ask students to think about the political issues that motivate them and the relationships they have, or would like to have, with other women, with other men, and with people of other races and ethnic backgrounds. Probably the most pointed question I ask them is to think about where and how they are going to invest themselves in the future. The last time I taught this course, students were preoccupied with only a few female musicians/singers: Madonna, Tracy Chapman, k.d. lang, and the Indigo Girls. Next time I teach the course I'd like to talk about women in punk and other nonmainstream female artists.

The final section of the course focuses on the novel *The Female Man*, in which Joanna Russ (1975) offers four different narratives of gender identity that describe different permutations of heterosexual, homosexual, and asexual gender relations. Russ's novel explodes some of the more persistent myths of contemporary culture: technology isn't always benevolent; women aren't always gentle, compassionate, powerless, or afraid of conflict; and history doesn't guarantee absolution or progress. I discuss the relationship between science fiction and contemporary culture, suggesting that these stories express not so much the possibilities of some distant fictional future, but rather, the preoccupations of the contemporary moment. The final exercise for the course asks students to construct a discursive analysis of a cultural issue that represents, in their opinion, a contemporary cultural anxiety about gender identity, sexuality, or gender relations. Recent reports have investigated the adult relations between mothers and daughters, the relationship of reproductive technology and the female body, and the artifactual nature of gender itself.

"Literary Analysis": Cultural Studies and the English Major

The Institutional Story

As one of only three courses required of all English and English education majors at a large state university, English 103: "Literary Analysis II:

Poetry and Drama" serves an important role in defining for students the appropriate conceptual frameworks and working practices of the discipline of English studies. As part of a two-semester introductory sequence (in conjunction with English 102, which focuses on prose fiction), English 103 is conceived of as a course in "literary analysis"— generally read as "close reading" and "explication"—and is usually taught as a combination genre and historical survey course. As my discussions with other instructors of this course confirmed for me, English 103 is generally viewed as a course which teaches students "how to be English majors," or, as the departmental guidelines for the course state, serves to "introduce students to the skills they will need both to excel in subsequent upper-level English courses and to participate in our professional community." English 103 functions explicitly as a course whose project is to define the disciplinary boundaries, concerns, and practices essential to literary studies, and it thereby marks a crucial site for the intervention of cultural studies.

During the 1990–91 academic year, our department designated an ad hoc committee to review and reevaluate the English 102–103 sequence in light of recent changes in the discipline of literary studies. As our discussions in this committee progressed, it became evident that there was little or no consensus regarding the nature of the discipline itself, and, therefore, about what English 103 should address or how it should be taught. Those of us on the committee with a commitment to theory and cultural studies argued that the discipline had changed substantially over the past two decades, that the genre-coverage model implicit in the naming and constitution of the course had been superseded by a notion of English studies as critical practice and discursive analysis, and therefore we asserted that the two-semester sequence should be completely rethought. Several alternative models for the sequence were proposed, including one plan which suggested we divide the sequence differently: rather than organizing the courses by genre, we suggested instead a one-semester course in "practical criticism"—essentially a course in writing, critical practice, and research skills—to be followed by a second course in literary theory, cultural studies, and the history of the discipline. Others on the committee argued that a firm grounding in the historical traditions of the basic genres, as well as in "close reading" and "writing about literature," were essential for English majors before they could be expected to engage the kinds of "theoretical" issues some of us were proposing. It became clear to all involved in this process that the English 102–103 sequence had become a focal point for a much larger and more involved debate about the discipline itself and about the curriculum we would employ to teach it. What strikes me now, however, in a way it didn't then, was the degree to which even our alternative proposals were themselves structured by a powerful institutional logic and the discourse of professionalization—we were still thinking of the course in terms of the internal logics of the English department, rather than conceiving its intersections with the social and cultural domain at large. In the end, the existing description of the course remained substantially unchanged, except for the addition of a sentence on "issues and conflicts in the history of the discipline, and the concepts and implications of literary theory." It had, however, become clear that no individual course in our department could any longer be addressed outside of broader debates about the cultural politics of literary studies itself.

While the course description remained fully a product of the discourse of canon and coverage, our own reconfigurations of this course were acknowledged; we had at least succeeded in putting into play a series of discursive options and alternative frameworks governing one of the most important courses in our undergraduate program. The version of English 103 that I will outline below is in part a product of the debates that took place in that committee, debates which dramatized for me the terms, conflicts, and impulses motivating different visions of literary education. This brief history suggests to me that pedagogical theory and practice emerge out of a dual dialogue: we frame our teaching texts and methods through debates with both our colleagues and our students.

In my own sections of English 103, I wanted to find a way to foreground the institutional debate I was participating in, and to make it part of the "material" we would study and discuss in the classroom. In this project, I was informed by Gerald Graff's imperative to "teach the conflicts," and in part motivated by a broader ethical impulse grounded in telling students about what I thought was actually happening in the discipline called English (see Graff 1989). Courses like English 103 may usefully be seen in terms of institutional discourse, as a set of stories we tell ourselves and our students about the history, social position, and cultural functions of the profession of literary studies. It was clear to me that there were in fact a number of competing narratives available concerning English studies, and that the best thing I could do was attempt to tell as many of them as possible and to highlight the differences among them. Staging English 103 as a single-plot narrative, grounded in a stable model of the literary tradition, was simply not an option I could choose.

My thinking about English 103 thus began with an impulse to present literary studies as a discipline and an institution with a specific history of its own and a set of current debates and issues before it. Institutional history and conflict, then, rather than "primary texts" and the canon, formed the essential backbone of the course. I wanted to find a way to historicize literary studies for my students, and it seemed to me that cultural studies itself offered the most useful vantage point from which to construct such a historicized conception of the field. In addition, it is my conviction that we need to historicize our curricular aims and projects: there is no single, ideal model within which to teach literary and cultural studies today, but rather a series of strategic and tactical moves that can be made in any particular moment.

One point needs to be emphasized: The undergraduate literature course can be significantly reconceptualized once the centrality of literary texts within the broader terrain of culture is questioned, but this by no means suggests that such has "become" cultural studies. A commitment to cultural studies requires that we respect the specificity and history of the cultural studies tradition in its own right and that we remain wary of literature professors' claims to be always already "doing" cultural studies in literature courses (see Nelson 1991). Above all, cultural studies, in this context, represents a commitment to a broadly politicized and historicized view of culture as a realm of ideological struggle, in which literature can play an important but not necessarily central role.

The Shape of the Course

"Literary Analysis," the name and ostensible subject matter of the English 103 course, represents for me a set of practices and a cluster of intellectual problematics which, taken together, construct, define, and identify "literature" as an object of academic inquiry. The object of study in this course is thus a set of critical practices and discourses that constitute the field of "literary studies"; I explain to students early in the semester that this course is not so much about "literature itself" as about the ways in which we read literature and the social and cultural work we make it do. The concept of "cultural work" forms one of the primary theoretical axes of my teaching practice: I am interested in exploring the different kinds of cultural work literature can and might do in contemporary society. Thinking of literary analysis in terms of an inquiry into the "cultural work" of literature shifts attention in the course from formal analysis to the various signifying and material economies in which "literature" has circulated; it conceives of the "meaning" of a literary text relationally and socially—literary texts begin to "mean something" when they are taken up and rearticulated within a given sociohistorical context.

By beginning with a selection of articles on the canon, I immediately pose "literature" as a contested term through which various social agents struggle to find voice, representation, validation, and cultural authority. Cultural studies enables me to see literature as one of many cultural terrains upon which social actors strive to articulate themselves and their view of their relationships to the social formation.[17] "Meaning," I argue, is produced *around* texts and does not reside *within* them. This statement, a long-established critical truism within cultural studies, generates both anxiety and excitement in the undergraduate literature course. It means that there is no final guarantee of a text's "meaning," and that formal analysis is useful only insofar as it is articulated within a discussion of the time and place in which a particular reading or interpretation is produced or reproduced. Literary studies thus becomes inseparable from social and cultural history—a fact which, in itself, leads students to question their own lack of basic historical knowledge.

"Literature" as we read it in the undergraduate classroom is in fact a construction, and I begin the course by asking students to reflect on the process by which certain texts come to be known as "literature" and the mechanisms by which certain models of literary history and tradition are produced and reproduced. This discussion is framed by a series of key questions: Who decides what "counts" as "literature"? What criteria are used in making these decisions? Whose view of the world is "represented" in the texts we call "literature"? Whose views are excluded from "the literary"? Why would some people be interested in challenging the canon as it currently exists? What is at stake in the struggle to define what counts as "literature"?

Charles Altieri's essay "An Idea and Ideal of a Literary Canon" (1983) prompts students to reflect on the aesthetic and cultural functions canons are designed to serve: in contrast to a view of "cultural history as a tawdry melodrama of interests pursued and ideologies produced," Altieri seeks to recuperate at least the concept of a canon, arguing that "it is possible to recover some of the force in classical ideals of a canon" (41–42). Altieri's self-conscious idealizing of the canon-function in cultural history contrasts usefully with Dale Spender's "Women and Literary History," for example, in which Spender analyzes "the power of a tradition" which, in her view, has actively and aggressively excluded women. In juxtaposition with one another, these two essays immediately pose gender as a point of reference in any discussion of "the literary" or "literary history," demonstrating that the concept of "literature" is always the product of a specific cultural agency, and that that agency is always gendered.

Articles by Henry Louis Gates and Mary Helen Washington, for example, turn students' attention to the problematics of race as it relates to the canon. These essays encourage students to reflect on the role of literary studies and higher education itself in terms of the reproduction of a thoroughly racist view of "mainstream" American culture. How much writing by African American writers have they read in their survey courses? How might an intelligent engagement with literary texts by African Americans and other ethnic/cultural groups contribute to the projects of antiracism? Why is it important for us to argue for the inclusion of African American writers in the literary canon? In a predominantly white, middle-class university, these kinds of questions can pose both an intellectual and moral dilemma for students, and I try to encourage discussion to turn toward uncomfortable issues about the pervasively racist nature of higher education.

I have dealt in some detail with the materials for the first section of the course because they establish in crucial ways the terms within which my "cultural studies" approach to literary analysis will be presented. They pose "literature" as a specific historical and disciplinary problem and suggest some of what is currently at stake in the field of literary and cultural studies. The discussion of the canon also poses useful questions about the politics of representation which effectively displace formal analysis as the sole focus of the course or the field. I incorporate our discussion of these essays into a brief lecture on the history of English studies since the 1950s, suggesting how literary studies has been transformed and problematized by changes in the culture at large as well as the demographics of higher education in the U.S. Cultural studies frames and informs these discussions by placing institutional critique in the foreground of the study of "literature."

Catherine Belsey's *Critical Practice* (1980), the main text for the second section of the course, engages students in a dual project: the book encourages them to think explicitly and critically about "commonsense" modes of reading and the theory of literature ("expressive realism") which underlies those modes, and, at the same time, through an elaboration of a poststructuralist/post-Saussurean, language-theory model, to propose alternative strategies for interpreting literary texts. Belsey argues that "obvious" and "natural" modes of reading can be approached more self-consciously, proposing that "the 'obvious' and the 'natural' are not *given* but *produced* in a specific society by the ways in which that society talks and thinks about itself and its experience" (3). Ultimately, Belsey argues that "common sense betrays its own inadequacy by its incoherences, its contradictions, and its silences" (3). The challenge in teaching this view, of course, is to discover ways of demonstrating these incoherences, contradictions, and silences in concrete and specific terms.

For many students, Belsey's book offers a first encounter with "theory." "Theory" has become a loaded term among English majors in our program: they know which faculty "do theory" and which "don't," and they base a number of choices and evaluations upon this knowledge. My practice is to engage these presumptions explicitly, asking students "What do you think *theory* means? Do you think we should be doing *more* or *less* of it?" These perhaps banal questions can move into more interesting territory surrounding the issues of common sense and experience versus intellectual discourses as a basis of knowing and evaluating cultural texts; questions about the authority of different kinds of writing; primary versus secondary texts; ultimately, about what it means to "interpret" a cultural text. From here, we can return more specifically to Belsey: "What is interpretive theory for her? Why is 'theorizing' interpretation important for her?" In this segment of the course, I am not so interested in transforming students into Belsey-ite "critical practitioners" who can crank out ideological critiques of the subject positions offered by any literary texts that come along; rather, I am interested in engaging them in a discussion about how reading is a productive and ideologically overdetermined activity.

The concept of subject positions offers a link between the second and third sections of the course, in which critical practice becomes feminist practice, and the reading subject becomes a gendered subject. *The Feminist Reader* (Belsey and Moore 1989) offers a selection of essays on feminism and its relationship to literary history, theory, and criticism. The book is structured as an expanding series of debates and issues as they have been addressed by feminist literary scholars, moving from questions about the exclusion of women writers from the canon, to issues of language and gender, and finally into more difficult essays on subjectivity and critical theory. Rather than focusing on a single genre within feminist criticism—radical, psychoanalytic, socialist-Marxist, etc.—the book aims to suggest the diversity of feminist inquiry as it intersects with literary studies. For an audience of English majors, most with no prior exposure to feminism, *The Feminist Reader* is a useful way to learn about feminism itself as well as the more specific field of feminist criticism and literary scholarship.

Foregrounding feminism in a "core" course remains, sadly, an intervention in its own right. Within a department that offers a number of specific courses on women in literature and feminist theory, feminism is still often considered a localized discourse, and it would conceivably be possible for English majors to graduate without ever having to read and engage feminist work. By placing a five-week unit on feminist criticism and poetry in the middle of my required English course, I thus implicitly, and explicitly, make the argument that feminism—no longer an "alternative" or "radical" discourse on the margins—is an essential and pervasive element of any project calling itself literary analysis. I structure this unit around both poems and critical articles and aim to suggest "gender" and "women" as terms which disrupt and problematize our notions of reading and authorship. I ask students to read the poetry as an exploration of the concept of gender and women's identity along the lines marked out by the critical essays from the reader. A poem like Adrienne Rich's "Diving into the Wreck" could be read in gender-neutral terms, as a psychological allegory of self-exploration (a popular interpretation among students, especially males). Conversely, our reading of the poem could foreground "Diving" as a specifically feminist poem, one that finds the names of those whose names do not appear in "the book of myths" Rich repeatedly invokes to be women's names. I ask students not which reading of the poem is "right," but which one enables them to do more interesting or useful things with the poem. Any literary analysis, I believe, must take a stand on issues of gender and must take gender into account as part of the process of reading itself.

The final section of the course turns to Cary Nelson's book on the cultural politics of modernism. Although its ostensible focus is on American poetry of the modern period, *Repression and Recovery* (1989) is deeply informed by cultural studies and aims to contest prevailing definitions of "the literary" as it challenges specific and strategic exclusions from the modernist literary canon. Nelson gives special attention to conventionally marginalized or forgotten texts of the modern period, including labor songs and protest poetry, poetry by women, and poetry by African American writers. Nelson's project is to intervene in our "cultural memory" by offering us a new and potentially unrecognizable vision of modern poetry—poetry as it was actually written, read, and taken up within cultural struggles of the period—and to remind us of what we, as English scholars and literary historians, no longer know we have forgotten. *Repression and Recovery* represents what literary history looks like when written from within cultural studies. For these reasons, and because I felt students needed to be exposed to the kinds of texts *Repression and Recovery* foregrounds, I chose to make the book a central text in a six-week unit on literary history and the cultural politics of modern poetry. It is in this portion of the course—the last six weeks—that I think English 103 comes closest to achieving a productive fusion of literary and cultural studies.

The trajectory I have conceived for this course can be seen in terms of progressively expanding frames of reference. *Critical Practice* is focused largely on the practice of reading itself, offering a forced interruption of students' unconscious assumptions and consumptive habits. *The Feminist Reader* begins to connect literary texts to the social formation by posing gender as a problematic construction rather than a biological given, one of the fundamental axes of signification which links literature to a cultural history. And *Repression and Recovery*, besides adding race and class as further analytical coordinates, argues that literature is but one form of social discourse among many, regrounding literature within cultural and ideological struggles. "Literature" emerges at the end of sixteen weeks as a term that has no inherent or essential meaning whatsoever: it is a term which represents an irreducible variety of cultural projects in specific historical contexts. Rather than following some critics' arguments that politically responsible teaching demands we abandon "literature" as a useful concept and refrain from teaching primary texts altogether, I argue that "literature" is instead an infinitely rearticulatable concept, which has served a number of political and social functions throughout cultural history. Part of my aim in this course is to demonstrate that as a radical possibility.

Pedagogy as Social Technology

In summary, we would like to argue that it is not simply the case that cultural studies needs to be "brought to" the undergraduate literature classroom, but rather that cultural studies is, itself, produced through the kind of dialogic exchange that occurs in teaching. In many ways, the undergraduate classroom is, in fact, an ideal space in which to produce cultural studies. Because cultural studies remains grounded in the practices of everyday life as well as the forms and discourses which constitute "the popular," it can empower students to think and speak about their own experiences, consumer habits, relationships to the media, and the processes of identity formation central to all of these activities. As teachers, we feel a need to remain accountable to our students' experiences and perspectives while at the same time to articulate a challenge to unmediated personal experience as a secure ground of cultural or social truths. The complex dialectic of authority and empowerment that structures the undergraduate classroom is itself an important site of cultural and political analysis, and theorizing cultural studies *through* pedagogical practice remains a useful and important way to think cultural studies "from the ground up." In this sense, the pedagogy of cultural studies involves (1) the broadening and theoretical "rethinking" of such notions as "reading," "writing," "text," and "culture"; (2) the investigation of the production and reproduction of disciplinary and disciplining knowledges; and (3) the recognition and understanding of the political nature of pedagogy itself. In turn, cultural studies offers a framework for understanding how pedagogy functions as part of the social apparatus whereby individuals are constructed as autonomous, exploitable, disciplined (if not current, then future) laborers who are also fully functional members of economic, racial, and gendered hierarchies.

This notion of the "politics of pedagogy"—which would see it as a social technology that produces ideologically "fit" citizens—suggests two related issues that must also be addressed in the context of thinking through the relationship between pedagogy and cultural studies that we have not had the opportunity to elaborate in our descriptions of our courses in this essay; the first concerns the desirability of constructing a "model" of pedagogy, and the second suggests the importance of constructing broader institutional analyses. In that we make a deliberate attempt to influence students in terms of the knowledges and identities they encounter and take up, our courses are, fundamentally, politically staged events. This is not, of course, a unique characteristic of cultural studies courses, but rather a defining characteristic of all educational events. More to the point though, we argue that the cultural studies classroom is a place where the distinctions between theory and practice, politics and scholarship become hopelessly muddled. Moreover, the construction of a space for cultural studies within the institutional place of literature and English departments requires the reassessment of a range of entrenched institutional practices and policies that are going to make the construction of a "model of pedagogy" even more muddy and more complex. The first polemic of this conclusion, then, argues that cultural studies undermines the desire for an instrumental strategy toward pedagogy that would render a pedagogical "model" for undergraduate teaching wherein the roles/positions of the teacher and those of the students are clearly defined or determinable in advance of the discussions that take place in the classroom. We would argue, instead, that cultural studies requires a pedagogy that is focused on the process of the production of cultural knowledge and cultural capital, a process which it is ambiguously implicated in as well.

Secondly, and relatedly, this pedagogy-as-process approach not only requires the ongoing analysis of the specific features of the social/cultural identities of all educational participants, but also the analysis of

the institutional relations that structure the possibilities of those participants, the course, and the broader educational system. This latter concern demands that cultural studies teachers become more involved in
institutional discussions about institutional access, student recruitment
and retention, educational economics, as well as more familiar discussions about general education requirements and curriculum restructuring. In this way, cultural studies is not simply a debate about
representation on required reading lists, or the implementation of multicultural curricula—it is, more importantly, an imperative to become
involved in the power relations that structure the educational system in
the U.S.[18] With respect to the English studies department in a school like
Illinois State University, this runs the range from rethinking the rationale of required courses, to understanding that the classroom is not an
autonomous space separate from the rest of culture, to recognizing how
the institution is implicated in the ideological work of the U.S. educational system to produce quiescent laborers and intact social hierarchies. Such a polemic implies a number of related projects, including
the production of specific institutional analyses—about race and ethnic
student retention, financial aid for minority students, and threats to
academic freedom—to be used in the articulation of cultural criticism
that could, at the very least, help teachers develop a strategic plan
for educational reform in the institutions in which they are already
located.[19]

Notes

1. For a critical assessment of the way U.S. English departments have
taken up cultural studies recently, see Cary Nelson's "Always Already Cultural Studies" (1991). Nelson argues that "of all the intellectual movements
that have swept the humanities in America over the last twenty years, none
will be taken up so shallowly, so opportunistically, so unreflectively, and so
ahistorically as cultural studies" (25). See also Paul Smith's "The Political
Responsibility of the Teaching of Literature" (1990). We agree with Smith's
analysis of the present situation, in which "we are surrounded by the melan-
cholia of those who still want to talk about the literature they love and about
the importance of their feelings in relation to what they fear will become a lost
object," and we have tried to take seriously his argument that "perhaps we
now have a political responsibility *not* to teach literature in any context where
literatures, teaching itself, and the teaching of literatures are understood as not
political" (87–88).
2. The institutional specificity of cultural studies has been further emphasized in our more recent experiences in the School of Literature, Communication, and Culture at Georgia Institute of Technology in Atlanta. Here, the

domain of "the literary" and "the cultural" are quite differently situated with regard to the production of technological and scientific discourse.

3. It is in the work of Ernesto Laclau and Chantal Mouffe that the theory of political practice as "rearticulation" is most fully developed: see especially their *Hegemony and Socialist Strategy* (1985). Stuart Hall's work is also crucial: see Hall's *The Hard Road to Renewal: Thatcherism and the Crisis of the Left* (1988). Cary Nelson, in *Repression and Recovery* (1989), offers a useful brief definition of the term: "Hall, Laclau, and Mouffe employ rearticulation as part of a cluster of concepts they develop from Antonio Gramsci. It enables them to describe how political discourses either become dominant or organize for resistance by rearticulating existing terms [in this case, "literature"], concepts, arguments, beliefs, and metaphors into new configurations that are persuasive to people in a particular historical context. . . . The struggle to gain control over the production of meaning in social life is thus dependent on this competition to articulate and rearticulate relations between the valued and devalued concepts and languages in circulation in the culture" (250, *n*2).

4. Statements from "The Course Proposal: English 160–Women and Literature" (proposal filed 5/24/74; approved 8/22/74) Illinois State University, Normal, Illinois. Catalog copy from *Illinois State University Undergraduate Catalog*, 1990–1991, 104.

5. For a fuller elaboration of the relation of feminist cultural studies to feminist literary studies see my essay "Feminism and Cultural Studies" (1991).

6. Specifically, Illinois State University's "Goals of the Major in English" state that students who major in English should demonstrate the following abilities: (1) The ability to read a familiar or an unfamiliar text in any of several genres and from any of several cultural or historical origins in such a way that the act of reading incorporates literal comprehension, aesthetic responsiveness, informed awareness of the tradition(s) and context(s) with which the text may be most productively read, rhetorical and logical analysis of its argument, and critical reflection on the implications of its origins, tradition, aesthetics, rhetoric, and argument; (2) The ability to write about various kinds of texts in such a way that one's own writing articulates and embodies the multiple dimensions of the complex act of reading described above in clear, accurate, and effective prose. (Source: "Statement of Goals for the Majors in English and English Education at Illinois State University," mimeographed handout, approved 4/17/89 by the department faculty.)

7. Though their work differs in scope and emphasis—from offering a marxist-feminist analysis of the role of women in the family in late capitalism (Barrett), to exploring the constitution of gendered subjectivities (Walkerdine, Coward)—collectively these scholars demonstrate the importance of a cultural framework for the study of the social reproduction of gendered identity. Here I am referring to the following works: the Women's Studies Group's *Women Take Issue* (1978); Rosalind Coward's *Patriarchal Precedents* (1983); Henriques, Hollway, Urwin, Venn, and Walkerdine's *Changing the Subject* (1984); Coward's *Female Desires* (1985); Michele Barrett's *Women's Oppression Today* (1988); Carolyn Steedman's *Landscape for a Good Woman* (1987); and Cora Kaplan's *Sea Changes* (1986). A more extensive treatment of the body of work now identified as feminist cultural studies that served as the deep background for this course is found in Balsamo (1991).

8. For one class session, students read excerpts from Kramarae and Treichler's *A Feminist Dictionary* (1985) and then discuss the gendered elaboration of different words such as "academic," "autobiography," "feminism," "literary criticism," "heterosexuality," and "writing."

9. This editorial was only the first of several by the same writer that appeared during the semester (see Hinnen 1991).

10. My contribution to the discussion drew on Barbara Herrnstein Smith's essay "Contingencies of Value" (1983).

11. I also assign two excerpts from Dale Spender's *Women of Ideas and What Men Have Done to Them* (1983): "Aphra Behn: A Case Study" (32–42) and "Tough Politics: Virginia Woolf, 1882–1941" (672-81).

12. The statement about "timeless truths" comes from the introduction to Catherine Belsey and Jane Moore's *The Feminist Reader* (1989, 3).

13. The deep background for this section includes McConnel-Ginet, Borker, and Furman's *Women and Language in Literature and Society* (1980); Moraga and Anzaldúa's *This Bridge Called My Back* (1981); Belsey and Moore's *The Feminist Reader* (1989); and hooks's *Talking Back* (1989).

14. For this lecture, I use a variety of sources for statistical descriptions of the dynamics of these systems. For example, Paula Rothenberg's *Sexism and Racism* (1987) includes many tables that display evocative information. One set of tables offers a statistical profile of blacks in the United States that shows that while they have gained ground in education, political representation, and white-collar employment, they have not gained in terms of overall employment or income, demonstrating that the poverty gap between whites and blacks still persists (82–83).

15. Although both essays are reprinted in *Heresies* #15 (1982), they first appeared in other places: the first essay in Hull, Scott, and Smith (1982); the second in *Radical Teacher* no. 18. The exercises I conduct are based on suggestions offered in these articles. The deep background for my treatment of black women's literature and black feminist criticism draws on the many essays, bibliographies, and syllabi from Hull, Scott, and Smith (1982); hooks (1989); Lorde (1984); and Carby (1982).

16. On the second day, students work in pairs to discuss a series of questions that probe their experiences with people of different races; the list of questions I distribute is based on the questions described in Cross, Klein, Smith, and Smith (1982). Before the students begin, I outline the ground rules for their interactions: what they tell each other must be kept confidential, and they must listen nonjudgmentally.

17. This terminology draws on the work of Alain Touraine, whose *Return of the Actor* (1988) offers some crucial analyses of the concepts of historicity and cultural agency, which have yet to be taken up adequately in either literary or cultural studies.

18. Hazel Carby (1982) offers an example of this kind of cultural analysis of the institutional context of cultural studies. Also, see her comments in Jones (1991).

19. For example, articles in the journal *Black Issues in Higher Education* suggest a number of institutional practices and policies that demand faculty attention. See particularly Bruce Anthony's "Multicultural Education, Racism

and Reason for Caution" (1990); L. Eudora Pettigrew's "Recruiting Students of Color: Some 'Do's' and 'Don'ts'" (1991); and the "Special Report on Recruitment and Retention" (1991).

Works Cited

Altieri, Charles. 1983. "An Idea and Ideal of a Literary Canon." *Critical Inquiry* 10.1 (September): 37–60.

Anthony, Bruce. 1990. "Multicultural Education, Racism, and Reason for Caution." *Black Issues in Higher Education*, 22 November.

Balsamo, Anne. 1991. "Feminism and Cultural Studies." *Journal of the Midwest Modern Language Association*, 24.1 (Spring): 504ND73.

Barrett, Michele. 1988. *Women's Oppression Today*. New York: Verso.

Batsleer, Janet, et al., eds. 1985. *Rewriting English: Cultural Politics of Gender and Class*. New York: Methuen.

Belsey, Catherine. 1980. *Critical Practice*. New York: Routledge. 2nd ed., 1988.

———, and Jane Moore, eds. 1989. *The Feminist Reader: Essays in Gender and the Politics of Literary Criticism*. New York: Blackwell.

Brooker, Peter, and Peter Humm, eds. 1989. *Dialogue and Difference: English into the Nineties*. New York: Routledge.

Bunch, Charlotte, and Sandra Pollack, eds. 1983. *Learning Our Way: Essays in Feminist Education*. Trumansburg, NY: Crossing Press.

Campbell, Cathy. 1989. "A Battered Woman Rises: Aunt Jemima's Corporate Makeover." *Village Voice*, 7 November: 45–46.

Carby, Hazel. 1982. "Schooling in Babylon." In *The Empire Strikes Back: Race and Racism in 70s Britain*, 183–211. Centre for Contemporary Cultural Studies, University of Birmingham. London: Hutchinson.

Coward, Rosalind. 1983. *Patriarchal Precedents: Sexuality and Social Relations*. Boston: Routledge & Kegan Paul.

———. 1985. *Female Desires: How They Are Sought, Bought, and Packaged*. New York: Grove Press.

Cross, Tia, Freada Klein, Barbara Smith, and Beverly Smith. 1982. "Face-to-Face, Day-to-Day Racism, CR." *Heresies #15: The Issue is Racism*, 4 (3): 66–67.

Culley, Margo, and Catherine Portuges, eds. 1985. *Gendered Subjects: The Dynamics of Feminist Teaching*. Boston: Routledge & Kegan Paul.

Doyle, Brian. 1989. *English and Englishness*. New York: Routledge.

Ehrenreich, Barbara, and Deirdre English. 1978. *For Her Own Good: 150 Years of the Experts' Advice to Women*. Garden City, NY: Anchor.

Ericksen, Charles, ed. 1981. "Bilingual Life in an Anglo Land: Seventeen Hispanic Voices." *Perspectives: The Civil Rights Quarterly*, 13.1 (Spring): 30–35.

Frank, Francine, and Frank Anshen. 1983. *Language and the Sexes*. Albany: State University of New York Press.

Frank, Francine Wattman and Paula A. Treichler. 1989. *Language, Gender, and Professional Writing: Theoretical Approaches and Guidelines for Nonsexist Usage*. New York: The Modern Language Association of America.

Graff, Gerald. 1989. "Teach the Conflicts." *South Atlantic Quarterly,* 89: 51–67.

Hall, Roberta, with Bernice Sandler. 1982. "The Classroom Climate: A Chilly One for Women?" Project on the Status and Education of Women. *Association of American Colleges.* Washington, D.C.

Hall, Stuart. 1988. *The Hard Road to Renewal: Thatcherism and the Crisis of the Left.* New York: Verso.

Haraway, Donna. 1985 "A Manifesto for Cyborgs: Science, Technology, and Socialist Feminism in the Last Quarter." *Socialist Review,* no. 80 (March/April): 65–107.

Henriques, Julian, Wendy Hollway, Cathy Urwin, Couze Venn, and Valerie Walkerdine. 1984. *Changing the Subject: Psychology, Social Regulation, and Subjectivity.* New York: Methuen.

Hinnen, Brian. 1991. "Watch Out, Big Sister May be Watching You." *Daily Vidette,* 10 October.

hooks, bell. 1989. *Talking Back: Thinking Feminist, Thinking Black.* Boston: South End Press.

Hull, Gloria T., Patricia Bell Scott, and Barbara Smith, eds. 1982. *All the Women Are White, All the Blacks are Men, But Some of Us are Brave: Black Women's Studies.* Old Westbury, NY: Feminist Press.

Jacobus, Mary, Evelyn Fox Keller, and Sally Shuttleworth, eds. 1990. *Body/Politics: Women and the Discourses of Science.* New York: Routledge.

Johnson, Richard. 1986. "The Story So Far: And Further Transformations?" In *Introduction to Contemporary Cultural Studies,* edited by David Punter, 277–313. London: Longman.

Jones, Lisa. 1991. "Civilization's Discontent: Professor Hazel Carby on Canons, Curricula, and Change," *Village Voice,* 24 January.

Kaplan, Cora. 1986. *Sea Changes: Essays on Culture and Feminism.* London: Verso.

Kramarae, Cheris, Muriel Schulz, and William M. O'Barr, eds. 1984. *Language and Power.* Beverly Hills: Sage.

———, Paula Treichler, with assistance from Ann Russo. 1985. *A Feminist Dictionary.* Boston: Pandora Press.

Laclau, Ernesto, and Chantal Mouffe. 1985. *Hegemony and Socialist Strategy: Towards a Radical Democratic Politics.* London: Verso.

Lorde, Audre. 1984. *Sister Outsider: Essays and Speeches.* Trumansburg, NY: Crossing Press.

Martin, Jane Roland. 1985. *Reclaiming a Conversation: The Ideal of the Educated Woman.* New Haven, CT: Yale University Press.

McConnel-Ginet, Sally, Ruth Borker, and Nelly Furman, eds. 1980. *Women and Language in Literature and Society.* New York: Praeger.

McDowell, Deborah. 1985. "New Directions for Black Feminist Criticism." In *The New Feminist Criticism,* edited by Elaine Showalter, 186–99. New York: Pantheon.

McRobbie, Angela, and Trish McCabe, eds. 1981. *Feminism for Girls: An Adventure Story.* Boston: Routledge & Kegan Paul.

Mildred Pierce. 1945. Michael Curtiz (dir.). 109 min.

Moraga, Cherríe, and Gloria Anzaldúa, eds. 1981. *This Bridge Called My Back: Writings by Radical Women of Color.* Watertown, MA: Persophone.

Nelson, Cary. 1989. *Repression and Recovery: Modern American Poetry and the Politics of Cultural Memory, 1910–1945.* Madison: University of Wisconsin Press.

———. 1991. "Always Already Cultural Studies: Two Conferences and a Manifesto." *Journal of the Midwest Modern Language Association,* 24.1 (Spring): 24–38.

Newell, R. C. 1981. "Giving Good Weight to Black English." *Perspectives: The Civil Rights Quarterly,* 13.1 (Spring): 25–29.

Pettigrew, L. Eudora. 1991. "Recruiting Students of Color: Some 'Do's' and 'Don'ts.'" *Black Issues in Higher Education,* 11 April.

Rich, Adrienne. "Compulsory Heterosexuality and Lesbian Existence." *Signs,* 5 (4).

Rothenberg, Paula, ed. 1987. *Sexism and Racism: An Integrated Study.* New York. St. Martin's.

Russ, Joanna. 1975. *The Female Man.* New York: Bantam.

———. 1983. *How to Suppress Women's Writing.* Austin: University of Texas Press.

Sandler, Bernice. 1982. "The Classroom Climate: A Chilly One for Women?" Project on the Status and Education of Women of the Association of American Colleges. Washington, D.C.

Schuster, Marilyn R., and Susan R. Van Dyne, eds. 1985. *Women's Place in the Academy: Transforming the Liberal Arts Curriculum.* Totowa, NJ: Rowman & Allanheld.

Shaw, Linda L. and Diane G. Wicker. 1982. "Teaching about Racism in the Classroom." *Heresies #15: The Issue is Racism,* 4.3: 67–71.

Smith, Barbara. 1985. "Toward a Black Feminist Criticism." In *The New Feminist Criticism Essays on Women, Literature, and Theory,* edited by Elaine Showalter, 168–85. New York: Pantheon.

Smith, Barbara Herrnstein. 1983. "Contingencies of Value." *Critical Inquiry,* 10 (September).

Smith, Paul. 1990. "The Political Responsibility of the Teaching of Literature." *College Literature,* 17.2/3: 80–89.

———. 1991. "A Course in 'Cultural Studies.'" *Journal of the Midwest Modern Language Association,* 24.1 (Spring): 39–49.

"Special Report on Recruitment and Retention." 1991. *Black Issues in Higher Education,* 7.24 (31 January).

Spender, Dale. 1983. *Women of Ideas and What Men Have Done to Them: From Aphra Behn to Adrienne Rich.* Boston: Ark Paperbacks.

Steedman, Carolyn Kay. 1987. *Landscape for a Good Woman: A Story of Two Lives.* New Brunswick, NJ: Rutgers University Press.

Thompson, E. P. 1963. *The Making of the English Working Class.* New York: Vintage.

Touraine, Alain. 1988. *Return of the Actor: An Essay in Sociology.* Minneapolis: University of Minnesota Press.

Treichler, Paula, A. 1987. "Escaping the Sentence: Diagnosis and Discourse in 'The Yellow Wallpaper.'" In *Feminist Issues in Literary Scholarship,* edited by Shari Benstock, 62–78. Bloomington: Indiana University Press.

————, Cheris Kramarae, and Beth Stafford, eds. 1985. *For Alma Mater: Theory and Practice in Feminist Scholarship*. Urbana: University of Illinois Press.

Walker, Alice. 1983. *In Search of Our Mother's Gardens: Womanist Prose*. New York: Harcourt.

Wall, Cheryl A., ed. 1989. *Changing Our Own Words: Essays on Criticism, Theory, and Writing by Black Women*. New Brunswick, NJ: Rutgers University Press.

Widdowson, Peter, ed. 1982. *Re-Reading English*. New York: Methuen.

Williamson, Judith. 1986. "Woman Is An Island: Femininity and Colonization." In *Studies in Entertainment: Critical Approaches to Mass Culture*, edited by Tania Modelski, 99–118. Bloomington: Indiana University Press.

Women's Studies Group. 1978. *Women Take Issue: Aspects of Women's Subordination*. Centre for Contemporary Cultural Studies, University of Birmingham. London: Hutchinson.

Woolf, Virginia. 1989 [1929]. *A Room of One's Own*. San Diego: Harcourt Brace Jovanovich.

Appendix A

Women and Literature
English 160
Professor Anne Balsamo

Required Texts:
How to Suppress Women's Writing, Joanna Russ;
This Bridge Called My Back, Cherrie Moraga and Gloria Anzaldúa;
A Room of One's Own, Virginia Woolf;
The Awakening and Selected Stories, Kate Chopin;
Their Eyes Were Watching God, Zora Neale Hurston;
The Female Man, Joanna Russ;
Wonder Woman, by Trina Robbins;
Reading Packet;
Required Film: *Mildred Pierce*, directed by Michael Curtiz, w/Joan Crawford.

COURSE SCHEDULE
Part I: Beginning Terms and Framework
Introduction to course
Literary terms and guiding questions;
Reading as a feminist cultural practice;
How to Suppress Women's Writing, Russ;
"The Story of an Hour," Kate Chopin.

Short Stories: Guiding Themes
"A Jury of Her Peers," Susan Glaspell;
"The White Heron," Sarah Orne Jewett;
"A New England Nun," Mary E. Wilkins Freeman;

"The Only Rose," Sarah Orne Jewett;
"The Other Two," Edith Wharton;
"The Storm," Kate Chopin.

Part II: Women and Language

The Feminist Dictionary (selections), Cheris Kramarae and Paula Treichler;
"Introduction to Feminism"
　and "A Quiet Life," Angela McRobbie and Trisha McCabe;
"Talking Like a Lady" and
"Of Girls and Chicks," Francine Frank and Frank Anshen;
"Common Problems of Sexist Usage," Francine Wattman Frank and Paula A. Treichler;
"Woman Is An Island: Femininity and Colonization," Judith Williamson;
"Black Language as Power," Geneva Smitherman;
"Giving Good Weight to Black English," R. C. Newell;
"Bilingual Life in Anglo Land: Seventeen Hispanic Voices," Charles Ericksen, ed.;
"The Campus Climate: A Chilly One for Women," Bernice Sandler;
"The Yellow Wallpaper," Charlotte Perkins Gilman.

Part III: Feminist Frameworks

A Room of One's Own, Virginia Woolf;
"Aphra Behn: A Case Study" and
"Tough Politics: Virginia Woolf," Dale Spender.

Racism, Heterosexism, and Ethnocentrism

"Compulsory Heterosexuality and Lesbian Existence," Adrienne Rich;
From *This Bridge Called My Back*:
"Introduction,"
"Racism in the Women's Movement,"
"Across the Kitchen Table: A Sister-to-Sister Dialogue,"
"Lesbianism: An Act of Resistance";
From *Heresies: The Issue Is Racism*:
"Face-to-Face, Day-to-Day Racism, CR," Tia Cross, Freada Klein, Barbara Smith, and Beverly Smith
and "Teaching about Racism in the Classroom," Linda L. Shaw and Diane G. Wicker.

Part IV: Identity and Writing

"When I Was Growing Up," Nellie Wong;
"on not bein'," Mary Hope Lee;
"I Am What I Am," Rosario Morales;
"And When You Leave, Take Your Pictures with You," Jo Carillo;
"Beyond the Cliffs of Abiquiu," Jo Carillo;
"A Poem about Intelligence for My Brothers and Sisters," June Jordon;
"I Have Come to Claim Marilyn Monroe's Body," Judy Grahn.

Women's Agency/Women's Awakenings

The Awakening, Kate Chopin;

Their Eyes Were Watching God, Zora Neale Hurston.

Part V: Representations of Women in Popular Culture

The Women's Film

Mildred Pierce viewing

Women in Popular Culture

"The Society Page," *Heresies #14,* collective statement;

"A Battered Woman Rises: Aunt Jemima's Corporate Makeover," Cathy Campbell;

"Barbie and Tammy: The Real Story," Carole Nicksin; Women in popular music (bring audio or video selection); Female Heroes: *Wonder Woman;*

Visual Artists: Laurie Anderson, Barbara Kruger, Cindy Sherman, Trinh T. Minh-ha.

Part VI: Feminist Futures: Alternative Narratives of Gender Identity

The Female Man, Joanna Russ.

Appendix B

Working Questions on Reading Fiction

Developed by Michael Greer

Story and Plot

1. How does the opening of the story serve to establish the dramatic situation? How much background material (exposition) is presented? What tensions or potential conflicts are present in the opening of the story?

2. What constitutes "action" in the story? Is the pacing of incidents fast or slow? How is tension, suspense, or mystery sustained by the plot? To what extent does the plot rely on surprise or the unexpected?

3. To what extent does the plot's arrangement conform to chronology? What other patterns of order or arrangement (spatial, visual, metaphorical, symbolic, mythic, etc.) are used?

4. How does the story end? Is there a strong sense of "closure" or resolution? What is left unresolved? Which questions remain unanswered? How does the plot prepare readers to accept its resolution? Does the ending suggest that some sort of judgment or decision has been rendered?

5. How might one describe the overall shape or form of the plot? Is it circular? Linear? Episodic? Are there multiple plots or subplots? To what extent does the plot conform to narrative conventions? Does the plot move toward clarity and resolution, or toward complexity and ambivalence?

6. What demands does the story make on readers? What does the story assume or understand about its readers? Does it aim to confirm or to challenge readers' presuppositions? How might one describe the "ideal audience" for the story?

Character and Characterization

7. How important is character development in the story? Do characters function primarily as agents of the plot, or is the plot primarily a means of delineating character? Is the story "plot-centered" or "character-centered"?

8. Which characters are presented sympathetically? Which antagonistically? What values or ideals inform choices about character presentation?

9. Does the story encourage us to see the characters as "real people"? Are characters in the story "bigger than life," mythic, or heroic? Are they "life-size," players in a realistic drama? Or are they inferior to us, the objects of irony or satire?

10. How are characters defined and represented by the text? Is direct or indirect presentation predominant? Which modes of character development are most effective or important (action, speech, external appearance, environment, analogy, inner life, etc.)?

11. Are characters presented "objectively" or "subjectively"? To what extent are readers encouraged to participate in characters' inner lives? What about the central characters in the story is left *un*said?

12. What assumptions about "human nature" does the story's characterization rely on or support? What motivates the main characters? What do they fear? Know? Desire? Believe? Are we encouraged to read them as reflections of ourselves?

13. To what extent does the fictional "environment" control or determine characters in the story? Which characters manage or master their environment? Which succumb to it? Who in this story are the products of their world, and who are the producers?

14. Which characters speak? Whose are the different "voices" in the story? How are they distinguished?

Narration and Point of View

15. Who narrates the story? Is the narrator a participant in the story? How much influence does the narrator exert on the events of the story? How does the narrator's involvement (or lack of it) influence the way the story is told?

16. Do we "see" the events of the story through the eyes of a single character? Through many characters? Which characters seem to be at the narrator's center of attention? How does the choice of point of view affect or depend on the plot?

17. How much of the story is retold or summarized by the narrator? How much of the story is dramatized through scenic presentation? Why does the narrator choose to represent some incidents directly and others indirectly?

18. What other ways might this story have been narrated? How would a different choice of narration or point of view change the way we interpret the story? What purposes or assumptions would appear to inform the choice of narrator and perspective?

19. Does the story reflect on its own narration? How much is the act of writing or telling a part of the story itself? Is the plot "framed"? What questions

about narrative are raised? What does the story assume to be the role of fiction, or of literature itself?

Language and Style

20. How would one describe the style in which the story is written? What can one assume about the gender, social class, race, and education of the narrator from the way the story is written? How is the sentence used in the story?

21. What images and metaphors are important in the story? How does the imagery relate to the plot? Are certain characters repeatedly associated with certain kinds of imagery? What do we learn from this?

22. To what extent does the story rely on traditional kinds of symbolism? Are religious or cultural symbols important? Does the story "invent" symbols anew? How is the use of symbols related to the themes of the story?

23. What view toward language itself does the story take? Is language primarily a tool for communication and information in the story? What other functions or purposes does language serve in the story? Is the narrator "comfortable" with his or her language? What is not possible in language as it is understood in this story?

24. What mode/s of fiction is/are predominant in the story? Does the story reinforce or subvert conventions of genre and style? How does this story seem to understand its relationship to literary history and convention?

25. What kind of relationship does the story seek to establish with its audience? What kind of "position" are we encouraged to take in relation to the characters and their stories? Are we drawn into the story, or placed at an analytical or judgmental distance? How is this reflected in the style of the story?

Appendix C

Syllabus

Literary Analysis II: Poetry and Drama

(English 103)

Michael Greer

I. Current Debates in Literary Studies: The Canon and Literary History (weeks 1–2)

1. Charles Altieri, "An Idea and Ideal of a Literary Canon"; Dale Spender, "Women and Literary History."

2. Henry Louis Gates, Jr., "The Master's Pieces: On Canon Formation and the African-American Tradition";
Mary Helen Washington, "'The Darkened Eye Restored': Notes Toward a Literary History of Black Women."

II. Interpreting Literature: Reading as Critical Practice (weeks 3–7)

3–5. Catherine Belsey, *Critical Practice*;

6. Shakespeare, *Macbeth*;

7. Shakespeare, *The Tempest*.

III. Writing Women: Feminist Theory, Literary Criticism, and Women's Poetry (weeks 8–11)

8. Belsey and Moore, "Introduction: The Story So Far";
   Rosalind Coward, "The True Story of How I Became My Own Person";
   Adrienne Rich, "Diving into the Wreck," "Natural Resources," "North American Time";
   Judy Grahn, "Ah Love, You Smell of Petroleum," "I Have Come to Claim Marilyn Monroe's Body."

9. Toril Moi, "Feminist, Female, Feminine";
   Helene Cixous, "Sorties: Out and Out: Attacks/Ways Out/Forays".

10. Barbara Smith, "Toward a Black Feminist Criticism";
    Gwendolyn Brooks, "The Lovers of the Poor," "Young Afrikans";
    Audre Lorde, "Coal," "Need: A Choral of Black Women's Voices," "Stations";
    June Jordan, "Excerpts from a Verse Diary," "Moving Towards Home."

11. Gayatri Spivak, "Three Women's Texts and a Critique of Imperialism";
    Julia Kristeva, "Women's Time."

IV. Literary History and the Cultural Politics of Modern Poetry (weeks 12–16)

12. Cary Nelson, *Repression and Recovery*, 3–41;
    Langston Hughes, "Afro-American Fragment," "The Negro Speaks of Rivers," "Freedom's Plow".

13. *Repression and Recovery*, 41–97;
    Joy Davidman, "Twentieth-Century Americanism";
    Sol Funaroff, "What the Thunder Said";
    John Beecher, "Ensley, Alabama: 1932," "News Item."

14. *Repression and Recovery*, 97–130;
    **student presentations.

15. *Repression and Recovery*, 131–81;
    **student presentations.

16. *Repression and Recovery*, 181–246;
    **student presentations.

Index

Abcarian, Richard, 48, 50
Abrams, M. H., 6–8, 9, 28, 30, 32
Abstract theory, 12, 13, 15, 60
Academic escapism, 62
Academic narcissism, 48
Accident, 47
Acculturation, 9, 24, 25, 28, 31, 280–282
Adams, Henry, 50
Advocacy teaching, 55–56, 190
Aesthetic perfectionism, 38
Affirmative action, 81, 97
Agnosis, 41
Ain't I a Woman?, 76
Albert, Michael, 49, 50
Alcoff, Linda, 124, 146, 157, 164, 195, 200
Alienation, 264
Allen, Deborah, 91, 100
Allison, Alexander, 71
Alperin, Davida, 49, 50
Alternative pedagogy, 96
Althusser, Louis, 16, 143
Altieri, Charles, 290, 299
America by Design, 45
Analysis, 253
Anderson, Margaret, 272, 273
Anecdote, 19
Anshen, Frank, 299
Anthologies, 53
Anthony, Bruce, 298, 299
Antifoundationalism, 4, 5, 7, 9, 11, 13, 30
Anzaldua, Gloria, 48, 50, 80, 97, 100, 102, 298, 301
Applebee, Arthur, 30, 32
Applebroog, Ida, 141
Aptheker, Bettina, 106, 119
Ardis, Ann, 155, 164
Arguing from Sources: Exploring Issues through Reading and Writing, 247, 249, 250
Argumentation, teaching, 247, 249, 252, 254–255, 258
Aronson, Elliot, 97, 102
Artificial intelligence, 47
Arts of the contact zone, 25

Asante, Molefi Kete, 273
Atkins, G. Douglas, 13
Atwood, Margaret, 46, 49, 50
Authority, x, 5, 21, 23–25, 32, 61, 149, 164, 182, 194–200, 283
Autonomous classroom, 187
Autonomy, x, xiv
Ayyoub, Dhu'l Nun, 204, 225, 231

Baca, Judy, 141
Bakhtin, M. M., 160, 162, 163, 165
Balsamo, Anne, xi, 27, 28, 264, 273, 275, 277, 297, 299, 323
Banking model of education, xiii, 9, 23, 134, 169–170, 181, 183
Banks, Cherry, 272, 273
Banks, James, 272, 273
Barbin, Herculine, 259
Barrett, Michele, 131, 146, 297, 299
Barth, John, 252, 261
Barthes, Roland, 60, 71
Bartholomae, David, 17, 193
Batsleer, Janet, 299
Baudrillard, Jean, 141
Bauer, Dale, ix, xi, 22, 23, 94, 96, 100, 104, 105, 109, 110, 115, 119, 149, 155, 157, 165, 225, 231, 323
Baym, Nina, 99, 100
Beaven, Mary H., 230, 231
Belenky, Mary Field, 118, 119
Bell, Thomas, 45, 50
Bell-Scott, Patricia, 272, 273
Belsey, Catherine, 291–292, 298, 299
Benjamin, Jessica, 206, 231
Benmussa, Simone, 139, 146
Berlin, James, vii, 27–28, 32, 195, 207, 231
Berman, Paul, 97, 100
Bernal, Martin, 273
Bernays, Anne, 92, 100
Berry, Ellen, viii, 22, 94, 100, 104, 118, 119, 122, 267, 273, 323
Bever, Thomas, 98, 100
Beyond the Culture Wars, 193

Bias, 205, 211, 282
Bifurcation, 38
Bingham, Sallie, 122*n*
Bizzell, Patricia, ix, 23, 25, 30–31, 151, 165, 186, 194, 200, 323
Black feminist perspective, 27, 263–272
Black studies movement, 272
Bloom, Allan, xi, 183
Bloom, Harold, 13, 164, 165
Bluest Eye, The, 210, 259
Blurred genres, 20
Bodenheim, Maxwell, 71
Bodnar, Ann Marie, xi, 22, 25, 49, 116, 119, 202, 264, 274, 324
Bohmer, Susanne, 115, 119
Bontemps, Arna, 70, 71
Booth, Wayne, 7
Borderlands=La Frontera, 48
Borker, Ruth, 78, 102, 298, 300
Bowles, Samuel, 213, 231
Boyle, Kay, 71
Bradstreet, Anne, 109
Brannon, Lil, 17, 29, 31, 33
Braxton, Joanne, 266, 273
Bridge person, 238–239
Brodkey, Linda, 23, 151, 157, 165
Bromwell, Nicholas, 48, 50
Brooker, Peter, 299
Brooks, Cleanth, 8
Brooks, Gwendolyn, 41
Brown, Elsa Barkley, 272, 273
Brown, Sterling, 68, 71
Brown Silk and Magenta Sunsets, 210, 219
Bruffee, Kenneth, 26, 186
Bully/wimp syndrome, 24, 181–182, 185, 186
Bunch, Charlotte, 49, 50, 299
Burke, Kenneth, 19, 29, 30, 32, 164, 165, 255
Burney, Frances, 259
Burnout, 178
Butler, Octavia, 46, 50
Bynner, Witter, 71

Cahalan, James, 8, 33
Cain, William, 49, 50
Call Me Woman, 266
Campbell, Cathy, 299
Campbell, Nancy D., 142, 146
Carby, Hazel, 132, 298, 299
Carpenter, John, 94, 100
Carroll, Berenice, 85, 100
Catcher in the Rye, 210
Cazden, Courtney, 89, 100

Ceasar, Terry, 24, 33
Centered Teacher, The, 177
Chaplin, Charles, 45, 50
Charters, Ann, 231
Chinweizu, 273
Chittenden, Patricia, 50
Christian, Barbara, 49, 50
Cixous, 139
Clarke, Arthur C., 47
Class, defined, 49
Class consciousness, 21, 39
Class discussions, 70
Class participation, 83
Classroom
  dissension in, x–xi
  as a laboratory of culture, 22–23, 94, 122, 267
  as a participatory democracy, 25, 198
  student-centered, 23, 26
  as a theater of contesting interpretations, 21
Class system of the intellect, 85
Clinchy, Blythe, 116, 117, 119
Close reading, 287
Coalition building, 43
Cohen, Ralph, 20, 33
Coherence, 236
Cole, Johnetta, 266
Collaboration, between teachers and students, 22
Collaborative classroom practices, x, 26, 198, 206
Collaborative community, 26
Collaborative teaching, 190
Collective stereotypes, 79
Collins, Patricia Hill, 132, 137, 146
Complementary holism, 49
Composition, 32, 199
Condry, J., 79, 100
Condry, S., 79, 100
Conflicts, 192, 288
Conflicts in Feminism, 125, 144
Contaminated logic of identity, 89
Content, 259
Contextualism, 117
Conversion experiences, 150
Conversion narratives, 159
Coordinates of art criticism, 6, 7–8
Correct terminology, 79
Counterauthority, 23, 115, 150, 159, 185–186
Coward, Rosalind, 297, 299
Crane, Hart, 71
Creative writing, teaching of, 236, 261

Crisis Management in American Higher Education, 48
Critical Practice, 291, 294
Critical Teaching and the Idea of Literacy, 29
Critical textuality, 60
Critical thinking, 220
Crosby, Harry, 66, 67, 71
Cross, Tia, 284, 298, 299
Cross-course conferences, 193
Cross-race communication, 78–79
Cross-sex communication, 78, 82
Cullen, Countee, 59, 68, 71
Culler, Jonathan, 13
Culley, Margo, 299
Cultural diversity, 78
Cultural feminist, 140
Cultural illiteracy, 11
Cultural literacy, 8, 12, 27, 271
Cultural memory, 293
Cultural pragmatism, 8, 9, 16, 30
Cultural representation, 251
Cultural studies, xi, 11, 16, 27–28, 189, 236, 255, 275, 276, 291
  teaching of in a literature department, 275–296
Cultural transformation, 9
Cultural transmission, 6, 9
Cultural work, 289
Culturation, 11, 12
Culture, 276
  as canonical text, xi
  as everyday experience, xii
Culture wars, 29
cummings, e. e., 68, 71
Curricular integration, 116–117
Curriculum revision, 25, 26
Cutting edge negation(s), 13–14, 16, 19
Cyborg myth, 43, 46, 137

Daedalus, Stephen, 94
Dakar Childhood, A, 266
Dangarembga, Tsitsi, 266, 273
Davison, Alice, 98, 100
de Certeau, Michel, 48, 50
Deconstructionism, 13, 15, 16
de Lauretis, Teresa, 126, 133, 139, 142, 144, 146
de Man, Paul, 3, 13, 33
D'Emilio, John, 98, 100
DeMott, Benjamin, 49, 50
Derrida, Jacques, viii, 8, 13, 16, 17, 60, 71, 126, 131, 147
Desert Shield/Desert Storm, 49. *See also* Persian Gulf War

Dewey, John, 30
De-centering, 272
Dialect, 68
Diallo, Nafissatou, 266, 273
Dialogue, feminist theorists in, 137–138
DiBernard, Barbara, ix, xi, 22, 96, 101, 104, 105, 107, 324
Differences
  facing up to in the classroom, x–xi, 23
  tensions and, 128–129
Difference without/difference within, 128
Discipline, theory of, 16
Discourse communities, 186
Discursive modes, 30
Dissemination of knowledge, 4
Diversity, 197
Domestication of consciousness, 42
Donahue, Patricia, 33, 100, 101
Doro, Sue, 46, 51
Double consciousness, 48
Downing, David, viii, xi, 3, 8, 30, 33, 321
Doyle, Brian, 299
Drama of the Gifted Child, The, 171
D'Souza, Dinesh, 56
duBois, Page, 151, 162, 164, 165
Du Bois, W. E. B., 48, 51
Duncan, B. L., 97, 101
Dunn, Kathleen, 116, 117, 118, 119
Duster, Troy, 81, 97, 101
Dworkin, Andrea, 140, 147

Eagleton, Terry, 183
Eames, Charles, 101
Eames, Ray, 101
Eckert, Penelope, 98, 100
Economically disengaged knowledge, 41
Economic determinism, 42
Ede, Lisa, 193
Education of Henry Adams, The, 44
Educational equality, 75
Ehrenreich, Barbara, 41, 49, 51, 299
Eisenberg, Susan, 46, 51
Eisenhart, Margaret, 98, 101
Eisler, Benita, 44, 51
Eliot, T. S., 70
Ellison, Ralph, 48, 51
Ellmann, Richard, 71
El-Khawas, Elaine, 97, 101
Emotion, 175
Empty idealism, 59
Enculturation, 4, 9
English, Deirdre, 299
English majors, 287, 297
Entrustment, 133

Equivocating teaching persona, 24
Erdrich, Louise, 225, 231
Ericksen, Charles, 299
Essentially Speaking: Feminism, Nature and Difference, 129, 138, 157
Ethos, 153, 203, 228
Evans, Margaret, 45
Experience, as basis for critical analysis, 284
Experiential knowledge, 267
Experimental classroom, 57
Expressive realism, 291

False self, 170
Fear, 170–171
Fear of Falling, 49
Fearing, Kenneth, 62, 63, 71
Feldman, Jamie, 97, 101
Female Man, The, 286
Feminist Dictionary, A, 22, 96, 97, 104
    New and Needed Words, 114
    use of in the classroom, 104–118
    Word of the Day reports, 113, 115
Feminist Ethic of Risk, A, 41
Feminist experience, ix, 278. *See also* Black feminist perspective
Feminist mentors, 84
Feminist narratives, lessons from, 75–96
    narrative of identity, 77–81
    narrative of power, 82–85
    pedagogical narrative, 85–93
    theory in the classroom, 93–96
Feminist pedagogy, 87, 96
    need for, 22
Feminist postmodernism, 86
Feminist Reader, The, 292, 294
Feminist sophistics, 23, 96, 109, 149–164
    changing classroom practices, 159–163
    origins of, 150–155
    reactions to in the classroom, 155–159
Feminist subject, defined, 126–128
Feminist theory
    assignments related to, 136–146
    course outline for, 148
    in the classroom, 122–146
    origins of, 131
Feminist Theory: From Margin to Center, 48, 137
F/feminism, defined, 124–126
Fetterly, 29
Finley, Karen, 139, 147
First generation mentors, 84
First-year English curriculum, 235–260
Fish, Stanley, 4, 8, 13, 29, 30, 33

Flatliners, 209
Flower, Linda, 235, 238, 242, 243, 244, 247, 252, 260, 261
Flowers in the Attic, 209
Flynn, Elizabeth, 99, 101
Ford, Charles Henri, 68, 71
Foucault, Michel, viii, 5, 13, 16, 17, 60, 71, 85, 87, 96, 101, 126, 143
Foundationalism, 4, 5–6, 31
Fowler, Lois, 235
Frank, Francine, 79, 101, 282, 299
Freire, Paulo, 8, 23, 33, 134, 147, 162, 169, 178, 181, 183, 193, 263, 274
Freud, Sigmund, 8
Frey, Olivia, 32
Frye, Marilyn, 111
Funaroff, Sol, 67, 68, 71
Furman, Nelly, 99, 298, 300
Fuss, Diana, 129, 138, 147, 157, 165, 195, 200

Gabelnick, Faith, 190, 193
Gabriel, Susan, 98, 101
Gallop, Jane, 125, 147, 259
Gates, Henry Louis, 291
Geertz, Clifford, 17, 20, 33
Geisler, Cheryl, 247, 250, 253, 254, 261
Gender, 45
Gender-neutral language, 79–80
Gender stereotypes, 83
Genre(s), 3, 20, 136
Gibson, P. J., 219, 231
Gilbert, Sandra, 96, 101
Gilman, Charlotte Perkins, 109
Ginguly, Keya, 88, 89, 98, 101
Gintis, Herbert, 213, 231
Giroux, Henry A., 228, 231
Giving Up the Ghost, 139
Goldberger, Nancy, 119
Goodwin, Marjorie H., 78, 101
Gordon, Dane, 49, 51
Goswami, Dixie, 33
Graff, Gerald, 24, 28, 33, 66, 150, 159, 164, 165, 179, 189, 193, 237, 238, 261, 288, 300, 324
Gramsci, Antonio, 297
Graywolf Annual Six: Stories from the Rest of the World, The, 203, 222
Greenblatt, Stephen, 8
Greer, Michael, xi, 27, 28, 264, 273, 275, 277, 324
Grimke, Angelina Weld, 68, 71
Gubar, Susan, 96, 101
Guerrilla semiologist, 142

Guy-Sheftall, Beverly, ix, 27, 263, 272, 273, 274, 324

Hairston, Maxine, 196, 198, 199, 200, 245–246, 261
Hall, Roberta, 300
Hall, Stuart, 60, 297, 300
Hamilton, Mykol, 101
Hammer, Barbara, 116
Handmaid's Tale, The, 46, 49
Hansen, Karen, 49, 51
Happy consciousness, 82
Haraway, Donna, viii, 43, 46, 51, 137, 138, 139, 146, 147, 300
Hard Core, 140
Harkin, Patricia, viii, xi, xiii, 3, 17, 18, 33, 324
Harlow, Barbara, 48, 51
Harris, Charles B., 275n
Harrison, Michelle, 112
Hartsock, Nancy C.M., 48, 51, 138, 139, 147
Havelock, Eric, 153, 165
Hawthorne, Nathaniel, 44, 51
Heart, Home & Hard Hats, 46
Hegemony and Socialist Strategy, 60
Heinlein, Robert, 47
Hendricks, Gay, 177, 178
Henley, Nancy M., 101
Henricksen, Bruce, 33
Henriques, Julian, 297, 300
Heresies: The Issue is Racism, 284
Heteroglossia, 163
Hill, Anita, 91, 92
Hine, Lewis, 45, 51
Hinnen, Brian, 297, 300
Hirsch, E. D., xi, 27, 271
Hirsch, Marianne, 125, 144, 147
Historians of letters, 8
Historical criticism, 7
History, 153
Holland, Dorothy, 98, 101
Hollingdale, R. J., 153, 158, 165
Hollway, Wendy, 297, 300
Holzer, Jenny, 141
Honey, Maureen, 70, 71
hooks, bell, viii, 48, 51, 76, 79, 80, 102, 132, 137, 138, 147, 151, 156, 160, 161, 162, 165, 263, 268, 272, 274, 298, 300
Houston, Marsha, 78, 102
Howe, Florence, 104, 119
Huff, Cynthia, 278
Hughes, Langston, 68, 70, 71
Hull, Gloria, 298, 300

Human experience, 37
Humanities, 237, 255
Human labor, as a subject of literary study, 37–48
Humm, Peter, 299
Hungry Wolf, Beverly, 266, 274
Hurlbert, C. Mark, xi, 22, 25, 49, 116, 119, 202, 206, 231, 264, 274, 325
Hutcheon, Linda, 42, 51

Identity, popular cultural determinations of, 285
Identity politics, 157
Ideology as apparatus, 16
Illiteracy, 8
  as inarticulateness, 11
  solution to, 12
Indoctrination, 158
Informed reader, 29
Institute for the Study of Social Change, 80–81, 97
Institutionalization, 75, 283
Institutional stereotyping, 241, 245
Integrated curriculum, 187
Intellectual intimidation, 196
Interest, and writing ability, 246
Interpretive analysis, 247
Interpretive communities, 8
Interpretive theory, 250
Intersubjective space, 206
Intertextuality, 15
Intratextuality, 15
In Visible Light: Photography and the American Writer, 1840–1940, 38
Invisible Man, The, 48
Irigaray, Luce, 60, 137, 138, 139
I, Rigoberta Menu, An Indian Woman in Guatemala, 266
It's a Good Thing I'm Not Macho, 46

Jackson, Elaine, 231
Jacobus, Mary, 259, 300
Jaggar, Alison, 175, 178
James, William, 30
Jameson, Frederic, 8, 141
Janangelo, Joseph, 198, 200
Jarratt, Susan, ix, xi, 22, 23, 94, 96, 100, 104, 105, 109, 110, 115, 119, 149, 153, 165, 225, 231, 325
Jemi, Onwuchekwa, 273
Jerome, V. J., 68, 71
Johnson, Barbara, 3, 33
Johnson, Richard, 275, 277, 300

Jolas, Eugene, 66, 67, 71
Jones, Lisa, 300
Justify My Love (video), 139, 142

Kaplan, Cora, 297, 300
Kaufer, David, xi, 26, 235, 247, 250, 253,
    254, 260, 261, 325
Kecht, Maria-Regina, 33
Keller, Evelyn Fox, 125, 144, 147, 259, 300
Kelly, Mary, 141
Kennedy, Alan, xi, 26, 33, 235, 260, 325
Kentucky Foundation for Women, 122*n*
Khudayyir, Mohammed, 204, 231
Kimball, Bruce, 198, 201
Kimball, Roger, 56
Kimmel, Stanley, 71
Kindred, 46
King, Stephen, 209
Kingston, Maxine Hong, 266, 274
Kiniry, Malcolm, 50
Klein, Freada, 284, 298, 299
Klotz, Marvin, 48, 50
Knapp, Peggy, 235
Knoblauch, C. H., 17, 29, 31, 33
Knowledge
    dissemination of, 4
    procedural *vs.* propositional, 18
    reconceptions of, 4, 5
Kramarae, Cheris, 85, 96, 97, 98, 102, 106,
    113, 118, 119, 298, 300, 302
Krishnamurti, J., 169
Kristeva, Julie, 97
Kruger, Barbara, 95, 141, 142, 147
Kuhn, Thomas, 96
Kuzwayo, Ellen, 266, 274

Labowitz, Leslie, 141
Lacan, Jacques, 8, 13, 16, 126
Laclau, Ernesto, 60, 71, 297, 300
Lacy, Suzanne, 141
Landscape for a Good Woman, 40
Language, and the conditions of
    knowledge, 282
Language, Gender, and Professional Writing,
    79
Larson, Richard, 17
Lasser, Carol, 98, 102
Learning communities, 190–191
Learning Communities, 190, 191
Leavitt, David, 208, 225, 231
Left teaching, 58
Liberal neutrality, 66
Libertarian education, 183
Like a Prayer (video), 139, 142

Lindsey, Vachel, 71
Lindzey, Gardner, 97, 102
Linguistic left, 48
Linguistic turn, xiii
Linguistic Society of America, 84, 98
Literacy, 248
    crisis, 11
    as normalization, 11, 12, 31
    and power, 249
Literary Analysis II: Poetry and Drama
    course, 286–294
    course content, 289–294
    feminist criticism in, 292–293
    origins of, 286–289
    syllabus, 306–307
Literary research, changing classroom
    practices and, 6–12
Literary studies, 289
Literary theory, 20
Literature, in creating social change, 212,
    229–230
Literature and Technology course, 44–47
Literature of the contact zone, 199
Literature: The Human Experience, 48
Lloyd-Jones, Richard, 17
Local action, 16
Local coherence, 238, 241
Local struggles, 125
Lord of the Flies, 209, 210
Lorde, Audre, 49, 51, 161, 298, 300
Lore
    as an alternative to foundationalism, 18
    anecdotal character of, 19–20
    about changing classroom practices,
        21–28
    defined, 12, 17
    as genre, 20
    as a reconception of research, 17–20
*Lowell Offering: Writings by New England
    Mill Women, 1840–1845, The*, 44, 46
Lowry, Don, 49, 51
Lubiano, Wahneema, 99, 102
Lunsford, Andrea, 49, 51, 193
Lyotard, Jean François, 5

MacGregor, Jean, 190, 193
Machine in the Garden, The, 44
Machine-age poetics, 46
Madonna, 147
Madubuike, Ihechukwu, 273
Magil, A. B., 71
Maher, Frances, 116, 117, 118, 119
Maher, Frinde, 272
Mailloux, Steven, 30, 33
Maimon, Elaine, 186

Mainstream pedagogy, 96
Major, Lana, 132, 146, 147
Making of Knowledge in Composition:
 Portrait of an Emerging Field, The, 17
Male critical theory, 94
Male defined theory, 140
Male-dominated institutions, 82
Maltz, Daniel, 78, 102
Mandela, Winnie, 266, 274
Manet, Edouard, 93
Manic mode of teaching, 134
Marcuse, Herbert, 82
Marcussen, Andrea, 50
Marginality, 48
Markandaya, Kamala, 266, 274
Martin, Biddy, 97, 102, 123, 147
Martin, Jane Roland, 300
Martindale, Kathleen, 132, 146, 147
Marx, Karl, 45, 51
Marx, Leo, 44, 51
Master discourses, 6
Master narratives, 123
Master reader, 8
Master teachers, 4
Maternal/coaching model of teaching,
 134, 179
Matthews, Dorothea, 71
Matthews, Roberta, 190, 193
Matthiesson, F. O., 8
Maupin, Armistead, 97, 102
McCabe, Trish, 300
McClaren, Peter, 259, 261
McConnel-Ginet, Sally, 298, 300
McCormick, Kathleen, 235, 238, 242, 243,
 251, 252, 260, 261
McDowell, Deborah, 300
McGuire, William, 97, 102
McKay, Claude, 71
McRobbie, Angela, 300
*Me and Mine: The Life Story of Helen
 Sekaquaptewa,* 266
Meaning, 290
Melville, Herman, 44, 51, 283
Menchu, Rigoberta, 266, 274
Merod, Jim, 42, 49, 51
Middle class, 41, 49
Mildred Pierce, 285, 300
Miller, Alice, 171, 178
Miller, Jean Baker, 112
Mills, C. Wright, 45, 51
Minh-ha, Trinh T., 48, 51, 127–128, 137, 147
Minnich, Elizabeth Kamarck, 272, 274
Mirror and the Lamp, The, 6, 7
Mirror stage, 16
Miseducation, 27, 264, 265, 271
Misinterpretation, 216

Mixed genre, 20
Modern Times, 45
Moffett, James, 41
Moglen, Helene, 49, 51
Mondo New York, 139
*Money, Sex, and Power: Toward a Feminist
 Materialism,* 48
Montano, Linda, 140, 147
Moore, Jane, 292, 298
Moraga, Cherrie, 80, 102, 139, 147, 298,
 301
Moran, Charles, 34
Morgan, Thais, 33
Morrison, Toni, 210, 259
Morton, Donald, 34
Mouffe, Chantal, 60, 71, 123, 144, 146,
 147–148, 297, 300
Mukherjee, Bharati, 215, 231
Multicultural literacy, 27, 271–272
Multiculturalism, myths of, 97
Multiplism, 117
Myers, Craig, 262

Nassar, Joseph, 50
Natoli, Joseph, 34
Nectar in a Sieve, 266
Negation, 13–14, 16, 19, 31
Nelson, Cary, ix, 21, 34, 53, 70, 71, 98, 100,
 102, 265, 274, 289, 293, 296, 297, 301,
 325
Neopragmatist movement, 30
Nervous Conditions, 266
Neuwirth, Christine, xi, 26, 235, 245, 247,
 250, 253, 254, 260, 261, 326
New Criticism, 7, 8, 15, 30, 180, 236, 255
New Masses, 65
Newell, R. C., 301
Nielsen, Aldon Lynn, 70, 72
Nietzsche, Friedrich, 153, 157
Noble, David, 45, 52
Noncanonical modern poetry, teaching
 of, 53–70
Nonsexist language, 79
Norms, 12
North, Stephen M., 17, 18, 34
Norton Anthology of Modern Poetry, 53, 65
Norton Anthology of Poetry, 53

O'Barr, William, 300
O'Brien, Tim, 215, 231
O'Clair, Robert, 71
Objective knowledge, 150
Objectivity, 4, 56, 194
Of Grammatology, 60

Off the rack solutions, 254
Okawa, Judy Bessai, 91, 100
Olsen, Tillie, 64, 65, 68, 72, 109
Omolade, Barbara, 272
One-course concept, 237–238, 245, 260
Oppression, 42, 138
Orators, 198
Order of Things, The, 60
Orwell, George, 283
Out of This Furnace, 45
Overassertion, 24, 150
Owen, Maureen, 216, 231

Paper Chase, The, 93
Partial explanations, 125
Partial knowledge, 157
Parting Glances, 98
Part of My Soul Went With Him, 266
Patchen, Kenneth, 68, 71
Patraka, Vivian, viii, 22, 94, 100, 104, 118,
    119, 122, 267, 273, 326
Paull, Irene, 62, 63, 64, 72
Pedagogical turn, xiii, xiv
Pedagogy
    fear of, overcoming, 169–178
    research and, 6, 8
    as social technology, 294–296
    traditional discussions of, 3
Pedagogy-as-process approach, 295
Pedagogy of the Oppressed, 169, 263
Penfield, Elizabeth, 34
Penley, Constance, 99, 102
Performance model of teaching, 24, 134,
    170, 171
Persian Gulf War, 25, 49, 50
    teaching against backdrop of, 202–230
Personal pronouns, manipulation of, 127
Pettigrew, L. Eudora, 299, 301
Phelps, Louise Wetherbee, 18, 34
Philipson, Ilene, 49, 51
Philosophers, 198
Phronesis, 18
Piercy, Marge, 47, 52, 210, 214, 231
Pivoting the center, 272
Plato, 152, 164
Player Piano, 45
Pluralism, 7, 43
Poetics, 236
Poetry of the Negro, The, 70
Political correctness, 4, 21–22, 23, 69, 75,
    79, 97, 150, 164, 191, 197, 283, 284
Political Responsibility of the Critic, The, 42
Political values, ix
Politics of location, 105, 118
Politics of pedagogy, 295
Politics of visibility, 109
Politics of Postmodernism, 42
Pollack, Sandra, 299
Pornography, 140
Portuges, Catherine, 299
Positionality, 195
Postfeminist era, 97
Postmodernism, 42, 140–141
Poststructuralism, 126
Poulet, Georges, 60
Powers of Ten, 94
Practical criticism, 287
Practice of Everyday Life, The, 48
*Practicing Theory in Introductory Literature
    Courses,* 3, 8
Practitioner inquiry, 17
Pragmatic, 30
Pratt, Mary Louise, 25, 34, 199, 201
Predispositions, 218, 219
Primary texts, 289
Principle of Scientific Management, The, 45
Problem-solving approach, to writing, 244
Procedural knowledge, 18
Professor Romeo, 92
Progressive movement, 30
Propositional knowledge, 18
Psychoanalytic criticism, 7
Psychological possibility, 218

Quandahl, Ellen, 33, 100, 101
Quin, Mike, 62, 72

Race, 80
Racism, 22, 59, 69, 77, 80, 81, 285
Radhakrishnan, R., 15, 34
Radway, Janice, 8
Rankin, Elizabeth, 17, 34
Rationality, 152
Ravenel, Shannon, 231
Raymond, James, 17
Reader-oriented criticism, 7
Reader-response theories, 29
Reading fiction, working questions on,
    304–306
Reading Race, 70
Reading Texts, 242, 243, 260
Reagan's kids, 40–42, 215
Reagon, Bernice, 49, 52
Real-world problems, 26, 59
Rearticulation, 61
Rebuttals, 14, 31
Redistributed transformation, 96
Refutation, 14, 31
Reiter, Sheila, ix, xi, 22, 96, 101, 104, 326

Relative autonomy, 61
Remedial courses, 239, 240
Representative anecdotes, 19, 22, 29
Repression and Recovery: Modern American Poetry and the Politics of Cultural Memory, 1910–1945, 53, 70, 293, 294
Research paper, 247
Resistance Literature, 48
Resistance postmodernism, 141
Resistance teaching, 58
Resisting reader, 29
Re-vision, 123
Revolution, 212, 213–214, 226
Rhetorical authority, 195, 196
Rhetorical Traditions and the Teaching of Writing, 17
Rhymes of the Revolution, 62
Rich, Adrienne, 57, 105, 118, 119, 123, 137, 148, 293, 301
Richards, I. A., 8
Riffaterre, Michael, 29
Right answer, 117
Ringgold, Faith, 141
Roberts, Craige, 83, 84, 102
Rochester Institute of Technology, 49, 50
Rolfe, Edwin, 64, 72
Room of One's Own, A, 75, 284
Rorty, Richard, 4, 17, 30
Rose, Mike, 32, 34
Rose, Richard, 50, 52
Rosenblatt, Louise, 8, 30
Rothenberg, Paula, 298, 301
Royster, Jacqueline Jones, 272, 273
Ruprecht, Terry W., 99
Russ, Joanna, 286, 301
Russo, Vito, 98, 102

Said, Edward, 49, 52
Sandburg, Carl, 68, 69, 71, 72
Sandler, Bernice, 283, 300, 301
Sandoval, Chela, 272, 274
Sarachild, Kathie, 111
Sarett, Lew, 71
Sarris, Greg, 258
Schilb, John, 193
Schloss, Carol, 38, 52
Schmidt, Gladys, 235
Scholes, Robert, 13
Schooling in Capitalist America, 213
Schulz, Muriel, 300
Schuster, Marilyn, 301
Schwarzenegger, Arnold, 13
Scott, Barbara Ann, 48, 52
Scott, Patricia Bell, 298, 300
Self-reflection, 124

Segal, George, 47
Sekaquaptewa, Helen, 266, 274
Sensational Designs, 179
Sexism, 22
Sexual harassment, 90–93
Sexuality, 140
Shadowed Dreams, 70
Shakespeare's Sisters, 96
Shaughnessy, Mina, 17, 18
Shaull, Richard, 263
Shaw, Linda, 284, 301
Shea, Susan, 132, 146, 147
Sheldon, Sidney, 209, 211, 215, 232
Sherman, Cindy, 141
Sherwood, Bill, 98, 102
Shifting Gears: Technology, Literature, Culture in Modernist America, 45
Shirley MacLaine Principle, 177
Shuttleworth, Sally, 259, 300
Significant Others, 97
Simmons, Laurie, 141
Singular Life of Albert Nobbs, The, 139
Situation, 89
Slevin, James, 49, 51
Smith, Barbara, 284, 298, 299, 300, 301
Smith, Barbara Herrnstein, 298, 301
Smith, Barbara Leigh, 190, 193
Smith, Beverly, 284, 298, 299
Smith, Paul, 296, 301
Smithson, Isaiah, 98, 101
Social relations, 16
Society for the Humanities, 88
Soelle, Dorothee, 39, 52
Sosnoski, James, viii, xi, xiii, 3, 326
Souls of Black Folks, The, 48
Sowing the Body, 162, 164
Speas, Margaret, 84, 102
Specialized language, 86, 87
Spellmeyer, Kurt, 26, 31, 34
Spencer, Anne, 68, 71
Spender, Dale, 290, 298, 301
Spillers, Hortense, 132, 140, 148
Spivak, Gayatri, 131, 137, 148
Spivey, Nancy, 247, 262
Sprague, Rosamond Kent, 164, 165
Stafford, Beth, 302
Steedman, Carolyn Kay, 40, 52, 297, 301
Steinberg, Erwin, 235
Stephans, Walter G., 97, 102
Stereotypes, 69, 79, 83, 142, 219
Stevens, Wallace, 68, 70
Stewart, Jo Moore, 272, 274
Stillman, Peter, 33
Stimpson, Catharine, 119
Storytelling, 258

Stotsky, Sandra, 196, 197, 198, 199, 200, 201
Straub, Kris, xi, 26, 235, 245, 247, 259, 260,
    326
Strickland, Ron, 275*n*
Strong reader, 242–243
Stuckey, J. Elspeth, 12, 34
Student-centered classroom, 23, 26
Style, 153
Suleiman, Susan, 259
Summary, learning to write, 249–250
Superreader, 29
Survey of Women's Literature course, 108
    readings for, 120–121
Synthesis tree, 252
S/Z, 60

Taggard, Genevieve, 68, 71
Tales of the City, 97
Talking Back, 160
Tannen, Deborah, 78, 103
Tarule, Jill, 119
Taylor, Frederick, 45, 52
Teacher-as-acculturator, 25, 196–197, 200
Teacher-as-propagandist, 196
Teaching
    against the backdrop of war, 202–230
    fear of, 171–172
    as the foundation of culture, 6
    manic mode of, 134
    maternal/coaching model of, 134, 179
    performance model of, 24, 134, 170, 171
    sociopolitical significance of, xiv
    student-teacher equality, 184
    as the transfer of information, 5, 6, 8, 19
    as a vehicle for social change, 172
Teachers, as moral voices, 228
Teach the conflicts, 66, 192, 238, 288
Team teaching, 134–135, 159
Tension(s)
    productive, creating sites for, 128–129
    strategies for keeping productive,
        135–146
    in theory and practice, 129–135
Tetreault, Mary Kay, 116, 118
Textuality, 15, 31, 60
Theorized classroom, 57
Theory
    enactment of in the classroom, 122
    notions of, 292
    and teaching practices, writing about,
        3–4
    value of, viii
They Live, 94
*They'll Never Keep Us Down: Women's Coal
    Mining Songs*, 46, 52

Thick descriptions, 20
This Bridge Called My Back, 80
Thomas, Clarence, 91, 92
Thompson, E. P., 276, 301
Thomson, Garrett, 207, 232
Thoreau, Henry David, 47
Thorne, Barrie, 101, 116, 119
Tichenor, Henry Mulford, 62, 72
Tichi, Cecilia, 45, 46, 52
Tompkins, Jane, 13, 23, 26, 32, 130, 134,
    148, 169, 179, 185, 193, 327
Touraine, Alain, 298, 301
*Tradition and Reform in the Teaching of
    English: A History*, 30
Transformative pedagogies, 190
Treichler, Paula, ix, 22, 71, 85, 96, 97, 98,
    101, 102, 103, 106, 118, 119, 131, 135,
    146, 148, 282, 298, 299, 300, 301, 327
Trent, Lucia, 62, 63, 71, 72
Trickle-down theory of theories, 12–17,
    22, 23
Trimbur, John, 182, 186, 193
*Triumph of Literature/The Fate of Literacy,
    The*, 49
Tropes, 139
Troublesome narrative, 253
True Colors, 49
Turing, 12
Turow, Scott, 87, 93, 103
Tutoring, 240
Twentieth-Century Women Novelists
    course, 107, 108
    readings for, 120

Underassertion, 24, 150
Urwin, Cathy, 297, 300
Utopia, 46, 54

Valian, Virginia, 83, 98, 103
Value-neutral inquiry, 30
Value-neutral teaching, 25, 194, 196
Value-positive teaching, 25, 194
Values
    in grading papers, 59–60
    of student *vs.* teacher, 56–57, 58,
        194–195
Van Dyne, Susan, 301
Vasilyuk, Fyodor, 217, 218, 220, 232
Venn, Couze, 297, 300
Vietnam War, 57, 58, 227
Visibility, unequal distribution of, 38
Vivion, Michael, 27–28, 32
Vold, Edwina Battle, 220, 232
Voloshinov, V. N., 261, 262

von Neumann, John, 12
Vonnegut, Kurt, 45, 52

Walden, 47
Walker, Alice, 302
Walker, Scott, 203, 232
Walkerdine, Valerie, 297, 300
Wall, Cheryl, 302
Waller, Gary, 235, 238, 242, 243, 252, 260, 261
Walsh, Dorothy, 30
Warren, Douglas, 79, 97, 103
Washington, Mary Helen, 291
Watney, Simon, 259
Watt, Stephen, 48, 52
Ways of My Grandmothers, The, 266
Weedon, Chris, 94, 103
Welch, Sharon D., 41, 52
Wheelwright, John, 71
White, Hayden, 60
Whitman, Walt, 46
Wicker, Diane, 284, 301
Widdowson, Peter, 302
Wilkerson, Margaret, 232
Williams, Linda, 140, 148
Williams, Raymond, 60
Williams, William Carlos, 46
Williamson, Judith, 259, 282, 302
Willinsky, John, 41, 49, 52
Wilson, Deborah, 275n
Windmills of the Gods, The, 210–211, 214–215, 216–217
Winters, Yvor, 180
Wolf, Christa, 47, 52
Woman, Native, Other: Writing Postcoloniality and Feminism, 48

Woman on the Edge of Time, 47, 210, 214
Woman Warrior, The, 266
Women and Literature course, 277–286, 302–304
  acculturation, forms of, 280–282
  course schedule, 302–304
  critical frameworks, 283–285
  cultural determinants of identity, 285–286
  language and the conditions of knowledge, 282–283
  required texts, 302
Women for Racial and Economic Equality, 138
Women's Bill of Rights, The, 138
Women's Studies Group, 297, 302
Women's Ways of Knowing, 118
Woodson, Carter G., 272, 274
Woolf, Virginia, 75, 82, 103, 284, 302
Working-class identity, ix, 38–40, 65
Wright, Richard, 68, 71
Writing about literature, 287
Writing labs, 240
Writing skills, 259
Wuthering Heights, 281

Yearning, 80
Yonnondio, 109
You Can't Judge a Book by Its Cover, 219, 229
Young, Richard, 235

Zandy, Janet, ix, 21, 37, 215, 232, 327
Zavarzadeh, Masud, 34
Zimmerman, Claire, 116, 117

Editor

David B. Downing has taught since 1988 in the English department of Indiana University of Pennsylvania, where he regularly teaches introductory literature classes, research writing, and the core doctoral courses in the history and theory of criticism and literary theory for the teacher and scholarly writer. Previously he taught for nine years at Eastern Illinois University. With James Sosnoski, he has recently organized graduate teleseminars exploring the possibilities for collaborative research/teaching in electronic educational environments. He is the editor of *Works and Days: Essays in the Socio-Historical Dimensions of Literature and the Arts;* co-editor, with Susan Bazargan, of *Image and Ideology in Modern/Postmodern Discourse;* and co-editor, with James M. Cahalan, of *Practicing Theory in Introductory College Literature Courses.* He has published numerous articles and book chapters in the areas of critical theory and pedagogy, cultural criticism, and American literature. In 1990, he organized and directed the conference at IUP on "The Role of Theory in the Undergraduate Literature Classroom: Curriculum, Pedagogy, Politics," which led to this book.

Contributors

Anne Balsamo teaches courses in the Science, Technology and Culture Program of the School of Literature, Communication, and Culture at Georgia Institute of Technology. Her area of specialty is feminist cultural studies. In addition to being published in journals of sociology, communication, literary and film studies, she is completing a book for Duke University Press called *Technologies of the Gendered Body*. Her more recent work concerns the role of new information technologies in the reinvention of humanistic education for the twenty-first century.

Dale M. Bauer has taught, since 1990, in the English department and the Women's Studies Program at the University of Wisconsin–Madison, where she also currently serves as associate chair of the Women's Studies Program. Her published work ranges from her study of Bakhtin, feminist theory, and the American novel in *Feminist Dialogics* (SUNY Press, 1988) to her essays on film, American culture, and nineteenth- and twentieth-century fiction. She has completed a study of Edith Wharton's late fictions entitled "Edith Wharton's Brave New Politics," and published essays on feminist pedagogy, women's studies administration, and feminism and cultural politics.

Ellen E. Berry is associate professor of English and director of the Women's Studies Program at Bowling Green State University where she teaches courses in contemporary women's writing and critical theory. She is author of *Curved Thought and Textual Wandering: Gertrude Stein's Postmodernism* and co-editor of *Re-Entering the Sign: New Critical Languages in the Soviet Union*. Her essays on feminist pedagogy, film, women's experimental writing, and the international avant-garde have appeared in *Novel, Women's Studies Quarterly, The Mid-American Review,* and *Genders,* where she is an editorial associate.

Patricia Bizzell is professor of English and director of Writing Programs at the College of the Holy Cross. She and Bruce Herzberg have published the *Bedford Bibliography for Teachers of Writing,* now in its third edition, and *The Rhetorical Tradition: Readings from Classical Times to the Present,* which won the NCTE Outstanding Book Award in 1992. Among her many other publications is a collection of her essays, *Academic Discourse and Critical Consciousness.* She has served on various national professional bodies, including the NCTE Commission on Composition and the Executive Board of the Council of Writing Program Administrators. She is presently working to develop multicultural materials for teaching writing.

Ann Marie Bodnar is a graduate of Indiana University of Pennsylvania, where she obtained her Bachelor of Arts degree in sociology and her Master's degree in education in secondary school guidance. While at IUP, she organized and took part in student organizations, demonstrations, and other forms of student activism in response to social issues such as reproductive rights, the Persian Gulf War, and racism. She was a graduate assistant in the Women's Studies Program, and, with a grant from the IUP Graduate School, she completed an independent research project on the exclusion of women's issues in Master's-level counselor training programs. She is currently working in a public secondary school as an advocate for young people.

Barbara DiBernard teaches in the English department and directs the Women's Studies Program at the University of Nebraska–Lincoln. Her major interests are twentieth-century women's literature, including autobiographical writings of all kinds, lesbian literature, and literature by women with disabilities; and feminist pedagogy. She recently published an article on Audre Lorde's *Zami* in the *Kenyon Review.*

Gerald Graff is George M. Pullman Professor of English and Education at the University of Chicago. He is the author of *Professing Literature: An Institutional History* (1987) and *Beyond the Culture Wars: How Teaching the Conflicts Can Revitalize American Education* (1992).

Michael Greer is assistant professor in the Department of English at Illinois State University in Normal. He has published essays on contemporary American poetry in *Boundary 2, Meanjin* (published in Australia) and *Centennial Review,* in addition to other articles on literary theory and cultural studies. A forthcoming article on the history of Sun and Moon Press will appear in a special issue of *Critique* devoted to the small presses and the avant-garde tradition(s) in the U.S. During the 1992–93 academic year, he worked as a visiting assistant professor in the School of Literature, Communication, and Culture at Georgia Institute of Technology in Atlanta, teaching interdisciplinary courses in the Science, Technology, and Culture Program.

Beverly Guy-Sheftall is Anna Julia Professor of Women's Studies and English, and director of the Women's Research and Resource Center at Spelman College. She is co-editor of *Sturdy Black Bridges: Visions of Black Women in Literature* and *Double Stitch: Black Women Write about Mothers and Daughters;* author of *Daughters of Sorrow: Attitudes toward Black Women, 1880–1920;* and founding co-editor of *SAGE: A Scholarly Journal on Black Women.* She consults and speaks widely on issues relating to race and gender and multiculturalism.

Patricia Harkin is associate professor of English at the University of Toledo. Her writing on composition and rhetoric has appeared in *College English, Pretext, Journal of Advanced Composition,* and *Works and Days.* She is co-editor, with John Schilb, of *Contending with Words: Composition and Rhetoric in* *a Postmodern Age,* and she is at work on a textbook called *Acts of Reading* for Blair Press of Prentice-Hall.

C. Mark Hurlbert is associate professor of English at Indiana University of Pennsylvania, where he teaches in the graduate programs in rhetoric and linguistics and literature and criticism, and in the undergraduate programs in secondary education and liberal studies. He has co-edited, with Samuel Totten, *Social Issues in the English Classroom* (NCTE), and, with Michael Blitz, *Composition and Resistance* (Boynton/Cook-Heinemann). He has written and co-written various articles for such books and journals as *Cultural Studies in the English Classroom; Practicing Theory in Introductory College Literature Courses; Pre/Text; Works and Days: Essays in the Socio-Cultural Dimensions of Literature and the Arts;* and *The Writing Instructor.* He is currently writing, with Michael Blitz, *Utopia Notebook,* a study about actions that any teacher might take—or have taken—in response to political realities in America today.

Susan C. Jarratt is professor of English and Lillian Radford Chair for Rhetoric and Composition at Texas Christian University. She taught high school English for six years and served as director of College Composition at Miami University of Ohio for two years. In addition to articles in *College English, College Composition and Communication, Rhetoric Review, Pre/Text,* and *Philosophy and Rhetoric,* she published a special issue of *Rhetoric Society Quarterly* on feminist histories of rhetoric. Her book, *Rereading the Sophists: Classical Rhetoric Refigured,* was published in 1990 by Southern Illinois University Press.

David Kaufer is professor of English and rhetoric at Carnegie Mellon and director of the writing programs. He has recently published a book called *Communication at a Distance: The Influence of Print on Socio-Cultural Organization and Change* (co-authored with Kathleen Carley).

Alan Kennedy is professor of English and head of the English department at Carnegie Mellon University. He has served as the chair of the English department at Dalhousie University in Canada and was editor of *The Dalhousie Review* for five years. His most recent book is *Reading Resistance Value.* He is also the author of *The Protean Self: Dramatic Action in Contemporary Fiction,* and *Meaning and Signs in Fiction.* An essay entitled "Committing the Curriculum and Other Misdemeanors" has just appeared in *Cultural Studies in the English Classroom* (Boynton/Cook), edited by James Berlin and Michael J. Vivion.

Cary Nelson is Jubilee Professor of Liberal Arts and Sciences and professor of English, criticism, and interpretive theory at the University of Illinois at Urbana-Champaign. He is the author of *The Incarnate Word: Literature as Verbal Space* (1973); *Our Last First Poets: Vision and History in Contemporary American Poetry* (1981); and *Repression and Recovery: Modern American Poetry and the Politics of Cultural Memory, 1910–1945* (1989). His books as editor or co-editor include *Theory in the Classroom* (1986); *Marxism and the Interpreta-*

tion of Culture (1988); *Cultural Studies* (1992); and Edwin Rolfe's *Collected Poems* (1993). He is currently gathering together a volume of his theoretical essays, writing a book on modern poetry, and completing a biography of Edwin Rolfe.

Christine M. Neuwirth is associate professor in the English department and in the School of Computer Science at Carnegie Mellon University. She directs one of the first-year English courses. She has published articles on writing and the pedagogy of writing, primarily with an emphasis on computers. Two of her recent co-authored essays related to the pedagogy of writing have appeared in the journal *Written Communication* and in Bruce, Peyton, and Batson's *Electronic Networks for Interaction*. She has been a member of the Conference on College Composition and Communication's Committee on Computers in Composition and Communication, 1988–1993.

Vivian Patraka, professor of English at Bowling Green State University, teaches drama, performance and feminist studies. Her work has appeared in *Theatre Journal, Modern Drama, Discourse, The Drama Review, The Journal of Dramatic Theory and Criticism, Women & Performance, The Michigan Quarterly Review* and *The Kenyon Review* and in the books *Critical Theory and Performance, Acting Out: Feminist Performances, Performing Feminisms,* and *Making a Spectacle.* She is completing a book entitled *Spectacular Suffering: Theatrical Representations of the Holocaust and Fascism* for Indiana University Press.

Sheila Reiter is a writing teacher/researcher at Doane College's campuses in Crete and Lincoln, Nebraska. She has taught in the University of Nebraska–Lincoln Writing Lab, and tutors international students in a private ESL program. She has presented papers at conferences for writing instructors and facilitated writing workshops for area colleges and universities and public and private businesses. Her dissertation is an ethnographic study of the place (regard *and* location) of writing assignments in the lives of college students.

James J. Sosnoski is professor of English at Miami University in Oxford, Ohio. He is the author of *Token Professionals and Master Critics: A Critique of Orthodoxy in Literary Studies* as well as various essays in literary theory, and he has just completed *Modern Skeletons in Postmodern Closets: A Cultural Studies Alternative to the Disciplining of Literary Study.* He was the executive director of the Society for Critical Exchange (1982–1986) and is, at present, the executive director of Alternative Educational Environments, a national organization for the development of computer-assisted learning in cultural studies. He is editing a special issue of *Works and Days,* "The Geography of Cyberspace," and collaborating with David Downing on a book dealing with the cultural studies teleseminars they have taught, which is tentatively entitled *Cultural Jazz: The Cycles Project.*

Kris Straub is associate professor of English at Carnegie Mellon University where, with Christine Neuwirth, she directs the first-year writing program.

She is the author of numerous articles and a book on feminist theory and eighteenth-century British literature and culture. Her most recent book, *Sexual Suspects: Eighteenth-Century Players and Sexual Ideology* and an anthology entitled *Body Guards: The Cultural Politics of Gender Ambiguity* (co-edited with Julia Epstein), are in the fields of queer theory and the history of sexuality.

Jane Tompkins teaches English at Duke University. She is the author of *Sensational Designs: The Cultural Work of American Fiction, 1790–1860* (Oxford University Press). She studies the relationship of literature to its cultural and political contexts and is currently completing a book on the way Western novels and films have formed thought and behavior in the twentieth century.

Paula A. Treichler teaches on the faculty of the University of Illinois at Urbana-Champaign in the College of Medicine, the Institute of Communications Research, and the Women's Studies Program. She is co-author of *A Feminist Dictionary* (1985) and *Language, Gender, and Professional Writing: Theoretical Approaches and Guidelines for Nonsexist Usage* (1989); she is co-editor of *For Alma Mater: Theory and Practice in Feminist Scholarship* (1985) and *Imaging Technologies, Inscribing Science,* two issues of the journal *Camera Obscura* (1992 and 1993). Her work on AIDS has appeared in many journals including *Cultural Studies, October, Art Forum, Science,* and *Transition,* and in many edited collections; she is completing a books on AIDS. She has also published widely on feminist cultural studies, feminist theory, feminist pedagogy, and medical discourse.

Janet Zandy is assistant professor of language and literature at Rochester Institute of Technology. She is the editor of *Calling Home: Working-Class Women's Writings* (1990) and the forthcoming *Liberating Memory: Our Work and Our Working-Class Consciousness* (both from Rutgers University Press). She is engaged in the development of "working-class studies" and is petitioning the Modern Language Association for a permanent discussion group. She will guest-edit a special issue of *Women's Studies Quarterly* on teaching working-class studies.